CARING FOR OLDER PEOPLE

Caring for Older People
An assessment of community care in the 1990s

LINDA BAULD
JOHN CHESTERMAN
BLEDDYN DAVIES
KEN JUDGE
ROSHNI MANGALORE

Ashgate

Aldershot • Brookfield USA • Singapore • Sydney

Published by
Ashgate Publishing Ltd
Gower House
Croft Road
Aldershot
Hants GU11 3HR
England

Ashgate Publishing Company
Old Post Road
Brookfield
Vermont 05036
USA

Ashgate website: http://www.ashgate.com

British Library Cataloguing in Publication Data
Caring for older people : an assessment of community care
   in the 1990s
   1.Aged - Medical care - Great Britain 2.Aged - Care - Great
   Britain 3.Aged - Government policy - Great Britain
   4.Community health services for the aged - Great Britain
   I.Bauld, Linda II.PSSRU
   362.6'0941

Library of Congress Catalog Card Number: 99-76651

ISBN 0 7546 1280 5

Typeset by Jane Dennett at the PSSRU, University of Kent at Canterbury

Printed and bound by Athenaeum Press, Ltd.,
Gateshead, Tyne & Wear.

Contents

List of Tables, Boxes and Figures

xi

xiv

xv

Preface

What are the need-related circumstances of post-reform users of community care brokered by local authority social services departments? How similar are the interpretations of these by users, principal informal carers, and the persons undertaking the key assessment and care planning tasks when their care is being set up? What services do they receive? What changes in their states occur through time when they receive services? Evidence on which to base answers about these and related questions is key to understanding and evaluating the new community care.

Our evaluations of the success of community care differ partly because we have lacked the necessary findings from research of sufficient scale, depth, range and representativeness.

The most important aim of *Caring for Older People* is to provide such information of a range and depth not hitherto available. It is the core book providing the point of reference for the other items in a wide range of more focused descriptions and analyses, the first of which, *Equity and Efficiency Policy in Community Care: Needs, Service Productivities, Efficiencies and their Implications*, accompanies *Caring for Older People* to our publishers.

Our plans are nothing if not ambitious. It is the intention to compare post-reform with pre-reform community care, and so to evaluate change as well as the present. This study is the product of the second stage of a major programme on which the PSSRU has been working for twenty years. The programme was conceived in 1980. PSSRU experiments in budget-devolved care management were finding that equity and efficiency of community care could be greatly improved. But the experiments were focused on only some users. Therefore it was important to discover whether the problem of equity and efficiency applied to most users, to understand its nature, and to develop argument about how to tackle it. For this reason, PSSRU built into its quinquennial plan from 1980 a study of the whole range of elderly users of the community social services. The argument from that Domiciliary Care Project

[DCP] helped to define the challenge that had to be faced for the reforms to improve equity and efficiency. Evaluating Care for Elderly People ['ECCEP'] has been so designed as to replicate DCP sufficiently to form an 'after' stage of a before-after study of which the first stage was the DCP.

We could not possibly acknowledge all those who have made important contributions even to the collection, analysis and writing used in this volume. Most of the effort has been expended in collecting the data. First, there have been the users, carers, care managers, and the many other managers on whose cooperation we have depended. The design of the study asked a great deal of effort for only a distant and indirect reward. In particular, we made enormous demands on those who were our liaison persons with the collaborating authorities: June Barraclough, Gill Best, Tony Burks, Steve Cody, Duncan Henderson, Isabelle Houghton, April Lawler, Beverley McCann, Vivian Mellish, Barbara Priestly, Paul Richardson, Pam Satterthwaite, and Sandra Stapely. We cannot acknowledge the Directors of Social Services who sat on our Advisory Committee because we have promised the anonymity of their authorities. Neither do conventions allow us to name the twelve members representing the Department of Health. But we can acknowledge Lucianne Sawyer, and Terry Butler (who sat as Chair of the ADSS Service Evaluation Research and Information Committee), as well the academics Professors Shah Ebrahim, Elaine Murphy, and Claire Wenger.

Then there are those who have been part of the PSSRU team. The collection has been complex, vast, and difficult. Many people have contributed to the second stage of the project, taking place since 1995. Expectations are rising about how quickly research can be completed. This and its companion will appear within five years of the first collection of data on which they are based: a much shorter time than ever before, although the project experienced long delays because of an eighteen-month hiatus in mid-project because of recruitment difficulties. The acceleration is due only partly to new technologies for analysis and publication. We should acknowledge that is also due to the greatly increased pressure that research teams suffer.

During the collection period, and until the Department of Health made him an offer he could not refuse, Raymond Warburton was the manager and senior full-time academic member of the team. He brought great policy experience and imagination to the project, as well as driving us all forward with indefatigable energy and faultless organisation. Without that there would have been disaster, given the extremely tight time framework. Gail Goldstone, Steve Luckham, Alisoun Milne and Sherrill Stone were involved full-time over various periods during that period. Thanks are due to Research Services Limited, who undertook much of the field interviewing. Professor Bleddyn Davies has been principal researcher, designing the project, working with members of the teams at the LSE and Kent in all activities from framing analyses to drafting this book, and spending most of his time on the project throughout its entire history.

During the period between the departure of the collection team and the arrival of the analysis group, progress was made mainly by persuading colleagues to switch projects, and by employing casual and temporary staff. Dr John Chesterman was moved from his work on care management with Bleddyn Davies. Fortunately, *Community Care in England and France* had been completed, releasing José Fernández and Robin Saunders. José Fernández did much to organise the database. Robin Saunders contributed to the production of the early tables and has taken charge of the tracking of resources, needs and outcomes since the second interview with triad members. Sheila Kesby was engaged to fill gaps in our evidence about the utilisation of health services. By the end of the period, we had produced a large stack of tables analysing almost every variable in our collection within a few standard descriptors, so providing a foundation for the reanalysis and revision for this book. But from April 1997, the analysis team was brought up to establishment. We had the good fortune of being able to attract Professor Ken Judge back to be Director of the PSSRU at the University of Kent at Canterbury, and he took over the management function and, particularly, the management of the production of this book, with characteristic decisiveness and energy. The other new members of the analysis team were Dr Linda Bauld and Roshni Mangalore. Linda Bauld has been the critical member of the team responsible for producing this book. Her tireless efforts make it appropriate that she should be its first-named author.

No book from the PSSRU stable should fail to acknowledge the effort and professionalism of the PSSRU's team in its publications office, Nick Brawn and Jane Dennett. The quality of the work at that stage will be evident to all readers.

ECCEP is an extremely detailed study, with a unique collection of data. The length of this book reflects ECCEP's complexity. It is thus worth taking some time to consider how to approach this volume, depending on the perspective and requirements of the reader. The first point to emphasise is that this book has been written in such a way as to make the material accessible and relevant to a wide audience. It will be a particularly useful resource for students, teachers and researchers across the social sciences; those involved in developing health and social care policy and those working with older people. We hope it may also be of interest to older people themselves. Readers should however keep in mind that this volume is one of a set — and that in particular, it should be read in conjunction with another of the books being published at the same time, *Equity and Efficiency Policy in Community Care*, based on modelling the relationships between needs, resources and outcomes.

A selective approach should be considered by those first approaching *Caring for Older People*. Chapter 1 provides a useful summary of the development of community care from the post-war period to the present day. Chapter 2 outlines the design of ECCEP and places findings in a national context, and thus must be read in order for the results described in the rest of the book to be understood. Chapter 11 provides a conclusion, summarising the main descriptive findings from ECCEP and reflecting on their relevance to policy developments at the turn of the century. Readers who do not have adequate time to work through the whole volume should therefore consider paying particular attention to Chapter 2 and 11, in order to capture some of the key messages from the study.

The remainder of this volume presents findings from ECCEP in relation to a variety of themes. Chapter 3 and 4 describe the characteristics and circumstances of the older people in the study, and their principal informal carers. Chapter 5 describes findings in relation to care management, including the characteristics of care managers, aspects of assessment, monitoring and review, and outlines the costs of care management. Chapter 6 examines the concept of consistency. This involved analysing user, carer and care manager responses to a range of questions and then addressing areas of inconsistency between respondents. A study of consistency in social care — and the issues it raises in relation to user and carer involvement in assessment — has not been previously undertaken in the U.K. Chapter 6 thus provides a useful summary of some of the detailed analysis which Dr John Chesterman has conducted in relation to this theme. Chapter 7 and 8 outline the support provided to service users. Chapter 7 describes inputs from informal carers, and Chapter 8 from statutory, voluntary and private providers, with associated service and care packages costs. Finally, Chapter 9 and 10 present outcomes for users and carers. These last chapters should be read with some understanding of the needs-related circumstances set out in Chapter 3 and 4, and the informal and formal inputs described in Chapters 7 and 8.

1   The Development of Community Care

> 'Community care may be ... a sweeter smelling rose, a more promising health and social hybrid, but it has to grow in the soil we have...we do not indeed start, as some academic planners sometimes imply, with a clean slate. Reality starts with history'
>
> Richard Titmuss, *A Commitment to Welfare*, 1968.

The 1990 NHS and Community Care Act ushered in a new era for both health and social services. The changes it introduced were fundamental, altering the role of statutory and independent organisations, changing professional practice and boundaries, and transforming the experience of care for many users and carers. In relation to services for older people in particular, implementation of the reforms took place over several years and it is only now, at the close of the decade, that research and practice are beginning to assess the implications.

As a series of recent texts have highlighted, however, the origins of the 1990 Act are rooted in the development of social welfare and health services in preceding decades (Maclean, 1989; Means and Smith, 1998a, 1998b; Bernard and Phillips, 1998). Community care is not a new idea, and an understanding of its origins is essential to assess developments since the passage of the 1990 Act. While readers should turn to the work of Robin Means and Randall Smith (1998a, 1998b) for a more comprehensive survey of the history of community care, we introduce some of the main developments here, as several are of specific relevance to the care of older people, and to the particular approach adopted in the project Evaluating Community Care for Elderly People (ECCEP).

Origins

Community-based care for older people shares with all social welfare services in Britain a common origin in the Poor Law. The Poor Law reforms of 1834 established a general principle of segregation between the sane and able bodied and the other groups in the workhouses, with older people, children, the sick, the disabled and the insane housed in specialist institutions (Pilgrim, 1993). Subsequent legislation formalised the separation of these groups. Despite the early identification of older people as one of the groups requiring support, and the subsequent introduction of residual social policies such as means tested (1908) and contributory (1920s) pensions and national insurance (1911) it was not until the period following the Second World War that legislation specified the development of community-based services for the elderly. The post-war period is thus a natural starting point from which to examine the development of community care for older people.

The period from 1945-1951 laid the foundations of Britain's welfare state. Fuelled by a desire for social change following the experience of war, the Labour government introduced a series of pieces of legislation which owed much to the ideas of Beveridge and his reports describing how the 'five giants' of want, ignorance, disease, idleness and squalor should be addressed by universalist rather than selectivist solutions (Fraser, 1973). Three pieces of legislation in particular were to affect the lives of older people: the National Health Service Act (1946), the National Insurance Act (1946) and the National Assistance Act (1948). The new framework established free health care at the point of use and marked the decline of the old system of public assistance institutions under the Poor Law (Dalley, 1998). The National Health Service Act introduced a tripartite structure, with general practitioners as independent contractors, hospital services united for the first time and local authority public health departments retaining control of environmental health services and the employment of certain categories of nursing staff who worked in the community, such as health visitors and district nurses. Perhaps most significantly in regard to social care services for older people, Section 21 of the National Assistance Act established that it was the duty of every local authority to provide residential care for those who were in need of care, either due to their age, infirmity or other circumstances (Means, 1997). This provision marked the formal beginning of four decades in which institutional, rather than domiciliary, services were to form the bulk of public expenditure on social care services for older people.

As Means and Smith (1998b), Dalley (1998) and others have pointed out, the immediate post-war legislation established that residential care was the responsibility of local authorities, yet it did not balance this with the power to develop domiciliary services to allow older people to remain at home if they wished. Indeed, it was not until the passage of the 1968 Health Services and Public Health Act under which local authorities were given the responsibility for the overall welfare of older people that any centralised development of domiciliary services would begin, while a coordinated approach to social care provision for older people was not possible until the creation of social services departments following the Seebohm reforms introduced in 1971 (Davies and Challis, 1986; Tester, 1996; Means, 1997). Despite these changes and early efforts by particular local authorities to develop innovative approaches to providing home-based services (Ruck, 1958), institutional care remained dominant and attempts at comprehensive development of domiciliary care were slow to succeed. The reasons for this are well documented, but provide the necessary context for the reforms of the 1980s and 90s.

Early developments in community care

The shift away from the predominance of institutional care for older people towards the acceptance and expansion of community-based services took place slowly. In the years immediately following the war, general acceptance of existing institutional provision was first challenged by Nuffield Foundation studies in the late 1940s and early 1950s, particularly the work of the committee led by Seebohm Rowntree (1947). In his survey of old people's homes, he described conditions in local authority premises (predominantly the old workhouses), some of which housed more than 1,000 people in impersonal and austere surroundings (Maclean, 1989). Although the final recommendations of the committee proposed changes to the buildings and organisation of homes rather than suggesting a reduction in the supply of residential care, they did describe and recommend the expansion of 'an innovation', the local authorities home help scheme, which, along with meal services, was proving popular but was in short supply.[1] Later work by Sheldon in Wolverhampton (1948), Townsend in London and other parts of England and Wales (1957, 1962) and Isaacs and colleagues in Glasgow (Isaacs and Thompson, 1960; Isaacs et al., 1972) raised awareness of the poor living conditions of many older people and the scarcity of supportive services, other than residential provision. Table 1.1., taken from Townsend's *The Last Refuge*, illustrates the 'warehousing' of older people in the former workhouses which became residential care homes, with the majority of residents living in ward-type rooms with a large number of beds and with few personal possessions permitted. These accounts were to support the growth of a gradual consensus that alternatives should be available to institutional care.

Deinstitutionalisation began, however, not with old people's homes but with the psychiatric hospitals of the 1950s. Indeed, the first official mention of the term 'community care' is attributed to the 1957 Report of the Royal Commission on Mental Illness and Mental Deficiency, which preceded the 1959 Mental Health Act. The 1957 report stated that 'it is now generally considered in the best interests of patients who are fit to live in the community

Table 1.1
Distribution of beds, by size of dormitory (39 former public assistance institutions)

Number of beds, by size of dormitory	Total beds (%)
1	2.3
2	5.6
3-5	10.5
6-9	28.8
10-19	36.5
20-29	6.9
30 or more	9.4
Total	100
Number	9,933

Source: Townsend (1962).

that they should not be in large and remote institutions such as the present mental and mental deficiency hospitals' (cited in Pilgrim, 1993, p.171). A closure programme of psychiatric hospitals began, buoyed by concern from central government (expressed in the 1959 Guillebaud report) about the rising costs of hospital care. Targets for closure were formalised by the 1962 Hospital Plan for England and Wales. The Plan set out a programme for the closure of a significant number of hospital beds over a twenty year period. The number of inpatient beds for each category of patient (including geriatric patients) was stipulated and the remainder were selected for closure, with the intention being that the released resources would be made available for community health services (Dalley, 1998). The Plan was followed by a series of documents (such as the 1963 DHSS White Paper *Health and Welfare: The Development of Community Care*) which reaffirmed the government's commitment to deinstitutionalisation and the promotion of community alternatives. Indeed, Means and Smith (1998b) have argued that there was general agreement in policy documents from the 1950s onwards that older people in need of care should be allowed to remain in their own homes, but that this ideological shift was not matched by a corresponding shift in resources. Equally importantly, these early changes in legislation and practice did not amount to a *comprehensive* approach to the developing domiciliary provision, but were rather adaptations to existing structures and organisations, most notably the NHS. The creation of a policy model for community care was to come much later.

Thus by the late 1960s social policy in relation to older people remained focused on residential care. The community-based provision that did exist was patchy and of varied quality. The 1963 White Paper highlighted wide variations in home help provision across the country, insufficient supply of other services such as meals, and a shortage of staff (DHSS, 1963). Part of the problem stemmed from decisions made regarding the separation of responsibilities for different aspects of health services following the war. Responsibility for community-based, non-medical services was not clear and, as mentioned previously, local authorities were obliged by legislation only to provide residential care for older people.[2] Two important changes took place at the end of the 1960s which were to change how community services were provided. The first was the passage of the 1968 Health Service and Public Health Act, which stipulated that local authorities had the responsibility to look after the welfare of older people in their communities, including the obligation to provide a home help service. The second was the 1968 report of the Seebohm Committee, which was to shape the Local Social Services Act of 1970.

The post-Seebohm era

The Seebohm Committee was formed in 1965 with the remit of reviewing the responsibilities and organisation of local authority social services in both England and Wales. The recommendations which emerged from the committee in 1968 centred around one main issue: the need to form new local authority departments which would unite the previously fragmented social work functions (such as children's and mental health services) and provide a single point of entry for all clients. The legislative changes which followed Seebohm — the 1970 Social Services Act, 1972 Local Government Act and the 1974 reorganisation of the National Health Service — were to transform the organisation and administration of social work and complete the separation of health and social care services. Box 1.1 describes the committee's recommendations regarding the establishment of social services departments.

The reforms which Seebohm recommended were prompted by a variety of changes in public attitudes, central government thinking and the concerns of social workers themselves. A review of social work education and training had taken place in the late 1950s, chaired by Eileen Younghusband (Younghusband, 1959). In 1962 the core recommendations of the this report were implemented. They centred around the need for more formalised social work training to increase the number of qualified social workers with a generic training base. A national institute of social work training was formed, and a new two year professional certificate was introduced in higher education colleges in addition to existing university programmes. These changes reflected a growing desire among social workers for the development of a common core of knowledge and enhanced professional status.

Changes in other parts of the UK, most notably Scotland, were also influencing reform within social services. Following the report of the

---

Box 1.1
Seebohm Committee's recommendations for a unified social services department

A social service department

(3) We recommend a social service department, with responsibilities extending well beyond the responsibilities of existing local authority departments. They would include:

(a) the present services provided by children's departments;
(b) the welfare services provided under the National Assistance Act 1948;
(c) education welfare and child guidance services;
(d) the home help service, mental health social work services, other social work services and day nurseries, provided by local health departments;
(e) certain social welfare work currently undertaken by some housing departments.

Source: Seebohm (1968).

Kilbrandon Committee in 1964, the Social Work (Scotland) Act of 1968 had combined separate functions such as children's panels and social work services into the same departments within local authorities (Adams, 1996). These changes amounted to the introduction of the first comprehensive approach to providing social services in the UK. Adams also points out that wider societal factors were at work at this time in all parts of the country which supported moves towards expanded and less fragmented social services. He suggests that there was enhanced public expectation regarding what social services could deliver, driven by the demands of rising juvenile crime rates and awareness of the growing number of older people; changing public attitudes towards people with problems; growing popularity of community-based services and an increase in local authority spending on personal social services, with real expenditure doubling between 1960 and 1968.

The Seebohm reforms reflected the rising profile of social work and the need for a more coordinated approach to tackling social problems. Social service functions were combined into single social services departments following the local government reforms. This meant that social care services were now entirely separate from the local health service, and were administered by a new breed of professional social workers entirely separate from medical and nursing staff. This separation was finalised by the NHS reorganisation of 1974, which united hospital services, community medical services and public health services (the latter previously being within the remit of the local authority) and thus finally removed any medical presence from local government. The result, as Maclean points out, was that 'elderly clients or patients would thereafter be viewed in terms of their social work or their medical and nursing needs, however bewildering or arbitrary this severance might feel to the subjects of such divided attentions' (1989, p.25).

While the reforms changed the organisation and administration of social work, it is important to realise, as many critics have pointed out (Davies and Challis, 1986; Webb and Wistow, 1987) that there was little immediate improvement in organisation or quality of domiciliary services for older people. The idea of the social services department as a single point of entry for people with a variety of needs meant that workers with a range of skills were still required, from untrained welfare assistants to those with a professional qualification. Services such as home help and day care were thus still administered by untrained staff, with little resulting assessment of the overall needs of users (Means and Smith, 1998a). There was also the problem that work with older people retained a low status, despite developments in social work training. Services for older people also suffered from a lack of coordination post-Seebohm, as the single point of entry did not apply to many of the services required. Thus, access to home help still had to be negotiated through the home help organiser, access to home nursing was now through the GP, and meals on wheels was still operated largely by the voluntary sector. Dalley (1998) reminds us that this lack of progress was highlighted by reports and surveys in the 1970s — most notably the study of the home help service by Hunt (1970), who found patchy provision and evidence of unmet need — and government accounts such as the 1976 White Paper which reported a shortfall in home help, meals on wheels and day care provision (DHSS, 1976).

One of the main reasons why community care was slow to develop in the 1970s was undoubtedly due to the economic recession which followed the oil crisis of 1973. Spending cuts prevented the expansion of existing provision, and continuing inflation limited investment in any new services (Bernard and Phillips, 1998). Limited resources put further strain on the joint finance arrangements which had been made between health and social services following Seebohm. Despite encouragement from central government, collaboration between local agencies was limited, and mutual distrust between professional groups in health and social care persisted. Failures in joint working contributed to the continued fragmentation of services. By the time a Conservative government was returned to power in 1979, there was widespread criticism of welfare services and growing concern that spending needed to be controlled in the face of continued economic problems and demographic change.

Social security and institutional care

The economic downturn of the late 1970s had an effect on residential as well as domiciliary provision. Particularly following Britain's monetary crisis in 1976, local authorities found that capital for expanding residential provision ceased to be available. At a time when growth in the number of older people was increasing demand, this shortage of funds also affected voluntary organisations running homes, who depended on local authority grants. As Laing (1993) has pointed out, in 1974 local authorities paid for 60 per cent of voluntary residential care places in England, yet this had dropped to 34 per cent by 1983. The explanation was that both voluntary and private sector homes began to receive a growing proportion of their funding from central government in the 1980s, through a loophole in the supplementary benefits (later income support) system. This loophole permitted anyone who had less than £3,000 capital and who qualified on income grounds to apply for supplementary benefit to pay for their care in a residential or nursing home of their choice, in either the private or voluntary sector. No assessment of need was required. In effect, the central government had set up a voucher system for the public funding of private and voluntary care homes (Laing, 1993). Although there is some debate about the extent to which politicians and officials were aware of what they were doing (Walker, 1993; Lewis and Glennerster, 1996), the effects of the policy soon became clear. The number of income support recipients in private and voluntary homes rose from 11,000 in December 1979 to 155,000 in November 1988, while public spending on these recipients grew from £10 million in 1979 to £958 million in the same period, and continued to rise until policy changes were implemented in 1993 (Laing, 1993). Thus, as Maclean states: 'as hospital doors closed, the doors of private nursing homes had conveniently opened' (1989, p.44). Table 1.2 illustrates this escalation in expenditure on private residential and nursing homes.

Two main consequences arose from the practice of using benefits to pay for independent sector institutional care. The first, and most obvious, was the rapid growth of the private nursing and residential home sector, particularly in areas where there were a high density of older people, such as along the south coast of England. The second was that the development of community care had been further hindered by the practice. While policy documents had continued to promote the desirability of community-based alternatives, public money had been directed towards the expansion of institutional care. This irony was highlighted in a highly influential report released by the Audit Commission in 1986, *Making a Reality of Community Care*. In contrast to an earlier report from the Commission which had highlighted weaknesses in services for elderly people but had been attacked for its managerial focus and assumptions regarding informal care, the 1986 publication was acclaimed as a 'cogent and highly critical document' (Lewis and Glennerster, 1996, p.5). The report spelt out the weaknesses of the current system, including the 'perverse effects' of the use of social security funding to pay for private institutional care. It also described a number of other weaknesses in existing community provision, including the fragmented nature of care, lack of collaboration between health and social services, problems of staffing, and the incidence or

Table 1.2
Income support recipients in private and voluntary residential and nursing homes (all client types), Great Britain

Year	Numbers	Average payment, £ per week[1]	Annuitised expenditure, £ million
December 1979	11,000	18	10
December 1980	13,000	27	18
December 1981	13,000	34	23
December 1982	16,000	47	39
December 1983	26,000	77	104
December 1984	42,000	92	200
December 1985	70,000	96	348
February 1986	90,000	98	459
May 1987	117,000	110	671
November 1987	130,100	114	772
May 1988	147,000	115	878
November 1988	155,000	119	958
May 1990	189,000	129	1,270
May 1991	231,000	156	1,870
November 1991	253,200	-	2,400

1 Income support payments are net of other social security benefits and therefore do not give an accurate picture of total charges met from all social security sources.
Source: Department of Social Security, cited in Laing (1993).

inappropriate or insufficient care packages (Means and Smith, 1998a; Lewis and Glennerster, 1996). The report concluded with a call for a comprehensive review of community care and stated that 'what is not tenable is to do nothing' (Audit Commission, 1986).

Griffiths

Writing at the end of the decade, the authors of ECCEP's predecessor, the Domiciliary Care Project (Davies et al., 1990, p.8) noted that 'the late 1980s may well prove to have been climacteric in the history of long-term care for elderly people'. Real changes in community care policy were indeed begun during this period, evidenced by a series of review documents in addition to the Audit Commission reports. The Social Services Inspectorate published two national inspections of home care during this period, which revealed continued weaknesses in the system (1987, 1988). The Firth Report was published by the DHSS in 1987, outlining the importance of a needs-led assessment for people entering residential care (DHSS, 1987) and the Wagner Report (1988) reviewed existing residential care policy and highlighted, among other things, that people who moved to institutional care should do so by choice (Bernard and Phillips, 1998). Most significant, however, was the 1988 report compiled by Sir Roy Griffiths, *Community Care: An Agenda for Action.*

In 1985 Griffiths had reviewed the introduction of general management into the NHS. From the government's point of view, the resulting NHS reforms had met with some early success, and thus Griffiths was asked to turn his attention to community care immediately following the publication of the 1986 Audit Commission report. The remit he was given was to review the way in which public funding was being used in community care, and to report back to the Secretary of State with options to improve its use.

The Griffiths report contained a series of specific recommendations which were to heavily influence the subsequent White Paper and the 1990 Act. His recommendations were on the themes of responsibilities of existing agencies, funding structures, planning and management, supporting people in the community rather than in long-term care, the use of public finance for institutional care, the role of the private sector, registration and inspection of homes, and suggestions for implementation. Overall, he recognised the failures of the current system, stating that 'the ways in which money is spent on community care do not enable a comprehensive approach to needs assessment, planning and delivery of services to be achieved' (Griffiths, 1988, 4.17). Griffiths' recommendations amounted to the first attempt to develop a *policy model* for community care, one which considered the functions of all relevant agencies and proposed how their roles should change. He recommended that the practice of using income support to pay for institutional care cease, and outlined an alternative structure for the funding and delivery of care to older people. Three themes in the report were to prove to be of particular significance in the years that followed: the responsibilities of the local authority, the concept of care management, and the promotion of the mixed economy.

Griffiths was not in favour of the fundamental reorganisation of central government departments or significant changes in the level of existing public expenditure. Instead, he advocated an alternative way of managing existing resources, with the local authority taking a lead role (Maclean, 1989). He felt that local authorities should be responsible for assessing the needs of both their local population and individual clients, and then mobilising resources to meet those needs. Key in this assessment process was the care manager who, 'in cases where a significant level of resources are involved ... should be nominated from within the social services authorities' staff to oversee the assessment and re-assessment function and manage the resulting action' (Griffiths, 1988, 6.6). Rather than relying on services directly provided by the local authority, the care manager should be able to put in place a care package drawn from services in the private, voluntary and public sector. Griffiths argued that the growth of the independent sector in community care would 'encourage choice, flexibility and innovation in a climate of competition' (Ibid, 3.4). Encouragement of private sector involvement within public sector systems was consistent with policy pursued by the Conservative governments since 1980, when local authorities had been statutorily obliged to contract out a portion of their activities. This policy had been further evidenced first in the case of the care of older people by the 1981 DHSS report *Growing Older*, which had advocated the concept of the 'enabling authority' providing a framework of services to complement (rather than replace or explicitly support) existing assistance from family networks. Along with a key role for the local authority, formal structures for assessment and the promotion of the mixed economy, however, Griffiths also argued that the failure of over three decades of community care policy suggested that specific funds had to be *earmarked* as separate from health, social security or other local authority funding and should be allocated specifically to domiciliary services. As he stated 'it is essential that the transferred funds reach their intended destination, ie. local social services authorities, and do not end up in the general grant pool' (Ibid, 5.13). Along with a number of other specific ideas in the Griffiths report, this was one recommendation which was not destined to be put into practice.

The White Paper and the Act

There was a delay of eighteen months between the submission of the Griffiths report and the publication of the White Paper, *Caring for People*, in November 1989. This has been attributed to the mixed reaction from central government regarding the contents of the report. Commentators argued that the Treasury resisted the idea of earmarked funds for community care, while Mrs. Thatcher in particular disagreed with the suggestion that the Labour local authorities should have an expanded role (Means and Smith, 1998a; Henwood et al., 1996). Thus, the government looked for other alternatives to Griffiths. When it eventually became apparent that no quick solutions were forthcoming, the White Paper was released. In most respects it reflected Griffiths' proposals, with the exception of his suggestion that a Minister of Community Care be appointed to manage the new structures, and minus the concept of an earmarked grant for local authorities.

Means and Smith have argued that the White Paper and subsequent changes lacked a 'positive spirit of implementation'. Griffiths himself felt his other suggestions for reform would be undermined by the absence of ring fenced funding (Lewis and Glennerster, 1996). Despite these and subsequent criticisms, *Caring for People* did introduce a significant set of changes that would later become part of the 1990 Act. As a document, it centred around a series of principles — which explained the government's approach to reform

— and followed these with six key objectives and some description of the changes required to achieve them.

The central principles in the White Paper centred around the themes of *home*, *choice* and *independence*. In relation to the concept of home, the main aim of community care policy was described as 'enabl[ing] people to live as normal a life as possible in their own homes or in a homely environment in the community' (Department of Health, 1989, 1.8). Unnecessary admissions to institutional care were to be avoided, on the basis that appropriate services for older people, people with a mental illness or learning disabilities, or people with a physical or sensory disability could be arranged in the community. Choice was also a central principle in *Caring for People*, with a specific focus on providing users with more say in how they lived their lives and the services they needed, through the explicit aim of providing 'services that allow a range of choice for consumers' (Ibid, 1.10). Thus, the concept of choice was explicitly tied to a mixed economy of care, consistent with government policy in other areas and Griffiths' recommendations.[3] Finally, independence was included as a central principle, 'by provid[ing] the right amount of care and support to help people achieve maximum possible independence and, by acquiring or requiring basic living skills, help them to achieve their full potential' (Ibid, 1.8).

It is worth noting that there is a fourth guiding theme in the White Paper, which is not singled out as a central principle but nonetheless influences the approach taken. This concerns carers, and the government's perception of their role in community care. Consistent with policy documents from the early 1980s onwards, the White Paper acknowledges that the majority of care is provided by the informal sector. Throughout the document, the fact that the caring role is taken on as a 'choice' is recognised and the worthy nature of this decision is emphasised. Carers are very clearly conceptualised as what Twigg would call 'resources', forming part of a network also made up of statutory, voluntary and private sources of support (Twigg, 1989). The White Paper does not go as far as to recognise carers as clients in their own right within this new system (this came with the Carers Act in 1995) but does underline the need to support their efforts, stating 'The majority of carers take on these responsibilities willingly, but the government recognises that they may need help to manage what can become a heavy burden' (Ibid, 2.3). In this way, the White Paper does go further than Griffiths, who acknowledged the importance of informal care but did not state explicitly that specific services should support them. This slight shift in emphasis has been attributed by Parker (1999) to pressure from carers' organisations, supported by research evidence, in the period between the submission of the Griffiths report and the publication of *Caring for People*.

Guided by these general principles of the desirability of life at home, the choice available from a mix of services, the independence that could be achieved with the right support, and the recognition of carers, the White Paper set out six clear objectives, all of which were reflected in the 1990 legislation. Box 1.2 illustrates these objectives.

Box 1.2

Objectives of **Caring for People**

• To promote the development of domiciliary, day and respite services to enable people to live in their own homes whenever feasible and sensible
• To ensure that service providers make practical support for carers a high priority
• To make proper assessment of need and good case management the cornerstone of high quality care
• To promote the development of a flourishing independent sector alongside good quality public sector services
• To clarify the responsibilities of agencies and so make it easier to hold them to account for their performance
• To secure better value for taxpayers' money by introducing a new funding structure for social care

---

Griffiths' recommendation that local authorities become the lead agency for assessing need, coordinating care packages and 'securing the delivery of services' (rather than directly providing them) was adopted in *Caring for People*. The concept of the enabling authority, making the best use of existing informal sources of support and encouraging the growth of independent sector services was a key mechanism for achieving objectives. Case management[4] was confirmed as the means which authorities would use to 'design services to meet individual need' and specific reference was made to the approach taken in PSSRU projects.[5] A new funding structure for community care underpinned all other recommendations, based not on ringfenced funding but on a single unified budget for domiciliary and residential/nursing home care drawn from the Revenue Support Grant and the transfer of funds from social security.

In 1990 the NHS and Community Care Act was passed with the reforms to be implemented in both health and social care by April 1991. Yet the planned implementation timetable was stalled at an early stage. Henwood et al. (1996) have argued that the delay was unintended but representative of the tension between explicit policy goals on the one hand, and the pressures of routine political management on the other. The reforms involved significant change for local authorities, who argued that the expectations of central government were unrealistic, particularly given the vague nature of some of the changes. In addition, the substantial reforms to the NHS (including the forming of Trust hospitals and the introduction of GP fundholding) were intended to be implemented within the same time scale, yet were in many ways incompatible, with considerable uncertainty regarding the boundary between health and local authority responsibilities (Hunter, 1994). As a result of this confusion, central government began to issue a stream of policy and practice guidance, in an effort to inject greater clarity. The result was implementation in stages. Some changes, such as new complaints procedures and arrangements for the inspection of care homes, proceeded in 1991 as planned. Others, such as the mandatory publication of health and social services community care plans, went ahead in 1992. The most significant changes however, including the new funding framework, the introduction of care management, and the requirement to divide purchasing and providing functions within SSDs, were implemented in April 1993 (Means and Smith, 1998a; Gostick et al., 1997).

The years following implementation have witnessed a growing body of research which has began to evaluate one or more aspects of the reforms. In addition to inspections by the Social Services Inspectorate, reviews by the Audit Commission and a series of studies funded by the Department of Health (of which ECCEP is one), a wide range of other research has been conducted. In October 1998, the Royal Commission on Long Term Care commissioned a series of papers to distil key findings from these varied post-reform studies in England and Wales and address the question: What have we learned about the impact of the 1993 reforms on the care of frail elderly people? (Henwood and Wistow, 1999) This evidence, and that from other research not reviewed by the Commission in detail but of particular relevance to the first three years of the post-reform period, provides a valuable context for ECCEP.

Issues in post-reform community care

As the Royal Commission papers reflect, research relating to the reforms and their impact on the care of older people can be grouped into several main themes, all of which relate to the original aims of *Caring for People*. Three of these themes are of particular relevance to ECCEP: the extent to which services have been developed which allow older people to remain at home; evidence relating to the provision of support for carers; and findings relating to the formation of assessment and care management arrangements.

There is a significant level of consensus in the post-reform literature that innovative and effective domiciliary services have been developed since 1993 (Harding, 1999; Audit Commission, 1997). There is now greater recognition among social services departments of the wish of older people to remain in their own homes which has resulted in concerted efforts to make that possible. The requirement that users and carers should be involved in assessment and care planning has provided older people who wish to remain at home with greater opportunities to state their views and play a role in choosing appropriate forms of support (Lewis and Glennerster, 1996). Forms of care previously provided in institutional settings (most notably personal care services) can now increasingly be provided at home, and developments in new forms of housing and in aids and adaptations have made remaining in the community a more viable option for a growing number of older people. Reviews by the Social Services Inspectorate suggest that the development of independent sector domiciliary services has also met with some success, particularly in some parts of the country.

The growth of community-based services, new forms of assessment for services and the new funding arrangements have also had an effect on residential and nursing homes. There has been some shift away from the dominance of institutional forms of care: the rapid growth in residential and nursing home placements which took place during the 1980s and early 1990s began to stabilise after 1993 (Department of Health, 1996b). The government's wish to stem the flow of public money from social security into institutional care has been largely achieved through the introduction of the new funding structure, which requires an assessment of need as well as financial eligibility for support. The implication of the old funding structure was that people who did not necessarily require institutional care were still admitted. Post 1993, many less dependent older people are being directed towards community-based services rather than residential alternatives. An ongoing PSSRU study is able to illustrate the resulting change in the dependency profile of older people in institutional care by comparing results from a 1996 national survey of homes with those from a parallel survey conducted in 1986 (Netten et al., 1997a). As Figure 1.1 illustrates, the profile of older people in all three types of independent sector homes, and particularly those in nursing homes, is one of significantly higher dependency than a decade before.

Despite the changes in institutional care, research has also shown that overall progress in the development of domiciliary services since 1993 has

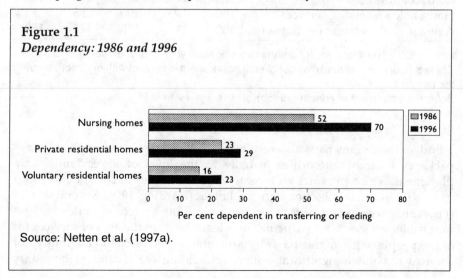

Figure 1.1
Dependency: 1986 and 1996

Per cent dependent in transferring or feeding

Source: Netten et al. (1997a).

been slow. As the programme of monitoring work by the Nuffield Institute/Kings Fund and studies conducted during the first two years of the reforms demonstrate, authorities focused much of their early attention on processes and systems, rather than on changing the nature of services (Henwood et al., 1996; Lewis and Glennerster, 1996). The process of short-term development and adjustment that was required to adapt to the reforms varied between local authorities, but there is no doubt that it was a difficult and prolonged process in many parts of the country. Even following this difficult initial period, however, more recent research suggests that there remain significant gaps in existing services for older people. One of the most prevalent criticisms of the reforms has been that as a consequence of the emphasis on targeting services to those most in need of assistance (without providing local authorities with new funds to do this) 'low-level' support — such as cleaning and shopping — has been withdrawn from a significant number of service users (Clark et al., 1998; Blackman and Atkinson, 1997). In the case of the local authority home help service, the result of targeting is that a more intensive service is being provided, but to fewer households overall. Table 1.3 illustrates that while the number of households receiving home care services dropped by 7 per cent between 1993 and 1997, the total number of contact hours per household increased by 50 per cent. Thus, services began to be concentrated on fewer users who required more frequent or concentrated support.

Table 1.3
Trends in local authority home care provision, 1993-1997

Home care trends	1993	1994	1995	1996	1997
Contact hours	100	124	135	140	148
Households receiving services	100	105	100	95	93
Average contact hours per household	100	119	135	146	159

Index 1993 =100. Data are for a sample week each year in September or in October. Contact hours are the total number of staff hours spent in contact with or directly serving the client(s).
Source: Department of Health (1998b).

Budget limitations have also resulted in cost ceilings being applied to care packages in most authorities, usually at the level of a residential care placement, which provides an incentive for authorities to continue to admit users with more complex needs to care homes (Harding, 1999). Several studies report that some users and carers are continuing to receive inflexible and unreliable services, with particular problems noted in the area of services for older people with dementia (Moriarty and Webb, 1997b). Eligibility for services remains a significant issue, highlighting the continued boundary disputes between health and social care (Challis, 1999; Means and Smith, 1998a). Research has also raised the issue of charging policies for domiciliary care, with the prevalence of charges levied varying significantly across local authorities (Baldwin and Lunt, 1996; Chetwynd et al., 1996). Regional variation in general remains a major theme in post-reform reviews. Which services are available, at what cost, to whom, is a matter of postcode as much as level of need, suggesting the tenacity of a service-led system (Gostick et al., 1997).

Carers occupy a different position in post-reform community care than they did prior to the reforms. The White Paper's recognition of their need for support was followed in 1995 by the passage of the Carers (Recognition and Services) Act, which formalised their right to ask for a separate assessment. Research and programme development relating to carers and issues around caregiving has grown substantially since 1990. Evidence from the Social Services Inspectorate and the Kings Fund Carers Impact programme suggests that the number of carer assessments are increasing and special initiatives, such as support groups and designated workers for carers, are developing. Despite greater awareness of carers and their needs, however, there is limited research evidence of improved outcomes in the post-reform period, or even of adequate support from services. The Royal Commission summary, referring to a recent SSI inspection of services for carers, states: 'the quality of support that carers receive remains a matter of chance. Support depends far more on where carers live and who they are in contact with in social services than on what they need.' Gillian Parker, in her review for the Commission, argues that evidence to date suggests that only marginal improvements have been made to the 'core' services that carers need for support (Parker, 1999). She attributes this, as other researchers have done, to both to the nature of the reforms — which made continued assumptions about the role and availability of family carers — and the lack of available finance to support their implementation (Twigg, 1998).

The introduction of care management involved significant structural change for social services departments. The White Paper itself provided few details regarding how these changes were to be made, or even a definition of what constituted care management. These details were contained in the substantial body of guidance material issued between the passage of the Act and implementation in April 1993 (SSI/SWSG, 1991). However, even the guidance allowed authorities significant flexibility in how they would interpret and thus implement the changes. A series of Social Services Inspectorate reports, plus studies conducted in a small number of authorities (Hoyes et al., 1994; Lewis and Glennerster, 1996) reflect the early confusion experienced and report on the variation in care management models which began to emerge. A Department of Health-funded study conducted by the PSSRU from 1997 is currently mapping these forms of care management and evaluating their

---

Box 1.3
Key features of care management development

1   Definition of the nature, structure and goals of care management
2   Influence of external contextual and environmental factors
3   Target population, including user group; targeting methods including assessment
4   Care management as process and intensive case management; the balance between these two activities
5   Location of care management; SSD, NHS, external; access to NHS staff.
6   Style of care management: administrative or more extensive?
7   Operational aspects of care management; role specificity; balance of activities between assessment and review; caseload size; continuity; documentation
8   Influence over providers; devolution of budgets; range of service mix
9   Management of care management; quality assurance; supervision; peer group review
10 Clarity of organisational arrangements; practice incentives; logical links between values, goals, care management service

Source: Challis (1999).

---

implications (Challis et al., 1998a). Box 1.3 summarises the key features of care management development.

David Challis, drawing on previous research, summarised how care management has developed since 1993 in his submission to the Royal Commission (Challis, 1999). While some benefits were clear, such as a more planned approach to assessing need and arranging care, greater involvement of users and carers, and an expansion of the role of trained social workers in the care of older people, there were a considerable number of problems identified. These centred around the way in which authorities defined and differentiated care management, and how care management arrangements interacted with existing structures and other aspects of the reforms. Problems with the model of care management adopted involved a tension between the performance of the core tasks[6] and the role of the individual care manager. Early studies indicated that a growing number of authorities were adopting an administrative model of care management, in which the performance of the core tasks formed a process which all users went through, and in which these tasks were conducted by a variety of staff within the SSD. Many authorities were not differentiating between this process and the original model of intensive care management, which involved the provision of one designated care manager to users with complex needs (Davies and Challis, 1986; Davies, 1992; Challis, 1994a). The consequences of this lack of differentiation were that many of the potential benefits of care management for users with more complex needs were lost, including emotional support and counselling, while continuity of contact between users and one key worker was rare. Separation of tasks also contributed to a focus on assessment at the expense of monitoring and review. Other organisational problems were also identified in early studies, such as difficulties with assessment documentation and the provision of information to users and carers, lack of involvement of health professionals in assessment, and limited evidence of devolved budgets, due to the absence of adequate financial monitoring systems and concerns about the control of scarce resources.

Central to the analysis of developments in care management following the reforms is an understanding of the origins of the concept, and its introduction into the British social care system. In order to do this it is necessary to take a step back from the current changes and briefly examine the demonstration projects and studies which were conducted by the PSSRU in the 1970s and 80s. Findings from these studies played an important part in shaping community care policy in the 1990s. In conjunction with the Unit's distinct theoretical framework for examining resources, needs and outcomes in social care, the studies also provide the context for the design and development of *Evaluating Community Care for Elderly People*. We now turn to genesis of ECCEP at the PSSRU by reviewing the early work of the Unit, and in particular the Domicilary Care Project.

Notes

1   Both the home help service — whose origins were as a form of assistance to new mothers — and meals provision began as developments in local authority public health departments, which at that time also administered community nursing, midwifery and health visiting services. For a concise history of the home help service, see Dexter and Harbert (1983).
2   A 1962 amendment to the National Assistance Act had formalised local authority meals on wheels services, but surveys illustrated that provision was still patchy by the early 1970s and dominated by the voluntary sector (Harris, 1968).
3   It is important to recognise that the agenda relating to *empowerment* for users and carers, as distinct from choice alone, emerged from the guidance issued following the White Paper, rather than from *Caring for People*.
4   Griffiths had employed the term 'care' rather than 'case' management in his report. Guidance following the 1990 Act was to return to the use of care management in response to criticisms that users were not 'cases' to be arranged, but rather individuals with varied needs.
5   See Chapter 2 for an explanation of the Kent care management project and subsequent PSSRU studies.
6   The core tasks of care management, as set out in the 1991 guidance, include case finding and screening, assessing need, care planning, monitoring and review.

Evaluating Community Care for Elderly People is the most recent of a series of studies conducted around a distinct theoretical framework which has been developed at the PSSRU since the Unit's establishment at the University of Kent in 1974. This framework (the Production of Welfare, or POW) has been applied consistently in the Unit's work over the years, in relation to a range of policy areas. The Production of Welfare approach is introduced in this chapter, as is some of the Unit's earlier research upon which ECCEP builds: most notably the Kent Community Care Project and its successors, and the Domiciliary Care Project. The second part of this chapter describes the design and methods of ECCEP, and the third and final section places the study's findings in a national context by comparing them with nationally representative data from surveys of older people living in the community.

The Production of Welfare

When the PSSRU was established, the then Department of Health and Social Security and the Unit's founder, Bleddyn Davies, agreed that the programmes of work to be undertaken would focus on the analysis and research of needs and the 'production relations' of community care. Production relations referred to the economic theory of production which was to be adapted at the PSSRU to take into account the processes and consequences involved in the provision of social care services (Davies and Challis, 1981; Davies and Knapp, 1988). The first comprehensive use of the POW approach in the Unit's work was in relation to residential services for older people, in a 1981 study authored by Bleddyn Davies and Martin Knapp (Davies and Knapp, 1981). While acknowledging and building upon important developments in gerontological research (particularly E.M. Goldberg's 1970 study, *Helping the Aged*, and work on the relationship between needs and outcomes in American

Figure 2.1
The Production of Welfare

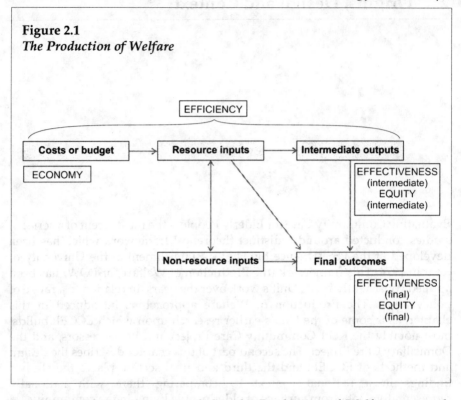

social gerontology), they argued that the Production of Welfare approach filled a gap in the existing literature by focusing on the relationship between causes and consequences in social care, and provided both a set of questions and a series of tools to guide evaluation. The POW approach has been consistently used in Unit research since that first study, and is a key device for realising the main aim of PSSRU work, which is to undertake research which improves equity and efficiency, and the use of resources in community and long-term care and related areas.

The Production of Welfare centres around a series of questions about who gets how much of what support and resources, at what cost to whom, and with what effects of evaluative significance (Davies, 1994b). Figure 2.1 illustrates the relationship between the different components of the Production of Welfare. These consist of *inputs* — including 'resource inputs' (such as buildings and staff) and 'non-resource inputs' such as client characteristics and management procedures — and, on the other side of the equation, *outputs* — including 'intermediate outputs' (such as services received by users and service quality) and 'final outputs', which represent final outcomes such as improvements in health or quality of life.

Application of the POW approach in the Unit's work is guided by three important assumptions. The first is that the *focus of analysis is the impact of resources on final outputs*. These are outcomes for users and carers which are important for the evaluation of effectiveness. One example of such an output would be the length of time the user is able to remain living in the community rather than entering residential or nursing home care. The second assumption is that broadly interpreted *equity and efficiency*, rather than effectiveness, are the appropriate evaluative criteria in a POW study. This means that faced with a budget constraint it is not sufficient to demonstrate that resources can yield a benefit. What is required is that resources are distributed in relation to needs in ways that maximise the total potential for welfare gains given the weighting of equity and other objectives. To do this requires a clear understanding of the differences between average and marginal costs and benefits, and the fact that variations in the relative prices of inputs can and should influence technological assumptions about the interventions to select in responding to individual needs.

Third and finally, POW studies are guided by the assumption that *the relationship between resources and outputs varies greatly between individuals*. This implies that the type and mix of service inputs must reflect quite subtle differences in the need-related circumstances of individuals in order to achieve an optimal level of equity and efficiency in social care. This has two enormously important implications for analysts and practitioners. The first is the failure to investigate important differences between subgroups of users runs the risk of making invalid assumptions about the appropriate technological response to particular configurations of need-related circumstances. The second is that those responsible for assessing need-related circumstances need to be sufficiently well-trained to identify these differences. This final assumption regarding the relationship between individual circumstances, inputs and the resulting outputs has profoundly affected PSSRU analysis, from the first POW studies onwards.

ECCEP is a 'classic' Production of Welfare study. Central to ECCEP's design are the POW questions, which are in simple terms about how resources affect outcomes, given the needs and circumstances of users, carers and the local service system. Thus, ECCEP describes in detail the individual characteristics of users and carers and examines the structure and variation in care management arrangements (non-resource inputs), determines which types of services, from which source, make up the care package (resource inputs), and analyses a range of intermediate outputs and final outcomes which arise from the combination of different inputs.

While knowledge of the Production of Welfare approach is useful in understanding both the study design and types of analysis used in ECCEP, it constitutes only part of the tradition which shaped the types of questions and issues addressed in the study. ECCEP's origins also lie in the early work of the

PSSRU and its role in shaping social policy reform. Of particular relevance was the Kent Community Care Project, and its successors.

Origins of the Kent Community Care Project

The establishment of the PSSRU took place in 1974, during a time when several broad shifts in health and social care were occurring, changes which raised questions about the capacity of the existing system to meet the demands of the future and make efficient use of available resources. Chapter 1 outlines some of these developments through the 1960s and 70s. These included the process of deinstitutionalisation from long-stay hospitals, a growing awareness of the increasing elderly population and developments in policy, particularly the implementation of recommendations from the Seebohm Committee report in 1971. The policy discourse which followed the committee's recommendations provided an important context for the PSSRU's early work. Three strands within this discourse were particularly important: the emphasis on the need to develop a broader policy for community care; the changing role of local authorities; and the importance of coordinating services at the field level by including users, their families and others in the planning, organisation and delivery of services.

In its discussion of social care for elderly people, the Seebohm Committee emphasised the need to develop a broader policy or 'overall plan of action' in social care, rather than continuing to provide services under 'a variety of functions scattered through legislation'. Thus, rather than continuing to provide fragmented services from a variety of agencies as prescribed by national policy, the committee called for more ambitious local policy-making. A change of this kind would require a new type of relationship between local authorities and national government, one which was also reflected in the reform of local government begun by the work of the Maud Committee in the late 1960s (Committee on the Management of Local Government, 1967). This changing role for local authorities would include two important shifts. One was from loosely constituted service providing departments to more 'corporate' bodies who would contribute to coordination across public agencies and in some cases into the private sector. The second was from a narrow focus on administration towards a greater emphasis on management, meaning both that elected representatives were to be engaged more consistently in aspects of policy rather than the details of administration, and that specific programmes were to be better coordinated and managed.

A third strand of policy discourse following Seebohm concerned the need to coordinate services at the field level while including users, their families and other members of the community in both the planning and the delivery of services. This needed to occur for several reasons. First, there was a growing recognition at the time that local government more generally was insufficiently responsive to the needs, values and preferences of local people. Second, territorial justice studies had shown that variations in the needs profile of populations were only one of many factors influencing patterns of spending and provision between authorities (Davies, 1968, 1992). Third, a growth in demand for services highlighted the need for authorities to support caregivers and where possible recruit other informal helpers to complement professional workers. While the committee report itself offered no real sense of how older people and their families could be involved in decision-making about services, it did emphasise the importance of needs-based assessment and planning. One component of this was the vision of a 'community-orientated family service' which would not only consider the needs of the elderly in the context of their social circumstances but also aim to support caregivers, which the report's chapter on the elderly advocated. Informal sources of support for service users were to be encouraged, not only in terms of family caregivers but also community volunteers.

It was with this background of policy developments and discussion that the then Director of Kent Social Services made a speech at the University of Kent shortly after the Unit's establishment. He argued that new approaches were required to make social services more flexible and more responsive to users' wishes and needs. Subsequent discussions with Bleddyn Davies led to the protocol for the Kent Community Care Project, which began in 1976 (Davies, 1974).[1] The project turned out to be one of the first care management projects for older users anywhere in the world, coinciding with the establishment of demonstration projects in the U.S.A. preceding the National Long Term Care Channeling Program, which established pilots in ten states to coordinate services for older people.

The Kent Community Care Project

The Kent Community Care Project (KCCP) was designed with the aim of improving equity and efficiency in social care by concentrating the authority and accountability for matching resources to users' and carers' need on care management teams. The study had a quasi-experimental design, and was based in three towns in the Thanet area of Kent. Older users of social services received the new service in one town (n=92), while users in two other towns received standard services (n=116). Carers were also interviewed. Those older people in the experimental group received their services in a framework designed to improve each of the three aspects of efficiency central to an economic theory of care-managed care: namely input mix, output mix and technical efficiency.

Input mix efficiency was improved in the experimental group by decentralising responsibility for all core management tasks to workers, and providing them with an individual budget to mobilise resources in a flexible way. Workers were accountable for the resources used and what they achieved. Services could be commissioned from new or innovative sources, a wide range of user and carer needs were to be taken into account, and divisions of labour were set up to reduce burden on carers. In order to encourage input mix efficiency, trained social workers were recruited as care managers. These workers' caseloads were kept low in order to facilitate careful and thorough assessment and the performance of other care management tasks. Output mix efficiency involved the care manager developing a 'holistic' care plan for users which would widen the range of benefits possible. Reflecting the ideals of some of the practical commentaries of the time, this included supplementing available services with quasi-informal 'helpers' from within the community who were recruited and matched to users by the care management team. These helpers were employed to assist users. They were selected based on their motivation and experience, and to match users as individuals as well as for their ability to provide practical assistance (Qureshi et al., 1989). Technical efficiency was improved in the experimental group by encouraging innovation among workers and managers more broadly. This included activities such as home-based day care for a small group of users, and the establishment of a block contract for low-level assistance to a group of helpers from a community church. The operational features of the KCCP approach are shown in Table 2.1.

Table 2.1 illustrates the key components of the community care approach. Detailed explanation of each of these features can be found in the two books from the original study (Davies and Challis, 1986; Challis and Davies, 1986) as well as contemporary and subsequent articles (Challis et al., 1995; Davies, 1990a,b, 1995). It is worth emphasising here the importance of one key aspect of the model in particular, which was the targeted caseload. Targeting was central to the study's overall objective, which was to improve equity and efficiency in the form of welfare gains without raising lifetime costs to either health or social care services. Because the model intended to demonstrate that older people with complex needs could be maintained at home without the need for admission to residential care, those selected to take part in the study were those deemed to be at risk of admission. Care packages for this targeted group were subject to budget caps, in order to contribute towards achieving budget neutrality. Weekly costs had to be limited to two-thirds the cost of residential care (higher expenditure was permitted, subject to managerial approval) and thus care managers had to be aware of the unit costs of services (Davies, 1992; Challis et al., 1993).

The operational features of targeting and devolved budgeting with expenditure limits were key to reducing some of the vagueness regarding ends and means which had been identified as a characteristic of social work and social care practice at the time (Goldberg and Warburton, 1979). Subsequent interpretations of the KCCP's findings assumed that the model could be equally successfully applied to all older service users. This

Table 2.1
The community care approach, service objectives and aspects of efficiency

Service objectives and efficiency criteria	Approach
1. Improved uptake and outreach to areas of unmet need (Horizontal Target Efficiency)	(i) Decentralised budget: more flexible and responsive services (ii) Coterminous with other key services/known in locality
2. Improved assessment and screening (Vertical Target Efficiency) (Input Mix Efficiency) (Market Efficiency)	(i) Staff more experienced and qualified (ii) Specialisation: improved knowledge base (iii) Key worker: coordinate contributions of others (iv) Manageable caseload (v) Respond to elderly person and carers' definition of problems (vi) Targeted caseload — margin of institutional care
3. Improved care planning: overcome fragmentation (Input Mix Efficiency) (Market Efficiency)	(i) Key worker approach (ii) Decentralised budget: more flexible and responsive service (iii) Risk-taking more legitimate (iv) Closer contact with other agencies (e.g. NHS) (v) Involve elderly person and carers in defining solutions (vi) Gap filling — develop services where none at present (vii) Enhanced status of work with elderly: job satisfaction (viii) Opportunities for continued learning — peer review (ix) Remove negative incentives to staff
4. Continued monitoring and review (Input Mix Efficiency) (Market Efficiency)	(i) Key worker — continuity of contacts in network (ii) Manageable caseload (iii) Recording system — feedback to workers and managers
5. Improved accountability (Vertical Target Efficiency) (Input Mix Efficiency) (Market Efficiency)	(i) Budget limit (ii) Recording system — caseload reviews, and costs (iii) Scheme integrated into SSD (iv) Introduce peer review (v) Targeted caseload — margin of institutional care
6. Make better use of resources (Vertical Target Efficiency) (Input Mix Efficiency) (Market Efficiency	(i) Targeted caseload — margin of institutional care (ii) Knowledge of costs (iii) Services normally charged to budget

Source: Challis and Davies (1986, p.12).

interpretation failed adequately to recognise that the scheme included a particular group of users for whom the potential productivity of care management could be realised given the study's design.

Despite the varied inferences subsequently drawn from the results, findings from the KCCP were clear. They suggested that care managers with devolved budgets could improve the effectiveness of social care for older people in several important ways. First, lower rates of admission to residential and nursing home care were found amongst the experimental group. Second, comparisons across several measures of quality of life revealed that both users and their carers receiving the care management model showed greater improvements that those receiving standard services. Finally, these benefits were realised at no greater cost than for existing services. Given these findings, replications of the study were implemented in other parts of Kent, and new demonstration projects were set up in other parts of the country. The model was taken one step further in an extension of the Gateshead replication of KCCP, and then in Darlington (Challis et al., 1990, 1995). The first Gateshead study permitted testing of the community care approach in an urban setting, with a second later study in the city based in primary care. The Darlington project implemented the care management model in geriatric care, providing a home care package to older people who might otherwise have remained in long-stay care. These successors to the KCCP found similar improvements in destinational outcomes and quality of life for older people and their carers at no greater cost than existing services, and with resulting care management costs remaining low in relation to the cost of better coordinated care (Davies, 1992; Davies et al., 1990).

The Kent Community Care Project and its descendants had important implications for both policy and practice. Within the UK and abroad, the model was used in further demonstration projects, most notably in Scotland with the EPIC scheme (Bland, 1994; Bland and Hudson, 1994) as well as in New York State, the Netherlands and in Australia (Davies, 1990a,b, 1992). Discussion of the model in British social policy began from the late 1970s onwards, particularly within the Department of Health and Audit Commission reports and the work of the Social Services Inspectorate. The Unit's findings and the POW approach were acknowledged to have an important effect on the design requirements for projects funded under the Care in the Community project during the early 1980s. The initiative funded a series of 28 community care demonstrations for different client groups across the country, which the PSSRU was later responsible for evaluating (Renshaw et al., 1988). Most significantly, arguments regarding care management were to influence the recommendations put forward by Sir Roy Griffiths in his 1988 report *Community Care: An Agenda for Action*. The result was the inclusion of care management as the 'cornerstone' of the policy proposals put forward in the 1989 White Paper and subsequently implemented following the 1990 NHS and Community Care Act.

The Domiciliary Care Project

While the PSSRU was conducting further care management projects following the initial success of the KCCP, other related research was also being undertaken. One of the largest studies of the 1980s was the Domiciliary Care Project. DCP was first proposed in 1979, and fieldwork began in 1984. Like the Kent Community Care Project, it aimed to address issues in the system of care for older people, but on a broader basis. While KCCP and its descendants had focused on specific communities of older people, helping to define the nature of problems, allowing the testing of a new model of care management and providing the basis for policy arguments, these studies had not gathered evidence reflecting the national picture. DCP, in contrast, was proposed as a large study which would be conducted across a range of local authorities and produce statistically full, reliable and representative evidence (Bebbington et al., 1985).

The study had several central aims. One of the underlying issues that it aimed to address was the prevalence and consequences of local variations in patterns of care. While community care policy was being developed by central government, local authorities were responsible for organising and providing services. By the early 1980s it was evident that, despite the changes in social services departments following Seebohm, local variations had grown rather than diminished (Bebbington and Davies, 1983). A study which aimed to gather information about differences in the relationship between needs, services and outcomes for both older service users and their carers across local authorities would, it was thought, shed some light on the causes and consequences of local variation as well as arrive at results regarding the equity and efficiency of the system as a whole. The central aims of DCP are summarised in Box 2.1.

As a study focusing largely on outcomes, a longitudinal research design was required which would assess users, carers and the service system before services were provided, and subsequently as effects from the care package became evident. Additional and ongoing data would also need to be collected regarding resource flows over time. Most importantly, the study needed to be located in a range of local authorities reflecting varying area characteristics. Criteria used to select local authorities were status (shire, metropolitan or London borough), political control and level of expenditure.[2] Based on these criteria, ten authorities were selected and agreed to participate in the study. Table 2.2 illustrates the breakdown of authorities by the three selection criteria.

Once the local authorities had been selected, it was necessary to identify area social services offices within these authorities which could serve as a source for the cases to be recruited to participate. Criteria were again applied in area selection. First, in addition to being willing to participate, the areas had to be judged large enough to generate sufficient cases of older users during a three

Table 2.2
Characteristics of local authorities in the Domiciliary Care Project

Local authority	Status	Political control	Domicilary care expenditure
1	Inner London	Labour	High
2	Inner London	Conservative	Low
3	Outer London	Conservative	High
4	Metro. district	Labour	High
5	Metro. district	Conservative (marginal)	Medium
6	Metro. district	Conservative (marginal)	Low
7	English shire	Conservative	High
8	English shire	Conservative (marginal)	Medium
9	English shire	Conservative	Low
10	Welsh shire	Labour	High

Source: Bebbington et al. (1986).

Box 2.1
Objectives of the Domiciliary Care Project

- To describe the consequences for clients in different circumstances, and those who care for them, of the main types of community-based services.
- To estimate the resources required and the costs of achieving specific outcomes by particular means.
- To understand better substitutability between services, and between personal social services and other services.
- To examine different social service organisations in terms of four different criteria of efficiency.
- To explain how different systems have evolved, how organisational goals are developed, and the ways in which the process of creating welfare is enabled or constrained.

Source: Twigg (1985).

---

to four month period. In two local authorities the area offices were fairly small, and for this reason two offices in these authorities took part in the study. Second, areas were also selected on the basis of the form of social work and home help organisation they had (patch versus specialist teams, area or central control of home help offices) and, finally, areas were selected on the basis of evidence of one or more innovatory approaches to care of the elderly, from specialist discharge schemes to night-sitting services.

Following the selection of the twelve study sites within ten local authorities, recruitment of interviewees for DCP began. It was decided that older users would be interviewed as close to their assessment for community care services as possible, and then six months afterwards in order to examine the effect of the care package. The resulting users sample across authorities at Time I was 589 older people, or just under 60 users in each authority. In cases where the user had a main carer, these individuals were also interviewed (n=210). Telephone interviews with the care manager of each user were also conducted. In this way, the perceptions of three key actors — the user, carer and care manager — were captured in the study. This triadic design provided DCP with a unique field-level perspective.

In addition to the survey material gathered by DCP, other data were collected. Interviews with social service department staff and district health authorities were conducted and a documentary review undertaken to gain information about policies, practices and procedures in each authority (Bebbington et al., 1986). Data were extracted from the 1981 census to provide contextual information about the population and profile of each area in the study, and secondary analysis of the 1985 General Household Survey and DHSS statistics was also undertaken. Perhaps most significantly, resource flows (consisting of information regarding changes in the services provided to users, as well as costing data) were tracked in some detail over time. This information was central in estimating the outcomes of variations in inputs, the substitutability of inputs and in conducting other statistical analyses to address themes such as targeting and marginal productivities.

DCP findings

Findings from the Domiciliary Care Project were published in Resources, Needs and Outcomes in Community Care (Davies et al., 1990).[3] While readers should turn to this text for a detailed analysis of results, it is worth highlighting several important findings here, as they directly contributed to the design of ECCEP in the early 1990s.

Despite developments in community care policy and resulting changes in local authority provision, DCP findings suggested that there was a poor relationship between the resources available and the needs of older service users. There was a failure to allocate services such as home care between users in order to maximise benefits, and indeed it was found that a significant proportion of users were receiving assistance with tasks which they could manage for themselves. DCP was the first study to estimate marginal productivities from services, and found that they were much weaker than expected. This finding of low, or in some cases non-existent, productivities meant that a policy of concentrating more resources on fewer users would be doomed to failure unless productivities changed. In order to achieve this change, the nature of the service system would have to be reformed in ways which would be more far reaching than merely adapting patterns of targeting.

In particular, DCP found that domiciliary provision remained ineffective in preventing admission to residential care. Interviews with care managers revealed that preventing institutionalisation was not a primary aim of the care package, and this (combined with the fact that the supply of residential care was plentiful) was reflected in admission rates. Some services in particular were poorly developed (such as respite care) while others were distributed in such a way as to reduce potential benefits. Interviews with informal caregivers and analysis of resource provision for carers found that their needs were not being met in many cases. Levels of stress and burden identified in the study were higher than expected, and the mix of services being provided was found to have little effect on these carer stress levels over time.

In addition to evidence relating to a mismatch between resources and needs in the mid-1980s, DCP also found that the regional variation in levels of service provision, types of service available and local policies regarding charging was evident across authorities. These local factors were found to have greater impact on the amount and type of services received by users (and related outcomes) than the needs and circumstances of users themselves. In short, DCP identified a number of areas in which the service system of the mid-1980s was failing to meet the aims and objectives of early community care policy.

ECCEP

Like the Kent Community Care Project, initial findings from DCP also contributed to the policy reform process of the late 1980s, particularly through the PSSRU's contact with Sir Roy Griffiths and the dissemination of findings at seminars within the Department of Health and Social Services Inspectorate. Following the passage of the 1990 NHS and Community Care Act, it was clear that new research was required to assess changes in the system in the post-reform period. Policy guidance following the Act stipulated that in-depth evaluation was needed to monitor the impact of the new policy, and the Department of Health's own research strategy for 1991-3 described as a 'particularly important objective' the assessment of the extent to which the objectives of the community care reforms had been met.

Thus, in 1992 the PSSRU submitted a proposal to the Department of Health to conduct a replication of DCP, in the same ten local authorities, in order to evaluate the new system and identify changes in pre-reform patterns. The second part of this 'before-after' study was to be entitled *Evaluating Community Care for Elderly People*. The study would be unique in its range and breadth, meeting the needs of the Department for monitoring and evaluation of some of the central aspects of the reforms, particularly in relation to issues of equity, effectiveness and efficiency. Like DCP, ECCEP was expected to produce information about the relationship between the needs of older people and their carers, the resources available and the outcomes achieved, with the aim of improving both policy and practice in relation to needs-based planning and care management.

Design

Consistent with the design of a before and after study, and in order to ensure that findings could in the future be compared with pre-reform patterns, ECCEP was structured to replicate the design of the DCP. The study was to take place in the same twelve areas within the same ten local authorities in England and Wales. Users, their principal carers and care managers were to be interviewed following the user's referral to social services, and, consistent with the longitudinal design of DCP, follow-up interviews were to take place with the same triad of informants six months later. The aims of ECCEP also reflect the emphasis on the relationship between resources, needs and outcomes that was central to DCP and constitute an integral component of the Production of Welfare framework common to both studies. The study, therefore, aimed to collect data relating to which users and carers, living in what circumstances, received which resources, at what cost, and with what effects. Evaluation of patterns and effects between and across authorities was also expected, as well as comparisons with DCP findings. A range of more complex analyses linking patterns of provision and outcomes in relation to issues such as targeting and productivities was also a central part of the ECCEP design (Davies and Fernández, 1999).

The ECCEP sample

In order to address the aims of the study, a representative selection of the caseloads of care managers working with older people in each local authority was sought. This process began in 1994. As the study is longitudinal, users were eligible for inclusion only if care managers believed that their service package would last more than two months. These older people also had to be either new referrals to social services, or review cases in which the older person's needs were going to be reassessed and significant changes made to their care package.

The collection of data in the local authority areas was complex, and elderly people were selected to take part in the study on the basis of a multi-cell sampling matrix based on such factors as interval need (described below), the extent of service provision and living arrangements. By the time that initial data collection was completed at the end of July 1995, the total number of elderly people identified as being eligible for inclusion in the study across all ten authorities was 597. Of those eligible, interviews were achieved with 492 users: a response rate of 82 per cent. Data obtained from these interviews have been weighted using information obtained during the screening process to achieve population representativeness where appropriate.

Users who agreed to take part in the study were asked to identify a principal informal carer (PIC), who was defined as someone who provides the older person with assistance on a regular basis, at least once a week. Those carers were then asked to participate in the study, and constitute the ECCEP carer sample.

A small proportion (15 per cent) of the older people recruited to the study moved to residential or nursing homes upon referral. Findings presented in this book focus on the remaining 419 users and their carers who were assessed for domiciliary services. These users, their carers and care managers constitute the sample of community-based responses. Table 2.3 illustrates the number of interviewees associated with this community sample at each stage of the ECCEP project.

Longitudinal design

As Table 2.3 illustrates, there were two initial stages of ECCEP data collection. Time I interviews took place following the (re-)referral of the user. For users and carers, this interview took place on average 14 weeks after referral, while care manager Time I interviews took place on average 25 weeks after the referral date of the user. Time II interviews took place with users who were still resident in the community approximately six months after the initial interview. Their carers and care managers were also interviewed a second time.

The majority of evidence presented in the chapters that follow is drawn from Time I user, carer and care manager interviews. Time II data are employed in

Table 2.3
Community-based responses

	Time I (1995)	Time II (1996)
	n	n
Users	419	299
Carers	238	186
Workers	425	418

Chapters 9 and 10. These two chapters deal with outcomes for users and carers, employing evidence gathered by comparing Time I with Time II data. By the second interview, all users had been receiving community-based services for more than six months, and thus it was possible not only to identify changes in needs and circumstances, but also begin to draw conclusions about the effect of services. Some Time II data are also employed in Chapter 5 relating to care management — these data relate to the final core tasks of the care management process (monitoring and review) which take place after all services are in place, and thus information regarding these activities was gathered during the second care manager interview.

Following Time II interviews, further ECCEP data collection continued to take place. A tracking exercise was commenced, in which the circumstances of users and the services they were receiving were monitored at four-monthly intervals. Tracking forms were filled in by care managers or from social service records. Tracking continued in 1999, with 20 per cent of the original sample remaining in the community and still receiving domiciliary services as of December 1998. Tracking data will be employed in future analyses relating to longer-term outcomes for users and carers.

An additional data collection exercise also began following Time II interviews, which related specifically to the collection of *utilisation of health services*. This Health Research Module was conducted by a registered nurse researcher who had carried out a similar exercise during DCP. The aim of the exercise was to confirm the accuracy of ECCEP health service utilisation data, which were obtained from users, carers and care managers at Time I and Time II. It was expected that care managers would be able to provide basic information regarding the health inputs that users were receiving, but this did not occur in all cases. In addition, users themselves were not always able to provide utilisation data, particularly in cases of cognitive impairment. Thus, the Health Research Module was a retrospective exercise, which returned to the health authorities in which ECCEP users had been treated, and collected more detailed information regarding which NHS resources had been used, for how long and with what frequency. In future ECCEP work, these data will be used in conjunction with the findings presented in Chapter 8 to provide a more comprehensive picture of the health care resources used by older people, and the relationship between health and social care services.

Interview schedules

One final point that applies to Time I and Time II interviews relates to the type of interview schedules used. While the vast majority of users and carers were interviewed using one schedule at Time I and another at Time II, some proxy interviews did take place, and data from these are included in some tables throughout this book. Proxy interviews occurred when the user was unable to provide certain types of information. In most cases, this occurred when the user was cognitively impaired or had a behavioural disorder. In these instances, the carer completed a proxy schedule on the user's behalf.

The system used to interview care managers was more complex, which should be noted when reading Chapter 5. While all workers received the same schedule at Time II, four types of interviews took place at Time I. The largest group of care managers at Time I were interviewed in depth, for over an hour. This type of interview used a 'standard' schedule (n=200). A second group of interviews was conducted using a 'brief' schedule (n=106), while a third group of care managers or a member of the same fieldwork team was interviewed using 'short' schedules (n=38). Finally, a small group of care managers were interviewed using 'proxy' schedules (n=81). Proxy care manager schedules were completed when the worker primarily responsible for the case was not available, but a colleague was present who was able to answer basic questions and consult the relevant case files to supply other information.

Dimensions of analysis

Findings in the chapters that follow are presented in text and tables. Tables are weighted to achieve user population representativeness. Most tables follow a standardised format, which reflects ECCEP's aim to explore the relationship between the needs of users and carers, and the type and amount of services they receive. Most tables present findings in relation to the interval need of the user, the social support available, and whether or not the user is cognitively impaired or has a behavioural disorder. In relation to social support, tables differentiate between 'PIC', indicating that the user has a carer, and 'No PIC', indicating that no principal carer is involved. The concepts of interval need and cognitive impairment are, however, more complex and merit explanation here.

Interval need

The health and functional ability of users affects the type and amount of services they require. As a result, ECCEP analysis distinguishes between three main groups of users, based on level of functional dependency. Dependency was measured according to the frequency with which the user needed help performing a number of daily activities. Table 2.2 illustrates the basis for this classification, devised originally by Isaacs and Neville (1976), used in DCP and other PSSRU studies, and referred to as 'interval need'.

There are three types of interval need: critical, short and long. Critical interval need users are the most dependent, requiring assistance on a frequent and unpredictable basis. Short interval need users also need help, often at unpredictable times, but less frequently. Long interval need users are more independent, requiring assistance with several activities, but on a more predictable basis. The concept of interval need is thus closely related to the older person's ability to perform activities of daily living (ADLs) and instrumental activities of daily living (IADLs). The relationship between these two concepts helps to illustrate further the interval need classification, as shown in Table 2.4 As the table demonstrates, critical interval need users have the highest level of dependency and are identified as such if *any* of the *ticked* cells apply. Users with critical interval needs account for 35 per cent of the ECCEP user sample. Short interval need users are those with the characteristics indicated by the *crossed* cells in the table, provided that none of the ticked cells applies. These users constitute 27 per cent of the sample. Finally, long interval need users are a residual category representing the least dependent users: they constituted 38 per cent of the total.

Cognitive impairment

Table 2.4
Interval need

ADLs & IADLs	Type of interview[1]			
	User	Carer	Proxy	Care manager
Needs help getting into/out of bed/chair	✔	✔	✔	
Needs help getting to/using toilet	✔	✔	✔	
Loses control of bladder at least once a day	✔			
Loses control of bowels at least once a day	✔			
Inappropriate/anti-social/violent/risky behaviour				✔
Needs help getting complete wash/bath/ shower	✖	✖	✖	
Needs help preparing, cooking or serving a main meal	✖	✖	✖	
Needs help preparing a light snack	✖	✖	✖	

1 Information is taken from other respondents only if a user response is not available.

Tables in the chapters that follow also distinguish between 'CI/BD' and 'No CI/BD' which refers to whether or not the user has a cognitive impairment or behavioural disorder. Cognitive impairment was measured among all users in the sample, using a standardised tool known as the Katzman scale. This scale has a range of 0-28 and groups respondents into three categories: no cognitive impairment (scores below 11), moderate cognitive impairment (scores above 11) and severe cognitive impairment (scores above 22). Users who demonstrated either moderate or severe impairment were classified as being cognitively impaired during ECCEP analysis. Further discussion of this measure, and the proportion of users in question, can be found in Chapter 3.

The national context

Although ECCEP is taking place across ten local authorities, and thus reflects a national picture, the study's user sample does not purport to be representative of all older service users in England and Wales. There are several reasons for this, the most important being that ECCEP (as a longitudinal study) aimed to include older users who would require services for a minimum of two months, which would exclude a proportion of users from the sample. Given this distinction, it is useful to place study findings in a national context. One way to do this is to present information from nationally representative datasets as a baseline for comparisons with the picture emerging from ECCEP. Three sources of data are particularly useful for this exercise: local authority performance indicators, Department of Health (DH) community care statistics and the General Household Survey (GHS). To begin, the ECCEP authorities are compared with all local authorities in England to establish whether their levels of expenditure on services for older people are comparable. The ECCEP user sample is then compared with nationally representative data regarding the needs of older service users, and finally levels of service receipt (from the formal sector generally and the independent sector) are compared between Department of Health statistics, the GHS and ECCEP.

Local authority expenditure

Nine of the ten local authorities in which ECCEP is taking place are in England. By using local authority performance indicators to compare expenditure on social services across the ECCEP areas with expenditure across *all* local authorities in England, it is possible to determine to what extent the authorities in the study reflect national spending patterns. This comparison is illustrated in Table 2.5.

Table 2.5 compares average expenditure per capita, expenditure on specific services and charges levied across all English SSDs in the year Time I interviews took place (1995) with average expenditure in the nine English ECCEP authorities. The pattern that emerges is one of only minor differences between national expenditure levels and spending in the study areas.

The first comparison in Table 2.5 concerns gross expenditure per capita on *all* social services. While the average across all SSDs is £172 per person, the

Table 2.5
Local authority per capita expenditure on social services 1994-1995

Indicator	All SSDs				ECCEP SSDs			
	Min £	Max £	Mean £	CV %	Min £	Max £	Mean £	CV %
Gross expenditure per capita	108.4	382.0	172.3	35.0	116.0	370.0	180.9	49.0
Gross expenditure per capita on services for the elderly	612.0	2872.0	1228.3	36.0	862.0	2722.0	1295.7	45.0
Home help in a sample week	245.0	1635.0	749.9	39.0	409.0	1194.0	774.4	35.0
Provision of meals in a sample week	51.0	597.0	232.0	52.0	163.0	491.0	261.5	47.0
Day care for elderly in a sample week	1.0	157.0	28.9	91.0	6.0	71.0	26.5	80.0
All charges (%)	0.7	21.4	10.5	47.0	2.6	19.8	9.0	59.0
Elderly charges (%)	1.0	31.0	8.9	61.0	1.0	27	10.4	89.0

1 CV = coefficient of variation.
Source: Key indicators of local authority social services, 1994-95; Department of Health/Government Statistical Service (1996).

mean for ECCEP authorities is slightly higher — at £180. The range from minimum to maximum levels of expenditure is very similar between ECCEP authorities and all local authorities. Similarly, if gross expenditure on services *for the elderly* is considered, the per capita average is just slightly higher in the ECCEP areas (£1,295 per person) than nationally (£1,228 per person).

When specific service expenditure is examined, mean levels of per capita spending on home help and meals are again very slightly higher in the ECCEP authorities (£774 and £261 respectively) than among all local authorities (£750 and £232). For day care, ECCEP authorities spend slightly less (£26) than the national average (£29). The differences are, however, very small. What is also important to note is that the range (from minimum to maximum) of expenditure on these services is very similar between all SSDs and the ECCEP authorities. One good comparative indicator of the distribution of values around the mean is the coefficient of variation (CV). Table 2.5 shows that this statistic has very similar values for all SSDs and the nine ECCEP study areas for all performance indicators given.

Table 2.5 also presents some information about resources recouped through service charges. On average across all SSDs, 10.5 per cent of gross current expenditure on *all* services was recouped through fees and charges in 1995. In ECCEP authorities, the proportion was very slightly lower: 9 per cent. In contrast, the proportion of gross expenditure on services *for the elderly* recouped through charges across all SSDs was almost 9 per cent, compared with just over 10 per cent among the ECCEP authorities. Thus, with some minor variations, spending in the areas participating in the study is broadly representative of national patterns.

ECCEP users in context

The General Household Survey is one of the most comprehensive and representative sources of information about individuals and families in the UK. The GHS surveys a stratified random sample of private households (6,000 households which include 25,000 individuals) every year. In addition to the annual collection, supplementary information on particular groups of people is collected on a regular but less frequent basis. One of these groups is older people. The last GHS special survey of older people took place in 1994/95, when ECCEP began. It thus provides a particularly valuable context for comparison, specifically in relation to the subsample of GHS respondents who were identified as service users (n=459). Older service users in the GHS were defined as those in receipt of one or more standard community care services. This subsample can be compared with the community sample of ECCEP respondents (n=419).

In interpreting results from this comparison, readers should keep in mind important differences between the two surveys: while ECCEP is a cohort study, the GHS contains cross-sectional data. This means that users in the GHS sample will have begun receiving community care services at various points in time, in comparison with the cohort of new referrals who make up the ECCEP sample. Direct comparisons between cohort and cross-sectional data should be treated with caution. Despite methodological limitations, however, comparing ECCEP users with those in the GHS does shed light on similarities and differences between the older people in the study and other users across the country.

On the whole, the socio-demographic characteristics of the ECCEP and GHS samples are fairly similar in terms of age, gender, living arrangements and tenure. However, the ECCEP group — representing a cohort of users receiving services for the first time or receiving a significantly different package of services due to a change in needs — is much more dependent when assessed in terms of need for assistance with common activities of daily living (ADLs) and instrumental activities of daily living (IADLs). Table 2.6 compares the proportion of elderly users of community care services who need help with various aspects of daily functioning in the GHS and the ECCEP samples. In both surveys respondents were asked similar (but differently worded) questions 'about everyday things that we all have to do'. Some of these activities such as bathing, feeding and ambulatory ability are listed in Table 2.6. All respondents were asked to indicate: (a) whether they were able to perform a task with relative ease, or (b) with difficulty, or (c) whether they needed help, or (d) whether the task was not done. Unfortunately, the final response category of not done can be interpreted in one of two ways in both surveys. It could either mean that the task is not done and cannot be done or that it could be done if required but that in practice it is done by someone else. To reflect this potential ambiguity, Table 2.6 presents two different estimates of the proportion of users who need help with different tasks. The minimum estimate is based on explicit responses about needing help whereas the maximum responses add in those who report not done. Whichever estimate is taken, however, it is very clear that the proportion of users needing help with selected tasks in the ECCEP sample is considerably greater than in the GHS sample.[4]

Formal services in context

Relatively few older people living in the community are recipients of formal community care services. Table 2.7 shows two sets of estimates of the proportions of the elderly population who were in receipt of formal community care services in 1994, immediately prior to the collection of the first round of ECCEP data. The national data are obtained from statistical returns collated by the Department of Health during the autumn of 1994 and from the elderly supplement of the 1994/95 GHS. The two sets of data are not

Table 2.6

Comparisons of the proportions of community care users needing assistance with daily activities between GHS and ECCEP

Daily activity	ECCEP Minimum %	Maximum %	GHS Minimum %	Maximum %
Bathing	49.0	54.6	22.0	25.1
Washing hands and face	13.2	14.9	1.3	1.3
Dressing	32.9	36.5	6.3	6.7
Transfer	17.5	19.0	4.1	5.2
Toilet	18.0	18.0	2.2	3.3
Feeding	10.9	10.9	1.1	1.3
Getting about the house	12.4	15.9	3.1	4.6
Climbing stairs	28.8	50.9	7.2	26.4

completely compatible — the DH data do not contain information about the use of district nurses — but they do show broadly similar patterns of overall utilisation once various methodological differences are taken into account. For example, the DH collects data about utilisation during a one-week survey period whereas the GHS asked respondents about consumption 'during the past month', which might be expected to record higher rates.

At any one time, about 6 or 7 per cent of elderly people were in contact with a district nurse or a home help, whereas rather smaller proportions of the population were in receipt of meals or attended day centres. A rather larger proportion of the elderly population, however, was in receipt of one or more of the services listed in Table 2.7. It is not possible to produce such estimates from administrative returns, but the GHS data suggest that 15 per cent of elderly people were in receipt of one or more mainstream community care services during 1994/95. Almost two-thirds of these elderly people were in receipt of a single service, a little less than one quarter (24.8 per cent) had access to two services, and 10 per cent were in receipt of three or more. The evidence presented in Table 2.7 suggests that rates of consumption of mainstream community care services among GHS elderly respondents are broadly similar to national patterns.

Another way of showing that the GHS sample of elderly users is broadly representative of all consumers is to compare data about the frequency and intensity of service consumption. Table 2.8 compares the proportion of GHS users and national consumers by categories of visits per week and contact hours per week of home help, the only community care service for which such data are available. The patterns of consumption are very similar in many

Table 2.7
Estimated receipt of community care services, England 1994

Service	Department of Health[1,2] %	General Household Survey[3] %
District nurses	n.a.	6.0
Home help	6.5	7.1
Meals on wheels	2.7	2.8
Luncheon clubs	1.2[4]	3.4
Day centre attendance	1.9	3.1
One or more of the above	n.a.	15.0

1 Information is obtained from statistical returns relating to services purchased and provided by local authorities during a survey week in the autumn.
2 Population base calculated by taking the 1994 estimated elderly population for England (7.7 million) and deducting the estimated number of places for elderly people in residential and nursing homes (360,000), i.e. a total of 7.34 million.
3 Services used by survey respondents in the month prior to interview.
4 Estimated number of people served with meals at luncheon clubs in Department of Health study *excludes* meals provided to elderly people at day centres for which statistics are not available.

Table 2.8
Patterns of home help utilisation, 1994

Contact hours per week[2]	Modest		Substantial		Intensive	
	DH %	GHS %	DH %	GHS %	DH %	GHS %
Modest	34	47	11	11	3	6
Substantial	4	1	23	15	6	7
Intensive	-	-	3	3	15	10

Visits per week[1]

1 Visits per week: Modest: DH = 'once per week', GHS = 'once per week'; Substantial: DH = '2-5 visits', GHS = '2-3 times per week'; Intensive: DH = '6 or more visits', GHS = 'daily or nearly'.
2 Contact hours per week: Modest: DH = 'up to 2 hours', GHS = '1-2 hours'; Substantial: DH = '2-5 hours', GHS = '3-4 hours'; Intensive: DH = '5+ hours'; GHS = '5+ hours'.
Source: Department of Health (1997); Office of National Statistics (1995).

respects although a larger proportion (47 per cent) of the GHS fall into the modest/modest category compared with 34 per cent of national users.

Given the higher level of dependency evident among ECCEP users when compared with those in the GHS, it would be expected that the older people in the ECCEP sample would be using a wider range of services on a more frequent basis.

Table 2.9 compares the usage of social and health care resources between the GHS and ECCEP samples. The left-hand column illustrates what proportion of *all* older people aged 65 and above are in receipt of specific services. Fewer than one in ten are receiving any one social care service, with home help (8 per cent) the most commonly received. Two selected health care services are also shown here: the GHS found that one in five older people had seen a hospital doctor or attended an outpatients clinic in the past three months, while just under one in four had seen a chiropodist.

Columns two and three compare two groups of services users: those in the GHS receiving one or more services, and ECCEP users. With the exception of lunch clubs, a higher proportion of ECCEP users are receiving all social care services. For instance, while just under half (47 per cent) of GHS service users receive home help, this proportion rises to 70 per cent among ECCEP users. Similarly, while 18 per cent of GHS users get meals on wheels, the service is received by 28 per cent of the ECCEP sample.

The bottom portion of Table 2.9 also compares ECCEP and GHS findings relating to the usage of three health care services: chiropody, hospital services and GPs. The figures illustrate the proportion of GHS respondents who report that they received these services in the past three months, and the proportion of ECCEP users who said that they had received these service either on an ongoing basis, or only when necessary. Results indicate that a slightly higher proportion of ECCEP than GHS users visit a chiropodist and a general practitioner, while outpatient or specialist medical visits are actually received by a smaller proportion of ECCEP than GHS users. With this exception, what Table 2.9 suggests is that not only are higher proportions of ECCEP users receiving services, but that these users are also more likely to be receiving a combination of resources. This is consistent with the poorer health and functional ability of the ECCEP sample when compared with older people receiving one or more services in GHS.

Table 2.9 does raise one important issue which is relevant to the remainder of this report. Comparisons with GHS and other national data are not straightforward for ECCEP *health* utilisation data. This centres around question wording in the ECCEP user and care manager questionnaire. Users and care managers were asked if health services were received on a current or ongoing basis. This phrasing implies consistent usage. Information regarding continuous utilisation is important, as it is central to many of the issues which the ECCEP study hopes to illuminate. However, the question wording means that information regarding episodic contact is not as comprehensive. For

Table 2.9

A comparison between ECCEP and the General Household Survey for 1994/95 regarding usage of resources

Resource	General Household Survey		ECCEP
	Whether received in last 1 month		Whether received
	Total sample	Sample receiving at least 1 service	
	%	%	%
Local authority home help	7.7	47.1	70.3
Private home help	6.8	13.1	19.2[1]
Meals on wheels	2.7	18.5	28.1
Lunch club[2]	3.2	22.2	3.6
Day centre	3.2	20.7	24.4
Helper from voluntary organisation	0.7	4.4	7.4
Visit by district nurse/ health visitor	5.9	39.5	38.5

Resource	General Household Survey		ECCEP
	Whether received in last 3 months		Whether received
	Total sample	Sample receiving at least 1 service	(ongoing/current or just when necessary)
	%	%	%
Hospital doctor/ outpatients clinics	20.0	34.4	20.7
Chiropodist	23.9	47.7	56.8
General practitioner	-	69.9	91.0
Total n =	3,501	459	425

1 Excludes private individuals not formally arranged and paid for but includes provision by voluntary organisation.
2 Lunch club includes provision by social services department or voluntary organisation but not private provision.

example, just 15 per cent of care managers said that the user visited their GP on a *current or ongoing basis*, yet an additional 76 per cent reported that contact *occurred when necessary*. The issue of ECCEP health resource data is raised again in Chapter 8.

Table 2.10 compares GHS and ECCEP data regarding the level of service which users were receiving in 1995. The general pattern observed is that

ECCEP users are receiving a higher level of service — either more frequent visits or provision — than GHS users. Again, this is consistent with the more complex needs of the older people taking part in ECCEP. The most striking contrast is in the provision of home help. Just one in five recipients of home help in the GHS sample was receiving a visit every day, compared with two out of three ECCEP users. Although not shown here, this difference in service intensity is also evident when the average number of hours of home help received per week by GHS home help users (just under three hours) is compared with that received by ECCEP users (just over six hours for those receiving the service). While the differences in the receipt of other services are not as significant, ECCEP users are still receiving a higher level of provision. For example, as Table 2.10 shows, just over half of GHS users receiving meals on wheels got them each day, compared with more than two-thirds of ECCEP users. Regarding domiciliary visits by a district nurse or health visitor, just under half of GHS users of this service receiving this service are visited less often than once a week, whereas under a third of ECCEP users are visited less than weekly.

Thus, comparisons of ECCEP data with the General Household Survey and DH statistical returns suggest that older users in this study are more likely to be receiving a wider range of services, on a more frequent basis, than users nationally. ECCEP thus has a potentially unique contribution to make in expanding knowledge about process and outcomes in community care. ECCEP contains information about the impact of services on the users and carers whom the reforms were particularly aimed at supporting: those older people and their families with complex needs, who require and receive a combination of services on a regular basis.

Independent sector services in context

One final contextual comparison relates to the mixed economy of care. A growing proportion of social care services, and some health care services, are being provided to older people by voluntary and private agencies. The most recent (1997) DH community care statistics indicate that, in relation to home care, 44 per cent of service hours were now being provided by the independent sector, compared with just 2 per cent in 1992. Meals services now account for the independent sector's biggest proportionate contribution: in 1997 private or voluntary agencies were providing 41 per cent of meals delivered to people's homes, and 65 per cent of those served at lunch clubs.

In 1995 when ECCEP Time I interviews took place, the role of the independent sector as service provider was growing. However, it is important to establish whether care packages received by users in the study reflected that growth, or were instead disproportionally reliant on statutory services. One

Table 2.10

A comparison between ECCEP and the General Household Survey for 1994/95 regarding the frequency or quantity of provision for those receiving resources

Resource	General Household Survey (Sample receiving at least 1 service) If received in last month,[1] frequency of visits				ECCEP If received, frequency of visits			
	(Nearly) every day %	2/3 times a week %	Once a week %	Less often %	(Nearly) every day %	2/3 times a week %	Once a week %	Less often %
Local authority home help	20.5	25.6	43.3	10.7	67.7	15.0	17.3	0.0
Meals on wheels	54.1	35.3	5.9	4.7	68.2	27.6	4.2	0.0
Lunch club[2]	6.9	27.5	43.1	22.5	0.0	78.6	21.4	0.0
Day centre	6.4	33.0	45.7	14.9	7.8	43.1	49.1	0.0
Helper from voluntary organisation	5.0	0.0	35.0	60.0	3.5	10.6	45.7	40.2
Domiciliary visit by district nurse/health visitor	9.4	18.8	23.2	48.6	10.1	13.6	44.9	31.4

1 Samples were for those receiving each service, given by the proportions shown in the previous table.
2 Lunch club includes provision by social services department or voluntary organisation but not private provision.

Table 2.11
Proportion of resources provided by independent sector

Type of resource provided	DH statistical bulletin[1] 1995 %	ECCEP Time I care manager interview[2]	
		%	missing (n)
Home help/care contact hours[3]	30	25	6
Day centre places[4]	18	18	0

Number of (ECCEP) cases: 425
1 DH statistical bulletin. Community care statistics 1996. Day and Domiciliary Personal Social Services for Adults, England. This bulletin contains information on services purchased or provided by local authorities for people at home, at luncheon clubs or in day centres.
2 These ECCEP interviews were carried out between April 1995 and February 1996 with a median date of 10 September 1995. Only 8 per cent occurred in 1996, so the data are comparable with those given by the DH bulletin for 1995.
3 Independent sector home care in ECCEP was provided by voluntary organisations, private organisations and private individuals formally arranged and paid for, excluding informal carers.
4 Independent sector day centre places were provided by voluntary or private organisations.

way of determining this is to compare the proportion of services received by ECCEP users from independent providers with findings from the 1995 DH statistical bulletin.

Table 2.11 illustrates the proportion of social care resources provided by the independent sector to ECCEP users and to users nationally, as defined in DH community care statistics. The two services for which data are directly comparable are home help and day care. In relation to these two services, it is evident that ECCEP care packages reflect national patterns at the time. The proportion of home help hours provided by the independent sector to ECCEP users was 25 per cent, compared with 30 per cent nationally. The proportion of day care places provided by the independent sector is the same as that reported in the DH statistical bulletin — 18 per cent.

Comparisons with nationally representative datasets thus provide an important context for interpreting ECCEP findings. While the local authorities in the study are broadly representative of the national picture in terms of overall expenditure and spending on services for older people, it is evident that when they first received services the ECCEP users tended to be more dependent than the national cross-section of users. Comparisons with the user sample of the 1995 GHS demonstrate that, although the socio-demographic characteristics of the two samples are similar, ECCEP users are significantly more dependent in terms of ADL and IADL limitations. Not surprisingly, this higher level of need is reflected in patterns of service usage. With reference to social care resources, those taking part in ECCEP are receiving a larger number of services, on a more frequent basis, than users nationally. The next chapter begins to illustrate the personal and environmental factors which contribute to this need for services, by introducing the need-related circumstances of the older users in the study.

Notes

1 Though not having its implementation team in post until mid-1976 and an additional evaluator appointed until late1976, the KCCP was designed in outline during late 1974 during the early months of the Unit. Reflecting the Kent proposal to give vouchers for children to attend nursery schools and classes, the new Director of Social Services in Kent originally discussed a voucher scheme for community services, but that was replaced by a PSSRU suggestion for what amounted to a care management team provided with menus of prices, a budget, and freedom to purchase or commission services. In the field from early 1977, the KCCP was one of the small group of first generation of care management programmes for elderly people whose early results were the subject of a special issue of *The Gerontologist* in 1980 on the eve of the launch of the American long-term care channelling demonstration (Davies and Challis, 1980).

2 Levels of expenditure per capita of the elderly population on home help services in each authority area were obtained from CIPFA Actuals for 1983-84.

3 *Resources, Needs and Outcomes* (Davies et al., 1990) focuses largely on findings from the statistical modelling carried out as part of DCP analysis. As such, this book should not be viewed as an earlier equivalent to this ECCEP monograph. It has more in common with the productivities and defensibility analyses from a concurrent stream of ECCEP work (Davies and Fernández, 1999). Descriptive findings from DCP can also be accessed through two PSSRU discussion papers (Bebbington et al., 1985, 1986).

4 This difference in dependency between the cohort and cross-sectional samples is what would be expected were the evolution of the group to be the same as that recruited to take part in DCP in the mid-1980s. Findings from DCP showed how changes in disability and the loss of some users from the sample due to death or institutionalisation caused the profile of remaining the users to become less disabled through time.

3 Need-Related Circumstances of Users

Introduction

Most older people live independent lives, and when they need assistance they rely on their relatives and friends. But for those individuals who are the most dependent, or the least able to access informal care or both, community care is essential to the maintenance of quality of life. This chapter focuses on a group of older people who were living in private households, using community care services, and who took part in the first stage of ECCEP, in 1995. It outlines their personal characteristics and explores some of the circumstances which gave rise to their need for community care interventions.

Personal characteristics such as age and health status, environmental factors such as living arrangements, and social circumstances such as the availability of informal support and the attitudes of the older person him/herself are all referred to as *need-related circumstances*, due to the fact that they all potentially influence the nature of the older person's need for community care interventions. This chapter details the most important need-related characteristics of users obtained from the community sample of ECCEP respondents (n=419). These characteristics are grouped together under the following headings: basic characteristics; living environment and finances; functional ability; physical health; mental health; social support; and anxieties and attitudes.

It is important to note that the information outlined here was obtained directly from the older people who took part in ECCEP. This has two implications. First, some of the tables and statistics presented are not representative of the whole sample because a number of users with cognitive impairment were unable to provide information and in many such cases it was not possible to conduct proxy interviews. Second, even where users did provide information directly, there are grounds for believing that in certain circumstances they under-report problems that they experience. In Chapter 6 we will examine in greater detail the extent to which the need-related characteristics of users are reported differentially by users, carers and care managers.

Basic characteristics

The typical ECCEP respondent is a female widow in her eighties who is living alone with an identifiable informal carer. The average age of respondents in the ECCEP sample was 80.8 with women (81.2) being slightly older than men. The average age of elderly users in the GHS sample of the same year was very similar at 79.3. Three-quarters of users in the ECCEP community sample are women compared with 70 per cent in the GHS. Slightly fewer (20 per cent) ECCEP users are married or partnered than in the GHS (23 per cent). These statistics can be compared with the gender and marital status distribution of all elderly people in the 1994/95 GHS. Among the elderly group as a whole, the gender balance was more even, with men representing 42 per cent and women 58 per cent of the total sample. Similarly, a larger proportion of the total sample (53 per cent) were married.

Table 3.1 shows the distribution of ECCEP respondents by age group, marital status and gender. For both men and women the highest proportion of individuals are widowed, although proportionately more men remain married/partnered than women. Widowed women constitute more than half (53 per cent) of all ECCEP users. The comparable proportion in the GHS sample of users was very similar (49.7 per cent).

Table 3.2 shows the proportion of users who live alone by whether they have a principal informal carer or not, and levels of dependency. The great majority of service users live alone: 62.9 per cent in the ECCEP sample compared with 68 per cent in the GHS. One very noticeable feature of the ECCEP sample, however, is that the great majority of elderly users identified a principal informal carer (81 per cent). There is no directly comparable information obtainable from the 1994/95 GHS, but it is of interest to note that almost 30 per cent of elderly users in that survey reported that they had not had any visitors in the week prior to the survey.

Table 3.2 also shows that there is a clear association between interval need and the living arrangements of ECCEP users. Relatively few people in the critical interval need category, whether cognitively impaired or not, live on their own without an identifiable principal informal carer. By contrast, almost 60 per cent of such users live with others. Overall, the proportion of users who live alone increases as the severity of need diminishes, whereas the proportion living with others increases as the needs of users become more severe.

Table 3.1
Marital status by age category and gender

Marital status	Under 70 M %	Under 70 F %	70-75 M %	70-75 F %	75-80 M %	75-80 F %	80-85 M %	80-85 F %	85-90 M %	85-90 F %	90 & over M %	90 & over F %	Total M %	Total F %	Total M n=	Total F n=
Single	22.2	40.0	-	11.6	12.5	8.3	20.0	7.6	14.3	14.7	-	13.2	13.0	12.6	12	35
Married/ partnered	55.6	20.0	40.0	23.3	50.0	12.5	48.0	16.7	21.4	5.9	10.0	5.3	40.2	12.9	37	36
Widowed	22.2	26.7	40.0	58.1	37.5	2.9	32.0	75.8	64.3	76.5	90.0	78.9	44.6	70.5	41	196
Separated/ divorced	-	13.3	20.0	7.0	-	6.3	-	-	-	2.9	-	2.6	2.2	4.0	2	11
Total n =	9	15	10	43	24	48	25	66	14	68	10	38	92	278	92	278

Valid cases: 370. Missing cases: 48. Out of the 48 missing values, 20 were due to missing information on age and marital status for cognitively impaired cases with Katzman scores of at least 22 when proxy interviews were not available.

Table 3.2
Social support/living group, by interval need and cognitive impairment[1] or behavioural disturbance[2] of user

Presence of PIC & living arrangements	Interval need									
	Critical		Short		Long		Total		Total
	CI/BD %	No CI/BD %	CI/BD %	No CI/BD %	CI/BD %	No CI/BD %	CI/BD %	No CI/BD %	n =
No PIC — living alone	10.9	14.7	-	20.9	17.6	29.6	9.5	23.0	77
PIC — living alone	31.3	25.3	50.0	47.3	41.2	56.8	37.1	45.7	172
PIC — living with others	57.8	60.0	50.0	31.9	41.2	13.6	53.3	31.3	147
Total n =	64	75	24	91	17	125	105	291	396

Valid cases: 396. Missing cases: 22. Out of the 22 missing values, 20 were due to missing information on living group for cognitively impaired cases with Katzman scores of at least 22 when proxy interviews were not available.

1 The presence of cognitive impairment was defined as a Katzman score of at least 22.

2 The presence of behavioural disturbance was defined as:

a) For cases with a PIC who was interviewed: Whether PIC found user's behaviour difficult, demanding or embarrassing.

b) For cases without a PIC who was interviewed: Whether care manager reported inappropriate/anti-social/violent/risky behaviour of user.

Living environment and finances

Just as the extent of social support available to older people in the community varies, so do their living environments and financial resources. All users were asked about the type of accommodation they live in, either alone or with others. Thus, in the case of owner-occupied properties for instance, the carer, rather than the user, may be the owner. Table 3.3 shows how the ownership of housing depends on housing type. From the left-hand column for all types of housing combined, the most frequent types of ownership were social housing (43 per cent) and owner-occupied housing (44 per cent), although 7 per cent (of the total) still had a mortgage. However, ownership varied considerably with type of housing. Thus, while 58 per cent of houses were owned outright, this proportion fell to 36 per cent for bungalows, 21 per cent for flats or maisonettes and only 3 per cent for sheltered housing units. In contrast, the proportion in social housing rose from 17 per cent for houses to 56 per cent for bungalows, 58 per cent for flats or maisonettes and 93 per cent for sheltered housing units. Accommodation was most frequently privately rented for flats or maisonettes (12 per cent) and houses (6 per cent). Social housing is in many cases more likely to be adapted to the needs of older people and can include purpose-built flats, bungalows and sheltered units.

The ownership of housing in the ECCEP study closely resembles that from a comparable sample in GHS, where once again 43 per cent of older service users were in social housing, 49 per cent in owner-occupied housing (comparable with 44 per cent in ECCEP) and 8 per cent were living in private rented accommodation (compared to 7 per cent in ECCEP).

Housing problems can inhibit the ability of some older people to continue living independently in the community, and can limit the potential for social care services to improve outcomes. Users were asked a series of questions about the facilities available to them inside the home. One finding, supporting evidence from other research, is that almost one in four users (24 per cent) reported that they had trouble keeping warm. These problems were particularly prevalent among users living in homes with little or no central heating. More than one in five users (23 per cent) did not have any central heating or storage heaters in their home, while an additional 8 per cent had this type of heating in only some rooms. The partial or total absence of central heating was related to housing type and ownership, with occupiers of privately rented accommodation much less likely to have central heating than other occupiers. Thus, not surprisingly, a higher proportion of those in privately rented housing (39 per cent) reported problems keeping warm than those in other types of housing (22-24 per cent). Another factor leading to problems keeping warm was low income, as measured by the user claiming income support or housing benefit, this information being available for users who were not severely cognitively impaired. Thus, while only 21 per cent of

Table 3.3
Housing type, by ownership

Ownership	House %	Flat/maisonette %	Bungalow %	Sheltered unit %	Other[1] %	Total %	Total n =
Owned outright	58.0	21.2	36.1	3.4	7.7	37.2	143
Owned with mortgage	12.1	3.5	4.2	3.4	-	7.0	27
Social housing[2]	16.6	58.4	55.6	93.1	46.2	43.0	165
Private landlord	5.7	11.5	1.4	-	38.5	7.3	28
Other[3]	7.6	5.3	2.8	-	7.7	5.5	21
Total n =	157	113	72	29	13	100	384

Valid cases: 384. Missing cases: 34. Out of the 34 missing values, 20 were due to missing information on living group for cognitively impaired cases with Katzman scores of at least 22 when proxy interviews were not available.

1 Other types of housing, including bedsit and studio flat.
2 Social housing covers council housing and housing association.
3 Other owners include son/daughter, other person and other organisation.

users not claiming benefit had problems keeping warm, this proportion rose to 30 per cent for benefit recipients.

Other research has examined the relationship between the income of older people and their use of social services (Ginn and Arber, 1992; Bernard and Phillips, 1998). Poverty or low income is related to need in a variety of different ways and it is, therefore, of value to know the types of income older people receive, together with their total levels of income and savings. Because users are frequently reluctant to divulge such data, there is missing information for this particular theme within ECCEP, and it is possible that some of the information gathered was unreliable or inadequate.

The types of income received by the ECCEP users who responded to these questions are shown in Table 3.4. This information was available only for users who were not severely cognitively impaired: those who had Katzman scores below 22. As expected, the vast majority received at least one pension (90 per cent). Moreover, 16 per cent of all cases received no other type of income. Thirty-eight per cent received income support and/or housing benefit. Substantial proportions received attendance allowance (40 per cent) and interest from savings (31 per cent). One quarter of users received one type of income, a third received two types, leaving 42 per cent with three or more types.

Table 3.4
Types of income received

	%
Pensions	90.0
Income support	26.0
Attendance allowance	39.6
Housing benefit	24.5
Mobility allowance	7.4
Disability allowance	9.1
Interest from savings	31.3
Earned income	0.3

Valid cases: 325. Missing cases: 0. The sample excluded the 93 with Katzman scores of at least 22 (severely cognitively impaired). Of those cases living alone, 20.3 per cent received pension(s) but no other source of income.

Weekly income was considered separately for those living alone and those living with others. Users or their proxies were presented with a show card asking them into which of the categories in Table 3.5 their income fell. A common indicator of basic adequacy is income support, which can be used as a reference level. Typically users would be eligible for a 'higher pensioner

Table 3.5
Income, by whether living alone

Income	Living alone %	Living with others Personal income %	Household income %
£60 per week or less	6.8	16.0	12.5
£61-£100 per week	53.3	32.8	19.6
£101-£175 per week	33.6	42.5	40.0
£176-£275 per week	5.3	5.5	16.9
£276-£325 per week	-	0.8	3.7
£326-£450 per week	1.1	2.4	2.7
£451-£600 per week	-	-	1.8
More than £600 per week	-	-	2.7
Valid cases	188	123	106
Missing cases	54	32	49

The 20 cases with a Katzman score of at least 22 (severely impaired) and no proxy interviews data were excluded from the sample.

premium', which provides a minimum income support level at 1995 prices of approximately £71.60 for a single person and £108.85 for a couple. More generally, a measure of relative poverty could be defined as having savings of no more than £3,000 and income not exceeding £100 for those living alone or a household income not exceeding £175 for those living with others. Using this criterion, 42 per cent of users overall were found to be in relative poverty, this amounting to 35 per cent of users living alone and 56 per cent of those living with others.

In considering the savings of users, it is helpful to separate results for users with personal savings from users with shared savings. This is done in Table 3.6. Because some users would not or could not divulge this information, it was available only for 57 per cent of the total sample, so the percentages quoted may be subject to sampling errors. For those cases with missing information on savings, it was possible that this was deliberately withheld, perhaps because users with substantial savings were afraid of being charged excessively if details became known to the local authority. To shed some light on this, the distribution of personal income for these cases with missing information on savings was compared with that for the whole group, since larger savings were likely to be associated with higher income. In practice, for cases living alone, users who would not disclose savings had a slightly higher

Table 3.6
Savings

Savings	All users	Users with personal savings	Users with shared savings
	%	%	%
Up to £3,000	31.3	55.2	53.5
£3,001-£8,000	12.0	22.4	16.1
£8,001-£20,000	7.4	13.1	13.0
£20,001-£50,000	4.8	6.6	15.2
Over £50,000	1.5	2.7	2.2
Don't know/refused	43.0	-	-
Valid cases	398	182	45
Missing cases	0		171

Sample: The 398 cases for which user or proxy information was available. The 20 severely cognitively impaired cases with Katzman scores of at least 22 and no proxy interviews were excluded.

percentage in the *lower* income groups, an opposite trend to that expected, while for cases living with others the distributions were very similar. It can, therefore, be concluded that for cases with information on income but not savings, the missing savings information is unlikely to be appreciably biased in comparison with the remainder of the group. However, a group remained of 54 users living alone and 32 living with others for which neither income nor savings was known. These users may have atypical income or savings.

As Table 3.6 shows, among users with personal savings, over half had savings below £3,000 which would not have been taken into account in calculating any income support due. A further 22 per cent had savings between £3,000 and £8,000, which would have resulted in a reduction in the level of any income support to which they were entitled. Users with personal savings above this level could not have been entitled to any income support. Thirteen per cent had savings between £8,000 and £20,000; 7 per cent had savings of between £20,000 and £50,000; and just 3 per cent had savings above this level. For users with shared savings, the percentages of users in each of these categories were fairly similar to those for users with individual savings. This suggests that users with shared savings were proportionately worse off. The exception was for those better off users with shared savings of between £20,000 and £50,000 who constituted 15 per cent of the group (as compared with 7 per cent for those with personal savings).

Functional ability

Ability to carry out the range of tasks required to live independently is most commonly measured using an index of activities of daily living (ADLs), with the addition of instrumental activities of daily living (IADLs). The former relate to basic tasks such as bathing and dressing, while the latter are household activities such as cleaning and shopping. The extent to which the user can perform these daily tasks is one of the most reliable indicators of the amount and type of assistance that will be required, either from informal carers, formal services, or both. Although not shown here, there is a strong correlation between interval need and ADL/IADL scores. This is due to the fact that the dependency categories used are derived from the frequency with which the user needs help performing ADL/IADL tasks. Thus, critical interval need users would have difficulty with a greater number of activities than short and long interval need users.

Table 3.7 shows the proportion of users who needed help in performing twelve key tasks by the presence or absence of a principal informal carer and by living arrangement. Users whose performance of a particular task was classed as 'not done' were assumed to be 'able'. By identifying other tasks for which the need for help was highly correlated with that for the task in question, it was possible to demonstrate the validity of this assumption.

As Table 3.7 illustrates, the tasks for which help was most frequently required were bathing (49 per cent), dressing (33 per cent), shopping (27 per cent) and handling money (25 per cent). The need for help with tasks was generally much more frequent among users with a PIC who live with others particularly with ADLs. For instance, 67 per cent of this group needed help with bathing, compared with 36 per cent of those with no PIC, and 39 per cent of those with a PIC living alone. Users with a PIC living alone had a slightly more frequent need for assistance with most tasks than those with no PIC. Indeed, it is clear that users with informal support, particularly support within the same household, were more frail. They were less likely to be able to manage on their own and would be more likely to enter institutional care if this informal help was not available.

Overall ADL scores can be obtained by adding one for each of the five ADL items with which the user required help. In other words, an individual with an ADL score of 5 would require assistance with all activities, in contrast to someone with a score of zero, who would be able to perform all ADLs independently. Similarly an IADL score ranging from 0 to 7 can be obtained.

Table 3.8 shows the effect of breaking down the mean ADL and IADL scores by interval need and the presence of cognitive impairment or behavioural disturbance. The overall ADL score for the ECCEP sample was 1.28, while the overall IADL score was 1.21. Although these aggregate scores are fairly low, suggesting that users are able to perform most activities, it is important to note that the comparisons between the proportion of ECCEP and GHS users able to

Table 3.7
Physical functioning

ADLs/IADLs	No PIC	PIC living alone	PIC living with others	Total	
	%	%	%	%	n =
Needing help with ADLs					
Bathing	36.1	38.7	66.9	48.8	385
Transfer	6.8	5.4	35.4	17.0	388
Dressing	17.8	22.0	51.7	32.5	388
Toileting	4.1	9.5	34.2	17.8	387
Feeding	1.4	3.0	23.1	10.3	387
Needing help with IADLs					
Shopping	17.8	32.1	25.9	27.1	388
Meal preparation	9.9	16.0	20.4	16.5	387
Preparing snack	5.5	6.0	15.6	9.6	387
Preparing hot drink	4.1	5.4	16.3	9.3	387
Heavy housework	26.0	20.1	21.4	21.7	387
Light housework	8.2	10.1	19.1	13.2	385
Handling own money	16.7	24.1	29.9	24.9	382

Out of the 30 or more missing values, 20 were due to missing ADL and IADL information for cognitively impaired cases with Katzman scores of at least 22 when proxy interviews were not available.

perform certain tasks (described in Chapter 2) found that the ECCEP sample overall require more assistance with a wider range of activities than GHS users.

ADL and IADL scores vary depending on the needs of the user, as Table 3.8 clearly illustrates. Scores increase rapidly from long through short to critical interval need. In addition, users who were cognitively impaired or behaviourally disturbed had much higher scores. Thus, overall the presence of cognitive impairment or behavioural disturbance increased the combined score from 2.07 to 3.73. The greater dependence of the confused group provides one reason why they were generally supported by a principal informal carer. This subject is investigated further in the section on mental health.

Physical health

The health characteristics of users affect their ability to carry out activities of daily living, and can thus influence their need for assistance. It is possible that

Table 3.8
Mean ADL and IADL scores, by interval need and cognitive impairment[1]/behavioural disorder[2]

ADLs/IADLs	Critical		Short		Long		Total		Overall total
	CI/BD	No CI/BD	CI/BD	No CI/BD	CI/BD	No CI/BD	CI/BD	No CI/BD	
Mean ADL score	2.71	2.30	1.15	1.25	0.30	0.05	2.06	1.01	1.28
Mean IADL score	1.66	1.42	2.19	1.41	0.61	0.56	1.63	1.05	1.21
Mean ADL + IADL score	4.39	3.72	3.43	2.64	1.00	0.61	3.73	2.07	2.49
Total n =	62	76	22	87	12	120	97	283	379

Valid cases: 379. Missing cases: 39. Out of the 39 missing values, 20 were due to missing information on living group for cognitively impaired cases with Katzman scores of at least 22 when proxy interviews were not available.

1 The presence of cognitive impairment was defined as a Katzman score of at least 22.

2 The presence of behavioural disturbance was defined as:

a) For cases with a PIC who was interviewed: Whether PIC found user's behaviour difficult, demanding or embarrassing.

b) For cases without a PIC who was interviewed: Whether care manager reported inappropriate/anti-social/violent/risky behaviour of user.

health needs may go unrecognised among older people, as symptoms can be interpreted as being the result of ageing rather than disease. Redmond et al. (1996) point out that generally a high proportion of elderly have unreported illnesses or disabilities which require attention. ECCEP users were asked questions about their physical health to assess the level of health needs among users in the community and to look for the effects of health problems on the ability to perform activities of daily living. Another aim was to see whether users with more severe health problems were less likely to survive in the community without the support of a principal informal carer, or conversely, whether users without such support were more likely to become neglected and hence develop health problems. Physical health was described in relation to the type and number of health problems the user had experienced.

Overall, 89 per cent of users indicated that they had experienced health problems in the year preceding the interview and frequently had more than one problem. The presence of multiple and interacting health problems undoubtedly adds to the complexity of the needs of users. Users overall had an average of 2.74 health problems, with this score varying little between the three interval need categories or by presence of a carer.

Table 3.9 lists the prevalence of user's health problems in the year preceding the first interview. The health problems reported most frequently by users were arthritis and rheumatism (40 per cent) and other musculo-skeletal problems including back and knee problems, and fractures (36 per cent), followed by heart disease (25 per cent). Respiratory problems were reported

Table 3.9
Medical problems in the last twelve months

	%		%
Stroke	12.2	Urinary incontinence	7.2
Other nervous system	5.9	Faecal incontinence	2.2
Eyes	24.2	Other genito-urinary	8.1
Ears	18.0	Arthritis or rheumatism	40.4
Coronary and other heart	24.6	Other musculo-skeletal	35.7
Hypertension	6.6	Cancer, tumour or growth	4.7
Varicose veins and other circulatory	15.7	Diabetes	7.8
Respiratory	21.3	Other	20.0
Digestive	17.5		

Sample: The 325 cases whose Katzman scores were below 22.
By excluding all cases with severe cognitive impairment (Katzman scores of at least 22), the percentages shown in this table may not be representative of the whole sample.

by 21 per cent of users; 12 per cent reported a stroke. All these could affect the user's ability to carry out personal and household tasks. Some of the other problems reported by fairly significant proportions of users were those relating to the digestive system, the circulatory system, and visual and hearing impairment. These results are fairly similar to those found in other studies, such as Parker et al. (1997) and OPCS (1991).

The clearest association between these health problems and interval need of the users was in the case of incontinence of urine and faeces, for which the proportions increased sharply with interval need. This was expected as incontinence was included in the definition of interval need. A strong relationship was also found for strokes, with weaker effects for Parkinson's disease, hip fracture or damage, and diabetes.

It is, perhaps, important to note that the self-reported prevalence of health problems in Table 3.9 will differ slightly from the true rates in the community, as these are based on responses from only those users who are not severely cognitively impaired (Katzman score less than 22), which constitutes approximately 78 per cent of users.

In addition to these health problems, 19 per cent of users reported a serious accident or injury in the three months preceding the interview, such as a fall at home or road accident. The proportions are lower for users with a principal informal carer in the critical and long interval need categories. Twenty-seven per cent of critical interval need users living without a principal informal carer had had an accident or injury as compared to 13 per cent among those with a principal informal carer. The corresponding figures in the long interval need category were 25 per cent and 14 per cent respectively. The result is likely to reflect the increased supervision and number of check up visits received by users with a PIC, with help more likely to be available when the user was in difficulty.

When a subsample of the 115 hospital discharge cases was examined, the overall mean number of health problems remained almost unchanged, although there was more variation with interval need, from 2.17 for long interval to 3.83 for critical interval. For hospital discharge cases without a PIC, this variation was still greater, ranging from 2.00 for long interval need to 4.86 for critical interval need.

Mental health

The presence of dementia and other mental health problems in older people has serious implications for the type and amount of both formal and informal help they require in order to remain living in the community. ECCEP addressed both organic and functional mental disorder in the elderly. Organic disorder was measured using the Katzman score which has already been described. For the overall group, 18 per cent had a Katzman score of between

Table 3.10
Mean Katzman score of cognitive impairment, by interval need, social support and living group

Presence of PIC/ whether living alone or with others	Critical	Short	Long	Total	n =
No PIC	12.02	6.16	5.76	7.32	77
PIC — living alone	12.45	8.04	6.37	8.28	171
PIC — living with others	13.86	13.83	12.98	13.71	147
Total	13.23	9.80	7.30	10.12	395
Total n =	139	114	141	395	

Valid cases: 395. Missing cases: 23. Of the 23 missing values, 20 were due to living group being missing, for users with Katzman scores of at least 22 when proxy interviews were not available. By excluding these cases, the mean Katzman scores of at least some of the cells will be underestimated. These mean Katzman scores may be compared with the cut-off levels defining moderate cognitive impairment (11-21) and severe cognitive impairment (22 and over).

11 and 21 indicating moderate cognitive impairment, and 22 per cent were severely cognitively impaired with scores of at least 22. In view of the difficulty traditionally experienced in coping with the cognitively impaired both in the community and in institutional care, it is therefore significant that 40 per cent of the ECCEP sample were in this category.

Table 3.10 shows how the mean Katzman score depended on interval need, the presence of a principal informal carer and living group. Examining the total row it is clear that, overall, the mean score rises rapidly from 7.30 for long interval need to 13.23 for critical interval need. This last value is above the cut-off level of 11 indicating the presence of moderate cognitive impairment. The total column in Table 3.10 shows that users with a principal informal carer have a greater Katzman score, particularly when the user is living with others, for which the score of 13.71 is above the cut-off level. Indeed users with both a principal informal carer and living with others had a mean score which hardly increased at all with interval need. This result suggests that in order for the cognitively impaired to remain at home, the support of informal carers is essential, whatever the user's level of dependence. This can be understood in terms of the high degree of supervision normally required.

Results on functional mental disorder are presented through the Philadelphia Geriatric Center (PGC) morale scale (Lawton, 1975) and the geriatric depression scale (GDS). Table 3.11 presents results for both the full PGC score, obtained by summing the responses to seventeen questions, and

Table 3.11
PGC morale and its components, by self-assessed health

Mean scores of PGC morale and its components	Better than other people of user's age	About right for user's age	Worse than other people of user's age	Don't know[1]	Total
Full morale score[2]	10.34	9.91	6.51	7.53	8.68[3]
Agitation	2.57	2.44	4.13	4.06	3.20
Positive attitude to own ageing	3.34	2.97	1.55	1.25	2.62
Lonely dissatisfaction	1.70	1.88	3.04	3.16	2.38
Total n =	81	150	106	78	416

Valid cases: 416. Missing cases: 2.

1 Out of the 78 cases for which the user answered the self-assessed health question as 'don't know', 53 had Katzman scores of at least 22 so were severely cognitively impaired.

2 The full PGC morale score was based on the seventeen components described by Lawton (1975).

3 The ECCEP mean PGC morale score of 8.68 may be compared with that for cases accepted into the evaluated care-managed schemes for the frail elderly in Thanet (The Kent Community Care Project — Davies and Challis, 1986), Gateshead (Challis et al., 1990) and Sheppey/Tonbridge (extensions of the Kent Community Care scheme — Chesterman et al., 1994). The mean PGC morale scores for these studies were: Thanet 4.72, Gateshead 5.42, Sheppey 7.12, and Tonbridge 7.44.

three partial scores calculated by summing subgroups of these questions. These subgroups were those obtained by Lawton in a factor analysis of the seventeen responses. He named them 'agitation', 'positive attitude to own aging' and 'lonely dissatisfaction' and their definitions are given in the notes to the table. The means for these scales have been broken down by the self-assessed health of the elderly person, which reflects not only their overall physical health but also their morale.

The relationship between self-assessed health and morale is confirmed in Table 3.11 by the strong relationship with full PGC morale score which increases from 6.51 for users who felt their health to be worse than others to 10.34 for those who felt their health to be better. A similar trend is found for 'positive attitude to own aging'. As expected, the trends for 'agitation' and lonely dissatisfaction' are in the opposite direction since they are both measures of *lack* of morale. The middle category of self-assessed health, namely 'about right' had mean values which lay close to those for 'better than other people' for all four measures of morale. This suggests that those users who felt their health was worse than others had a level of morale which was depressed relative to the rest of the group. One explanation is that these users were indeed in a poorer state of physical health and that their morale was lowered as a result. This interpretation would be consistent with the finding by Roth and Kay (1956) that physical health and affective disorder are frequently associated in the elderly. Another is that their objective state of health was average but their lower morale caused them to view their own health more pessimistically. A third is a spiralling vicious circle of deteriorating physical and mental health caused by the interplay between mind and body.

To obtain an impression of how the PGC morale score for the ECCEP sample compares with that measured for frail elderly people in other studies, Table 3.11 also includes a comparison between the overall mean for ECCEP with those for users at the point of entry to four intensively care managed schemes. These all have morale in the range 5 to 7, somewhat lower than for ECCEP (8.7). One reason for the difference could be that in Thanet, Gateshead and Sheppey the users were interviewed by the evaluator before the care manager had become involved. In Tonbridge, where morale was found to be slightly higher, the users were interviewed just after the care manager's initial assessment, while in ECCEP the users had frequently been receiving a care package for weeks or months. The care manager's involvement could have already raised the user's morale. Another factor contributing to the difference could be that the intensively care managed schemes were targeted at cases at risk of entry to institutional care and such circumstances would be expected to lower their morale. When PGC morale score was broken down by the presence of a principal informal carer and whether the user was living alone, the mean scores of each subgroup were almost the same. This suggests that the ability of users to cope with relatively little informal support may boost their morale, compensating for the lower degree of informal contact.

Another measure of functional mental health is given by the shortened geriatric depression scale which yields a score obtained by summing the responses to fifteen items. Because it was not feasible to ask the fifteen questions of all users, these were asked for a subsample but with five of them asked for the full sample. These five questions were known to provide a score (referred to as the brief score) which is normally highly correlated with the full score. After verifying that the correlation was indeed high, the brief score based on the five questions was scaled up to what would be expected for a shortened score, using the scaling-up factor obtained for the subsample. Mean scores broken down by interval need and the presence of a principal informal carer and whether living alone are shown in Table 3.12, which also includes notes giving details of the scaling-up process.

Table 3.12 illustrates that the mean shortened depression score for ECCEP users increases with interval need, from 4.83 for long interval need to 7.38 for critical interval need. This trend is likely to be largely a result of higher levels of disability and risk, increasing degrees of reactive depression, although could also arise from an inability to perform ADL and IADL tasks as a result of endogenous depression. The total column shows increasing depression with increasing levels of informal support. It can be seen from the critical and short interval need cases that those without a principal informal carer are less depressed. This may be partly a selection effect whereby informal carers have become involved with users who have become depressed, perhaps through difficulties in coping. It could, however, also indicate that users who are able to manage living alone without a principal informal carer obtain satisfaction from achieving this, with the independence and autonomy which it offers them. Based on the standard scale of 30 items, Brink et al. (1982) suggest a threshold score of 11 indicating clinical depression. Assuming that the shortened scale of 15 items has a threshold score of apporximately half this (5.5), it can be seen that this level is close to mean values in the cells of Table 3.12. Therefore, approximately one-half of the ECCEP sample is suffering from depression. This level is consistent with the finding of Kay et al. (1964) that the prevalence of depression in the elderly is high. These authors in their Newcastle study identified approximately 30 per cent of elderly to be clinically depressed. As the ECCEP sample is significantly more dependent than the general elderly population, it is perhaps not surprising that an even higher prevalence of depression is evident.

Social support

The importance of principal informal carers in the support of the frail or cognitively impaired elderly has already been emphasised, and the nature of

Table 3.12
Mean geriatric depression score, by interval need, social support and living group

Presence of PIC/ whether living alone or with others	Critical	Short	Long	Total	Total n
No PIC	5.38	4.07	4.93	4.83	77
PIC — living alone	7.40	6.43	4.73	5.89	171
PIC — living with others	7.81	6.06	5.01	6.88	147
Total	7.38	5.91	4.83	6.05	395
Total n =	139	114	141	395	

Valid cases: 395. Missing cases: 23. Of the 23 missing values, 20 were due to living group being missing, for users with Katzman scores of at least 22 when proxy interviews were not available.

A brief geriatric depression score available for the full sample was first obtained by adding the number of the following five items which applied, with 'refused to answer' and 'don't know' counting as 0.5: (a) Do you feel that your life is empty? (b) Do you often feel hopeless? (c) Do you feel pretty worthless the way you are now? (d) Do you feel that your situation is hopeless? (e) Do you think that most people are better off than you are?

The shortened geriatric depression score based on fifteen items, including the five making up the brief score, was available for a subset of only 119 cases. However, the shortened score is highly correlated with the full score for this subset of cases. (Pearson correlation coefficient = 0.91, $p<.0005$) so could legitimately be used as a proxy for it on the full sample, when scaled up by the appropriate factor.

The mean scores for the subset of 119 cases were: shortened score 6.21; brief score 2.01. Hence the shortened score for a particular case or cell mean was estimated from the brief score through multiplying by a factor: 6.21/2.01 = 3.09.

Using the standard 30-item scale, a full score of at least 11 was taken by Brink et al. (1982) to be a threshold which can be taken as a possible indicator of clinical depression. Presumably the threshold for the shortened 15-item scale will be approximately half this (5.5). It can be seen that the means for all cells in the table are close to this value, suggesting that around half of the users are clinically depressed.

As a consistency check between results obtained using the shortened score on the full sample and the full score on the subsample, a similar table was prepared using the full score on the subsample. The cell means gave fairly close agreement between the two tables with the difference in means always being less than 2.

this support will be considered in subsequent chapters. However, older people are often assisted by a network of friends and relatives. It is thus important to examine more generally the varied sources of support available to an older person. This is commonly achieved by conducting an assessment of the social support network.

One of the most widely used British support network typologies is that developed by Clare Wenger and colleagues at the University of Wales (Wenger, 1989, 1994, 1995). Wenger proposed a classification of informal support based on the responses to eight questions covering the type of contact (relative, friend or neighbour), the distance which these individuals have to travel and the frequency of their visits as well as the user's attendance at religious meetings and other community or social groups. This information allowed users to be placed in one of five categories, named in terms of the type of relationship which the elderly person has to their network.

The *local family* dependent group are mainly focused on close local family ties with few friends and neighbours and generally low community involvement. They are often based on a shared household with, or close to, an adult child, usually a daughter.

The *locally integrated* users include close relationships with local family, friends and neighbours, in which many friends are also neighbours. Active community involvement in religious or voluntary organisations are also usual.

The *local self-contained* group typically has arm's length relationships with at least one relative living nearby, usually a sibling, niece or nephew, with reliance principally on neighbours. Community involvement tends to be low, with users keeping to themselves for much of the time.

The *wider community focused* users are typified by active relationships with both distant relatives, usually children, and friends and neighbours. Involvement in community or voluntary organisations is common, and users had frequently retired to the area.

The *private restricted* network typically has no local kin, although a high proportion of users are married. Contact with neighbours is minimal and there are few local friends and a low level of community contacts.

Table 3.13 illustrates how users in the ECCEP study are distributed between these five network types. Most ECCEP users fell into the locally integrated or private restricted categories, characterised by relatively high and low levels of informal support respectively. A very small proportion (only 5 per cent) relied on wider community focused help, reflecting the dependence of many elderly on family rather than friends in their support. This ECCEP distribution may be compared with two given by Wenger for her 'urban' sample drawn from Liverpool and her more general 'client' sample (drawn from the original study conducted in rural Wales), which are also included in the table. The distribution of the ECCEP sample appears to lie between that for the two Wenger samples. This becomes clear by comparing the ECCEP results with

Table 3.13
Comparing distributions of Wenger support networks for Wenger's samples with the ECCEP sample

	Family dependent %	Locally integrated %	Local self-contained %	Wider community-focused %	Private restricted %	Inconclusive %	Total n =
Wenger's urban sample	22	42	12	4	15	5	4,698
Wenger's client sample	16	21	12	8	40	4	355
Wenger's urban/client sample combined in equal weights	19	31.5	12	6	27.5	4.5	-
ECCEP sample	17	35	19	5	24	0	96

Each row of percentages adds up to 100 per cent. The ECCEP data were obtained by asking a subsample of 96 users about their support networks. This sample was biased since it excluded users who were severely cognitively impaired, with Katzman scores of at least 22.

Table 3.14
Whether user has a PIC, by network type (Wenger scale) and interval need for users without severe cognitive impairment

Wenger network type	Critical		Short		Long		Total	
	%	n =	%	n =	%	n =	%	n =
Family dependent	100	6	100	6	79	5	94	16
Locally integrated	100	10	78	11	89	13	89	34
Local self-contained	57	7	61	4	65	8	61	18
Wider community-focused	-	0	67	1	45	3	47	5
Private	83	9	61	6	78	8	75	23
Total n =	84	32	75	28	78	37	79	96

those obtained by combining the two Wenger samples by equal weight, when the resemblance becomes striking. The weighting towards an urban sample is consistent with the way in which the ECCEP users were selected.

As the principal carer is a key player in the older person's social network, it is not surprising that a close relationship was found between whether the user had a carer and network type. Table 3.14 illustrates this relationship.

As Table 3.14 shows, principal carers were present for the vast majority of users with family dependent or locally integrated networks, which is as expected in view of their definitions. It is perhaps surprising that as many as 61 per cent of users with a locally self-contained network had a principal informal carer. This result presumably reflects the rather weak definition of principal carer adopted here in which contacts of only once a week can be sufficient provided the carer is providing substantial support. In view of this, it can be understood how almost half of the rather small sample of the wider community focused group had a carer. When interval need is taken into account it can be seen that all critical interval need users who were in the family dependent or locally integrated groups had a carer. In contrast, the proportions of the other three groups having a carer showed little variation with interval need.

Anxieties and attitudes

Older people living in the community have the same concerns as other age groups, including worries about finances, crime, and/or the family. However, when poor mental or physical health begins to place limitations on the life of an older person, concerns regarding the ability to cope and the possibility of having to move into residential or nursing home care become more prevalent. ECCEP users were asked about their worries, and their opinions regarding institutional care.

Worries

Concerns regarding health, personal safety and other related issues can affect the user's quality of life, and moderate any benefits obtained from formal services. Table 3.15 illustrates what users worry about.

Table 3.15 details findings from a multiple response question asking which issues were of concern to users. A high incidence of anxieties was found, with most users reporting at least two worries. The most frequently mentioned worries were becoming too dependent to be looked after at home (47 per cent), becoming a burden on carers (40 per cent), and losing independence (39 per cent). Not surprisingly, users who have a principal informal carer were more concerned about becoming a burden than those without: 43 per cent of users

Table 3.15
What users worry about

Type of worry	%
Becoming too ill, dependent or forgetful	47
Putting too much burden/strain on family/friends	40
Losing independence and having others make decisions	39
Having an accident at home and no-one being around to help	33
Personal safety (burglars, being attacked, etc.)	25
Making ends meet	15
Not eating well enough	9
None	21
Total n =	315

Missing values: 11. Sample excludes users with severe cognitive impairment.

with a carer said they were concerned about putting strain on family and friends, compared with 29 per cent of users without a principal carer. Having an accident at home was mentioned as a worry by 33 per cent of users overall. It is interesting that the most prevalent concerns are all related to events that could contribute to the user having to leave his/her own home and possibly enter institutional care.

One in four users mentioned that they were concerned about threats to their personal safety — such as mugging or robbery — while smaller proportions were worried about finances (15 per cent) and not eating well enough (9 per cent). Users with a principal informal carer were less worried about crime (22 per cent) than those with a carer (35 per cent). This could be related to the fact that more users without carers live alone, or that users feel the presence of a carer offers some protection.

Attitudes to institutional care

Increasing frailty or confusion can result in some older people moving into residential or nursing home care, particularly if they do not have a carer. ECCEP users (excluding those with a cognitive impairment) were asked how they would feel about such a move.

Users were asked to choose which of five statements most accurately described their feelings about moving into a residential or nursing home. Table 3.16 shows that the single largest group of respondents — 38 per cent — were firmly against a move, stating that they wished to stay at home under all

Table 3.16

Users' feelings about moving into a residential or nursing home, by interval need and social support

User feels a move would be:	Critical		Short		Long		Total
	No PIC %	PIC %	No PIC %	PIC %	No PIC %	PIC %	n =
An attractive option	-	1.4	-	2.8	-	4.9	7
Would not mind moving	26.7	5.5	5.9	8.3	-	2.4	18
Prefer not to	20.0	24.6	29.4	22.1	45.9	27.4	80
Strongly against	20.0	23.2	35.3	22.1	32.4	28.1	75
Stay at home under all circumstances	33.3	45.4	29.4	44.8	21.6	37.2	111
Total n =	15	71	17	71	36	80	291

Missing values: 34. This question was not asked of cognitively impaired users.

circumstances. Opposition to a move was also voiced by 26 per cent of users who said that they were strongly against it, and 28 per cent who stated that they would 'prefer not to' move. Less than one in ten users described moving into care as positive, either as an attractive option (2 per cent) or something they would not mind doing (6 per cent). Carers were also asked to describe how they thought the user would feel about a move. When the sample of respondents common to both users and carers is compared (n=150), the level of agreement between the two groups is high. The only area in which carer and user responses differ, albeit very slightly, is in the intensity of opposition to care home admission. A slightly higher proportion of carers (70 per cent) said the user would be either strongly or completely against residential or nursing home admission, while the corresponding proportion among users was 66 per cent.

User attitudes to institutional care do not vary significantly between interval need categories. However, the presence or absence of a principal informal carer does reveal some differences in responses. Whereas 42 per cent of users with a carer were completely opposed to entering institutional care, just 26 per cent of users without a carer chose this option. This finding underlines the importance of informal care in allowing older people to remain at home, not just because of the assistance carers provide, but also because of the way in which informal support affects the perceptions of users. Older people who have a regular source of informal support may feel more secure and more able to do things for themselves, in the knowledge that someone is there to help them if they need assistance.

Table 3.17
Circumstances under which user might enter residential care

Reasons why users might enter a care home	%
Failing health	34.8
Increasing frailty or dependence	28.5
Carer can no longer care	19.3
Feeling unsafe at home	8.0
Loneliness, bereavement, grief	6.3
I'd be better off there	4.2
Something happening to home	3.8
If I wanted to	3.5
Other	0.3
Under no circumstances	39.7
Total n =	280

Missing values: 45. This question was not asked of cognitively impaired users.

Table 3.17 describes the circumstances which users felt could possibly lead to a move into institutional care. Those users (40 per cent overall) who refused to consider institutional care as an option did not answer this question, but are included in the table as 'under no circumstances'. Among those willing to think about a move, poor health is the most frequently mentioned reason for having to leave home. Over a third of users (35 per cent) said that failing health could be a reason for having to enter institutional care, while 28 per cent mentioned increasing frailty or dependance as a cause. Interestingly, it was users in the long interval need category who were most concerned that poor health would lead to admission. These are the users who are just beginning to adapt to a loss of functional ability or worsening health, and may view it as more of a threat to their independence than short or critical interval need users, who have remained at home despite increasing frailty.

Just under one in five users reported that admission to institutional care could occur if their carer was no longer able to offer assistance. Carers were also asked which circumstances could lead to admission for the user. Responses were again very similar to users' answers when a sample with both user and carer responses was selected. Although carers would not admit to the possibility of their future inability to care (29 per cent) significantly more frequently than their users (27 per cent), they were, however, more likely to identify increasing frailty and dependence on others as a cause of admission (31 per cent) than users (20 per cent). Moreover, loneliness, bereavement and grief were seen as factors which might lead to an admission more frequently by carers (16 per cent) than users (6 per cent). Spouse carers in particular might be afraid that they may die before the user. The views of principal informal carers, their personal circumstances, and their relationship with the user, are dealt with in the next chapter.

Appendix 3.1
The Measurement of Certain User and Carer Characteristics

Cognitive impairment

The user interview measured cognitive impairment using the Katzman scale. The answers to six questions testing orientation in time, short-term memory and various cognitive skills yield a score with a range of 0-28. Scores of 11-21 corresponded to moderate cognitive impairment and 22 and over to severe cognitive impairment.

Depression

The user interview measured depression using the shorter geriatric depression scale, the answers to 15 questions yielding a score in the range 0-15. Because scores of 11 and over on the full geriatric depression scale (score 0-30) were taken to indicate clinical depression, the corresponding threshold for the shorter scale was taken as 5.5.

4   Need-Related Circumstances of Carers

Introduction

It is estimated that 13 per cent of Britain's adult population are informal carers (OPCS, 1997). Both the 1990 and 1995 General Household Surveys included supplementary questions aimed at identifying these carers. The recent analysis of the 1995 findings found that 4 per cent of the population are providing informal care to someone in the same household, while 8 per cent of people are providing care to someone living in another household.

Informal care is the main source of support for older people. Families and friends, rather than services, provide the bulk of assistance. The 1994/95 GHS asked older people how often they visited or received visits from relatives and friends. More than three out of four people reported visits at least once a week, while only 3 per cent stated that they did not see friends and relatives at all nowadays. Walker and Maltby (1996) asked older people in Britain to list their main sources of assistance in a multiple response question: 40 per cent mentioned their adult children, 32 per cent their spouse, 16 per cent mentioned public services and voluntary organisations, 14 per cent other relatives, 12 per cent friends and neighbours, and 11 per cent mentioned private paid help.

While many older people benefit from the support of a large network of relatives and friends, those that require assistance on a regular basis often have one main helper, one person who provides most of the caregiving (Chappell, 1990). The ECCEP carers are drawn from this group of people who provide assistance on a regular basis: the 'principal informal carers'. More than 80 per cent of ECCEP users have such a carer, and just over 70 per cent of these carers were interviewed. These carers (n=238) were looking after an older user who was resident in the community at the time of the first interview. In this chapter, these carers are introduced and their personal circumstances described, including their living arrangements, employment, other caring responsibilities, and their mental and physical health. The carers' views of their relationships with users are also presented. The nature of the assistance they provide to older people will be dealt with in a subsequent chapter.

Carer's basic characteristics

Informal care is provided by both men and women, of all age-groups and within and outside the family. A growing literature has emphasised the many forms of the caregiving relationship, progressing from an earlier emphasis on caring as the activity of female relatives in mid-life (Walker, 1982; Finch and Groves, 1983) to more recent analyses of caregiving within marriage, male carers and the wider informal care network (Arber and Ginn, 1992; Fisher, 1994; Parker, 1993). The characteristics of each carer in the ECCEP study — such as age, gender and relationship with the older person — interact with the needs-related circumstances of the user to affect the type and amount of informal care that is provided.

Age

The Family Resources Survey (DSS, 1997) has pointed out that the likelihood of becoming a carer increases with age up to retirement. The Carers National Association surveyed their members in 1997 and found the single largest group of carers to be between the ages of 50 and 59, while one in 20 was over the age of 80. The 1995 GHS confirmed that the peak age for caring was from 45-64 (OPCS, 1997). Studies focusing specifically on the carers of older people in the community have found the average age of carers to be between 55 and 65 (Bland and Hudson, 1994; Fisher, 1994). The age profile of ECCEP carers highlights the role of older people in providing informal care. Carers below the age of 40 account for only 6 per cent of carers, and those aged 41-50 19 per cent. In contrast, almost half of the ECCEP sample (46 per cent) are between the age of 51 and 70, with an additional 29 per cent between the ages of 71 and 90.

Older carers are looking after the frailest group of users. While one in five carers of short and long interval need users is over the age of 71, the proportion is one in three when the user has critical interval needs. Older carers are also more likely to be looking after someone with a cognitive impairment, although the differences are less marked.

Gender

Women make up almost three-quarters of principal informal carers (72 per cent). The presence or absence of cognitive impairment or a behavioural disorder in the user makes no difference to this gender breakdown. However, the importance of male carers increases with the physical dependency of the user, from 22 per cent of those looking after users in the long interval need category, to 35 per cent of carers of critical interval need users.

It is important to note that both age and gender differences are heavily influenced by the large group of spouse carers in the ECCEP sample. The majority of male carers in ECCEP are spouses (53 per cent). As the spouses of older service users, these carers are themselves elderly. In many cases, it is their support that has been instrumental in preventing the admission of a frailer user to residential or nursing home care.

Marital status

Most carers (80 per cent) are married. Among male carers, the majority are married to the user, while the majority of female carers who are married are not spouse carers. Just under one in ten (8 per cent) of carers are single, a similar proportion are widowed (9 per cent), while just 2 per cent are divorced.

Table 4.1 shows the age group and marital status of male carers by interval need of the user. There are no widowed male carers in the sample, in part due to female longevity and the propensity of women to marry men older than themselves. A small proportion of male carers are single (12 per cent), and just two male carers are divorced; all but two of these individuals are living with the user, and thus potentially providing a high level of support.

The vast majority of male carers are married (85 per cent), with two-thirds of this group being the spouse of the user. The married carers are looking after the most dependent users; 83 per cent of this group are caring for someone in the critical interval need category. Male carers also tend to be older, with almost two-thirds (65 per cent) over the age of 61. There are no male carers under the age of forty.

Table 4.2 shows the age group and marital status of female carers by interval need of the user. Among female carers, a slightly lower proportion than their male counterparts are married (77 per cent). Only one-third of married female carers are the spouse of the user. Along with widowed carers (13 per cent of female carers), these married carers are most likely to be looking after users with critical and short interval needs. Only 7 per cent of female carers are single, with three who are divorced. The age profile of female carers is extremely varied. Their mean age is slightly younger than that of male carers; while two-thirds of male carers are over the age of 61, less than half of female carers have reached that age.

Table 4.1
Age group and marital status of male carers, by interval need of user

Age groups	Single			Married/Partnered			Divorced	Total
	Critical %	Long %	Short %	Critical %	Short %	Long %	Short %	n =
41-50	50.0	33.3	100	13.8	14.3	19.2	-	12
51-60	-	33.3	-	2.9	42.9	19.2	100	12
61-70	50.0	-	-	14.3	21.4	19.2	-	11
71-80	-	-	-	38.3	7.1	19.2	-	16
81-90	-	-	-	30.9	14.3	23.2	-	17
Total n =	2	3	3	34	14	10	2	68

Missing values: 0.

Table 4.2
Age group and marital status of female carers, by interval need of user

Age groups	Single			Married/partnered			Widowed			Divorced		Total
	Critical %	Short %	Long %	Critical %	Short %	Long %	Critical %	Short %	Long %	Critical %	Long %	n =
0-40	-	14.3	66.7	7.1	6.9	10.7	-	-	-	-	-	14
41-50	50	-	-	24.8	20.8	19.9	-	-	16.7	-	-	32
51-60	-	42.9	-	21.7	32.4	24.2	18.1	33.3	16.7	50.0	100	44
61-70	50	-	-	23.4	20.4	29.1	43.6	33.3	50.0	50.0	-	43
71-80	-	42.9	-	21.2	17.1	10.7	25.6	22.2	-	-	-	30
81-90	-	-	33.3	1.8	2.3	5.4	12.8	11.1	16.7	-	-	8
Total n =	2	7	3	55	42	36	8	9	6	2	1	171

Missing values: 0.

In summary, there are important differences to note between the male and female carers in this study. The majority of male carers are the spouse of the user, almost all of whom live with the user. There is also an important group of co-resident single or divorced male carers. In contrast, the age and marital status profile of female carers, who make up the vast majority of the sample, is more varied. A large group are over the age of 65, and are either the spouse of the user or a widowed or single relative. An equally large group are in mid-life and are the daughters or other female relatives of users.

Kinship

Age, marital status and gender all play a part in determining who will become a carer, yet these variables must be considered along with the relationship between the user and the carer, which also determines caring responsibility.

Relationship between the user and the carer

The single largest group of carers are looking after their parents or parents-in-law (45 per cent), while almost one in three (31 per cent) are looking after a spouse. Only 4 per cent of carers are the siblings of the user, while nearly 10 per cent are other relatives. Friends and neighbours account for 8 per cent of carers. Table 4.3 illustrates which carers are looking after users with different needs-related circumstances.

There is a connection between the dependency level of users and the relationship of user to carer. Carers who are sons and daughters (in-law) are more likely to be caring for users who are less physically dependent, in the short and long interval need categories. It is spouse carers who are most likely to be caring for those with critical interval needs. Despite the fact that spouse carers account for just under one-third of carers overall, they make up almost half (46 per cent) of carers of critical interval need users. Chappell (1990) has emphasised the importance of spouse carers in providing assistance to frailer older people in the community. She argues that older couples tend to redistribute domestic tasks when the health of one or both worsens, and spouses are more likely than others to provide care for greater disability and illness, especially for chronic conditions. The children of a user may become principal carers only when a spouse has not been or is no longer available. The 1994 GHS asked older people who had difficulty with various tasks who usually provided them with assistance. With the exception of cutting toenails, older people living with their husband or wife identified this spouse as the main source of help with all tasks (OPCS, 1994).

Spouse carers, along with other close family carers, are a particularly important source of assistance for users with a cognitive impairment or

Table 4.3
Relationship of user to carer, by interval need and cognitive impairment/behavioural disorder of user

Relationship of user to carer	Critical		Short		Long		Total
	CI/BD %	No CI/BD %	CI/BD %	No CI/BD %	CI/BD %	No CI/BD %	n =
Parent/parent-in-law	40.5	32.8	67.8	48.7	43.4	44.5	105
Wife	22.7	33.6	4.0	5.6	17.5	4.4	37
Husband	20.9	18.4	16.1	12.0	17.5	10.9	38
Sibling/sibling-in-law	3.5	2.9	4.0	5.6	0	6.5	10
Other family member	5.3	8.2	0	11.2	7.2	18.4	22
Friend/neighbour	3.5	4.1	8.1	11.2	14.5	10.9	19
Paid carer	3.5	-	-	5.6	-	4.4	7
Total n =	55	48	24	52	13	45	237

Missing values: 1.

behavioural disorder (CI/BD). Overall, 48 per cent of the carers of users with CI/BD are the sons or daughters of the user, and 36 per cent are spouses. Less close family members account for only 4 per cent of those caring for someone with CI/BD, compared with 12 per cent of those caring for someone without these mental health problems. The small group of friends and neighbours who are PICs (nineteen people) are caring primarily for less dependent users: those in the short and long interval need category, and those who are not cognitively impaired. This is consistent with the 'hierarchy' of caregiving described by some writers (Qureshi and Walker, 1989; Finch and Mason, 1993). The nature of the assistance required by more dependent older people, including help with personal care, means that it is largely close family members — a spouse, followed by the children and siblings of the older person — who are willing to provide support, or who are accepted by the user. Assistance with these tasks, along with behavioural problems, also means that friends and neighbours are rarely identified as the main carers of cognitively impaired users.

Gender plays an important role in determining who becomes a carer. As mentioned, three out of four carers in the study are women. The single largest group of women are the daughter of the user (45 per cent), while 21 per cent are the wife of the user. These proportions are reversed among male carers, where only 31 per cent are the son of the user, whereas 53 per cent are spouse carers. There are no male carers looking after an in-law, whereas 6 per cent of female carers are looking after someone related to them by marriage. This may be due to the social acceptability of women providing care, particularly intimate care, to older people of both genders, whereas male carers may only be comfortable or accepted providing this type of assistance to their closest relatives. That said, there is a gender congruence between carers and users, meaning that female carers are more likely to be providing assistance to an older woman, whereas male carers are more likely to be helping an older man. For instance, whereas only 6 per cent of female carers are looking after their fathers, 9 per cent of male carers are doing so. While 38 per cent of female carers look after their mother, 23 per cent of male carers identified their mother as the older person they care for.

Length of time carer has been providing assistance

As longevity increases, the number of years in which older people may experience health problems also grows. The implication for informal carers is that many will be providing assistance to an older friend or relative over a period of years, rather than months. The Carers National Association 1997 survey found that the average time their members had been caring was eleven years. Another recent study examining crossroads care attendant schemes in all parts of the UK (n=230) found that 52 per cent of carers using the service had been carers for five years, more than one-third had been caring for ten years or more, while 9 per cent had been looking after the user for more than twenty years (Centre for Health and Social Research, 1997). ECCEP carers were also asked to indicate whether they had recently begun caring, or whether they had been looking after the user for some time.

Table 4.4 illustrates how long carers have been providing their current level of assistance to the user. Over 70 per cent of respondents indicated that they had been caring for a year or more. There is no clear relationship between the dependency level of the user and the length of time the carer has been providing assistance, with 72 per cent of carers of critical interval need users, 64 per cent of carers of short interval need users and 75 per cent of carers of long interval need users stating that they had been providing assistance for more than a year. Carers of cognitively impaired users did, however, report that they had, on average, been providing care for a longer period than carers of users without a cognitive impairment.

The vast majority of ECCEP carers have thus been supporting the user for at least a year before social services became involved. This is consistent with evidence from other studies suggesting that many families have been caring for some time before they seek help from statutory services (Moriarty and Webb, 1997b). Taking on the role of carer is often a gradual process, particularly for those living with an older person with health problems. ECCEP carers were asked if the initiation of help they provide to the user had been gradual or sudden. Two-thirds reported that it had been a gradual process, whereas the remaining one-third of carers had suddenly had to help the user on a regular basis. The presence or absence of cognitive impairment/behavioural disorder in the user made little difference to carer responses. While 35 per cent of the carers of users with a cognitive impairment had suddenly had to provide help, 32 per cent of those looking after a user without cognitive impairment had suddenly become carers. The only clear relationship between the needs of the user and carer responses was found among the carers of long interval need users. They were much more likely than other carers to have found themselves suddenly in the role — 44 per cent — compared with 56 per cent who became carers gradually. As this is the least dependent group of users, the sudden onset of the caring role may have been due to a rapid deterioration in health among these users, or discharge from hospital.

For two-thirds of carers, a deterioration in the health of the user was the reason why the carer began providing help. When asked why they had begun providing assistance, 42 per cent of carers stated that illness or the user's disability had prompted them to become carers, while an additional 22 per cent mentioned a sudden fall or stroke. These proportions rose to 54 per cent and 23 per cent among the carers of critical interval need users. While 26 per cent of carers identified their reasons for becoming carers simply as 'a gradual process', others reported reasons related to events that would have unfolded over time. One in five carers (21 per cent) said that they had begun helping

Table 4.4

Length of time in weeks that the PIC has been providing the current level of help, by interval need and cognitive impairment or behavioural disorder of user

How long carer has been helping	Critical CI/BD %	Critical No CI/BD %	Short CI/BD %	Short No CI/BD %	Long CI/BD %	Long No CI/BD %	Total n =
Less than 4 weeks	-	-	4.0	-	-	-	1
4-12 weeks	3.5	10.2	8.1	13.1	-	8.7	19
12-52 weeks	21.6	18.4	36.3	16.8	6.7	19.6	48
More than a year	74.8	69.3	51.7	70.0	93.3	69.5	168
Don't know	-	2.0	-	-	-	1.6	2
Total n =	55	48	24	52	14	45	238

Missing values: 0.

when it became apparent that the user 'could no longer cope alone', while 16 per cent said the user's confusion was the deciding factor. Some carers (15 per cent), said that they and the user had 'always looked after each other' while 12 per cent reported that they had taken over the role of carer when the user had been widowed. Only a very small number of carers — 3 per cent — said that they had taken on the caring role because a previous carer had been able to cope no longer.

Living arrangements

The 1994 GHS reported that, since 1980, there has been an increase in the proportion of older people living alone, and a decrease in those living in 'miscellaneous' households, which includes those living with their children and others, either with or without a spouse. The proportion of older people living in these 'miscellaneous' households was 21 per cent in 1980, dropping to 16 per cent in 1991 and levelling off at 15 per cent in 1994. This decline in the proportion of older people living with others does have implications for the type and frequency of support that is available to them if their health deteriorates and assistance with daily activities is required.

Table 4.5 illustrates with whom the carer lives. Very few carers live alone (n=25). Most live with others and in many instances that includes the user. Overall, just under half of ECCEP carers, 42 per cent, live with the user. This is a fairly high proportion, certainly higher than that identified by the 1996 Family Resources Survey, which found only 35 per cent of carers living with the person they look after (DSS, 1997). Identification of principal informal carers was achieved by consulting users and care managers. The requirement to identify only one main carer may have resulted in a particularly high proportion of co-resident carers being interviewed.

There is a clear relationship between co-residency and the dependence of the user. Total proportions for CI/BD and non-CI/BD in each interval need category reveal that while 59 per cent of the carers of critical interval need users live with the user, only 35 per cent of the carers of long interval need users do so. If the user is cognitively impaired, the carer is also more likely to be co-resident. While 42 per cent of carers of users without a cognitive impairment said that they live with the user, over half — 55 per cent — of those caring for someone with a cognitive impairment are co-resident.

Qureshi and Walker (1989) and Twigg and Atkin (1994) have argued that co-residency is an important determining factor in defining who within a family becomes a carer. This is most obvious in the case of spouse carers, but also applies to other family members, in particular the children of the user. This is perhaps best illustrated by the fact that almost two-thirds of male carers are co-resident, whereas only one-third of female carers in the ECCEP sample live with the user. These male carers (primarily the spouses and sons of users)

Table 4.5

Who does the carer live with if they do not live alone, by interval need and cognitive impairment or behavioural disorder of the user

Co-residents	Critical CI/BD %	Critical No CI/BD %	Short CI/BD %	Short No CI/BD %	Long CI/BD %	Long No CI/BD %	Total n =
User	62.6	54.3	39.4	40.1	53.2	29.7	100
Spouse	44.5	52.1	65.0	59.9	46.8	64.1	119
Sibling(s)	2.1	-	-	-	7.8	4.8	4
Child(ren)	28.6	32.0	30.7	25.3	23.4	34.5	64
Grandchild(ren)	-	-	8.8	-	-	-	2
Parent(s)	2.1	-	-	2.1	-	2.4	3
Other relative(s)	2.1	-	-	-	-	1	2
Friend(s)	2.1	-	-	-	-	-	1
Other non-relatives	-	-	-	2.1	-	-	1
Total n =	47	46	22	46	12	40	213

Missing values: 0. One carer (long interval need, no CI/BD) reported that the user was living with him/her on a temporary rather than permanent basis. This case was included in the 'User' total.

may have become carers 'by default' as a consequence of not only their close relationship with the user, but also the fact that they live under the same roof (Arber and Ginn, 1995). In contrast, the expectation that females will provide informal care means that they assist relatives both within and outside their own household. The fact that living arrangements may have contributed to male family members becoming carers does not lessen the importance of the care they are providing, but it does emphasise, as Twigg and Atkin (1994) have stated, that caring is not just about the performance of tasks, but also concerns the consequences of a relationship.

Co-residency

Co-resident carers were asked how long they had been living with the user. For most, co-residency was a long-standing arrangement. Eight out of ten co-resident carers had lived with the user for more than ten years. Not surprisingly, among spouse carers all but one individual had been living with the user for a decade or more. Other female carers reported the shortest duration of co-residency, with just over half living with their older relative for ten years or more, while 24 per cent had been co-resident for less than a year. This suggests that female carers who are not the spouse of the user — primarily daughters — are the group most likely to make a change in either their own or the user's accommodation to adapt to increasing dependency.

Other recent British studies have reported that living in a son's or daughter's household is the least-preferred long-term care option of older people (Arber and Ginn, 1991; Allen et al., 1992). Moving in with a carer involves not only a loss of independence but also the worry of becoming a 'burden' on family members, which 40 per cent of ECCEP users reported was something they worry about. Thus, it is not surprising that only 5 per cent of carers reported that living with the user was a recent, rather than long-standing, arrangement. Among this small group of cases, all but one carer reported that the user had moved into their home, rather than vice versa. A recent study of co-residency among older people carried out for the Joseph Rowntree Foundation found that moving in with a younger relative was strongly related to age, widowhood and disability or illness (Healy and Yarrow, 1997). Among ECCEP users, it was those in the critical interval need category who were most likely to have moved into a carer's home.

Distance between user/carer residences

Although older people may prefer not to live with younger family carers, the proximity of these carers is nonetheless important. As needs change, the distance between the residence of the user and carer can have important implications for the amount and type of help that the carer can provide. ECCEP carers who do not live with the user were asked to describe the distance between their home and that of their older person they support.

Table 4.6 illustrates the distance between the home of the user and carer. More than two-thirds of non-co-resident carers live within five miles of the user, with 38 per cent living within one mile. Indeed, only one carer lives 30 miles or more away from the user. There is a clear gradient relating the needs of the user to the proximity of the carer. The highest proportion of carers living within one mile are supporting critical interval need users, reflecting these users' needs for care at unpredictable and frequent intervals. If the user is cognitively impaired or has a behavioural disorder, carers living separately are also more likely to live nearby, with 43 per cent of these carers living within a mile of the user, compared with 34 per cent of other carers. When users have a cognitive impairment and critical interval needs, the proportion of non-co-resident principal carers who live within a mile rises to 45 per cent.

Other caring responsibilities

Most carers in the UK look after one older person or younger person with disabilities. Arber and Ginn's (1995) secondary analysis of the 1990 GHS found that 80 per cent of carers look after one person, 17 per cent are responsible for two people, and just 3 per cent are caring for three or more people. Analysis of the 1995 GHS found that 18 per cent of carers were looking after more than one person.

Just under one in four carers have other dependants, almost two-thirds of whom live in the same household. There is no clear relationship between the needs of the user and whether the carer has other dependants, although carers of cognitively impaired users are overall slightly less likely to have these extra responsibilities.

Carers were asked specifically whether they had children under the age of eighteen who live in the same household. Overall, 13 per cent of carers have dependent children. Perhaps surprisingly, it is the carers of the frailest users who were slightly more likely to have children in their household. Among carers of critical interval need users, 16 per cent have children, compared with 12 per cent of the carers of both short and long interval need users. In addition, 17 per cent of carers of cognitively impaired users live with children, compared with 11 per cent of carers of users without a cognitive impairment. In short, there is a group of carers looking after children while also being responsible for an older relative or friend with complex needs. Balancing the role of carer to both younger and older family members is something that these carers do on a daily basis.

Table 4.6

Distance between the home of the user and the carer, by interval need and cognitive impairment or behavioural disorder of the user

Distance between user's and carer's homes	Critical		Short		Long		Total
	CI/BD %	No CI/BD %	CI/BD %	No CI/BD %	CI/BD %	No CI/BD %	n =
Less than one mile	45.0	34.2	31.6	41.9	62.5	26.9	52
1-5 miles	27.5	21.4	46.8	40.7	12.5	40.1	47
6-15 miles	13.0	23.1	8.9	11.6	25.0	26.9	25
16-30 miles	9.2	8.5	12.6	-	-	6.0	8
31-50 miles	-	-	-	2.9	-	-	1
Don't know	5.4	12.8	-	2.9	0	-	5
Total n =	26	23	15	33	8	33	138

Missing values: 0.

Table 4.7

People dependent on carer who may or may not live with the carer, by interval need and cognitive impairment or behavioural disorder of the user

Other dependants	Critical CI/BD %	Critical No CI/BD %	Short CI/BD %	Short No CI/BD %	Long CI/BD %	Long No CI/BD %	Total n =
Yes — live with respondent	32.4	19.3	16.1	15.0	27.0	14.0	44
Yes — do not live with respondent	13.8	2.0	25.8	16.8	6.7	8.7	29
No other dependants	62.7	78.7	58.1	68.2	66.3	77.3	165
Total n =	55	48	24	52	14	45	238

Missing values: 0.

Employment

Employment rates among carers vary, and are influenced by a variety of factors, including the age and health of the carer, the needs of the user and the availability of assistance from informal support networks and formal services. Carers are less likely to be in employment than non-carers (Green, 1988; Twigg and Atkin, 1994). The Social Work Services Inspectorate (SWSI) in Scotland interviewed older users of the home help service and their carers in 1995. They found just over half (53 per cent) of the carers interviewed were in some form of paid employment (SWSI, 1996). The most recent Family Resources Survey found that 44 per cent of carers were employed. Twigg and Atkin (1994) interviewed the carers of younger as well as older people and found that approximately one-third were in paid employment.

Table 4.8 shows the proportion of carers in employment. Carers were asked whether they were in paid employment, not in employment, or were in unpaid employment as a housewife. Just over one-third of carers are in paid employment, while an additional 12 per cent are housewives.

There is a relationship between the needs of the user and the carer's employment status. When the interval need of the user is considered, the carers of critical interval users were least likely to be in paid employment, with just over one in four reporting that they had a job outside the home. Carers of users with a cognitive impairment or behavioural disorder were also less likely to be employed, with 31 per cent of these carers reporting that they had a job, compared with 36 per cent of other carers. The impact of caring for someone with a cognitive impairment who is functionally more independent, and thus may have behavioural problems that require close monitoring, is most evident among the carers of cognitively impaired users who have long interval needs. Only 13 per cent of these carers are employed, despite the fact that they are the youngest group of carers, and thus have the greatest potential to be active in the labour market.

Table 4.9 illustrates the hours worked by carers in paid employment. Three out of four carers work full-time, defined as 21 hours or more per week. Again, it is apparent that caring for someone with a cognitive impairment or behavioural disorder can have an impact not only on *whether* a carer is in employment, but also on the *hours worked*. Carers of an older person with these mental health problems were less likely than other carers to be in full-time employment, with the differences most marked among the carers of short and long interval need users.

Balancing employment and other responsibilities

Among employed carers, 38 per cent have other dependants, compared with 27 per cent of carers who are not employed outside the home. While this

Table 4.8
Proportion of carers in employment, by interval need and cognitive impairment or behavioural disorder of the user

Is principal informal carer employed?	Critical		Short		Long		Total
	CI/BD %	No CI/BD %	CI/BD %	No CI/BD %	CI/BD %	No CI/BD %	n =
Yes	28.0	24.6	50.0	35.6	13.5	48.9	82
No	57.1	67.2	40.3	53.2	79.8	35.8	128
Housewife	14.9	8.2	9.7	11.2	6.7	15.3	28
Total n =	55	48	24	52	14	45	238

Missing values: 0.

Table 4.9

Carer working part-time or full-time, by interval need and cognitive impairment or behavioural disorder of user

Employment status	Critical		Short		Long		Total
	CI/BD %	No CI/BD %	CI/BD %	No CI/BD %	CI/BD %	No CI/BD %	n =
Full-time	68.4	50.0	56.4	94.7	50.0	84.8	61
Part-time	31.6	50.0	43.6	5.3	50.0	15.2	21
Total n =	15	12	12	19	2	22	82

Missing values: 0. Full-time = More than 20 hours per week, Part-time = 20 hours or less per week.

difference must be attributed in part to age — younger carers are most likely to be in employment and to have dependent children — it does highlight the multiple demands on some carers, particularly those who must remain in employment in order to support their families, while continuing to provide assistance to an older relative.

ECCEP carers were asked if they had taken any time off time off work in the past year to look after the user. Forty-four carers, just over half of those in employment, reported that they had taken time off work. For three out of four of these carers, this time off had been unplanned, rather than annual leave or flexitime. Taking unplanned leave to respond to the needs of the user both limits promotion and other work-related opportunities for carers, income and benefits will also be limited if the carer must permanently reduce their working hours. A small group of carers — 13 per cent of those not in employment at the time of the interview — reported that they had left their job specifically to look after the user.

Carers' physical health

A carer's ability to assist the user is restricted if his or her own health is poor. This is particularly the case if the carer suffers from any limiting or long-standing illness. In turn, caring can have an impact on the carer's health, both mental and physical. ECCEP carers were asked to assess their own health, and to describe any health problems they had experienced in the past year.

Self-assessed health

Carers were asked to compare their own health with the health of other people their own age. Table 4.10 illustrates whether carers felt their own health to be better, the same or worse than the health of others their own age. This perception is likely to reflect a combination of their objective state of physical health and their overall morale. Over 60 per cent of carers stated that their health was 'about right' for their age group, while 19 per cent described it as 'worse than others' and 20 per cent considered their health better than others their own age. The proportion of carers who were unhappy with the state of their health was higher among those caring for critical interval need users than short interval need users. Interestingly, the group of carers who had the worst impressions of their own health were the carers of long interval need users with a cognitive impairment or behavioural disturbance. This could be indicative of the pressures of caring for physically less dependent users with mental health problems, whose behaviour may make it very difficult for the carer to cope.

Table 4.10

Self-assessed health of the carers, by interval need and cognitive impairment or behavioural disorder of user

| | Interval need | | | | | | | | Total |
| Self-assessed health in relation to average for age | Critical | | Short | | Long | | Total | | |
	CI/BD %	No CI/BD %	CI/BD %	No CI/BD %	CI/BD %	No CI/BD %	CI/BD %	No CI/BD %	n =
Better	18.4	18.4	5.7	26.2	27.0	21.8	16.5	22.3	48
About same as	59.9	54.9	86.3	47.6	50.0	69.5	65.2	56.8	143
Worse than	19.9	22.5	8.1	26.2	23.0	8.7	17.3	19.3	44
Don't know	1.8	4.1	-	-	-	-	1.0	1.4	3
Total n =	55	48	24	52	14	45	94	144	238

Missing values: 0.

Table 4.11

Carers' health problems in the past twelve months, by interval need and cognitive impairment or behavioural disorder of user

Health problems in the past twelve months	Critical CI/BD %	Critical No CI/BD %	Short CI/BD %	Short No CI/BD %	Long CI/BD %	Long No CI/BD %	Total CI/BD %	Total No CI/BD %	Total n
				Interval need					
No problems	40.8	41.8	28.2	43.1	21.7	56.4	43.7	46.8	99
Musculo-skeletal problems	28.5	23.4	25.8	31.8	24.7	17.5	27.2	24.6	60
Circulatory system	14.4	16.4	16.1	20.6	17.5	8.7	15.3	15.5	36
Anxiety/phobias/depression	10.5	6.1	4.0	11.2	14.5	2.2	9.4	6.8	18
Respiratory problem	8.7	6.1	12.1	9.4	10.2	2.2	9.8	6.1	18
Deafness/other hearing problem	5.4	7.0	8.1	9.4	10.2	2.2	6.8	6.4	15
Digestive problem	5.4	13.1	4.0	8.3	2.2	-	4.2	8.0	15
Nervous system	6.9	2.0	9.7	5.6	14.5	4.4	8.7	4.1	14
Cataracts/other eye	5.4	7.0	4.0	9.4	7.2	2.2	5.3	5.4	13
Senile dementia/mental	2.0	3.7	14.5	2.2	-	-	2.1	2.7	6
Musculo-skeletal deformity/hip fracture	4.0	1.9	7.2	6.5	-	-	2.1	2.7	6
Kidney/urine/prostate	7.2	2.9	1.9	-	-	-	4.2	1.6	6

Incontinence of faeces/other excretory	1.8	2.0	4.0	1.9	-	-	2.1	1.4	4
Cancer/other internal growth	1.8	4.1	2.2	-	-	-	1.1	2.0	4
Reproductive disorders	1.8	2.0	-	-	-	-	1.1	0.7	2
Diabetes	4.0	-	-	-	-	-	1.1	-	1
Other health problems	10.5	6.1	16.1	11.2	7.2	10.9	11.5	9.5	24
Total n =	54	48	24	52	13	45	92	144	236

Missing values: 2.

Co-resident carers were more likely to report poor health: 28 per cent compared with 12 per cent of those living separately. Spouse carers were also more likely to assess their health as poor. Thus, it is those carers who provide the most hours of help per week, and who are looking after the most dependent users, who are most likely to view their own health as poor.

Health problems

All carers were asked if they had suffered from any health problems in the past twelve months. Over half — 58 per cent — said that they had. Carers of critical and short interval needs reported the highest proportion of health problems (59 and 62 per cent respectively). The presence of cognitive impairment corresponded with a higher proportion of reported health problems for carers in all three interval need groups. Co-resident carers were also more likely to report health problems in the past year: 70 per cent compared with 50 per cent of those living separately. When the relationship between the user and carer was considered, it was again spouse carers who had the poorest health: 75 per cent reported problems in the past year, compared with 55 per cent of other female and 35 per cent of male carers.

·Those carers who indicated that they had experienced health problems were asked to identify the nature of the problem. They were asked to select their responses from a list of possible problems, including some related to their mental health.

Table 4.11 illustrates the kind of health problems experienced by the carers against the interval need and mental health of the users. Due to the wide variety of conditions listed in the responses to this question, the number of individuals under each category is small. Despite this, clear patterns emerge.

The most frequently mentioned conditions were musculo-skeletal problems, such as osteoporosis, arthritis or back pain/injury (26 per cent overall), followed by circulatory problems, such as angina and hypertension (15 per cent). Both these conditions can have a potentially serious effect on the ability of carers to assist users, particularly when it comes to tasks such as lifting, bathing and heavy housework. Carers with these types of health problems may be in need of regular assistance with strenuous tasks, as well as training in techniques such as lifting. Other conditions including shingles, skin conditions or other unlisted problems were mentioned by 10 per cent of carers with health problems. It is, perhaps, surprising that anxiety or depression was mentioned by only 8 per cent of these carers. The proportion with these mental problems was higher for carers of critical and long interval need users with cognitive impairment or behavioural disorder (10 per cent and 14 per cent respectively).

Carers' health and the ability to care

Carers were also asked if their health affected their ability to assist the user. Just over half of those carers with health problems — 53 per cent — indicated that their health did have an impact on their ability to care. There was also a clear gradient across interval need categories. While 44 per cent of carers of long interval need users indicated that their health affected the tasks they could do for the user, 59 per cent of carers of critical interval need users said that this was the case. A higher proportion of those looking after someone with a cognitive impairment or behavioural disorder also stated that their health affected their ability to care. Clearly, the more dependent the user, the more outside help is required by carers with health problems.

Almost three out of four co-resident carers with health problems said that their health affected what they could do for the user, compared with less than one-third of carers living separately. Not surprisingly, spouse carers were also more likely to report limitations due to poor health: 70 per cent compared with 40 per cent of other female and 55 per cent of other male carers.

Table 4.12 demonstrates how the carer's poor health affects their ability to care. Lifting the user is the task which the largest group of carers with health problems found difficult to perform (37 per cent). The second most frequently mentioned problem was doing heavy housework, especially laundry. These findings are significant, specifically because these two tasks are those which local authority home helps traditionally would not perform, for insurance reasons in the case of lifting, and due to targeting or task specification, in the case of heavy housework (Dexter and Harbert, 1983; SWSI, 1996). Bathing was the third most frequently mentioned task which carers with health problems

Table 4.12
How PIC's health affects what he/she is able to do for the user

Effect of health problem	% of carers	Number of carers
Does not affect what carer does for user	46.8	62
Difficult/not able to lift user	36.7	49
Difficult/not able to do heavy housework	29.1	38
Difficult/not able to bathe the user	26.8	36
Difficult/not able to do light housework	17.2	23
Difficult/not able to do the shopping	16.4	22
Other	6.1	8
Total n=		238

Missing values: 0.

found difficult to perform. As Twigg (1997) has pointed out, responsibility for providing bathing services is blurred between community nursing and home care services in many parts of the country. The risk is that carers with health problems may not be receiving adequate assistance with this task.

Shopping and doing light housework were reported as difficult by 32 per cent and 31 per cent of these carers respectively. These 'traditional' home help tasks are currently being provided less frequently to some users. Carers with health problems may have to rely on friends or other family members to assist them.

Carers' mental health

There is now a significant body of literature relating to the mental health of carers, focusing primarily on concepts such as burden and stress. This research stems from the understanding that informal carers can be subject to extreme pressures resulting from the demands of providing care. The nature of these demands is determined by such factors as the dependency of the care recipient, the time and effort needed to meet their needs, the economic costs of providing care, and a lack of respite for the principal carer. Emotional strain and restrictions on time and freedom are prevalent, all of which have an impact on mental health.

ECCEP employed two well-validated instruments to measure the mental health of carers: the Rutter Malaise Inventory (Rutter et al., 1970) and the Kosberg Cost of Care Index (Kosberg and Cairl, 1986).

Rutter Malaise

The Malaise Inventory was introduced in 1970 by Rutter and colleagues as an adaptation of the well-tested Cornell medical index. The Malaise Inventory consists of a series of 24 questions which relate to the respondent's mental health manifested in physical symptoms (for example, 'Do you feel tired most of the time?' 'Are you easily upset or irritated?') The respondent is asked if he or she has had any of these feelings in recent weeks. The number of affirmative answers is taken as the total score. A score of 4 or less indicates that the respondent is 'not stressed', scores of 5 or 6 are indicative of emotional stress, while scores of 7 or more are considered 'critical'.

Most previous research used the scale on parents, mainly mothers of disabled children, although more recently it has been used on carers of elderly (Wright, 1986; Quine and Charnley, 1987). Grant et al. (1990) compared mean Rutter scores across studies and found wide variation, depending on whom the carers were. The predecessor to ECCEP, the Domiciliary Care Project (Davies et al., 1990) recorded a mean score of 3.9 among carers.

Table 4.13 illustrates the mean malaise scores for ECCEP carers. As the notes indicate, this scale was administered to carers who were providing users with a significant level of support: co-resident carers or those living separately who were helping with tasks such as personal care. A moderate to high level of malaise was recorded overall, with a mean score of 6.26. This is close to Quine and Charnley's mean score of 6.28 for a group of 40 carers looking after an elderly person with severe behavioural problems at home. It is also close to that found by Burden (1980) and Woods and Macmillan (1994), although not for the same kind of caring responsibilities. The former was a study of the parents of severely disabled infants while the latter was a survey of the relatives of patients with dementia cared for in a large Victorian psychiatric hospital.

Carers of users with cognitive impairment recorded slightly higher levels of strain, with a mean score of 6.56 overall as against a score of 6.03 for carers of users without these problems. Carers of long interval need users with a cognitive impairment/behavioural disorder had the highest mean score, 9.65. This again reflects the pressures of caring for someone with these mental health problems who is still in relatively good physical health.

Kosberg

The Kosberg Cost of Care Index was specifically developed as a care management tool for assessing the potential and actual consequences of caring for an elderly person by informal care givers (although the index can be used on those caring dependent persons of any age). The index was developed with twenty items to measure five dimensions found in the literature to be related to the 'costs' of providing care to dependent elderly persons, such as personal restrictions, economic costs and psychosomatic consequences. Each of these five dimensions is composed of four items, to which the carer responds by checking one of four categories: 'strongly agree', 'agree', 'disagree' or 'strongly disagree'.

Table 4.14 shows the Kosberg scores obtained by ECCEP carers. All carers were assessed using the scale. Carers overall had a mean score of 4.92, indicating a moderate level of stress. Kosberg scores also revealed a relationship between the needs of the user and the level of stress experienced by the carer. Those carers looking after the frailest users, those in the critical interval need category, recorded a mean score of 5.54, compared with 3.91 for those caring for someone with long interval needs.

However, it is between those caring for someone with a cognitive impairment or behavioural disorder and those caring for users without these mental health problems that we see the most marked differences in the Kosberg score. Whereas carers of users without CI/BD had a mean score of 3.85 overall, this rises to 6.57 for those caring for someone with CI/BD. Carers

Table 4.13

Carer malaise score, by interval need and cognitive impairment or behavioural disorder of user

| | Critical | | Short | | Long | | Total | |
	CI/BD %	No CI/BD %	CI/BD %	No CI/BD %	CI/BD %	No CI/BD %	CI/BD %	No CI/BD %
Mean score	6.36	5.59	5.74	6.33	9.65	6.26	6.56	6.03
Std. error of mean	0.65	0.64	0.71	0.61	1.44	1.00	0.50	0.41
Total n =	47	35	17	35	8	22	72	92

Missing values: 74. Sample=164. Only carers providing a high level of support to users were asked to complete the Rutter scale. These carers were either (a) co-resident, (b) living separately but making overnight visits or having the user stay overnight at least once a week, or (c) providing medical/toileting and/or personal care assistance to the user.

Table 4.14

Kosberg stress score for the carer, by interval need and cognitive impairment or behavioural disorder of user

	Critical		Short		Long		Total	
	CI/BD %	No CI/BD %	CI/BD %	No CI/BD %	CI/BD %	No CI/BD %	CI/BD %	No CI/BD %
Mean score	6.67	4.23	6.76	4.00	5.86	3.28	6.57	3.85
Std. error of mean	0.64	0.49	0.94	0.54	1.07	0.58	0.47	0.31
Total n =	55	48	24	52	14	45	94	144

Missing values: 0. Sample = 238.

Table 4.15

Frequency that carer had a break or holiday away from home, by interval need and cognitive impairment or behavioural disorder of user

	Interval need							
	Critical		Short		Long		Total	
Frequency of breaks	CI/BD	No CI/BD	CI/BD	No CI/BD	CI/BD	No CI/BD		
	%	%	%	%	%	%	n =	
More than once a year	48.6	45.9	59.7	56.9	47.2	66.4	129	
Less than once a year	18.1	14.3	20.1	11.2	9.5	13.1	35	
Never, but wish they could	23.7	23.4	8.1	15.0	43.3	9.6	44	
Never, and do not want to	9.6	16.4	12.1	16.8	-	10.9	30	
Total n =	55	48	24	52	14	45	238	

Missing values: 0.

looking after a user who is physically dependent and has a cognitive impairment recorded the highest levels of stress: 6.76 for those caring for a user with a cognitive impairment and short interval needs, and 6.67 among those caring for critical interval need users who are cognitively impaired.

What both Rutter and Kosberg scores illustrate most clearly is the impact of looking after someone with a cognitive impairment on the mental health of carers. These are the users who have the most unpredictable needs, who need support on an almost continual basis. Without adequate respite and support from other sources, the carers looking after these users are forced to continue caring under significant strain.

Breaks from caring

A break from caring is important for both the mental and physical health of the carer, particularly for those who live with the user and may be providing many hours of assistance. Carers were asked how often they had taken a break, away from home, in the past year.

Table 4.15 shows the frequency with which carers take a holiday or break away from home. Just over half of all carers (54 per cent) stated that they take a holiday more than once a year. A smaller group of carers (15 per cent) has a holiday less than once a year. However, a significant proportion of carers, almost one-third, state that they have never had a holiday, either because they choose not to (13 per cent) or because they are unable to but wished that they could (18 per cent). The carers (almost one in five) who stated that they had not had a holiday but wished they could take one were also asked if their inability to take a break was due to the help they provide to the user. Over two-thirds of these carers stated that their caring responsibilities were the reason they could not get away.

Carers of users with a cognitive impairment are less likely than other carers to have taken a holiday, with 23 per cent stating that they had not taken a break but wish they could, compared with 16 per cent of those looking after someone without a cognitive impairment. Carers of more physically dependent users were also less likely to have taken a holiday, with 24 per cent of the carers of critical interval need users stating that they had not had a break but wished they could take one. Thus, the frequency of assistance required by users who are less physically able, and the less predictable needs of someone with a cognitive impairment can place significant restrictions on the ability of carers to get away for a holiday. This was particularly the case for co-resident carers, 31 per cent of whom stated they had not had a break but wished they could have one, compared with just 9 per cent of carers living separately.

The quality of the user/carer relationship

Results from statistical modelling of ECCEP data to investigate the equity and efficiency of resource allocation (Davies et al., 1998) indicate that the quality of the user/carer relationship can affect not only the amount of informal support available to a user, but can also influence the effect of formal services on outcomes such as length of stay in the community, carer stress and user satisfaction. Three important indicators of relational quality between user and carer are: whether the carer feels he/she can confide in the user; whether the carer gets on well with the user; and whether there have been any recent changes in the relationship. Carers were asked about each of these three indicators.

Almost two-thirds of carers (64 per cent) said they could confide in the user. An additional 59 per cent of carers got on 'very well' with the user. Only 8 per cent of carers said they got on 'not at all well' with the user. Two-thirds (67 per cent) said their relationship with the user had not changed in recent years, 19 per cent said it had deteriorated, while 13 per cent said it had improved. Overall, therefore, carers have a positive relationship with the older people they support. However, factors which influenced responses were the presence of cognitive impairment or behavioural disorder in the user and, to a lesser extent, the physical dependency of the user and whether the carer lives with the user.

Carers of cognitively impaired users were less likely to state that they could confide in the user. Less than half of these carers (48 per cent) said the user was a confidante for them. Communication of this kind was particularly difficult if the user was cognitively impaired and frail, with just 42 per cent of the carers of critical interval need users with a cognitive impairment agreeing that they could confide in the user. Similarly, when carers were asked if they got on well with the user, those looking after someone with a cognitive impairment were less positive than other carers, with 12 per cent stating that they got on 'not at all well' with the user. This group of carers also reported the most marked change in the quality of their relationship with the user over the last few years. One in four carers of users with a cognitive impairment or behavioural disorder reported that their relationship had deteriorated in recent years, as the competence of the user diminished. There was also a clear gradient across interval need categories when it came to recent changes in the user/carer relationship. While no carers of long interval need users said the relationship had deteriorated, 28 per cent of those caring for a critical interval need user said that things had worsened. This proportion rose to 33 per cent of carers looking after someone with both a cognitive impairment and critical interval needs.

Who the carer is and where they live also appear to affect the quality of the user/carer relationship over time. Co-resident carers were much more likely to describe the user as a confidante: 82 per cent did so, compared with 53 per

Table 4.16
Why does carer care for the user, by interval need and cognitive impairment or behavioural disorder of user

Reasons for caring	Critical		Short		Long		Total
	CI/BD %	No CI/BD %	CI/BD %	No CI/BD %	CI/BD %	No CI/BD %	n =
Out of love	80.1	79.9	77.3	80.2	93.3	82.2	189
Out of duty	49.6	26.6	47.9	43.6	27.0	26.8	88
Financial reward	1.8	–	–	2.0	–	4.5	4
User has cared for carer	35.8	26.6	25.2	43.6	33.7	22.3	74
No one else to do it	36.5	22.5	37.8	29.8	50.0	24.5	72
Expected of carer	27.7	20.5	25.2	27.8	20.2	8.9	51
Expected by user	6.0	4.9	12.6	11.9	13.5	4.5	18
Always cared	26.2	36.5	31.1	53.6	23.0	27.7	81
Total n =	55	48	23	49	14	44	233

Missing values: 5.

cent of carers who live separately. Responses were also more positive among co-resident carers when asked how well they get on with the user, with only one co-resident carer saying they got on 'not at all well' with the user. Spouse carers were, not surprisingly, more positive about the relationship, compared with other female or male carers. Co-resident carers were also generally more positive about their relationship with the user, except when it came to changes in this relationship over time, when co-residents were twice as likely as other carers to report a deterioration in the relationship. This finding is, however, closely related to the fact that co-resident carers are looking after the most dependent users, whose increasing frailty or confusion, and the resulting demands on the carer, could have been a cause of increasing relational problems.

Reasons for caring

The user/carer relationship is complex, but one thing that can affect both its quality and duration is the carer's motivation. Carers take on the role for different reasons. ECCEP carers were asked about their motivation for providing assistance to the user.

Table 4.16 lists the reasons why carers provide support to the user. As carers often have more than one reason for caring, this was a multiple response question. The vast majority of carers — 81 per cent — mentioned love for the user as a motivation for providing care, while the second most frequently mentioned reason for caring was 'out of duty' (38 per cent). Three other reasons — that the user had at one time cared for the carer, that the carer had always cared, and there was no one else to do it — were each mentioned by approximately one-third of carers. That others just expected the carer to provide care was mentioned by 22 per cent of the interviewees. Two remaining reasons — that the user expected it (8 per cent) or that caring was undertaken for financial reward (2 per cent) — were mentioned by only a very small proportion of carers.

There is no clear relationship between the needs of the user and the carer's motivation for caring. This is hardly surprising as personal motivation is more closely connected to the relationship between the user and carer, and the personal circumstances of the carer. That said, 'duty' as a motivation is mentioned more frequently by those looking after more dependent users (those with a cognitive impairment and those in the critical interval need category) than other carers. It may be that some of the relational problems caused by confusion can affect the carer's motivation, turning what used to be care provided out of love and past reciprocal support, to care provided out of duty.

The carer's relationship to the user, their place of residence, and their gender affect reasons for caring. Spouse carers are most likely to list love as their motivation. Carers living with the user are also more likely to list love as their motivation, rather than duty or the other choices (expectations and no one else to do it) which are strongly related to a sense of duty. Male carers were slightly more likely than female carers (84 per cent compared with 77 per cent) to describe love as their reason for caring, while female carers more commonly chose reasons relating to duty or expectations.

The benefits of caring

This description of the needs-related circumstances of carers has focused almost entirely on the problems and limitations placed on carers by their role. There are also positive aspects to caring: ways in which the carer can benefit as well as the user. The literature does acknowledge these benefits. For example, Fitting et al. (1986) found that 25 per cent of the male spouse carers in their sample claimed an improved relationship with their wife after assuming the role of carer. Lewis and Meredith (1988) found that the majority of daughter carers they interviewed were glad that they had taken on the role of carer and felt satisfied in having done it. Fisher (1994) reminds us that many carers choose their role, and would not change it.

ECCEP carers were asked about benefits accrued from taking on the role of principal carer. Findings were that 67 per cent of carers reported that becoming a carer had made them feel needed and wanted, while 48 per cent of carers felt that providing support had brought them and the user closer together, and 28 per cent agreed that helping the user had allowed them to develop new skills and abilities, and provided a welcome challenge. Thus, carers did acknowledge some benefits of caring, although it is interesting that the only statement that the majority could agree with was that helping the user made them feel needed and wanted.

The characteristics of individual users as well as carers did affect responses relating to the positive aspects of caring. Overall, carers of cognitively impaired users reported fewer benefits, as did those looking after someone with critical interval needs. For instance, only 59 per cent of carers of cognitively impaired users said they felt needed and wanted, compared with 83 per cent of other carers. While 57 per cent of those caring for less dependent, long interval need users agreed that helping the user had brought them closer together, just 44 per cent of those caring for someone with critical interval needs agreed with that statement. Just over one in five carers overall were willing to state that caring had allowed them to develop new skills, with the carers of cognitively impaired users with critical interval needs least likely to agree with the statement.

Co-resident carers, particularly spouse carers, were overall more willing to agree that there were benefits in caring. This is interesting as carers who live with the user, particularly spouse carers, are providing the most hours of support, to users with the highest level of dependency. It again suggests that knowledge concerning the relationship between user and carer is essential to understanding the dynamics of caregiving. An awareness or acknowledgement of the positive sides of the caregiving role, in the context of a close relationship, may moderate some of the difficult aspects of caring. This type of awareness needs to be included in the care management process designed to assess users' and carers' needs and design an appropriate care package to support what are not always compatible preferences. The different components of care management — from screening and assessment to care planning and review — constitute the topic of the next chapter.

Note

1 PICs were in most cases identified by social services and confirmed or re-identified by users, who were simply asked if they had 'someone who sees you at least once a week, looks after you and does a lot for you' . In cases where the user did not or could not (as in cases with cognitive impairment) clearly confirm the carer, the care manager interview alone was used. Care managers were also asked if there was a close family member, friend or neighbour who helped the user. However, if the care manager named more than one individual who provided the same level of assistance, they were asked to choose the one who was a close family member or, failing that, the one who lived with the user. Herein lies the argument that the ECCEP carer sample may be slightly biased towards co-resident carers.

5   Care Management

Introduction

One of the central aims of the community care reforms was the continued development of care management. Care management was described in *Caring for People* as the 'cornerstone' of community care, the main mechanism by which care packages could be 'designed in line with individual needs and circumstances' and 'secure better value for taxpayer's money' (Department of Health, 1989).

Care management itself is an umbrella term. It can be interpreted in a variety of ways. However, central to the concept is the notion of a coordinated response to assessing the needs of users and carers, and planning interventions to meet them. The approach is based on a body of logic which has developed over time, connecting variations in arrangements for the performance of care management tasks to particular contexts. This body of logic began to be constructed in the American and British literature in the late 1970s, and by the 1980s was well developed. There is now a large literature on the subject, which makes clear that there is no one ideal model of care management. Instead, it must be looked at in the context of community care at the field level: hence the design of ECCEP, built around user, carer and care management accounts which provide a case level perspective. Care management must be fitted to local system circumstances, and seen in the broader context of service arrangements. This logic has been applied in previous PSSRU studies, from the Kent Community Care Project onwards, and extended in the years that followed (Davies and Challis, 1986; Davies et al., 1990).

This chapter presents descriptive material from ECCEP which relates to care management. ECCEP does not separate care management from other factors influencing who gets what and with what impact at the field level. The study design does not expect a single care management model. Instead, it describes how care management tasks are fitted to the circumstances of individual users and local system priorities, structures and resources in a way that makes sense.

The chapter is divided into several sections. It begins with a description of the characteristics of care managers and findings relating to the various stages of the care management process. The costs of care management are then discussed, making the distinction between costs during the setting-up phase of a care package, and those involved in the subsequent, continuing care phase. Finally, the perceptions of care managers, users and carers are described, focusing on each group's views relating to the functions and goals of care management, as well as the nature of the relationship between care managers and clients.

Care manager basic characteristics

Care management is a process, made up of a series of core tasks which were, in the British context, mentioned in the 1989 White Paper and detailed in the guidance that followed (SSI/SWSG, 1991). The tasks themselves were defined more closely than the type of professionals who were to complete them. The label of 'care manager' was loosely applied to workers who carried out one or more functions of the process, despite differences in training and degree of involvement at various stages. Thus, in the post-reform period, the answer to the question 'Who is the care manager?' varies across local authorities, as findings from ECCEP demonstrate.

In 1993, the Joint Initiative for Community Care identified no less than 23 job titles given to care managers in the UK (JICC, 1993). By 1995 workers performing care management functions were still known by a variety of job titles. Thus, it is not surprising that ECCEP interviewees gave a wide range of responses when asked to state their job title. Table 5.1 illustrates the main responses, by interval need of users.

Eighteen job titles given to those carrying out care management tasks are shown in the table. The single largest group of respondents, over one-third, identified their job title as social worker. Social work assistants make up an additional 13 per cent of the sample. Other recent research has shown that, since the implementation of the reforms, social workers in some local authorities have fought to retain their job titles as a distinctive professional label, as have occupational therapists. Therapists, however, make up less than 1 per cent of ECCEP care managers. This is interesting as it demonstrates that, although the reforms officially welcomed the concept of health professionals becoming care managers, no real change in this direction had taken place by 1995.

The second largest group of care managers described their job title as home care manager (21 per cent) while an additional 8 per cent said it was home care

Table 5.1
Job title of staff member, by interval need among community-based sample

Job title	Critical %	Short %	Long %	Total n =
Social worker	43.2	33.7	29.1	149
Assistant social worker	15.4	16.5	8.0	55
Care manager	7.7	9.5	10.7	39
Care coordinator	5.1	5.6	4.9	22
Home care organiser	3.9	7.8	12.3	34
Home care manager	15.3	17.4	28.6	88
Occupational therapist	0.6	1.7	0.6	4
Senior home care assistant	0.6	-	-	1
Senior care coordinator	4.1	1.7	-	8
Senior community care worker	0.6	0.9	0.6	3
Assistant care manager	-	0.9	-	1
Assistant home care organiser	0.6	1.7	1.2	5
Community care assessor	0.6	-	1.2	3
Home care assessor	-	0.9	0.6	2
Home care support worker	-	1.7	1.2	4
Community care hospital social worker	-	-	0.6	1
Service manager	0.6	-	-	1
Unit manager	0.6	-	-	1
Other	0.6	-	-	1
Total n =	151	112	158	421

Missing values: 3. Source: All care manager interviews.

organiser. This group of workers have traditionally been responsible for managing and providing home help services. Their role has expanded in the post-reform period to include care management responsibilities. Just 9 per cent of workers stated that their job title was that of care manager, which may demonstrate the level of ambiguity which still exists concerning this job title.

It is clear from Table 5.1 that there is some relationship between the needs of the user and the type of worker who becomes their care manager. More dependent users — those in the critical interval need category — were most likely to have a qualified social worker as their care manager (43 per cent), while the least dependent users — those in the long interval need category — were most likely to have a home care manager/organiser (41 per cent). This suggests that the more complex the needs of the user, the more likely they are to have their assessment and care planning done by a worker with a professional qualification. The exception to this is for occupational therapists, where there is no clear relationship to interval need. However, the number of occupational therapists is too small for findings to be significant.

Care managers were also asked if the assessment they had carried out for the user was complex or simple. The complexity of assessment is determined by the user's needs-related circumstances, so examining complex and simple assessments by type of worker is another indicator of differences in the nature of care management. As would be expected, qualified social workers were responsible for the highest incidence of complex assessments (48 per cent), compared to just 10 per cent of complex assessments which were carried out by home care managers, and an additional 2 per cent by home care organisers.

Table 5.2 further illustrates the breakdown of responsibility for cases between social workers and home care organisers. The contrast between assessments carried out by social workers and by home care organisers is evident. Social workers are responsible for assessing a higher proportion of more dependent users. Indeed, they are responsible for 56 per cent of assessments among users with critical interval needs, compared with home care organisers who are responsible for just 19 per cent of assessments for users in the critical interval need category. The gap narrows as the needs of older people become less complex, with 44 per cent of long interval need users being assessed by a social worker, compared with 41 per cent receiving an assessment from a home care organiser. The presence or absence of informal support also plays a role in who is the assessor, with social workers more likely to be involved when a principal informal carer is present. As services must be arranged to meet the needs of the carer as well as the user, care packages designed to complement and support informal care may be by their very nature more complex, and thus require arrangement by a qualified social worker.

The evidence relating to the needs of users and the job titles of workers therefore suggests that, despite the fact that care management is a generic term, users with more complex needs are being assessed by workers with a professional qualification. Trained social workers are more likely to be responsible for assessing the needs of users who are more frail, have an informal carer and require a greater input of services and a broader service mix.

Assessment

The assessment stage of care management involves understanding the user's needs, relating them to agency policies and priorities, and agreeing the objectives for any intervention (SSI/SWSG, 1991). Prior to an assessment taking place, however, two initial stages in care management must be completed. These are case finding and screening, which involve determining

Table 5.2
Whether staff member (i) social worker or equivalent[1] and (ii) home care manager or equivalent, by interval need and social support

	Interval need			
Job title of staff member	Critical %	Short %	Long %	Total %
Social worker or equivalent				
Without PIC	50	53	37	44
With PIC	57	48	47	51
Total	56	49	44	50
Home care manager or equivalent				
Without PIC	27	37	50	41
With PIC	18	23	38	26
Total	19	25	41	29
Total n =	150	112	156	418

Missing values: 7. Source: All care manager interviews.
1 The category of social worker was applied to workers who had identified themselves as social worker, care manager or care coordinator. The category of home care organiser was used to describe home care organisers and managers, home helps and domiciliary care assessors.

whether the user in question is eligible for care planning and services, and which type of assessment the user will receive. Defining which older people have needs appropriate for care management is important, as not all users of services will require a full or complex assessment.

Table 5.3 illustrates the extent to which care managers believe that the user's problems fit SSD eligibility criteria. Petch (1996) has argued that the eligibility criteria that determine whom should proceed to care management were not made explicit by the reforms. As a result, many authorities sought generality in criteria, in order to avoid excluding those in genuine need of assistance. Despite this broad framework, not all ECCEP users were described as fitting eligibility criteria in each authority. Just over 15 per cent of users were described as fitting criteria to some extent, to a limited extent or not at all. The remaining majority of users (85 per cent) were described as fitting criteria to a considerable or very considerable extent. As Table 5.3 demonstrates, there is a clear relationship between the needs of the user and their eligibility.

Users in the critical interval need category most closely fit SSD eligibility criteria: 91 per cent to a very considerable or considerable extent. In contrast, one in four less dependent, long interval need users did not closely fit

Table 5.3
Extent that problems addressed fit SSD eligibility criteria by interval need

Problems addressed fit SSD eligibility criteria to	Critical %	Short %	Long %	Total %
Very considerable extent	64.3	47.4	40.3	50.4
Considerable extent	27.1	42.3	34.9	34.3
To some extent	7.9	7.9	15.7	10.9
Limited extent	0.0	1.1	7.4	3.2
Not at all	0.7	1.3	1.7	1.2
Total n =	102	84	115	301

Missing values: 5. Source: Standard and brief care manager interviews.

eligibility criteria. This does suggest that local authorities are targeting their services at frailer, more dependent older people who may be most at risk of admission to residential or nursing home care.

The practice and managerial guidance for care management (SSI/SWSG, 1991) made explicit the fact that not all potential service users will receive the same type of assessment, although, as Challis (1994a) has argued, there has been little subsequent development of methods of pre-assessment screening to assist workers in determining which type should be employed. The practice guidance describes six levels of assessment, ranging from simple to complex. ECCEP care managers were asked which type they had employed to identify the needs of the user. Seventeen categories of assessment were described, ranging from initial, simple or fast track, to full, multidisciplinary and complex. Other categories such as self-assessment and carer assessment were also mentioned by small numbers of care managers.

Table 5.4 illustrates the proportion of assessments which care managers described as complex, and relates this to the needs and social circumstances of users. Not surprisingly, there is a clear gradient across interval need levels in relation to complexity of assessment. Half of those with critical interval needs received a complex assessment, compared to just over a third of those with long interval needs. The presence or absence of informal support does not appear to have a significant effect on the type of assessment received. While a slightly higher proportion of those living with others rather than living alone received a complex assessment, this could be attributed to the greater level of dependency among these users. Similarly, whether the user lived with a spouse or had a carer while living alone made little difference to the type of assessment received. Thus, level of assessment is most closely related to the

Table 5.4
Incidence of complex assessments, by interval need and living group/social support among community-based sample

Type of assessment	Interval need			
	Critical Complex	Short Complex	Long Complex	Total Complex
Living with others				
Spouse %	49.6	34.9	48.3	45.6
Spouse n	25	12	9	46
Non-spouse %	54.9	43.5	23.0	45.9
Non-spouse n	32	17	11	60
Living alone				
PIC available %	49.9	48.2	33.9	41.8
PIC available n	28	34	55	117
No PIC %	39.1	51.2	38.4	42.8
No PIC n	7	16	25	49
Total %	50.7	45.8	35.1	43.6
n =	93	80	100	272

Missing values: 34. Sample: Cases receiving care manager standard or brief interviews (306).
Complex assessments were those indicated by the care manager as being complex, full, comprehensive or multidisciplinary. Simple assessments were those which were not complex and indicated by the care manager as being self-assessment, fast track, simple, initial, specific (service), core, standard, specialist, special form of assessment in hospital, carer assessment, no formal procedures for current cases, other.

functional ability and level of need for assistance, rather than the type and amount of informal support available.

User and carer participation in assessment

The assessment process itself is made up of a series of components, such as clarifying expectations, setting priorities and agreeing objectives. One important ingredient in the completion of this process is involvement of the user, and a carer where one is present. Indeed, carer involvement is increasingly recognised as an important part of comprehensive assessment, particularly since the passage of the 1995 Carers (Recognition and Services) Act.

Table 5.5
Extent to which user had a say in assessment and help received, by interval need

Extent to which user had a say	Critical %	Short %	Long %	Total %
Considerable	60.0	72.5	78.1	70.3
Some	19.1	20.6	12.3	16.9
Limited	13.5	4.3	6.4	8.2
No	7.4	2.7	3.3	4.5
Total n =	102	85	111	298

Missing values: 127. Sample: All care manager interviews, excluding cases with cognitive impairment.

ECCEP users, carers and care managers were all asked about the extent of user and carer involvement in the assessment process. Responses can be compared, and some differences observed, particularly between carers and care managers.

Table 5.5 details care managers' responses when asked to what extent users had been involved in the assessment process. Cases in which the user was cognitively impaired were excluded. Among the remaining care managers, over 70 per cent stated that the user had been involved in assessment to a considerable extent, with an additional 17 per cent reporting some involvement. Only 4 per cent of care managers said that no involvement had taken place.

Users without a cognitive impairment were also asked if they felt they had a say in the assessment process. Among users who did respond, however, there was a very similar result to that found for care managers, with 71 per cent of users reporting that they had a say in assessment. Responses from users and care managers regarding participation vary with needs-related circumstances. As Table 5.5 illustrates, there is a clear gradient across interval need categories, with 79 per cent of long interval need users reporting that they had a say in assessment, compared with 60 per cent of critical interval need users. Similarly, care managers reported that over 78 per cent of long interval need users had a 'considerable' say, compared with 60 per cent of critical interval need users.

The presence or absence of an informal carer also affects responses. Among users, 82 per cent of those without a carer reported that they were involved in assessment, compared with just 68 per cent of those with this informal support. Care managers also reported that users with carers had a proportionally lower incidence of involvement that those without one. While this can be partially attributed to the greater degree of frailty among users with carers, it may also suggest that some carers are becoming surrogate decision-makers in the assessment process, taking the place of the user. Indeed, carers were more willing to report that they 'had a say' in decision-making, with 89 per cent of carers stating that they were involved, compared with 71 per cent of users overall. Other research concerning care planning during hospital discharge has suggested that carers do in some cases take the place of the user in decision-making, even when the user is capable of participation (Abramson, 1988; Bauld, 1997).

The care management practice guidance emphasised the importance of involving carers in assessment and suggested that separate carer assessments should be offered in some cases (SSI/SWSG, 1991). However, it was not until the passage of the Carers Act in 1995 that a carer's right to a separate assessment was formally established. Despite the passage of the Act, recent research evidence suggests that the incidence of separate assessment remains low. A UK-wide study by the Carers National Association (1997) found that just 21 per cent of carers surveyed (n=1,655) had an assessment of some kind. It is important to point out, however, that ECCEP Time I data collection took place in 1995, before the implementation of the Act. Both carers and care managers were asked about the carer's role in the assessment process.

Table 5.6 presents the care manager's view of carer assessment. The responses were limited to care managers involved with users who had a carer. Just under three out of four carers did receive an assessment of some kind. The most common type was for the carer's needs to be assessed along with the user's, on the same form. Just 2 per cent of carers received an assessment on a separate form from the user's.

Care managers reported that carers of more dependent, critical interval need users were most likely to have their needs assessed, with just 17 per cent of these carers receiving no assessment, compared with 37 per cent of the carers of long interval need users. Interestingly, responses from carers themselves differed from care managers with regards to needs assessment. Only 16 per cent of carers thought that they had been 'offered a separate assessment of the pressures, if any, brought about by caring'. While the phrasing of the question does not make it directly comparable to responses from care managers, this finding suggests that very few carers were aware that their needs were being considered separately from the users'. When interval need is considered, it was actually the carers of long interval need users who were most likely to report that they had been offered a separate assessment (32 per cent) compared with the carers of critical (17 per cent) and short interval need users (4 per cent).

Table 5.6
Manner by which carer situation and needs were assessed, by interval need

Assessment	Critical %	Short %	Long %	Total %
No carer assessment	17.2	24.4	37.1	25.6
Combined interview with user:				
same form used	75.1	63.2	52.5	64.4
Separate interview from user:				
same form used	5.6	11.2	7.0	7.6
Separate interview from user:				
different form used	2.2	1.3	3.4	2.3
Total n =	76	56	62	194

Missing values: 58. Sample: Standard and brief care manager interviews (n=306); 54 cases not applicable, no informal carer.

Other aspects of assessment

Input from users, carers and care managers makes up the core of the assessment process. There are, however, other resources which can play a part in determining just how comprehensive or appropriate the assessment will be. Care manager training and experience, adequate time and a suitable environment in which to conduct the assessment can all influence outcomes.

Care managers were asked if there was anything lacking in the assessment process. Could they have benefited from extra resources of any kind? As Table 5.7 shows, the majority of workers (70 per cent) did not identify a need for additional resources of any kind during the assessment process. Among those who did identify gaps, it was time that was requested. Just over 12 per cent of care managers said they would have liked more time to fully assess needs. This was particularly the case among care managers assessing those with long interval needs (17 per cent). As Table 5.1 showed, home care managers and organisers are most likely to be the care managers of these less dependent users. Their caseloads may be particularly high, resulting in a shortage of time during assessment. More support from carers and/or the user's family was mentioned as an unmet need by 10 per cent of care managers, and more theoretical knowledge by 8 per cent. Better access to health professionals was mentioned as a need by only 6 per cent of care managers overall, but this proportion did rise to 12 per cent among those assessing critical interval need users. It seems surprising that so few care managers felt the assessment could have benefited from more health input, particularly (as evidence in the next

Table 5.7
Need for extra resources in assessment, by user's level of social support

Need for extra resources	Without PIC %	n =	With PIC %	n =	Total %	n =
More time to assess needs	11.2	4	12.4	19	12.2	23
More time to look for appropriate services	8.0	3	5.3	8	5.8	11
Better access to health professionals	0.0	0	7.1	11	5.8	11
More theoretical knowledge	3.4	1	8.8	13	7.8	14
More information on available services	4.6	2	6.2	9	5.9	11
More support from carer/family	5.1	2	11.0	17	9.9	18
None	82.3	29	67.8	102	70.5	131
Total n =		35		151		186

Missing values: 14. Sample: Standard care manager interviews (n=200); Multiple response question.

section of this chapter shows) when health worker involvement in assessment occurs in only a minority of cases.

Work with other professionals

The importance of multidisciplinary assessment increases as the user's needs, and the resulting care package, become more complex. As Hardy et al. (1996) have argued, comprehensive assessment is more likely if there is more than one professional involved. This type of assessment is more readily available when the care package has been set up as a result of hospital discharge. However, input from medical and allied professionals is frequently required for community-based assessments.

Table 5.8 lists the other professionals involved in assessment, along with the care manager. In 42 per cent of cases, the care manager conducted the assessment alone, without input from other professionals. In the majority of cases, however, there was input from at least one other source.

The most common contributions were from social services home care managers (19 per cent), with an additional 12 per cent mentioning home care staff. As over 80 per cent of ECCEP users receive home help as part of their care

Table 5.8
Other professionals involved in assessment with worker

Other professionals involved	Total %	n =
Area-based social worker	3.6	7
Hospital/clinic based social worker	6.0	12
SSD home care managers	18.7	37
SSD home care staff	12.2	24
Other SSD domicilary care managers/staff	4.8	9
SSD day care managers/staff	8.1	16
Day hospital staff	1.6	3
Community-based nurses/health visitors	11.3	22
Community psychiatric nurses	6.8	13
GPs	7.5	15
Hospital nurses	11.6	23
Psychologists	0.4	1
Psychiatrists/psychogeriatricians	3.0	6
Other hospital doctors/consultants	5.6	11
Physiotherapists	4.0	8
Occupational therapists and rehabilitation staff	17.0	34
Mobility officers and technical staff	1.0	2
Voluntary organisations	2.4	5
Housing department/associations	0.7	1
Department of Social Security	1.6	3
Sheltered housing wardens	1.9	4
Care home managers/staff	4.2	8
Independent agency	2.3	4
Others	2.4	5
None	42.4	83

Missing values: 3. Source: Standard care manager interviews (n=200).

package, it is not surprising that home care providers are involved in assessment, either as care managers themselves or in cooperation with social workers and others carrying out care management tasks. The second most commonly mentioned category of professional involvement in assessment was occupational therapy. Occupational therapy and rehabilitation staff were mentioned by 17 per cent of care managers. As the need for aids and adaptations cannot be accurately determined without input from therapists, their involvement is particularly important.

Other professionals involved in assessment were hospital nurses (12 per cent), community nurses (11 per cent), community psychiatric nurses (7 per cent), SSD day care managers (8 per cent) and GPs (7 per cent). The involvement of health care professionals such as therapists, nurses and psychiatrists/psychogeriatricians was mentioned more frequently by care managers of critical interval need users, who may have more complex health needs than other users.

Multidisciplinary input is not only required at the point of assessment. One of the identifying features of good care management is regular and consistent contact with other health and social care professionals in the community. Thus, ECCEP care managers were also asked which professionals they had been in touch with regarding any aspects of the case, since the point of referral or, in the case of those discharged from hospital, while the older person was an inpatient.

General contact takes place much more frequently than direct involvement in assessment. Only 5 per cent of care managers reported that they had no contact with other professionals regarding the case. Indeed, almost half of care managers (47 per cent) had contact with a home care organiser, and 40 per cent mentioned home care staff. Community-based nurses or health visitors were mentioned by 26 per cent of respondents, and occupational and other therapy staff by 25 per cent of care managers. GPs, hospital nurses and SSD day care managers were in general contact with one in five care managers.

Assessment in hospital can take place in very different circumstances from assessment in the community. A proportion of the ECCEP users were hospital discharge cases, meaning that their needs were assessed by hospital social work staff. Assessment and care planning in hospital often has to be done under time pressures, as the patient's bed may be required by others. Patient transfer between wards can also constrain the ability of hospital social workers to do a comprehensive assessment prior to discharge. In order for assessment to take place, care managers often require detailed information from other ward staff to accurately determine which services the user will require. This information may be obtained as part of a formal discharge plan, or merely provide a background for an assessment conducted entirely by the care manager. Effective communication between social services staff and health professionals in hospital is a key component of good discharge planning, and essential to the assessment process.

Table 5.9 shows the opinions of hospital-based care managers regarding their relationships with health professional and social services colleagues. Results show that, overall, very good relationships between the hospital care managers and others were more frequent with SSD colleagues than with medical and ward staff. The quality of relationships between care managers and medical staff in particular were not always positive, with 12 per cent of care managers describing it as mixed, poor or very poor.

What is perhaps most striking, however, is the proportion of hospital-based care managers who reported no contact between themselves and other professionals. Contacts between care managers, other social work colleagues

Table 5.9
Quality of care manager's relationship with hospital and SSD personnel with respect to the case

Quality of relationship	Medical staff %	Ward staff %	SSD colleagues %
Very good	14.1	17.6	31.4
Good	23.6	37.0	34.6
Mixed	8.3	5.5	5.9
Poor	1.8	0.0	0.0
Very poor	1.3	3.0	2.6
No contact	50.8	36.9	25.6
Total n =	73	75	72

Missing values: 30 for medical staff, 28 for ward staff, 31 for SSD colleagues. Source: Standard brief and short care manager interviews. Hospital discharge sample only.

and health workers are central to the development of multidisciplinary and multi-agency care plans in both hospital and community settings. Yet one in four of these hospital-based care managers had no contact with other SSD colleagues, and over a third had no contact with ward staff. Significantly, just over half of hospital based care managers reported no contact at all with medical staff. This raises questions about the comprehensive nature of assessment and care planning in hospital. As the vast majority of older people are admitted to hospital for health rather than social reasons, an account of their health status and future health needs should be considered when arranging post-discharge services. Contact between the care manager and health professionals is thus a necessary component of comprehensive assessment, yet it is a component that is missing in a significant proportion of ECCEP cases discharged from hospital to the community.

Autonomy and authority

The extent to which individual care managers have authority to make decisions — both budgetary and otherwise — about care planning varies significantly between local authorities. Budgetary devolution in particular has developed slowly. In her 1995 survey of Scottish authorities, Petch (1996) found that only one had devolved the purchasing role close to care manager level, and even in this case the actual budget was held by a senior, with the care managers operating within notional limits. Studies carried out in England since the reforms have found a similar lack of progress in budget devolution (Davies et al., 1995; Lewis and Glennerster, 1996; Challis et al., 1997).

The ability of a care manager to develop a care plan that meets the user's needs is dependent on a range of factors; most important among them are the services available in the community, the resources available to the care manager to pay for those services, and the authority the care manager has to negotiate with providers and other professionals whose contribution is necessary for assessment and care planning. ECCEP care managers were asked about each of these aspects of their position, and how the extent of their autonomy and authority affected the care plan.

Table 5.10 illustrates how care managers went about obtaining the services which make up the care plan. The extent to which workers were able to directly contact providers and arrange for services to be put in place is an indicator of the worker's authority to act, as well as the relationship between the SSD and other providers. Not surprisingly, the highest incidence of a direct approach by care manager to provider took place when in-house, SSD services were involved. Over half (56 per cent) of care managers were able to approach SSD providers directly, compared with just 18 per cent who were able to approach NHS services directly, and 19 per cent who were able to approach independent sector providers. It is important to note, however, that in 80 per cent and 73 per cent of cases respectively, extra NHS or independent sector services did not make up a portion of the care package. The vast majority of services provided came from the SSD directly.

Some care managers, as a result of their level of training or other organisational constraints, were not able to approach providers at all without first obtaining consent from a manager. This was the case for 16 per cent of care managers approaching SSD providers, 2 per cent approaching NHS providers, and 7 per cent approaching the independent sector. Care managers of critical interval need users were more likely than other care managers to have directly approached all three categories of provider. This may, however, be a function of the fact that these more complex care packages included services from a wider range of providers (rather than just SSD) and that the workers responsible for these cases were most likely to be trained social workers, who may have more authority to contact external services directly.

Care managers were also asked if providers or colleagues had amended the care manager's assessment or care plan. This is another indicator of autonomy, as it involves the care manager's ability to make final decisions regarding services, and therefore resources. Care managers' plans were amended in only 10 per cent of cases. There was, however, a clear gradient across interval need categories with regard to amendments. While just 2 per cent of care managers of long interval need cases had their plans amended, the proportion rose to 22 per cent for critical interval need cases. As these complex cases are more likely to be the responsibility of trained social workers, this finding is perhaps surprising. One explanation is that higher interval need cases consume more

Table 5.10
How services were obtained from SSD, NHS and independent providers

How services acquired	Service provider		
	SSD	NHS	Independent sector
	%	%	%
Approached providers directly	56	18	19
Approached providers only after approval of manager	16	2	7
Other SSD person approached provider	3	-	1
Not an issue — interior monies only SSD service provided	16	-	-
Not an issue — no (extra) SSD/ NHS/independent services required	11	80	73
Total n =	191	190	191

Missing values: 9. Sample: Standard care manager interviews (n=200).

resources, and thus curbs on expenditure may need to be implemented. This is supported by the fact that, when care managers reported who had made any amendments, it was most commonly the provider who was responsible for amendments to the assessments/care plans of users with critical interval needs.

The key factor, however, in the ability of the care manager to plan and implement a package of services is whether he/she can obtain the necessary resources. This involves the availability of services, the budgetary limits of the SSD (budget caps now being a widely accepted in order to avoid concentrating resources on a limited number of cases, at the expense of others in need of services), and the care manager's authority to spend or approve spending for each individual care package. This ability to spend, where present, allows the care manager a flexibility which is otherwise limited by the need for each component of the package to be approved.

Table 5.11 illustrates the extent of care manager's direct authority to spend on services (within budgetary limits) for users in each interval need category. Given that the workers responsible for more dependent, critical interval need cases are more highly qualified than those dealing with lower dependency cases, the gradient present is perhaps surprising. Just over 66 per cent of workers responsible for long interval need cases had direct authority to spend, compared with 40 per cent of those responsible for critical interval need cases.

One explanation for this is that there are a higher proportion of home care organisers or managers responsible for cases in the long interval need category. The services these workers deal with may be limited to meals on wheels and home care, and they may not have the same management structure — and thus issues of accountability — facing trained social workers within the SSD. In addition, home care organisers may not have the same budget limits as trained social workers, as less dependent users do not require care packages which consume as many resources as those in the critical interval need category. Almost one in four care managers of critical interval need users said they had authority, but only up to a specified spending limit, compared with just 7 per cent of those responsible for long interval need cases.

When authority to spend was not present, workers were asked whom they had to approach for approval. In two-thirds of cases, the worker approached their immediate line manager. Smaller proportions reported that another rank of manager (8 per cent) was approached, a service provider (8 per cent), or a colleague (7 per cent). Interestingly, 13 per cent of care managers who had to seek authority to spend required approval from a panel before implementing the care package. Approval from a panel was more prevalent for short or critical interval need cases (17 per cent, compared with 4 per cent for long interval need cases) which may reflect the increasing need for respite care among more dependent users.

Those care managers who reported lack of authority to spend were asked about its effects on the care planning and the resulting care package. Table 5.12

Table 5.11
Degree to which care managers had formal authority to spend or approve spending on the services for the case, by interval need

Degree of authority to spend	Critical %	Short %	Long %	Total %
Yes[1]	40.3	57.6	66.4	56.0
Up to limit	23.5	11.3	7.1	13.3
No	31.9	26.9	26.5	28.3
Other holds budget	4.2	4.2	0.0	2.4
Total n =	61	51	84	197

Missing values: 3. Source: Standard care manager interviews (n=200).
1 Presence of PIC increased the likelihood that there would be limits to the care manager's authority to spend.
No PIC: Yes: 77%; Up to a limit: 9%; No: 11%; Other person has budget: 3%; No. of cases: 37.
PIC: Yes: 51%; Up to a limit: 15%; No: 32%; Other person has budget: 2%; number of cases: 157.

Table 5.12
Degree to which care manager's lack of direct authority[1] limited effectiveness of service to user, by interval need

	Critical %	Short %	Long %	Total %
Considerably	3.2	0.0	0.0	1.5
To some extent	12.5	0.0	0.0	5.6
A little	5.7	9.1	19.5	10.3
Not at all	78.6	90.9	80.5	82.6
Total n =	21	13	12	46

Missing values: 10. Not applicable cases: 144 (care managers who indicated that they were not limited in their authority to spend). Source: Standard care manager interviews (n=200).
1 Directly to approach provider, to obtain information from SSD colleagues, to call health professionals to assessment and/or care planning meetings.

illustrates the extent to which care managers felt their lack of authority had an impact on the services provided. In the vast majority of cases — 83 per cent — these care managers reported that their lack of authority had no effect on the care package. Only in the case of critical interval need users was lack of spending power seen to limit effectiveness to any extent (16 per cent). This may be due to the cost of packages for more dependent users, and the wider range of services requiring approval before the care plan is implemented.

Care managers were also asked if their lack of budgetary authority had an impact on their resourcefulness. The 1991 guidance encouraged practitioners to 'give full rein to their creativity in devising new ways of meeting needs ... those that have some or all of the budget delegated to them, will have greater scope to create alternatives' (SSI/SWSG, 1991, p.63). Despite the apparent link between authority to spend and creativity in care planning, the vast majority of care managers who had restricted authority to spend said that this had not limited their resourcefulness at all (82 per cent). Resourcefulness is, however, not merely linked to budget holding but also to other factors such as overall spending limits, the availability of services and time, and contracting arrangements. The fact that the majority of services remain bulk-contracted may affect care managers' perceptions of the link between resourcefulness and authority to spend. The concept of directly controlling resources is in itself discordant with traditional conceptions of social work practice, which may also influence current views. This said, care managers responsible for more complex, critical interval need cases were more willing than others to state that their lack of authority to spend had limited resourcefulness. One in four of these workers reported that the need to seek approval on spending had limited their resourcefulness considerably or to some extent.

Time

Care management is made up of a series of stages, each of which account for a proportion of the worker's time. The initial stages of the process — case finding and screening, assessment and care planning — are commonly the most intensive activities, accounting for a larger proportion of care management hours than the monitoring and review which follow. However, the amount of time that care managers are able to spend at each stage of the process, on each case, is constrained by a variety of factors. The nature or extent of user needs, as well as overall caseload, are perhaps the most significant. Other factors also affect how the care manager's time is spent, such as administrative issues, travel time and coordinating contributions from other professionals and agencies.

Lewis and Glennerster (1996) have argued that, since the implementation of the reforms, two important changes have taken place in the way that social workers spend their time. First, an increasing proportion of time is spent taken up with clients who are heavily dependent, and second, there seems to be less time available for counselling and support. They found that, in their study of five local authorities between 1992 and 1994, just one-fifth of care manager's time was spent on direct work with clients, despite this activity being an important component of job satisfaction.

Challis (1994b) also warned that one consequence of the reforms (particularly the implementation of the purchaser/provider split) could be that direct contact between care managers and clients would diminish. Counselling and other related activities are a 'providing' task, constituting part of the care plan. Yet they are not services like any other, as they are supplied by the care manager, who is also the enabler or purchaser of services on behalf of the SSD. The danger is that the purchasing functions of care management, which are largely bureaucratic, will leave little or no time for face-to-face meetings with clients and the provision of direct assistance. ECCEP care managers were asked to describe how their time was spent on each case, both as services were arranged and once they were in place. They were also asked to comment on the nature of their direct input, which will be described in the next section.

The setting-up period in care management is the length of time between the (re-)referral of the user to social services, and all services being put in place. This is normally the most intensive period of involvement for care managers, accounting for a high proportion of their time. Table 5.13 describes the duration of the setting-up period, in weeks.

On average, the duration of the setting-up period was 4.31 weeks per case. The set-up period was, on average, longer for cases where a carer was involved. As Richardson and Higgins (1991) have indicated, time spent keeping carers informed and involved can be significant, particularly as services are being arranged. Setting-up time in weeks also differed according to interval need. Perhaps contrary to initial assumptions, it was actually the less dependent, long interval need cases that took longer to set up than short or critical interval cases. One explanation for this is that the need for assistance among critical and short interval need users is more urgent that for those in the long interval need category. This may result in the care package being put in place in a shorter period of time for more dependent cases. It is important to note, however, that this effect is moderated by the presence or absence of a principal informal carer. Long interval need cases with a carer took on average 6.22 weeks to set up, compared with 1.83 weeks for long interval need cases without a carer. Undoubtedly, support was required more rapidly for users without a carer, despite their relatively low level of dependence. This would be particularly the case for long interval need users discharged from hospital, who would require some support at home shortly after returning to the community.

When setting-up time in weeks among critical interval need cases is considered, the presence or absence of a carer is also important, but has the opposite effect on duration to that seen for long interval need cases. The mean set-up time for critical cases with a carer was 3.35 weeks, but this rose to 8.37 weeks for those without a carer. As all these users have significant need for support, often at unpredictable times, the setting-up period of over eight weeks for those without a carer must be attributed to the complexity of the package required, particularly when coordination with providers from the health and independent sectors is required. For critical interval need users with a carer, the average set-up time of just over three weeks is lower than the mean for all cases, and suggests that there was a need to put services into place quickly. Because of the demanding nature of caring for someone with critical interval needs, this shorter set-up time may also have been required to avoid the breakdown of informal support.

Table 5.14 shows the number of hours, rather than weeks, that care managers took to set up a case. On average, putting services in place took 9.3 hours. There is a clear gradient across interval need categories with respect to hours spent during the setting-up period, rising from 7.8 hours for long interval need cases to 12.54 for critical interval need cases. Again, this reflects the complexity of care packages for more dependent older people.

Cases were also broken down by whether they were a new referral, or a current case. It would be expected that care managers would take longer to set up services for a new referral, as current cases would already be receiving some services on which to build. Instead, the opposite is found. On average, new referral cases took 7.6 hours to set up, compared with 11.7 for current

Table 5.13

Length in weeks of setting-up period, by interval need and social support among community-based sample

| Setting-up period in weeks by presence of PIC | Interval need | | | | | | | | | |
| | Critical | | Short | | Long | | Total | |
	Mean	n =	Mean	n =	Mean	n =	Mean	n =
Without PIC	8.47	4	3.57	9	1.83	23	3.08	37
With PIC	3.35	47	4.04	34	6.22	52	4.65	133
Total	3.80	51	3.94	43	4.87	75	4.31	169

Missing values: 11. Not applicable observations: 20 (services not yet in place). Source: standard schedules (n=200).

Table 5.14

Total hours of care management during setting-up period, by interval need and whether referral or current case among community-based sample

Setting-up period in hours by whether new referral	Critical		Short		Long		Total	
	Mean	n =	Mean	n =	Mean	n =	Mean	n =
Current case	13.56	29	9.39	17	11.09	28	11.67	75
Referral	11.17	22	7.57	28	6.13	51	7.63	101
Total	12.54	52	8.27	45	7.87	79	9.34	176

Missing values: 4. Not applicable observations: 20 (services not yet in place). Sample: standard care manager interviews (n=200).

cases. One possible explanation is the complexity of current cases. Current cases were included in the study sample only if significant reassessment and changes in services were required. This suggests that the circumstances of these individuals had changed sufficiently to require a new care plan, perhaps as a result of an admission to hospital, or a sudden deterioration in health. These effects are not, however, reflected in differences between interval need categories. Thus, other changes must be considered, such as an alteration in the type or availability of informal support, changes in mental health or housing. One final explanation is that current case review may have been taken on by lower grade staff, such as a reviewing officer, who may require time to familiarise him/herself with the case before making changes, or may have a smaller caseload which allows a longer period of time to be spent arranging services.

Hours spent on setting up services were calculated by asking care managers how long they spent on six different types of activity. Table 5.15 lists these activities and summarises average care manager responses, broken down by interval need.

Care managers report that they spend approximately one-third of their time during the setting-up period in face-to-face discussions with users and carers, and an additional one-third of their time in face-to-face or other contacts with staff, colleagues and other agencies. Qualified social workers spent a higher proportion of their time on these activities than did other types of care managers. For all cases just 1.8 hours on average, approximately one-fifth of setting-up time, is spent on administrative activities. This suggests that care managers are still spending the majority of their time either with the client or negotiating with colleagues or providers on behalf of the client, rather than on administrative duties.

It is interesting to note, however, that 1.66 hours of care manager's time during this set-up period was spent travelling. There are important variations in travelling time between local authorities. Travelling time would be expected to account for a larger number of hours per week in the shire counties (where over one-third of cases were situated) than in metropolitan areas.

The number of hours spent on all activities rises with interval need, reflecting more intensive care management input for higher dependency cases. The difference between interval need cases is slightly smaller for paperwork and administration, however, suggesting that the extra hours required for more complex cases are largely being spent in contact with the user, carer, providers and other practitioners.

The continuing care period begins once all services are in place and the care plan has been fully implemented. Both monitoring and review take place during the continuing care period, which ends only when the user stops receiving services. Care manager input commonly diminishes during this period, and for some care managers (such as hospital-based practitioners involved in setting up services on discharge) it ceases shortly after the

Table 5.15
Hours spent by care manager during setting-up period on different types of activity for cases with services in place, by interval need for community-based sample

Type of management activity	Critical Mean	Short Mean	Long Mean	Total Mean
Face-to-face discussions with user and carer	3.92	2.81	2.38	2.95
Face-to-face discussions involving staff, colleagues and other agencies	1.49	1.39	0.94	1.22
Other contracts with users, carer, staff, colleagues and other agencies	2.31	0.86	1.46	1.55
Paperwork and administration	2.09	1.69	1.67	1.80
Travelling	2.51	1.43	1.24	1.66
Other	0.44	0.11	0.08	0.20
Total n =	52	45	77	173

Missing values: 7. Not applicable observations: 20 (all services not yet in place).
Source: Standard care manager interviews (n=200).

setting-up period, and transfers to other colleagues who then assume responsibility for the case.

Table 5.16 illustrates the average number of weekly hours care managers spent on each case during the continuing care period. As expected, care management input decreases significantly once services are in place. On average, care managers spent half an hour per week per case during the continuing care period. It is fair to assume that for many cases care managers would be in contact with the user/carer or providers on less than a weekly basis, instead maintaining contact once or twice a month and, in some cases, less frequently than monthly. Not surprisingly, however, continuing care hours go up with interval need, reflecting the need among more dependent users for monitoring and, in some cases, direct input from the care manager.

Direct input

Care management activity is not limited to assessment, care planning and review functions. Care managers themselves can and do contribute directly to the care package, by providing a variety of types of assistance to users and carers.

Table 5.17 illustrates the types of tasks which care managers perform for users and carers as part of the care plan. Not surprisingly, the most common function of the care manager following the set-up period is monitoring the user's situation. Over two-thirds of care managers reported that they are engaged in monitoring, either through face-to-face or telephone contact with the user and/or carer. Monitoring was a particularly prevalent activity among the care managers of critical interval need users. This is probably due to the more complex needs of these users, as well as the higher proportion of trained social workers responsible for these cases, whose involvement is likely to extend over a longer period than other types of care manager.

Only one in three care managers attributed time specifically to counselling. This proportion rises with interval need. Counselling was more prevalent among cases in which a principal informal carer was involved: 35 per cent of care managers responsible for cases with a carer provided counselling, compared with 24 per cent of care managers responsible for cases with no carer. Support for carers is an important component of many care packages, and the provision of counselling can provide one form of support, particularly if the carer has ongoing contact with one care manager, whom they can contact when necessary.

Care managers who provided counselling were asked, in a multiple response question, what form this therapeutic help had taken. Over half of these workers said that counselling had been offered as a form of general emotional support. A similar proportion of those who provided counselling — 50 per cent — said that it had been provided to help the user accept his or her need for assistance from formal services. A slightly smaller proportion of these care managers — 46 per cent — reported that counselling had aimed to help the user make decisions, and 47 per cent said it had aimed to help the user adapt to the change in their functional abilities. Other frequently mentioned purposes of counselling were helping the user adapt to change (39 per cent), helping the user to cope with fears of living at home (34 per cent), providing support following a bereavement (18 per cent), and helping deal with relationship problems (16 per cent). Overall, all types of counselling were more likely to be provided by a social worker than any other type of care manager. While just under half of trained social workers reported that they had provided some form of counselling to users (47 per cent), only one in four (26 per cent) care managers with other occupational backgrounds said they had provided counselling. This reflects differences in training between social workers and other types of care manager.

As Table 5.17 illustrates, tasks other than monitoring and counselling were provided by a much smaller proportion of care managers. Managing finances was something that 9 per cent of workers did, although this rose to 12 per cent among the care managers of critical interval need users. Housework was something that 6 per cent of workers reported they had done. Cleaning was provided by a higher proportion of the care managers of long interval need

Table 5.16
Total weekly hours spent by worker during continuing care period, by interval need and social support among community-based sample

Social support	Critical		Interval need Short		Long		Total	
	Mean	n =	Mean	n =	Mean	n =	Mean	n =
Without PIC	4.11	4	.24	8	.11	23	.65	35
With PIC	0.29	46	.24	35	.16	52	.23	134
Total n =	0.63	51	.24	43	.14	75	.31	169

Missing values: 11. Not applicable observations: 20 (all services not yet in place). Source: Standard care manager interviews (n=200).

Table 5.17

Types of direct input, by care manager by interval need among community-based user sample

Type of direct input	Critical %	Short %	Long %	Total %
Medical	2.3	0.9	-	1.1
Personal care	6.6	5.3	2.6	4.7
Housework/meals	4.7	6.1	8.7	6.5
Shopping, errands	5.3	3.5	4.8	4.6
Counselling	43.0	31.9	23.2	32.7
Company/leisure	6.9	3.5	3.2	4.6
Manage finances	12.2	5.3	8.4	8.9
Learn skills	2.8	1.8	0.6	1.7
Monitor situation	76.4	65.9	60.9	67.8
None	12.9	23.6	23.0	19.6
Total n =	146	111	151	409

Missing values: 16. Source: All care manager interviews.

users than others (9 per cent). There are several possible explanations for this. Less dependent users without personal care needs may no longer be eligible for cleaning services in some local authorities, a situation that may result in individual care managers providing cleaning help on a small number of occasions, perhaps during a home visit. Alternatively, the care managers of these long interval need users may themselves be home care staff, primarily home care managers, who may provide some assistance during an assessment or subsequent visit to the user.

Less than 5 per cent of care managers overall reported that they had assisted users with any medical or personal care tasks. Similarly low proportions have provided help with shopping, company/leisure, or helping the user to learn new skills. These are all activities which care managers may have neither the training nor time to engage in, although the proportion who have shopped or done housework for the user does rise slightly when there is no carer present. Again, these may be services which some users are not eligible to receive, yet find difficult to do alone, particularly when little or no informal support is available.

Monitoring and review

In the Domiciliary Care Project, monitoring and review were identified as activities which were carried out mostly by default, with few formal mechanisms. The majority of local authorities at that time failed to meet their own standards for reassessment in the home help service, in which six-monthly reviews were supposed to take place. Reassessment was most commonly undertaken when users or carers themselves indicated a change in their needs, rather than as part of a formal review process (Davies et al., 1990).

Since the introduction of the reforms, there has been a considerable effort within SSDs to formalise both monitoring and review, with the expectation that the practitioner responsible for assessment and care planning will, where possible, also assume responsibility for monitoring and review. Yet, as Challis (1994a) has indicated, in authorities where care managers have heavy caseloads or there is a staff shortage, the separation of care management tasks is occurring. As assessment is perceived as the most critical activity in care management, the most qualified or highly trained staff may be deployed in this activity, their involvement ending before the review stage. Other staff, such as review officers, may take responsibility for this later stage in the care management process. There are many arguments in favour of the separation of tasks, particularly with reference to effective targeting of resources (Davies, 1994b). Several of these arguments were elucidated in the Domiciliary Care Project as well as earlier PSSRU studies (Davies et al., 1990). The ongoing dilemma for authorities today is whether to risk the loss of continuity which can arise as a result of this separation.

During the second period of data collection for ECCEP (Time II), care managers were asked a variety of questions about the review process. It was assumed that reviews could have taken place for all cases by the time of the second interview, which was at least six months after the user's initial contact with social services.

Table 5.18 illustrates the proportion of cases which had been reviewed by the second care manager interview. In 60 per cent of cases, a review had taken place. As the absence of reviews or infrequent reviews can result in inefficient use of resources — with users receiving services they no longer require, and changing needs going unnoticed — the fact that the majority of cases at Time I had been reviewed by Time II suggests an improvement in care management practice when compared with findings from the Domiciliary Care Project.

Overall, reviews were more likely to have taken place for critical interval need users, particularly if they had an informal carer. This suggests that reviews are occurring most frequently for users with complex, and often less predictable needs. Among short interval need users, in 85 per cent of cases those without a carer were more likely to have had their case reviewed. Care managers may be responding to the risk of deterioration in the situation of

Table 5.18
Whether the user's situation was formally reviewed, by interval need and social support among community-based sample

Social support	Critical		Short		Long		Total	
Interval need								
	%	n =	%	n =	%	n =	%	n =
Without PIC	63	13	85	13	47	24	61	50
With PIC	72	83	50	71	57	80	60	233
Total n	71	96	55	84	55	103	60	283

Missing values: 55. Sample: All Time II care manager interviews except when user had died or moved away within four weeks of the date of the Time I interview.

these users, which may be particularly prevalent when informal support is not available.

Care managers who reported that a review had taken place were asked who had been involved. Table 5.19 lists their responses. It is encouraging to note that, in 80 per cent of cases, care managers report that the user was involved. This is consistent with the relatively recent emphasis on involving both users and carers in all aspects of care planning. Carers, family and friends were part of the review in 54 per cent of cases overall, with the proportion, not surprisingly, being slightly higher among cases where there was a principal carer (58 per cent).

Care manager interviewees were present at the review in two-thirds of cases. The fact that one-third were not involved does suggest that there has

Table 5.19
Persons actively involved in most recent review, by social support among community-based sample

Persons involved	Without PIC %	With PIC %	Total %	n =
User	88.6	77.7	79.6	132
Carer, family, friends	33.5	56.5	54.1	90
Interviewee	51.7	69.7	66.5	111
Care manager, social worker (excluding interviewee)	34.9	33.9	34.0	57
Line managers	3.4	6.7	6.1	10
Home care staff	45.0	23.7	27.5	46
Day centre, residential centre staff	4.7	16.8	14.7	24
Care home staff	13.4	17.6	16.9	28
Review, placement officers	0.0	2.4	2.0	3
GPs	6.7	4.9	5.2	9
Community nurses	6.7	5.7	5.9	10
Hospital consultants	3.4	1.4	1.8	3
Ward nurses	6.7	4.6	4.9	8
Occupational therapists	3.4	4.3	4.1	7
Physiotherapists	0.0	2.4	2.0	3
Other	13.4	3.1	4.9	8
Total n =	29	137		166

Missing values: 7. Sample: All Time II care manager interviews where the user's situation had been formally reviewed except when the user had died or moved away within four weeks of the date of the Time I interview.

been a separation of the care management tasks in some areas. Social work staff other than the care manager were present in just over one-third of cases, which is consistent with the transfer of responsibility of review from the original care manager to other colleagues within the SSD.

In the Domiciliary Care Project, it was observed that there was a reliance on home help staff during the monitoring and review stages of care management. Findings from ECCEP, that home care staff were involved in just 28 per cent of cases, suggests that this practice is in decline. Home care staff are, however, more frequently involved in the review of cases where a principal informal carer is not involved (45 per cent). This may reflect their knowledge of the user's home circumstances, information which is valuable in the review process.

Health care professionals were involved in only a small proportion of reviews, although frequencies do rise with interval need. GPs and community nurses were the most common participants, in 5 per cent of cases. As shown in Table 5.8, the incidence of health professional participation in the review process is lower than that at the assessment stage.

Care managers who reported that a review had taken place were also asked, in a multiple response question, what form it had taken. In 78 per cent of cases, a formal meeting was held with the user and carer. In 39 per cent of cases, a formal meeting was held with other professionals. Reviews over the phone with the user and carer took place in 18 per cent of instances, and 12 per cent of cases with other professionals. Telephone reviews were most frequent in the case of short interval need users with a carer (22 per cent). Reviewing based on written reports took place in very few cases, less than 10 per cent overall.

Table 5.20 lists the outcomes for cases that had been reviewed by Time II. In 41 per cent of cases, the review resulted in no change to the user's current care package. In over half of the cases reviewed, however, some change was made.

In 15 per cent of cases the most common alteration was in increase in services. A reduction in assistance was recommended for 10 per cent of cases. Admission to a residential or nursing home was the actual or predicted outcome of review in just 12 per cent of cases. The proportions facing a future admission to institutional care were slightly higher among users without a carer, particularly for residential care. Although the numbers are small, the difference does highlight the importance of informal support in helping the user remain at home, despite changes in health or functional ability.

It is interesting to note that only 2.9 per cent of cases were closed to care management at Time II. While cases which were closed completely to the SSD (3 per cent) suggest that the user either no longer required services, died, moved away or entered hospital, cases which were closed to care management are those which have become the responsibility of other workers within the SSD. The fact that so few cases are being reallocated to other staff (such as review officers) suggests that many care managers — at least in 1995/96 when the interviews took place — were retaining responsibility for a growing

Table 5.20

Conclusion of the most recent review, by interval need and social support among community-based sample

Conclusion	Without PIC %	Without PIC n =	With PIC %	With PIC n =	Total %	Total n =
Keep present package	31.6	9	43.9	61	41.2	70
Increase formal help at home	6.7	2	16.7	23	14.8	25
Reduce formal help at home	23.5	7	7.0	10	9.7	17
Care home sooner/later	17.2	5	10.1	15	11.8	20
Keep present placement	6.7	2	6.3	9	6.3	11
Change of placement	0.0	0	0.7	1	0.6	1
No clear conclusion	0.0	0	1.0	1	0.8	1
Close case to care management	6.7	2	2.1	3	2.9	5
Close case to SSD	3.4	1	3.5	5	3.4	6
Offer respite care	0.0	0	0.7	1	0.6	1
Other	4.7	1	7.7	12	7.9	13
Total n =		29		141		170

Missing values: 3. Sample: All Time II care manager interviews where the user's situation had been formally reviewed except when the user had died or moved away within four weeks of the date of the Time I interview.

number of cases long after the more intensive stages of care management (assessment, care planning and initial monitoring) had been completed. While this may be advantageous in terms of the user having contact with the same worker over time, it may contribute to the build-up of staff caseloads, resulting in fewer care management hours being available for each case.

All care managers were asked if a formal review was planned for some time in the future. Both workers who had stated that there already had been one review and workers who said there had been no review to date were asked this question. Two-thirds — 69 per cent — indicated that a future review was planned, in most cases within three to six months. There was a clear gradient across interval need categories, with just over half of those responsible for long interval need cases saying that there would be a review (54 per cent), rising to 85 per cent among care managers responsible for critical interval need cases. Cases without a carer (75 per cent) were slightly more likely to have a formal review planned for the future than cases in which a carer was not involved (68 per cent). Given that all cases should receive regular reviews, the fact that almost one-third of care managers stated that there was no future review planned suggests that reviewing is still a problematic area for local authorities.

The cost of care management

Care management is a process with associated costs, which must be included when calculating the overall cost of a care package. The primary source of care management cost is the time spent by the worker allocated to the case, and thus costs vary depending on the type or worker (qualified social worker or home care organiser, for instance) and the nature and intensity of activity required at different stages of the process. The level of care management costs depends strongly on whether a care package was still being set up, or whether a continuing care period had been reached when all services were in place. These two types of care management cost are treated separately here, an approach adopted previously in both the evaluation of an intensively care-managed scheme for the frail elderly (Davies and Chesterman, 1995, 1999) and a study of ECCEP resource deployment (Davies et al., 1995).

Care management set-up cost

In the history of a case, care managers normally spent most time each week during the setting-up period: namely the interval between the referral/review date and the date when all services were in place. Various studies of social work time use (for example, Carver and Edwards, 1972; City of Manchester, 1981) have indicated that workers tend to substantially underestimate the time they spend on their cases. In order to minimise such errors, care managers were asked how much time they had spent on various types of client-related activity. Moreover, the unit cost for the type of care manager involved social worker or non-social worker) included an element to allow for the additional cost of time spent on non-client-related activities. Information on the setting-up period was obtained for only a subsample of 201 cases and, of these, only 173 had all services in place, ensuring that the setting-up period was complete, hence the relatively low sample sizes in the tabulations.

Critical to the discussion of costs during the setting-up period is the length of the setting-up period. Table 5.21 shows how this length varies with interval need and social support. The mean setting-up period was 3.69 weeks for cases without a principal informal carer and 5.30 weeks for users with one. However, each of these two groups had setting-up periods which depended quite differently on interval need. While the setting-up period of users with a carer decreased with increasing interval need from 7.49 at long interval need to 3.67 at critical interval need, that for users without a carer increased from 2.10 at long interval need to 9.92 at critical interval need. As with tabulations relating to the allocation of care management time (see Tables 5.15 and 5.16), the shorter setting-up period for more dependent cases can be attributed to the urgency with which care managers were required to put services in place to support frail users.

The decreasing setting-up period with increasing interval need for users with a carer is likely to reflect the increasing urgency of having all services in place, as otherwise there would be a danger of the informal care network breaking down. The increasing setting-up period with interval need for users without a carer probably results from the larger proportion of hospital discharge cases at critical interval need, for whom the package was set up during a prolonged stay in hospital, while at long and short interval need there was a need to set up a package as soon as possible. Due to the absence of substantial informal help, the formal package had to be more comprehensive, so took longer to set up at short than long interval need.

There is a tendency for cases which have to be set up more quickly to have a higher weekly setting-up cost to the care manager, since the setting-up activities have to be squeezed into a shorter time interval. There are, therefore, some advantages in studying the total rather than the average weekly setting-up cost, since the total represents the care manager's time needed before all services are in place. When presenting costs, care managers have been categorised according to their job titles into social workers and non-social workers. Sixty per cent of cases in our sample had care managers in the social work category.

Table 5.22 shows how total and average weekly care management costs (in 1995 prices) during the setting-up period vary with interval need and social support. Total cost is also considered separately for cases with social workers and those with non-social workers. Examining the total columns, the set-up cost in cases where the care manager was a social worker was much more than for the non-social workers. The cost difference reflects their different hourly rates of pay of £27 and £16 respectively, and also the period of time they spent arranging the case. Overall, social workers spent eleven hours in setting up a case, while non-social workers spent eight hours.

Total setting-up cost showed little variation with interval need for cases with a carer, ranging from £203 to £241. However, those without a carer showed a vast jump from around £164 at long and short interval need to £726 at critical interval need. This high cost was the mean for just three cases of which two had protracted setting-up periods each lasting some three months, associated with a discharge from hospital, when care packages had to be set up virtually from scratch. Because this period was so long, the average weekly setting-up cost of £90 per week was not exceptional in comparison with lower interval need cases. Indeed, no clear pattern emerged regarding variation of average weekly cost with interval need and social support except that long interval need cases were less expensive.

Table 5.21
Length of setting-up period,[1] by interval need and social support

	Critical		Interval need Short		Long		Total		Missing
	No PIC[2]	PIC	No PIC	PIC	No PIC	PIC	No PIC	PIC	n =
Mean setting-up period (in weeks)[3]	9.92	3.67	4.76	4.59	2.10	7.49	3.69	5.30	23

Valid cases: 150. Source: Standard care manager interviews.

1 Setting-up period was defined as that between referral or review and when all services were in place. Cases for which services were not in place by the time of the first care manager interview were excluded from the sample.

2 PIC stands for principal informal carer.

3 The setting-up period is measured for the subsample with a standard care manager interview for which all services were in place by the time of the interview (n=173).

Total and average weekly setting-up costs by interval need and cognitive impairment of the user are shown in Table 5.23. Examining the total columns, cases who were cognitively impaired or behaviourally disturbed consumed more social work and non-social work time, the total cost of £272 comparing with only £218 for cases without this problem.

This contrast was particularly striking for social workers with long interval need users, for which the cost for cognitively impaired or behaviourally disturbed cases (£402) was much greater than for remaining cases (only £262). The former, due to their relatively good mobility, were more likely to wander or to be a danger to themselves or others, so may have been more problematic to care managers; for example, it might have been necessary to discuss possible risks with neighbours and relatives.

Continuing cost of care management

Care management time use during this period of continuing care was measured by asking the worker how much time they had spent on the case between the date that all services were in place and the evaluation interview date. Unfortunately, this question did not require the care manager to consider time spent on different types of activity, so is more likely to result in an underestimate. After the initial outlay of care manager time in setting up the package of care, involvement generally became much less, taking on a maintenance and monitoring role. This drop in the measured level of activity was far too great to have been caused simply by an underestimate in the time spent by care managers once all services were in place. As in the case of setting-up costs, data were obtained for only a subsample of 173 cases.

Table 5.24 shows how the weekly cost of care manager time varied with interval need and social support for social workers and non-social workers. Comparing the total columns with those of Table 5.22 for average weekly cost during the setting-up period, the sharp drop in weekly costs between setting up and continuing care is striking, with that for users without a principal informal carer falling from £106 to £6 and that for users with a carer from £109 to £7. This meant that in order to maintain cases once they had been set up, social workers were spending twenty minutes per week on each case and non-social workers fifteen minutes.

Weekly care management cost (in the total row) did however rise steadily with interval need whether or not there was a principal informal carer. It increased from £5.00 at long interval need to £9.37 at critical interval need for users with a carer, and more sharply from £4.18 to £11.89 for those without one. When the separate rows for social workers and non-social workers are compared, the weekly cost of non-social worker time for short and critical interval need users with a carer was much smaller than that for social workers. For example, social worker time spent on critical interval need users with a

Table 5.22
Cost of care management during setting-up period,[1] by interval need and social support

	Critical		Short		Long		Total		Missing
	No PIC[2] £	PIC £	No PIC £	PIC £	No PIC £	PIC £	No PIC £	PIC £	n =
Social worker or equiv.	725.87	251.06	223.47	300.16	273.98	272.88	374.58	269.73	29
Non-social worker	-	223.68	106.67	93.73	80.74	153.73	86.72	161.58	23
Total	725.87	241.11	165.07	203.40	163.01	228.36	235.09	227.14	52
Average weekly cost	89.52	153.08	138.49	83.64	96.84	80.14	105.90	109.19	33

Applicable cases: 173. Source: Care manager interview.
1 Setting-up period was defined as that between referral or review and when all services were in place by the time of the first care manager interview were excluded from the sample. The setting-up period is measured for the subsample with a standard care manager interview for which all services were in place by the time of the interview (n=173).
2 PIC stands for principal informal carer.

Table 5.23

Cost of care management during setting-up period,[1] by interval need and presence of cognitive impairment or behavioural disorder

| | Interval need | | | | | | | | Missing |
| | Critical | | Short | | Long | | Total | | |
	CI/BD[2] £	Not CI/BD £	CI/BD £	Not CI/BD £	CI/BD £	Not CI/BD £	CI/BD £	Not CI/BD £	n =
Social worker or equiv.	365.37	258.64	201.33	326.08	402.37	262.19	339.14	274.81	29
Non-social worker	226.93	219.81	66.13	101.83	131.20	124.34	173.54	134.82	23
Total	304.26	248.24	156.26	210.09	296.67	202.40	272.13	217.68	52
Average weekly cost	169.28	132.37	104.11	88.64	114.44	86.80	140.20	99.59	32

Applicable cases: 173. Source: Care manager interview. The setting-up period is measured for the subsample with a standard care manager interview for which all services were in place by the time of the interview (n=173).

1 Setting-up period was defined as that between referral or review and when all services are in place. Cases for which services were not in place by the time of the first care manager interview were excluded from the sample.

2 CI/BD stands for cognitively impaired or behaviourally disturbed.

carer cost £11.58 per week, while that for non-social workers cost only £4.18 per week. This suggests that the caseloads of non-social workers may be too great for them to be able to allocate sufficient time to these higher need cases. The corresponding cost differences during the setting-up period were less marked.

Table 5.25 shows weekly care management costs once services are in place when broken down by interval need and cognitive impairment or behavioural disorder. The totals columns show that cognitively impaired or behaviourally disturbed users cost rather more per week in care management time (£8.41) than those without these mental health problems (£6.39). For cases without cognitive impairment or behavioural disorder, the weekly care management cost increased from £4.09 at long interval need to £8.69 at critical interval need. However, when considering those with cognitive impairment or behavioural disorder, although those of short interval need cost substantially less (£2.05) than those at critical interval need (£10.46), those of long interval need were substantial (£8.73). This may reflect the greater difficulty of maintaining cases at home when the user is both cognitively impaired and of low disability so likely to be relatively mobile. These users could be prone to wandering or being a danger to themselves or others. The low care management cost of the short interval group suggests that these cognitively impaired or behaviourally disturbed users were sufficiently physically disabled to minimise the risk of dangerous behaviour while being insufficient to cause severe physical problems.

In summary, findings relating to care management costs suggest that they vary significantly between the set-up and continuing care phase, and are influenced by both the type of worker involved in the process, and the need-related circumstances of users. Overall, users without a carer had their care package set up more quickly, resulting in a higher initial care management cost. Care managers spend more time setting up care packages for users with a cognitive impairment or behavioural disorder. Overall set-up time and cost also rose with interval need. Costs during the continuing care phase or care management dropped fifteen-fold in comparison with those during the set-up period, reflecting the less intensive tasks of monitoring and review.

Perceptions of care management

Providers, practitioners and recipients of services can have very different views regarding the objectives of the care package or what constitutes a positive outcome. Similarly, those supervising, performing and receiving care management have different perceptions of the process and its benefits. In order to explore differences in perception, users, carers and care managers were all asked a series of questions regarding their view of the care

Table 5.24

Average weekly cost of care management once all services are in place, by interval need and social support

Weekly costs of care management[1] when all services in place	Critical		Short		Long		Total	
	No PIC[2,3] £	PIC £	No PIC £	PIC £	No PIC £	PIC £	No PIC £	PIC £
Social worker or equivalent	10.28	11.58	6.18	10.33	8.11	4.94	8.06	9.05
Non-social worker	15.77	4.18	5.86	2.61	1.03	5.12	3.25	3.94
Total	11.89	9.37	6.05	6.60	4.18	5.00	5.74	7.18

Number of cases: Valid: 129. Missing: 43. Sample: Standard care manager interviews, selecting only those users with all services in place (n=173).

1 Unit costs of care management were set at: social worker £27 per hour; non-social worker: £16 per hour.

2 PIC stands for principal informal carer.

3 One user of critical interval need with no carer received an exceptionally high level of care management input once services were in place, this amounting to an average of fifteen hours per week of social work time over a four-week period costing £405 per week, and this would have raised the corresponding mean costs considerably. This outlier was therefore omitted from the table.

Table 5.25

Average weekly cost of care management once all services are in place, by interval need and presence of cognitive impairment or behavioural disorder

Weekly costs of care management[1] when all services in place	Interval need							
	Critical		Short		Long		Total	
	CI/BD[2]	Not CI/BD	CI/BD	Not CI/BD[3]	CI/BD	Not CI/BD	CI/BD	Not CI/BD
	£	£	£	£	£	£	£	£
Social worker or equivalent	13.84	9.74	2.57	13.17	10.65	4.70	10.52	8.29
Non-social worker	5.18	4.69	0.48	3.38	4.96	3.23	4.49	3.49
Total	10.46	8.69	2.05	7.90	8.73	4.09	8.41	6.39

Number of cases: Valid: 131. Sample: Standard care manager interviews, selecting only those users with all services in place (n=173). Missing: 41.

1 Unit costs of care management were set at: social worker £27 per hour; non-social worker £16 per hour.

2 CI/BD stands for cognitively impaired or behaviourally disturbed.

3 One user of critical interval need without cognitive impairment or behavioural disorder received an exceptionally high level of care management input once services were in place, amounting to an average of fifteen hours per week of social work time over a four- week period costing £405 per week, and this would have raised the corresponding mean costs considerably. This outlier was therefore omitted from the table.

management process. Themes included: the aims and goals of care management, or the extent to which the care package could improve outcomes for users and carers; the balance between providing services to the user and support to carers; and the relationship between user, carer and care manager during the assessment and care planning process. This discussion of perceptions begins with a summary of findings from ECCEP's policy and practice discussions (PPDs), which asked managers and practitioners in each local authority about the goals of care management and service provision for older people.

Policy aims of care management

As care management is a key component of the community care reforms, it is not surprising that the goals and aims of the process embody those expressed in the reforms themselves: tailoring services to needs, promoting choice, improving joint working between agencies, and assisting people to remain in their own homes, to name just a few. In 1995, the ECCEP team undertook an exploration of some of the goals and objectives of both the reforms and the care management process in each of the ten local authorities taking part in the study. In order to do this, policy and practice discussions were held in each authority with senior and middle managers and fieldworkers: 134 respondents in total. One component of the discussions asked informants to give priority to a set of policy outcomes or goals. Findings relating to this aspect of the PPDs are worth summarising here, as they relate to care management objectives.[1]

Senior and middle managers and practitioners were presented with a series of statements relating to service outcomes for older people. They were asked to rank the outcomes in the order of priority to the local authority. Seven outcomes were presented, and informants ranked them in order of priority for the period 1992-1994, and then again for the period 1995-1997. A list of the seven statements is provided in Appendix 5.1.

For the period 1992-1994, the 'early implementation years', three outcomes were clearly rated as the highest priority by all three groups of professionals, across local authorities. Outcome C: ' a real chance for users to stay at home rather than enter a care home' was clearly ranked highest, with a rating of 1.88 (with 1 being the highest ranking). Outcome B: 'empowerment, choice and control over their own lives for users' was second, with an overall ranking of 2.53. Third, Outcome E: 'support for family carers to enable them to have respite' received a rating of 3.45. Two other outcomes — raising charges in order to generate income for subsidised services, and emphasising welfare gains for users irrespective of costs to the local authority — received ratings below 6, suggesting that they were not a priority for any grade of worker.

For the period 1995-1997, the same three outcomes which had received the highest rating for 1992-1994 were again chosen as most important, suggesting that overall policy priorities did not change dramatically through the reform period. Indeed, local authorities were more uniform in their rankings for this later period. The three outcomes did change in order of importance, however. In the 1995-1997 period, Outcome B became the most important (with a ranking of 2.85 overall), then Outcome C (2.96) followed by Outcome E (3.39). Outcome B related to empowerment, choice and control for users. It is interesting that this goal was chosen as most significant by both managers and fieldworkers for 1995-1997, and suggests that local authorities are taking the issue of user involvement in decision-making very seriously, at least at the policy level.

Workers' perceptions of care management

Individual care managers were also asked to reflect upon the aims and objectives of care management, and what they perceived as the welfare gains which could be realised for users.

Table 5.26 compares responses from workers for whom there was both a Time I and a Time II interview. The table illustrates the extent to which care managers felt that the care package would improve the welfare of the user when it was first set up, and how their views had changed over the six to nine months between interviews.

At Time I, just under two-thirds of these care managers thought that the care package would improve the welfare of the user to a considerable or to a very considerable extent. This was particularly the case for more dependent users: with 62 per cent of workers responsible for critical and 74 per cent of workers responsible for short interval need cases choosing these responses, compared to 53 per cent of those responsible for long interval need cases. At Time II, however, once services were all in place and had been for some months, the balance between care manager responses had altered slightly. Overall, care managers were more positive about the ability of the care package to improve the welfare of the user at Time II. Just over 71 per cent said the package would improve welfare to a considerable or very considerable extent. While optimism among the care managers or critical or short interval need users had remained steady, it was among care managers of long interval need cases that it had improved. As long interval need users commonly receive fewer hours of service and may not be eligible for some services, care managers may originally have been pessimistic about the ability of this level of service to realise significant welfare gains. It appears, however, that once services had been in place for several months welfare improvements were apparent for these users which caused care managers to alter their views. This may provide

Table 5.26

Extent that recently provided help at time of first care manager interview will improve welfare of user and extent that all help since assessment improved welfare at time of second care manager interview, by interval need

Extent that recently provided help will improve welfare	Critical Time I %	Critical Time II %	Short Time I %	Short Time II %	Long Time I %	Long Time II %	Total Time I %	Total Time II %
To a very considerable extent	27.8	25.0	27.9	32.8	18.3	23.9	24.5	27.0
To a considerable extent	34.7	36.1	45.9	42.6	35.2	53.5	38.2	44.1
To some extent	34.7	33.3	14.8	18.0	31.0	19.7	27.5	24.0
To a limited extent	2.8	5.6	9.8	4.9	11.3	1.4	7.8	3.9
Not at all	0.0	0.0	1.6	1.6	4.2	1.4	2.0	1.0
Total n =	72		61		71		204	

Missing cases: 0. Sample: Cases with standard or brief care manager interviews at Time I and with valid values for both Time I and Time II interviews.

evidence that even a small amount of assistance can make a real difference to the lives of users who might otherwise go without help and thus risk losing some of their independence.

The same group of care managers were asked at Time I and Time II how services would or had affected the users' independence. As Table 5.27 shows, care managers were slightly more likely to state that services were having a positive effect on the users' independence by Time II than at Time I. This suggests that several months of service receipt was benefiting users, either by facilitating a full recovery of independence (an answer chosen by 5 per cent of care managers at Time I, and 9 per cent at Time II) or preventing a further loss of independence (an answer chosen by 25 per cent at Time I, rising to 37 per cent by Time II). Indeed, whereas at Time I over 8 per cent of care managers had said that the care package would have no impact on the users' independence, this proportion had dropped to 3 per cent by Time II. The only exception to this more positive pattern at Time II was among care managers who hoped that services would 'achieve the best possible level short of full independence'. While over half of care managers hoped for this outcome at Time I, the proportion had dropped to 40 per cent by Time II. Thus, although the overall pattern is positive, the impact of services on independence was by no means perceived as uniformly beneficial.

When interval need is considered, it is apparent that the outcome of full recovery was seen as possible for a higher proportion of less dependent, long interval need users at both Time I and Time II. The role of services in helping the user emotionally adjust to the loss of independence was reported by a higher proportion of care managers of short and critical interval need users in both instances. What is most striking, however, is that more than one in ten (14 per cent) care managers of critical interval need users felt at Time I that the care package would have no impact on the users' independence. By Time II, this had dropped to 2 per cent, suggesting that services were much more effective in improving the independence of these frail users than workers had originally anticipated.

Balancing formal and informal support

Whether care managers perceive the help provided to be for the benefit of the user or the carer can significantly affect the type and frequency of service inputs in the care package. As other work from ECCEP has shown (Davies et al., 1997b, 1998) service mix differs when a carer is involved. Services which provide a break — such as day care and respite care — may be provided to users with a carer, rather than large amounts of home care and meals, which can substitute for rather than complement existing informal support.

Table 5.28 illustrates whether the care manager regarded the care package as being primarily to help the user or the carer. This question was intended to

Table 5.27
Extent that help provided since assessment affected users' independence, by interval need

Extent that help provided will improve welfare	Interval need						Total	
	Critical		Short		Long			
	Planned at Time I %	Achieved by Time II %	Planned at Time I %	Achieved by Time II %	Planned at Time I %	Achieved by Time II %	Planned at Time I %	Achieved by Time II %
Facilitates full recovery of independence	1.4	5.8	1.6	8.2	11.4	14.3	5.0	9.5
Achieves best possible level short of full independence	50.7	42.0	57.4	39.3	48.6	38.6	52.0	40.0
Prevents further loss of independence	21.7	36.2	24.6	36.1	30.0	40.0	25.5	37.5
Enables user to adjust emotionally to loss of independence	8.7	8.7	11.5	8.2	2.9	2.9	7.5	6.5
If terminally ill, it prepared user for death	1.4	2.9	0.0	1.6	0.0	0.0	0.5	1.5
No impact on independence	14.5	2.9	4.9	6.6	5.7	1.4	8.5	3.5
Other	1.4	1.4	0.0	0.0	1.4	2.9	1.0	1.5
Total n =	69		61		70		200	

Missing cases: 4. Sample: Cases with standard / brief interviews at Time I and with valid values for both Time I and Time II interviews.

apply both to users who had a principal carer and to those who did not, as a wider circle of family or friends who provide assistance were also defined in this instance as informal supporters.

In 46 per cent of cases, the care package was intended to support the user alone. In a similar proportion of cases (45 per cent), services were meant to benefit both the user and the carer. Not surprisingly, cases in which a principal informal carer was involved were more likely to receive services aimed at supporting both the user and the carer than cases without a PIC. The proportion of cases in which services are meant entirely for the carer is highest among critical interval need users with a principal carer (9 per cent). These principal carers are looking after the most dependent group of users, and are also the most likely to be older people themselves (primarily spouses) who may have health problems of their own, and thus require help from formal services.

Care managers were also asked about the interaction between formal and informal support. Care managers can have varying intentions when it comes to meshing together support from carers with services. In just 4 per cent of cases where the user had some informal support was the package intended to entirely replace that support. These cases could involve carers whose health had deteriorated so much that they could no longer continue caring, or perhaps include cases where the carer had to go into hospital or was for some reason unsuitable to assist the user. In 14 per cent of cases, however, help was meant to replace some carer inputs. Again, these cases could involve carers with health problems who find some tasks difficult (such as lifting the user) or who are at risk of giving up employment unless some of their caring responsibilities are alleviated.

In almost a third of cases, care managers stated that the service package was meant to complement support provided by carers by introducing different types of assistance. A good example would be a case where the carer is able and willing to do the shopping, provide transport and company, but is unwilling or cannot help with personal care tasks which the user now requires. An additional 15 per cent of care managers reported that services were aimed at providing help at different times from the carer (such as when the carer is employed outside the home). In 6 per cent and 9 per cent of cases respectively, formal services were provided with the intention of supporting carers, either by encouraging them to carry on and possibly increase their input, or to encourage them to continue while services mirrored their input.

Preventing admission

The care package coordinated by care managers is in many cases designed with the specific aim of allowing the older person to remain in his/her own home rather than be admitted to residential or nursing home care. However,

Table 5.28

Distribution of help between user and carer, by interval need and social support among community-based sample

Whose benefit	Critical		Interval need Short		Long		Total
	No PIC %	PIC %	No PIC %	PIC %	No PIC %	PIC %	n =
Mainly user	75.0	23.8	73.3	41.3	56.5	62.5	122
User & carer	12.5	61.9	26.7	49.2	43.5	30.6	120
Mainly carer	12.5	14.3	0.0	9.5	0.0	6.9	24
Total n =	8	84	15	63	23	72	266

Missing cases: 5. Sample: Standard and brief care manager interviews, excluding the 35 cases without informal support (n=271).

care managers also retained the responsibility for arranging suitable placements for older people who did require the type of support offered in residential or nursing homes. Thus, enabling people to remain at home may not be the eventual aim of every care package. As users' circumstances differ, so do care managers' perceptions of what constitutes a desirable outcome in each case.

ECCEP care managers were asked about their objectives for each case, and whether they believed that the help they were providing in the community would be sufficient to allow the user to remain at home. Table 5.29 shows the distribution of responses.

Two-thirds of care managers reported that they were confident that the care package would enable the user to live at home for the foreseeable future, without too many major problems. There was a clear gradient across interval need categories, with half (51 per cent) of care managers of critical interval need users being this confident, compared with eight out of ten care managers of long interval need users.

An additional 25 per cent of care managers were still optimistic that the care package could help the user remain in the community, although there would be some problems. Again, this response was chosen by a higher proportion of the care managers of less dependent users than those with more complex needs. Among workers responsible for critical interval need users, 9 per cent indicated that services were put in place with the intention of temporarily delaying care home admission, rather than preventing it. Just 4 per cent of short and 3 per cent of long interval need users were provided with services with this aim in mind.

Finally, care managers were asked how likely it was that the user would be admitted to a care home within two years of (re-)referral. Distributions are shown in Table 5.30. As this table illustrates, the majority of care managers conceded that there was a chance that the user would be admitted to a care home within the next two years. Over two-thirds stated that there was either a slim chance that admission would take place, or that it was possible or probable. The needs of the users and the availability of informal support did, however, significantly influence responses. Care managers responsible for arranging services for short and critical interval need users were more likely than those responsible for long interval need cases to report that there was a chance of admission. For cases with no carer, care managers were also more likely to report that admission was probable or possible than for those with a carer.

Events which the worker thought could contribute to admission to residential or nursing home care were also related to the level of dependency of the user and the availability of informal support. The most frequently given reasons for a possible admission were (in a multiple response question): failing health (23 per cent), a serious accident (16 per cent), the level of dementia (15 per cent) and the inability of a carer to continue caring (15 per

Table 5.29
Whether help provided can keep user at home, by interval need

Extent to which help provided can keep user at home	Critical %	Short %	Long %	Total n =
		Interval need		
Only delay admission	9.3	3.8	2.8	14
Keep at home with few problems	39.5	26.0	12.1	67
Keep at home with no problems	51.2	70.2	84.9	189
Total n =	86	77	107	270

Missing cases: 36. Source: Standard and brief care manager interviews (n=306).

cent, although this rose to 17 per cent for cases that did currently have a carer). Other possible reasons were problems with safety at home (8 per cent), loneliness (4 per cent), inadequate nutrition (4 per cent) and the carer no longer being there at all (4 per cent). Other research has found that physical and mental health, and particularly the availability of informal support, are the key determinants of who will be admitted to institutional care. Care manager responses suggest that workers are very aware of these causes, and thus the need to provide appropriate preventative services.

Users' perceptions of care management

As stated, promoting user and carer involvement in decision-making was described as a priority by the SSD managers and front-line staff who engaged in ECCEP's policy and practice discussions. While Table 5.5 above illustrated that the vast majority of users had a say in assessment, these same users were also asked a range of other questions about their interaction with care managers and their view of the process as a whole.

A random subsample of users who were not severely cognitively impaired were asked what their opinion was of their care manager and to what extent the worker seemed to understand their needs. When users were asked whether they felt that the worker understood their strengths as well as their problems (that is, what the user could do as well as what he/she could not do), 87 per cent agreed. Interestingly, agreement was highest among the most dependent, critical interval need users (92 per cent). This suggests that the care manager is considering the user's situation as a whole rather than focusing on

Table 5.30

Likelihood of admission to care home within next two years, by interval need and social support among community-based sample

	Interval need						Total	
	Critical		Short		Long			
Likelihood of admission	No PIC	PIC	No PIC	PIC	No PIC	PIC		
	%	%	%	%	%	%	%	n =
Probably	18.2	8.7	13.3	7.1	3.6	2.9	7.3	18
Possibly	45.5	27.5	40.0	28.6	21.4	11.8	24.3	60
Slim chance	27.3	39.1	33.3	42.9	21.4	48.5	39.7	98
No chance	9.0	13.1	13.3	16.1	50.0	33.8	23.1	57
Admission delayed	0.0	11.6	0.0	5.4	3.6	2.9	5.7	14
Total n =	11	69	15	56	28	68	100	247

Missing cases: 34. Not applicable cases: 25 (comprising 5 who had died and 20 who were already in care homes). Source: Standard and brief care manager interviews (n=306).

problems, even when the user is very frail. As critical interval need users were most likely to have a trained social worker as their care manager, their positive response may also indicate that the emphasis which social work training places on holistic assessment may be meeting with some success, at least in the eyes of older service users.

The same subsample of users were asked if there were any differences of view between them and the worker. Only 8 per cent of users indicated that there had been any problem. Interestingly, all these older people had a principal informal carer. This may suggest that differences regarding the extent and type of services proposed may have interfered with the user/carer relationship (a user who would prefer that the specific task in question be done by the carer rather than formal services, or a carer requesting services such as respite which the user was reluctant to accept). Also, care packages designed to support a carer as well as the user are by their nature more complex, which could have provided a wider scope for potential disagreements between any of the parties involved.

All users, again with the exception of those with a severe cognitive impairment, were asked their opinion of the care manager. The question was designed to determine just how much choice users felt they had in their dealings with the care manager. In other words, was the user given the impression that it was a meeting of equals and there was room for negotiation, or did meetings consist of the worker making decisions which the user then had to accept? Results are shown in Table 5.31.

In over two-thirds of cases (69 per cent) users felt that the care manager was someone with whom they could discuss alternatives, as an equal. An additional 16 per cent believed the care manager was there to elicit their views and then arrange the services that the user wanted. This suggests that the vast majority of ECCEP users believed that they had a role to play in decision-making during the care management process: a finding less evident in recent surveys of interaction between older people and health care professionals (Allen et al., 1992; Tierney et al., 1993).

Just under 9 per cent of users reported that they viewed the care manager as someone 'in charge', who would tell them what to do or what was best. A slightly higher proportion of users without carers chose this response, suggesting that the presence of informal carers may provide users with the confidence to disagree with the care manager or make alternative arrangements in the knowledge that there are friends or family members to 'fall back on'. Perhaps surprisingly, critical interval need users were least likely to describe the care manager as 'someone in charge, telling them what to do'. Instead, it was the more independent, long interval need users who more frequently chose this response. It is possible that some of these users had hoped for services (such as shopping or cleaning) for which they were ineligible, and could not therefore be negotiated.

Table 5.31

Users' opinion of their care managers' demeanour, by interval need and social support among community-based sample

User's opinion	Critical		Interval need Short		Long		Total
	No PIC %	PIC %	No PIC %	PIC %	No PIC %	PIC %	n =
Someone in charge, telling them what to do	0.0	7.8	12.5	7.9	10.3	9.7	21
Someone to discuss the alternatives with as an equal	77.8	72.2	50.0	69.4	62.1	72.2	171
Someone to get the service the user wants	22.2	16.2	25.0	14.8	17.2	13.9	40
Other	0.0	3.8	12.5	7.9	10.3	4.2	15

Missing cases: 78. Sample: Users who were not severely cognitively impaired (n=325).

Carers' perceptions of care management

The extent of contact between a carer and the care manager is an important determinant of whether the care package will complement rather than substitute for existing informal care inputs. In addition to carer involvement in assessment (which has been detailed above), carers were asked a series of questions about other aspects of the care management process.

Not all carers are involved in the care planning process. General contact with the care manager was, however, found to be high among ECCEP carers. As Table 5.32 shows, 78 per cent overall indicated that they had some contact with the social worker, either in person or by telephone. Table 5.32 breaks down responses by the relationship between the user and carer and the carer's place of residence, as there are interesting differences between these groups. Carers were more likely to have contact with the care manager if they were living with the user (86 per cent) rather than living separately (72 per cent). This is not surprising. Co-resident carers are more accessible to care managers: they are more likely to be present when the care manager makes a home visit, their contact details are the same as the users', and they are the group most likely to have care needs themselves, as a large proportion of co-resident carers are elderly spouses. Indeed, 85 per cent of spouse carers had contact with the care manager, compared with 76 per cent of carers who were other female relatives, and 72 per cent who were other male relatives. The fact that over a third of other male carers who live separately had no contact at all with the care manager does raise questions about the extent of effort made to find and involve carers who are not co-resident, particularly those of working age who may be occupied during social services office hours.

It is encouraging to note, however, that the vast majority of carers of the most dependent users had contact with the care manager. Indeed, there is a clear gradient across interval need categories with reference to care

Table 5.32
Whether carer had contact with care manager, by relationship to user and whether living with user among community-based sample

PIC relationship to user	Lives with user %	Lives separately %	Total n =
Spouse/partner	84	90	74
Other female	88	73	133
Other male	91	61	31
Total n =	86	72	238

Missing cases: 0. Sample: All carer Time I interviews.

management contact: 89 per cent of the carers of critical interval need users had contact, compared with 60 per cent of those looking after someone with long interval needs. Similarly, the carers of users with a cognitive impairment or behavioural disorder were more likely to have been in touch with the care manager (87 per cent) than the carers of people without these mental health problems (72 per cent).

Involving carers, particularly a principal carer, in care planning is important not only from the point of view of addressing and meeting the carers' needs, but also because the carer can provide valuable information not given by the user. Using the carer as an informant in this way is particularly important when the user is cognitively impaired. As a result, carers who reported that they had contact with the care manager were asked if they had been involved in any discussions which had not included the user.

Table 5.33 shows the incidence of contact between the carer and care manager without the user being present. Just over half of carers reported that this type of contact had taken place. Not surprisingly, the most striking difference in responses was between carers of cognitively impaired users and other carers. In 67 per cent of cases, carers of older people with a cognitive impairment or behavioural disorder had spoken to the worker without the user being present, compared with just 43 per cent of other cases. Contact excluding the user was also more likely to take place if the user was very frail, with 63 per cent of the carers of critical interval need users indicating that this had occurred. When the user is confused or particularly frail, or indeed when the user is in hospital and the care manager requires additional information regarding circumstances at home, the carer may be an invaluable source of information.

Table 5.33
Whether carer involved in separate discussions with social worker without user being there, by interval need and cognitive impairment or behavioural disorder of user among community-based sample

CI or BD	Critical %	Short %	Long %	Total n =
CI/BD	68	67	61	67
Not CI/BD	55	35	36	43
Total %	63	45	43	53
n =	90	57	35	182

Missing cases: 0. Sample: Carer Time I interviews for which carer had contact with care manager.

Like users, carers who had contact with a care manager were also asked about the role of this worker in arranging services. Responses were very similar to those given by users. Over two-thirds of carers (71 per cent) viewed the care manager as someone with whom they could discuss alternatives, as an equal. An additional 18 per cent viewed the care manager as someone who could get the services that the carer or user asked for. Just 9 per cent of carers thought the worker was someone 'in charge', dictating what was needed. Overall, this means that almost nine out of ten carers perceived care management as a process of negotiation, or a process designed to give carers and users access to the services they wanted. This suggests a high level of satisfaction among carers with this particular aspect of care management. This type of satisfaction is distinct from satisfaction with services, which will be discussed in Chapter 9. However, it does indicate that carers who come into contact with a care manager are generally pleased with the manner in which needs are assessed and service packages planned.

It is evident from these findings relating to user and carer perceptions that the views of one participant in the care management process may differ from those of others. Users, carers and care managers bring differing expectations and experience to the assessment and planning process, which can result in differences in outlook and opinions. Factors such as the user's mental and physical health, or the amount of stress experienced by the carer, can also affect perceptions. Where differences do occur, it is important that they are recognised, and if possible reconciled, in order to arrive at an agreed care plan that will appropriately address the needs of the user and carer. The next chapter examines these issues of consistency between user, carer and care manager views and highlights some of the implications for policy and practice in the post-reform period.

Appendix 5.1
Policy and Practice Discussions

Service Outcomes for Older People (list given to informants for ranking in order of priority to the local authority from 1992-1994, and again from 1995-1997)

A. Access to services to users who had previously done without either any help or appropriate help

B. Empowerment, choice and control over their own lives for users

C. A real chance for more users to stay at home rather than enter a care home

D. A chance for users to regain as much independence as possible through the provision of rehabilitation and skill-enhancing services

E. Support for family carers to enable them to have respite

F. Raising charges in order to generate income so that services can be extended to those who need subsidised care

G. Emphasising welfare gains for users irrespective of cost to the local authority.

Informants were asked to rank order choices from 1 (first choice) to 6.

Appendix 5.2
The Measurement of Certain User and Carer Characteristics

Cognitive impairment

The care manager was simply asked whether the user had senile dementia or other forms of cognitive impairment.

Depression

The care manager was asked whether the user was depressed.

Attitude to help

One type of factor influencing responses of users and carers is their attitudes to help. Information on these attitudes was obtained from the interview of the care manager. In this particular study it was decided to focus on whether users and carers had an independent or demanding attitude to help. This was deduced from the response to the following question: 'Compared with other elderly people in similar circumstances does user tend to ask for more help or less help. If the answer was 'more', the user was classified as having a demanding attitude to help, and if 'less' an independent attitude. A similar question was used to judge whether the informal carer had a demanding or an independent attitude to help.

Note

1 Findings relating to service objectives and outcomes are dealt with in some detail in Davies et al. (1998).

Introduction

The needs of frail elderly people are usually multifaceted and can be quite complex. This complexity can make the process of assessment a challenging one, requiring direct input from the user and carer, as well as the care manager. However, when care managers involve both users and carers in the assessment process, inconsistency of views can arise. In order to obtain as objective a picture as possible during assessment, it is helpful to be able to understand the different types of bias which can be introduced by users, carers and their care managers in their judgements of needs and the services required. ECCEP has proved a valuable source for investigating such bias. The user, carer and care manager interviews included a wide range of questions on different aspects of need and on informal and formal resource inputs. Sometimes a similar question was asked on more than one interview so that a response was obtained from more than one perspective. This approach resulted in a number of interesting differences in the assessments of needs and resources being identified.

This chapter begins with a discussion of some of the *background* issues relating to consistency, including: a definition of what is meant by inconsistency; a consideration of the ground rules which should apply for such comparisons to be valid; and a presentation of the means for measuring consistency. Other studies which have examined the issue of consistency also constitute part of the background to ECCEP analysis. Following this discussion, the *methods* used to examine consistency are explained, followed by *results* from the analysis. Results deal in detail with the need for help in performing ADL/IADL tasks as reported by users, carers and care managers. An outline of results relating to issues of consistency regarding the user's physical and mental health problems, the receipt of formal services, tasks performed by carers, problems caused by caring, and carer stress are then presented. Finally, this chapter concludes with a *discussion* and *conclusion* examining the implications of findings for both policy and practice.

Background

The issue of consistency arises when users, carers and care managers are asked the same question. Ideally the answer by an interviewee to an interviewer's question should concur with actual events or circumstances; in other words, some measure of 'objective reality'. In what follows it is generally assumed that when two interviewees agree in their responses, these are both consistent with objective reality. However, it is possible that they are both in error. Inconsistency arises when two interviewees give different answers to the same question. An ambiguity then arises as to which is correct. By investigating possible reasons for inconsistency, valuable insight can be obtained into the mechanisms leading users, carers or care managers to present different responses. This has important implications for how care managers should go about assessing users and their carers, and for how line managers interpret the levels of need reported by care managers. These matters relate to the wider issues of targeting, eligibility criteria and training.

Certain ground rules should be met in order for comparisons between responses to be valid. The respondents should be asked identical or very similar questions, phrased as precisely as possible. For example, 'Do you feel moderately anxious?' is vague and could be interpreted by different respondents in different ways, while 'Do you lose sleep through worry?' is more precise, since it pins down the concept in terms of something which can be measured. Moreover, interviewees should have understood the question and have the verbal and cognitive skills to respond. For this reason, users who were severely cognitively impaired were usually excluded from the comparisons. The measurement of cognitive impairment is explained in Chapter 2. The same amount of prompting should be offered, either verbally or using show cards, to both interviewees whose responses are being compared. Interviews should take place at about the same time so that the situation about which respondents are reporting is unlikely to have changed appreciably. In practice it was not always possible to satisfy all these criteria fully, in which case the results of comparisons have to be accepted subject to caveats.

All of the comparisons made related to yes/no answers, leading to four possible combinations of responses when the answers given by two interviewees were being compared. These combinations can conveniently be represented by a decision matrix of the type used by McNeil et al. (1975) in examining the accuracy of medical diagnoses. Thus, in the case of a user and care manager, these responses may be represented as:

		User response	
		Yes	No
Care manager response	Yes	a	c
	No	b	d

Here a, b, c, d represent the number of cases in each cell. The proportion of cases in each cell was then a/N, b/N, c/N and d/N, where the total number of cases, N=a+b+c+d. In the analyses which follow it was often more helpful to give the percentage of cases in each of the four cells as A, B, C, D, where A+B+C+D=100 per cent. By comparing the proportion of yes responses made by each interviewee to a particular question, a general picture is provided of which respondent is identifying most need. A convenient overall measure of consistency between two yes/no responses is given by Cohen's kappa statistic (Landis and Koch, 1977) which captures the proportion of agreement beyond what is attributable to chance alone. The coefficient can range from minus one for total disagreement through zero for a complete lack of association to plus one for total agreement.

Since it is of particular interest to compare the judgements of care managers with those of both users and carers, one choice of analyses would be to present comparisons first between care managers and users, and second between care managers and carers. However, results showed that carer responses tended to be closer to those of users than to those of care managers. Most comparisons were therefore made first between care managers and users, and second between carers and users.

When respondents do not agree, it is worth exploring the factors which might have led to disagreement. The approach adopted for each item being detected was, therefore, to find in what ways the cases for which respondents disagreed differed from those for which they agreed. First, cases were identified for which the first respondent gave a positive response and the second a negative response. Second, those were identified for which the first respondent gave a negative response and the second a positive response. Finally, characteristics of these subsamples showing disagreement were identified which distinguished them from the remaining cases. A pool of characteristics relating to user, carer and care manager which could be used to test for group differences between the cases showing disagreement and others for which the respondents agreed are shown in Appendix Tables 6.1-6.3. As well as finding user, carer and care manager characteristics which influenced bias between respondents over *individual* items of need (or resources), those characteristics which had an overall effect on a *group* of needs (or resources), such as physical health problems, were also determined. There were some effects which were likely to exert some influence on a substantial proportion of interviewees, yet had not been directly measured. For example, is the user likely to deny a particular problem out of embarrassment, such as incontinence, or is the care manager likely to exaggerate a problem as a result of the pressure on him/her to adhere to eligibility criteria.

In needs assessments it is sometimes necessary to interview a proxy in instances where the older person is unable to provide an accurate response. A growing number of studies include comparisons between the responses of older people and their proxies, with the aim of determining the reliability of proxy responses. Most earlier studies of consistency have been based on populations in the USA which were more restricted than in this present investigation (Long et al., 1998). One early example by Magaziner et al. (1988) compared responses of elderly patients and their proxies in measuring health and functional status. Another such study was made by Kanten and colleagues (1993) in relation to the reporting of falls in nursing homes by both staff and users, and important differences were apparent. The present authors have selected three previous studies of consistency in the measurement of the needs or resource inputs relating to the elderly in the community, all carried out in the USA, which allow some interesting comparisons with the present study to be made. Long et al. (1998) studied the differences in response between users and carers when asked about the need for help with activities of daily living (ADLs), instrumental activities of daily living (IADLs) and physical health problems, and discovered frequent discrepancies. Segal and colleagues (1998) tested differences between users and interviewers in the measurement of aspects of mental disorder — depression, anxiety and cognitive impairment — and again found substantial disagreement. Kasten and Tennstedt (1997) focused on resources, comparing users' and carers' reports of formal and informal resources received. Differences were again important, particularly in relation to informal resources. The ECCEP investigation also includes new comparisons not previously examined in any of these studies. These studies all provided measures of the degree of consistency. In addition, Kanten et al. (1993), Long et al. (1998) and Kasten and Tennstedt (1997) looked for the characteristics likely to predict inconsistency. Finally, Long and colleagues took the analysis one stage further by identifying characteristics which would contribute significantly to the overall inconsistency in a group of needs. All these techniques were used in the present study.

Extent of problems of consistency

In deciding which areas of consistency to examine, functional capacity and physical and mental health are included here in view of their importance and due to their inclusion in previous studies, allowing comparisons to be made. As well as investigating need, perceptions of informal and formal resource inputs are also examined. Finally, different perceptions of the problems experienced by users and carers as a result of informal support are investigated, as is the level of carer stress which resulted. These considerations led to the following comparisons, which all relate to data obtained from the Time I assessment interviews.

(a) Whether needing help to perform individual activities of daily living (ADLs) and instrumental activities of daily living (IADLs): user/care manager and user/carer.

(b) Identification of individual physical health problems: user/care manager.

(c) Aspects of mental health — cognitive impairment, depression and morale: user/care manager.

(d) Formal resources received: user/care manager.

(e) Tasks performed by carer: user/carer.

(f) Problems caused by the carer's help to either user or carer: user/carer.

(g) Identification of stress in carer.

Methods

For each group of problems or resources, analysis was undertaken by first obtaining an overall measure of the proportion of cases with a positive response for each item for each respondent. Next, the proportion of cases was placed in each of the four cells representing:

(a) both respondents identifying item

(b) first respondent and not second respondent identifying item

(c) second respondent and not first respondent identifying item

(d) neither respondent identifying item.

An overall measure of consistency of each item is given by Cohen's kappa, expressing the level of agreement over what might be expected by chance. In investigating the possible reasons for inconsistency, it was recognised that the causal factors leading to, say, a user and not a care manager reporting a particular item may be different from vice versa. Therefore, each of the two subgroups of inconsistent cases are examined separately. Logistic regression was used to identify items associated with each of these subgroups. Here the dependent variable was membership of the subgroup: for example, comparing cases for which user and not care manager identified an item with all other cases. Predictor variables were drawn from the pools shown in Appendix Tables 6.1-6.3.

For each group of dependent variables (for example, physical health problems) being investigated, two logistic regressions were carried out for each item, one predicting when the first but not the second respondent identified the problem, and the other predicting when the second but not the first identified it. The odds ratios[1] for the variables entering each regression equation were tabulated for the whole group of dependent variables. In this way, features common to each group of equations could readily be identified.

These two dependent variables for each item allowed a bias variable to be computed which took on the value of −1 when the first respondent but not the second reported the problem, 0 when both respondents agreed and +1 when the second but not the first reported it. This was the approach adopted by Long et al. (1998).The General Linear Model or GLM (SPSS, 1997)[2] was then applied to examine the overall effect of a pool of predictors[3] drawn from Appendix Tables 6.1-6.3 on a set of items, such as bias in measuring ADL needs. This approach would produce similar results to that of Long et al. (1998), although had the advantage of being relatively robust in situations where statistical conditions are not quite met or when certain combinations of values of factors lead to some cells having no cases. The result of using these techniques for each group of variables is now described.

Results

In presenting results, a full explanation of all the stages in the analysis has been offered only for the first comparison, regarding ADL and IADL needs as measured by user and care manager. In the remaining comparisons only the main tabulations have been included, with other results being referred to in the text. A full report relating to issues of consistency in ECCEP is given by Chesterman et al. (1999).

ADL and IADL tasks: user and care manager comparisons

It is easy to see how ambiguities might arise in detecting the need for help with daily tasks. The degree of help which an older person reports that he/she requires with activities such as cooking or bathing is not only dependent upon physical ability, but also upon the individual's perception of the level of assistance needed. For instance, if the user reported that they could perform a task unaided but with extreme difficulty, at what level of difficulty should the user be regarded as needing help? Factors such as the user's attitude[4] can influence responses. If the older person has an independent attitude to help, resisting intervention or being willing to downplay their need for assistance, this can affect their response to questions and can be viewed as a potential source of bias.

Results of a comparison of ability to perform ADL and IADL tasks as measured by user and care manager are shown in Table 6.1, which is typical of the way comparisons are presented in this chapter. The first two columns of figures show the total proportion of cases identified as needing help by the user and care manager respectively. The next four columns show how cases are divided into the four categories determined by whether or not the user and/or the care manager identify a need for help. The following three columns

Table 6.1
Consistency between ability to perform ADL and IADL tasks as measured by user and care manager

Task	Overall total User %	Overall total Care manager %	Both interviews (a) N %	User interview only[1] (b) N %	Care manager interview only[2] (c) N %	Neither interview (d) N %	Kappa Coeff	Kappa S.E.[3]	Sig. t	Missing cases n =
ADL activities										
Bathing	45.4	60.8	37.0	8.5	23.8	30.7	0.367	0.05	<.001	6
Dressing	28.3	49.8	22.5	5.9	27.2	44.4	0.336	0.05	<.001	5
Toileting	11.7	26.4	8.2	3.8	18.2	69.9	0.314	0.06	<.001	6
Transfer	13.1	25.2	8.2	4.7	17.0	70.1	0.313	0.06	<.001	7
Mobility at home	29.8	36.7	14.4	15.4	22.3	48.0	0.157	0.06	<.01	6
IADL activities										
Shopping/errands	27.6	49.8	12.9	14.7	37.0	35.4	-0.036	0.05	NS	6
Meal preparation	13.9	50.0	7.6	6.3	42.3	43.8	0.026	0.04	NS	8
Heavy housework	21.4	69.9	14.1	7.5	55.9	22.5	-0.034	0.04	NS	5
Managing finances	21.9	8.8	1.0	21.0	7.9	70.2	-0.071	0.04	.154	20

Total sample: 325. Only users who were not severely cognitively impaired were asked about performance of ADLs and IADLs
1 User interview but not care manager interview.
2 Care manager interview but not user interview.
3 S.E. = Standard error.

give Cohen's kappa statistic, the coefficient providing a measure of agreement between cases identified by the user and care manager respectively as needing help, together with its standard error and statistical significance.

From the overall totals it can be seen that care managers more frequently identified a need for help than users. The only exception was managing finances where the difference was sharply in the other direction. The two columns showing disagreement between user and care manager, marked b/N and c/N, indicate a substantial proportion of cases with disagreement for each activity. This proportion ranges from 22 per cent for toileting and transfer to 63 per cent for heavy housework. Cohen's kappa showing the level of agreement between the user and care manager in reporting a need for help was significant at the 1 per cent level or better for all activities of daily living but insignificant at the 5 per cent level for all instrumental activities of daily living. The poor agreement for IADLs may at least partly reflect the difficulty experienced by both users and care managers in assessing a need for help when an informal carer may carry out the task regardless of whether the user is capable of performing it unaided.

The groups of cases corresponding to the columns showing disagreement (b/N and c/N) have been analysed further in Table 6.2 to determine the characteristics predicting each type of disagreement. Examination of this table shows how certain characteristics can have a similar association with disagreement for several types of task. These patterns are now discussed in detail.

Users but not care managers identifying a need for help

Those cases where the user but not care manager identified a need for help (column b/N in Table 6.1) are dealt with in the top half of Table 6.2. The logistic regression equation predicting a need for help with any of the ADL or IADL items is represented by the corresponding row. Thus, the third row of figures with three numbers relates to the equation predicting whether the user but not the care manager identified a need for help with toileting. Just three predictors entered this logistic regression: age, ADL score and whether the care manager was a home care manager. The three numbers are the odds ratios for each term. In the case of age, the odds ratio of 1.08 implies that when a user's age is increased by one year, the probability that the user and not the care manager would identify a need for help with toileting goes up by a factor of 1.08. In addition, this probability would have been 3.50 times as great when the worker was a home care manager rather than when he/she had some other kind of professional background.

When a predictor had a significant effect on more than one dependent variable, more than one figure would enter that column. Thus, in the case of ADL score, as well as being a predictor of when user but not care manager

Table 6.2

Showing the factors associated with disagreement between user and care manager in identifying the need for help with ADL and IADL tasks

Significant predictors of disagreement showing odds ratios

							User					Care manager	
	Age	Female	Married	Living alone	Has a PIC	Income category	Gets income support/housing benefit	ADL score	Moderately cognitively impaired	Geriatric depression score	Independent attitude to help	Social worker	Home care manager
User but not care manager identified need for help													
Bathing								1.31[1]					
Dressing		0.28	0.026				2.26	2.92					
Toileting	1.08[1]						3.85	3.30					3.50[1]
Transfer								2.40					
Feeding			0.39			0.66[1]		3.60		1.11[1]			
Mobility in home								1.81		1.06[1]		0.58[1]	
Shopping					2.77								
Meal preparation			2.72[1]				2.21[1]	1.45				0.40[1]	
Heavy housework													
Handling own money	1.05									1.07			
Care manager but not user identified need for help													
Bathing		1.84[1]				1.48		0.34					0.41
Dressing		1.04						0.53				1.56[1]	
Toileting		1.06								0.93	2.30[1]		0.33
Transfer								1.23[1]					
Feeding													
Mobility in home				0.42	0.43	0.67							
Shopping		1.56[1]											

Table 6.2 continued

Significant predictors of disagreement showing odds ratios

	Age	Female	Married	Living alone	Has a PIC	Income category	Gets income support/ housing benefit	ADL score	Moderately cognitively impaired	Geriatric depression score	Independent attitude to help	Social worker	Home care manager
					User							Care manager	
Meal preparation				0.50		1.49			1.97				0.39
Heavy housework	2.09												
Handling own money	2.99[1]					0.52	0.222	0.65	2.91				

Sample: The 325 users who were not severely cognitively impaired.

Logistic regression was used to identify which of the user and care manager characteristics drawn from the pools in Appendix Tables 6.1 and 6.3 were significant at the 5 per cent level (unless otherwise stated) in predicting whether user but not care manager identified a need for help, or whether care manager but not user identified a need for help, for each ADL and IADL item in turn.

1 This term was only significant at the 10 per cent level.

Odds ratios are shown for the characteristics predicting each ADL and IADL item.

identified a need for help with toileting, it was also a predictor for the remaining dependent variables relating to ADL needs together with meal preparation. Moreover, since these odds ratios are all greater than one, a greater ADL score systematically increased the probability that the user but not the care manager would identify a need for help with the corresponding tasks. One explanation was that the user's perception of the first five individual ADL items are used in determining the ADL score, so are positively correlated with it. The result may also indicate that when users report a need for help with several ADL items, care managers are liable to identify only a proportion of these, and so fail to discover the full complexity of need.

Low income or the receipt of income support or housing benefit increased the likelihood that the user but not the care manager identified a need for help with bathing, dressing, mobility in the home or meal preparation. This may reflect the willingness of older people with lower incomes to accept assistance from statutory services. In relation to depression, the presence of depressed mood increased the likelihood that the user and not the care manager identified a need for help with feeding, mobility within the home and handling their own money. The odds ratio was greatest for feeding (1.11), meaning that for every unit increase in the geriatric depression score, the probability of the user but not the care manager identifying a need for help with feeding was increased by a factor of 1.11. This suggests that depression can substantially alter the user's perception of his/her ability to perform this activity.

Comparisons with users' responses thus suggest that, in some cases, care managers may be failing to identify a need for help. This may be due to many factors, such as caseload, training and experience. As the final two columns in Table 6.2 illustrate, the professional background of the care manager in some cases emerges as a significant factor in predicting the worker's ability to identify need. For two items, mobility in the home and meal preparation, the failure of a care manager to report a need for help identified by the user was much less when the care manager was a social worker (odds ratios of 0.58 and 0.40 respectively). Moreover, this type of disagreement over the need for help with toileting was much more likely when the worker was a home care manager. This finding suggests that social workers are less likely than home care managers to overlook the user's needs.

Care managers but not users identifying a need for help

Odds ratios for the set of logistic regression equations predicting whether the care manager but not the user identified a need for help with ADL or IADL tasks are presented in the lower half of Table 6.2. There was no evidence that these users asked for less help than other older people in similar circumstances, the one exception being needing help with toileting. Users with an independent attitude might have been more likely to withhold this information out of embarrassment.

In the case of bathing, shopping, heavy housework and handling money, the likelihood that care managers and not users identified a need for help was much greater when the user was female. It may be that some female users are underreporting their need for assistance, particularly in relation to tasks that they may always have taken responsibility for, such as shopping. Table 6.2 also shows that the likelihood of the worker but not the user reporting a need for help with two IADL items — meal preparation and handling own money — was greater when the user was moderately cognitively impaired.

A higher depression score made it less likely that the care manager and not the user reported a need for help with toileting. Care managers may have found it more difficult to identify this problem when the user was depressed, perhaps because the user would put the effort into performing the task while the care manager was visiting but not otherwise. Alternatively, depressed users may have been more likely to report this problem.

Once again, social workers appeared more likely than home care managers to identify certain needs. This may again be due to a range of factors, including social work training and caseload. Eligibility criteria may also be a factor; as findings in Chapter 5 illustrated, social workers deal with higher need cases and are generally under more pressure to meet eligibility criteria. Knowledge of these criteria may lead to social workers exaggerating some needs — such as in relation to personal care — in order to obtain services for the user. Conversely, users may be underreporting their needs due to other factors, including a reluctance to accept and acknowledge a deterioration in their health or ability to perform tasks. Alternatively, users may deny their needs out of fear of being made to leave home, perhaps in order to enter a care home.

User and care manager characteristics influencing ADL bias indicators

It can be seen from Table 6.2 that the pattern of predictors entering the logistic regressions to explain bias for individual ADL and IADL items suggest that IADL items as a group behave rather differently from ADL items. Therefore, when considering which characteristics predict items when taken as a group, ADL and IADL items were considered separately.

Results for ADL items are shown in Table 6.3. These were obtained using General Linear Model, the set of six ADL bias indicators acting as dependent variables, with predictors being drawn again from the pool in Appendix Tables 6.1-6.3. The first two rows of data show the overall effect of predictor variables entering the model: the F values and their corresponding significance levels. Statistical significance was not the only criterion used in modelling. Thus, inclusion of the insignificant geriatric depression score variable led to a model with more scope for interpretation and allowed 'being a home care manager' to enter significantly. This insignificant depression score term suggests again that depressed users may be more likely to overstate the need for help with ADL tasks. Once more, ADL score entered with a high level of significance. Living alone made it more likely that care managers would tend to understate the need for help with ADL tasks in comparison with users. Expressing this another way, users living with others may have been understating this need for help in comparison with care managers, perhaps because these users were afraid of having their informal support from a co-residing carer replaced by formal services. Once again, home care managers were apparently failing to identify certain ADL needs.[5] Thus, as expected, the characteristics which most frequently entered the logistic regressions for individual ADL items shown in Table 6.2, namely ADL score, geriatric depression score and home care manager, all entered the overall GLM model shown in Table 6.3.

The remaining rows in Table 6.3 show the significance levels for entry of the overall model predictors into a regression equation for each item of ADL bias in turn, considered independently of the remaining items. The first column of significance levels refers to the overall level of fit of each of these regression equations. This fit was significant at the 0.1 per cent level for all ADL items except transfer, for which the fit was insignificant, with none of the four predictors entering significantly. It can be seen that the only predictor which enters a majority of the individual regression equations significantly is ADL score, although being a home care manager and geriatric depression score enter two of the equations very weakly (p<.2) as well as entering one equation significantly. In confirmation of the results for the individual logistic regressions in Table 6.2, being a home care manager and a high geriatric depression score had the most significant influence on bias in measuring the need for help with toileting. Although the only equation which 'living alone' entered significantly was for bias regarding mobility within the home, it was still part of the overall model for the group of bias indicators given in the top two rows of data. This is because the strength of the effect of living alone on mobility was sufficient for it to significantly influence the overall model.

User and care manager characteristics influencing IADL bias indicators

Results for IADL items are shown in Table 6.4. The first two rows include the significance levels of individual user and care manager predictors entering the model. ADL score again enters, although not as significantly as in the case of ADL items. Married users appeared less likely than care managers to understate a need for help with IADL tasks, particularly in the case of meal preparation. Similarly, users with a principal informal carer appeared more likely than care managers to indicate a need for help, particularly with

Table 6.3
Multivariate model of user and care manager characteristics influencing ADL bias

F-tests on each characteristic		Model		Characteristics	
				User	Care manager
		Factors	Covariates		Factors
		Living alone	ADL score[1]	Geriatric depression score[2]	Whether a home care manager
Overall F-test F		2.34	20.10	1.40	2.11
P		*	***	0.22	*
Significance level, p, of F-tests on individual items of ADL bias					
Bathing	***	NS	***	NS	0.16
Dressing	***	NS	***	NS	NS
Toileting	***	NS	*	*	***
Transfer	NS	NS	NS	NS	NS
Feeding	***	NS	***	0.16	NS
Mobility within home	***	**	***	0.14	0.19

Valid cases: 310. Missing: 15. Sample: Users who were not severely cognitively impaired.

This General Linear Model used the individual items of ADL bias as dependent variables. The user and care manager characteristics listed along the top of the table were those drawn from the predictor pool in Appendix Tables 6.1 and 6.3 which entered significantly.

Significance levels: *** p<0.001, ** p<0.01, * p<0.05, NS not significant

1 ADL score with its high F-value dominates the model. If ADL score is excluded from the pool of predictor variables, the geriatric depression score term becomes highly significant (p=0.001), and the user's independent attitude to help also enters (p<0.1), though being a home care manager was no longer significant.

2 Geriatric depression score was included in the equation despite being statistically insignificant (p=0.22) in order that being a home care manager would enter significantly.

shopping. Perhaps care managers tended to overlook a need for help when a carer was involved who was likely to perform the task.

Table 6.4 also shows that users with a greater age were found to be more likely than care managers to express a need for help, suggesting that care managers are less likely to detect need in these cases. When income was high, users were more likely than care managers to understate the need for help, particularly with meal preparation. As mentioned earlier, one explanation could be that better-off users are less willing to accept help from statutory

Table 6.4
Multivariate model of user and care manager characteristics influencing IADL bias

	Model	Characteristics						Care manager
		Factors		User				Factors
					Covariates			
		Married	Has a principal inf. carer	Age	Income	ADL score	Perceived level of ill health	Whether a social worker
Overall F-test F		2.47	3.86	2.86	2.37	2.51	2.10	2.78
p		*	**	*	*	*	0.08	*
Significance level, p, of F-tests on individual items of IADL bias								
Shopping	0.09	0.13	*	NS	NS	NS	NS	NS
Meal preparation	***	**	0.15	*	*	NS	*	**
Heavy housework	NS	0.16	NS	NS	NS	NS	NS	NS
Handling own money	**	NS	NS	0.16	NS	**	NS	NS

Valid cases: 306. Missing: 19. Sample: Users who were not severely cognitively impaired.
This General Linear Model used the individual items of IADL bias as dependent variables. The user and care manager characteristics listed along the top of the table were those drawn from the predictor pool in Appendix Tables 6.1 and 6.3 which entered significantly.
Significance levels: *** p<0.001, ** p<0.01, * p<0.05, NS not significant.

services, for which they would be likely to be charged, so play down the need for help. Another explanation is that care managers were more aware of the IADL needs of users on higher incomes. When users rated their health as being below average, they were more likely than care managers to understate the need for help, particularly with meal preparation. Perhaps their poor health made them less effective at identifying needs in the interview. Alternatively, they may be denying problems out of fear of having to leave home. Finally, social workers were more likely to identify IADL needs in relation to users, implying that non-social workers may tend to overlook these needs. This was particularly important in relation to meal preparation.

The predictors dominating the columns of IADL items in Table 6.2 are generally those which enter Table 6.4, although being female, receiving income support or housing benefit and cognitive impairment failed to enter the overall model, suggesting that the effects of these characteristics applied only to one or two individual IADL items.

Some conclusions may be drawn from the results presented in Tables 6.2, 6.3 and 6.4. Overall, users tend to identify need less frequently than care managers, possibly due to reluctance to accept or acknowledge a deterioration in their ability to perform tasks. Alternatively, users may deny their need for help out of fear of being made to leave home, or of having informal help replaced by formal services. However, although users who rated their health as below average appeared more likely to understate the need for help with IADL items, depressed users seemed more likely to overstate the need for help with ADL tasks. Care managers may overlook a need for help with IADL tasks, particularly with meal preparation, when the user was living with a spouse, whom care managers may assume to be performing such household tasks, or with shopping, when the user had a principal informal carer, who may perform such tasks. The older the user, the less effective care managers appear to be in detecting need. A lack of awareness of the extent of depression could lead care managers to underestimate the need for help with such tasks as feeding, mobility in the home and managing finances. In relation to the professional background of the worker, home care managers tend to understate the need for help with ADL tasks, while social workers appear more likely to identify IADL needs.

Indeed, there was much evidence to suggest that good social work practice during assessment is likely to facilitate the identification of a need for help with ADL and IADL tasks. Factors contributing to this good practice include building up a relationship of trust with the user and carer so that they can speak freely with the care manager. Observing users performing tasks and not simply relying on their verbal report reduces the likelihood of error in the assessment process. Asking informal carers about the user's needs, and liaising with others involved with the user both within the SSD and in other formal agencies, particularly the NHS, allows the user's account to be balanced against those from other perspectives. Where specialist advice is still needed, obtaining a specialist assessment such as from a geriatrician can clarify a user's needs. Finally, the ability of care managers to perform these activities adequately depends on their being allowed to maintain low caseloads.

The implication of these results is that a failure by local authorities to appoint care managers who are social workers may result in a substantial proportion of the ADL and IADL needs of frail elderly people being overlooked. It might, therefore, be advisable to restrict the use of home care managers to cases with less complex needs. Further training of home care managers could also facilitate the identification of need.

ADL and IADL tasks: user and carer comparisons

This particular comparison was based on a much smaller sample of 64 cases, since only a selection of carers were asked about the user's performance of ADL and IADL tasks and severely cognitively impaired users were again excluded. However, despite this much smaller sample size, some clear trends are apparent. Most items were identified by both users and carers with roughly similar frequencies. The three exceptions were toileting, mobility at home and shopping, for which the user less frequently identified a need for help than the carer. In contrast with the user/care manager comparison, the disagreement between user and carer constituted a much smaller proportion of the total number of cases, ranging from 5 per cent for feeding to 25 per cent for mobility at home. This suggests that users agreed much more closely with carers than with care managers in the reporting of a need for help with ADL and IADL activities. The much closer agreement between user and carer is confirmed by the fact that the kappa coefficients are much higher and are all significant at the 0.1 per cent level. Moreover, kappa coefficients for IADLs are not much smaller overall than those for ADLs.

The agreement between user and carer regarding individual ADL and IADL items was also measured by Long et al. (1998) for the elderly person and their carer, so that kappa could be compared between the two studies for each item. In each study, agreement between user and carer for ADL items was on average better than that for IADL items. Overall, the kappa levels of Long and colleagues were not quite as high. The difference was particularly striking for bathing, where the high level of agreement for this study (0.67) compares with the very poor agreement for Long et al. (0.17), due to users in the American study being more than four times as likely as carers to rate themselves as completely dependent. This had worrying implications for the likelihood of falls in the bathroom. Our study shows that overall carers in Britain did not overlook this need to any extent, although evidence discussed below suggests that sons and daughters were less aware of bathing needs.

The much smaller time interval between user and carer interviews than between those of user and care manager will partly account for the closer agreement of the former, although the effect of the time lag between user and care manager interviews was too weak to be statistically significant. This agreement between users and carers also adds weight to the argument that part of the reason why care managers identify more ADL and IADL needs than users may be as a result of care managers exaggerating need through pressure to meet eligibility criteria rather than users underestimating need. The small overall sample size meant that numbers of cases reporting inconsistency were frequently too low for logistic regressions to be carried out for some ADL or IADL items.

User and carer characteristics influencing ADL bias indicators

Once again ADL and IADL items were considered separately. The four predictors in the model for ADL items have an important influence on the group, having a significant influence on half of the individual bias variables, on average. Three related to the user: their marital status, age and ADL score. Married users and older users tended to understate need relative to carers. This might occur since these users are likely to be more needy and cause greater demands on carers, who would sometimes be the spouses. These carers might then tend to exaggerate the level of need. As expected, ADL score was a predictor of users overstating need relative to carers, since this score was derived from individual items of ADL need as reported by the user. When individual logistic regressions were examined, carers who were sons or daughters appeared less aware that the user needed help with bathing or dressing, hence leaving the user more open to risk. This may have arisen partly because they were less likely to be living with the user and partly because users were less willing to place demands upon their sons and daughters.

The only carer characteristic to enter the model as a predictor was having paid employment, a term of high statistical significance which appeared to lead to carers exaggerating users' needs. Evidence from individual logistic regressions suggests that this bias increased with the hours worked. Presumably the extra demands of a job cause users' needs to appear unduly severe to their carers. In the study of Long et al. (1998), it was not paid employment but hours per week caring for user which led to disagreement between user and carer over ADL items. Both these commitments have in common the fact that they make demands on the time and energy of the user and may restrict the scope for relaxation and leisure activities, leading to a feeling of burden in the carer, which was the other predictor of disagreement identified by Long and colleagues. Individual logistic regressions also suggested that carers with a demanding attitude to help tend to exaggerate the help they provide.

User and carer characteristics influencing IADL bias indicators

Five predictors entered the overall model for IADL bias: user income and four carer characteristics — paid employment, age, hours per week caring for user, and Kosberg score of carer stress. None of these had a significant effect on 'handling own money' when considered separately, suggesting that causes of bias in this indicator were different from those for the remainder of the group.

A common feature with ADL items is that carers in paid employment appear to exaggerate needs, particularly in regard to shopping, although the reverse effect applied to heavy housework. Again, evidence from individual logistic regressions suggests that the bias increased with the hours worked. Similarly, the greater the time per week spent in caring for the user, the more likely the carer was to overstate need. Moreover, the presence of carer stress as indicated by the Kosberg score had a weak overall effect in causing carers to overstate needs. It was younger carers who appeared most likely to exaggerate need, particularly in regard to heavy housework and meal preparation. These results also make an interesting comparison with those of Long and colleagues. While our study shows the Kosberg score of carer stress to cause carers to overstate need in relation to users, Long and colleagues found carer burden to have a similar effect. Also while our study shows more hours per week caring to lead to carers overstating need with IADL items, Long and colleagues found hours per week caring to have a similar effect for ADL but not IADL items.

The main conclusions regarding user-carer consistency with ADL/IADL items are as follows. Agreement between users and carers was better than between users and care managers, with users identifying needs only slightly less frequently than carers. Carers who were sons or daughters of users appeared less aware of the need for help with bathing or dressing, although younger carers were more likely to overstate the user's IADL needs. Carers of older users may tend to exaggerate their needs, due to their additional demands. When users are married, carers appear more likely to exaggerate ADL problems, probably since many of these carers would be the spouses, who would be old themselves and normally living with the user, so feel under pressure. Carers with a demanding attitude to help may exaggerate the need for help with dressing and toileting. Carers with extra commitments or who were under stress appeared to overstate the user's needs, including those working for longer hours in paid employment, those spending longer each week in helping their users (IADL tasks only), those with children under eighteen at home (mobility within home only) and greater stress as measured by lifestyle problems in the Kosberg scale (IADL needs only). In order that care managers can maximise their ability to detect need, they should be aware of these circumstances when users or carers may wish to conceal or overstate problems.

Physical health problems: user and care manager comparisons

Users and care managers were also asked about the extent and type of physical health problems experienced by the user. As with ADL and IADL needs, reporting of physical health problems can also be compared between these two groups of respondents. Again, a full analysis of this comparison can be found in Chesterman et al. (1999), with findings being summarised here.

Overall analysis of consistency between users and care managers revealed that there were rather more health items for which the care manager identified a problem than the user. For most health items, the user and care manager disagreed for a larger proportion of cases than that for which both agreed their presence. The three exceptions were the fairly well-defined conditions of stroke, multiple sclerosis and diabetes. However, some other well defined conditions such as hearing impairment, blood pressure problems and speech problems led to user and care manager responses showing poor agreement, with values of kappa of less than 0.2. Indeed, in not one instance did users and care managers agree over the presence of faecal incontinence. This high rate of overall disagreement probably results from the fact that care managers and particularly users tend to report only a proportion of health problems, so that their combined reports are more likely to reflect the complete spectrum of health problems than either taken individually. This explanation could account for 30 per cent of the health items showing a level of agreement between user and care manager as given by their kappa statistics of less than 0.2.

User and care manager characteristics influencing physical health bias indicators

Results of a general model for health items are shown in Table 6.5. Only three predictors entered the model, all relating to the user. The geriatric depression score was included since it was almost significant at the 10 per cent level. The presence of cognitive impairment in the user made it more likely that they would understate their physical health needs, reflecting their reduced awareness of these problems, with significant effects on incontinence of urine, hip fracture/damage, visual problems and hearing problems.

The insignificant geriatric depression score term suggests that depressed users are more likely to overstate physical health problems: a similar pattern to that found for ADL tasks. Depression appeared to cause users to significantly overstate relative to care managers the presence of ulcerated legs and visual

Table 6.5

Multivariate model of user and care manager characteristics influencing bias in identifying health problems

	Model		Characteristics User	
	Factors		Covariates	
		Moderately cognitively impaired	Geriatric depression score	Perceived level of ill health
Overall F-test F		1.76	1.47	1.97
p		*	0.11	**
Significance level, p, of F-tests on individual items of health				
Stroke/hemiplegia	NS	0.14	NS	NS
Heart	**	NS	0.20	*
Blood pressure	*	NS	0.06	**
Bronchitis/ emphysema	NS	NS	0.16	NS
Asthma	NS	NS	NS	NS
Incontinence of urine	*	**	NS	NS
Incontinence of faeces	NS	NS	NS	NS
Other genito- urinary	*	0.09	NS	**
Arthritis/ rheumatism	*	0.19	NS	*
Muscular/skeletal deformity	NS	0.20	0.18	NS
Hip fracture/ damage	0.20	*	NS	NS
Cancer	NS	NS	NS	0.13
Diabetes	NS	NS	NS	NS
Ulcerated legs	0.08	NS	*	NS
Visual problems	**	*	**	NS
Hearing problems	***	**	NS	**

Valid cases: 325. Missing: 0. Sample: Users who were not severely cognitively impaired. This General Linear Model used the individual items of health bias as dependent variables. The user characteristics listed along the top of the table were those drawn from the predictor pool in Appendix Table 6.1 which entered significantly. No care manager characteristics entered.

Significance levels: *** $p<0.001$, ** $p<0.01$, * $p<0.05$, NS not significant.

problems. It is possible that if these users do not suffer from a particular health item, they may imagine they have it as a result of their depressed state. Alternatively, users may have become depressed as a result of their health problems. These two results illustrate the close interrelationship between mind and body. The greater the level of ill health as perceived by the user, the more likely the user was to overstate the number of health problems. This perception is likely to reflect the user's lower morale as well as their objective state of health (Roth and Kay, 1956), so is consistent with the greater depression associated with other health problems. This result is the reverse of that for IADLs, where users who rated their health low tended to understate need. An alternative interpretation of the depression and ill health terms is that these conditions made identifying the full range of health problems difficult for care managers.

Although not shown here, individual logistic regressions indicated other possible effects. The reporting by users of physical health problems was reduced when the user had an independent attitude to help (for strokes, asthma and arthritis) and increased with a demanding attitude (bronchitis, incontinence of urine and ulcerated legs). It is, therefore, likely that disagreement can arise through some users denying or overstating problems. In regard to strokes and incontinence of urine, denial was likely to have arisen out of embarrassment or, in the case of strokes, inhibition out of fear of the serious consequences of the condition. Care managers seemed more likely to overlook some health problems in male users. The exceptions were incontinence of both urine and faeces, where males were more likely to deny their presence as identified by care managers, suggesting that males may feel the embarrassment more keenly. Also care managers who were social workers appeared more likely to report certain health problems.

Thus, in relation to physical health problems, overall results indicated that care managers identified health problems slightly more frequently than users, and that agreement between users and care managers was poor. Users with a demanding attitude to help appeared more likely to exaggerate or less likely to conceal health problems. Equally, users may deny health problems out of embarrassment or fear of the serious consequences of the condition. Cognitively impaired users were less likely to identify certain health problems. Users who are depressed may imagine that they have health problems, while users with health problems appeared more likely to be depressed. Users who perceived their own health as being below average were more likely to identify their health problems or even exaggerate them. Care managers may tend to overlook some health problems among male users and seem poor at identifying visual and hearing impairments and asthma. Care managers who are not social workers were less effective in identifying health problems. These findings support the need for more multidisciplinary assessment, particularly with health professionals. Identification of user's' health problems could be improved by more frequent liaison with NHS personnel, particularly GPs and community nurses. Moreover, attachment to a specialist assessment team could improve a care manager's awareness of the user's health problems.

Mental health: user and care manager comparisons

Chapter 3 described the aspects of mental health addressed in ECCEP. These include cognitive impairment, depression and morale. Assessment of mental health problems can often lead to uncertainties. Fortunately, the levels reported for the user were based on standard scales, so that — provided the information was obtained under suitable conditions — the scores should be reliable.[6]

The presence of cognitive impairment as judged by the care manager is compared with that identified in the user interview by means of the Katzman scale, using first a cut-off score of 11 and over (moderate cognitive impairment), and second one of 22 and over (severe cognitive impairment). Depressed mood as identified by the care manager was compared with a shorter geriatric depression scale score which was obtained from the user interview. A score of 11 or over was taken to indicate the presence of severe depression. Low morale as judged by the care manager was compared with whether the user's PGC morale score (Lawton, 1975) was six or less. Because all the user measures of mental disorder were based on objective scales, it is likely that discrepancies with the care manager will reflect largely errors made by the care manager rather than the user. However, the rather arbitrary nature of the cut-off level chosen for each user scale could also contribute to error.

The incidence of cognitive impairment as identified by the care manager lay between the two user measures with the different Katzman cut-off scores. Depression as identified by the care manager was much less frequent (13.5 per cent) than the rates identified using a geriatric depression score threshold of 11 (21.5 per cent), despite the severity of depression above this level. Using the lower Katzman threshold of 11 and over, the proportion of cases for which user and care manager disagreed over the presence of cognitive impairment (22 per cent) was less than the proportion of cases for which they both identified cognitive impairment (23 per cent). However, using the higher Katzman cut-off of 22 and over, the proportion with disagreement (still 22 per cent) was much larger than that for which both reported severe cognitive impairment (only 14 per cent). Nevertheless the kappa coefficients were both significant at the 0.1 per cent level. The corresponding Kendall's τ_b correlations of 0.43 (p<.001) for the higher cut-off and 0.52 (p<.001) for the lower cut-off may be compared with the results of Segal et al. (1998) for memory in older adults, when the Pearson correlation coefficient between the self-reported CATI brain disfunction scale of memory and the interviewer DRS scale for memory was −.42 (p<0.05) so of the same order.

The proportion of cases for which user and care manager interviews were in disagreement over the presence of depression (25 per cent) was much greater than the proportion for which both identified the condition (only 5 per cent). The kappa statistic was much smaller than for cognitive impairment (only 0.148), although this was still significant at the 1 per cent level. The total proportion of cases identified by the care manager as being clinically depressed (13.5 per cent) was much smaller than that found for the elderly of around 30 per cent by Kay et al. (1964) in their Newcastle study of the elderly population as a whole. Again the corresponding Kendall's τ_b of 0.18 (p=.001) may be compared with results of Segal et al. (1998), when the Pearson correlation coefficient between the self-reported CATI depression scale and the interviewer SCID depression rating was 0.41 (p<0.05), although the coefficient for the self-reported BSI depression scale with the interviewer SCID depression rating was only 0.11 (not significant). Thus, our Kendall's τ_b is intermediate in value between these two correlation coefficients, showing overall comparability between the two studies.

When care managers failed to identify cognitive impairment or depression reported by the user, the user's ADL score tended to be high. This may have been as a result of mental disorder which the care manager had failed to identify. In the case of depression, these users were also likely to be younger and female and regard their health as below average for the frail elderly. It is unsurprising that the user's low perception of their health was associated with an above-threshold depression score, since physical ill health and affective disorder are frequently associated in the elderly (Roth and Kay, 1956). In relation to morale, findings suggest that when users but not care managers indicated low morale, the geriatric depression score of the user was naturally higher. However, these users were less likely to be cognitively impaired, probably since these cases were less able to express aspects of low morale measured by the PGC morale scale. Workers who were home care managers appeared less able to detect low levels of cognitive impairment or poor morale. In view of the importance of their detection in responding to the user's mental health needs, this points to a need for more training of home care managers or a greater use of social workers.

When care managers and not users identified mental health problems, the care managers were presumably able to detect these problems at a level below the threshold used for the user scales of measurement. When care manager but not user interviews indicated severe cognitive impairment, the user's geriatric depression score was lower. This might be because depressed users tend to have larger Katzman scores, due to the detrimental effect of depression on cognitive ability.

Overall findings on the consistency between users and care managers in detecting mental disorder suggest that care managers were apparently unable to detect moderate cognitive impairment or clinical depression in a substantial proportion of cases. Workers who were home care managers reported a particularly low incidence of levels of cognitive impairment or morale. Inability to identify mental health problems in the user can have a wide range of implications both for the type and amount of service offered, and the resulting benefit that user's obtain from the care package provided. Again, these consistency findings point to the need for more multidisciplinary assessment and input from health professionals on helping care managers to identify mental health problems and plan the resulting care package effectively. Training in relation to the identification and management of dementia and appropriate service intervention to cope with depression and low morale could also clearly benefit workers, as could the involvement of more trained social workers rather than home care managers/organisers in assessment and care planning.

Receipt of formal services: user and care manager comparisons

Discussion in this chapter has thus focused on issues of consistency relating to the detection and measurement of client problems. Another important area for analysis is the receipt and frequency of a selection of community resources received at the time of the initial user interview. For each resource considered, the user's and care manager's reports were compared concerning first whether the resource was received at all and second whether its frequency reached a particular threshold level.[7] This section casts some light on the care managers' awareness of the full range of resources which users received.

One source of error in these comparisons is that care managers were normally interviewed an average of eleven weeks after the user, in which time resource inputs could have changed. Another source of uncertainty is that if care managers are not sufficiently in touch with the health authority, they may be unaware of current levels of community nursing, regular GP visits or regular chiropody. Moreover, if care managers did not arrange the home help, perhaps because this was dealt with by a home care manager, they may not be aware of the level of service provided.

Care managers were detecting resources for more cases and in greater quantities than for users with regard to local authority home help, nursing visits and delivered meals. In the case of day care, both users and care managers were reporting this to comparable a extent. Finally, regular contacts with GPs and chiropodists were more frequently reported by users than care managers. The proportion of cases with disagreement was not always larger than the proportion for which both user and care manager identified the problem. Thus, while 25 per cent of cases showed disagreement in identifying the involvement of a local authority home help, there were 57 per cent of cases for which both user and care manager reported the service. Agreement was also good for the presence of delivered meals and day care. Agreement with regard to nursing visits was only fair. Disagreement was particularly bad regarding contacts with the GP and chiropodist. Nevertheless, when the kappa coefficients were examined, all except for the presence and frequency of chiropody were significant at the 1 per cent level. Coefficients for the presence of delivered meals and day care were particularly high at 0.616 and 0.733 respectively. The groups of cases showing disagreement have been analysed further to determine possible causes of bias. These are now discussed in detail.

User and care manager characteristics influencing bias in the frequency of a particular resource

Both users and care managers can introduce bias in reporting resource levels. Users who want more help may underestimate the amount of resources they receive. Alternatively, users might overestimate levels if they want less formal help either because they find it intrusive or prefer assistance from an informal carer. In relation to care managers, trained social workers may be more aware of resource levels than other workers. Thus, reporting of service receipt can be affected by similar sources of bias as reporting of user needs.

When the overall model showing the predictors of particular frequencies of the different resources were examined, married users were found to be more likely to understate resource levels compared to care managers, particularly in regard to receiving at least one community nursing visit a week. Users with a principal informal carer were also more likely to understate resource levels, particularly with respect to day care at least once per week and regular GP visits at least fortnightly. Some users may rely on their spouse or carer to monitor service levels, and thus they may be less aware of what they are receiving. Income may also play a part, as receipt of income support or housing benefit was found to have the most significant overall effect (p<.01), leading to more users overstating resource levels compared to care managers, especially the receipt of at least three delivered meals or one nursing visit per week.

When the individual logistic regressions were examined, female users appeared less aware than males of the presence and particularly the levels of resources, with the exception of community nursing. Also, an independent attitude to help tended to lead to the presence and frequency of NHS resources being underrecorded by users, although SSD resource levels were unaffected.

Returning to the overall model, care managers who were social workers were less likely to understate resource levels, particularly for receiving at least three delivered meals per week or regular GP visits at least fortnightly. One inference is that non-social workers were unaware of levels of contact with the GP so were probably seldom in touch with them, with worrying implications for the quality of care management provided. Moreover, individual logistic regressions showed that for frequent day care, regular GP visits and chiropody, home care managers were more likely to understate these resources. This is probably because home care managers may not have set up the day care and were out of touch with GPs over the frequency of their visits or of chiropody appointments.

To summarise some key findings regarding consistency over the receipt and frequency of resources, agreement between users and care managers over the presence and level of SSD resources was moderate, although for NHS inputs it was only slight. Users may underestimate the frequency of resource inputs particularly when they have an independent attitude to help. Moreover, female users may have been less aware of the levels of resources they received than male users, perhaps due to traditional role models. Users with a spouse or informal carer appeared liable to understate resource levels, perhaps because these users relied on them to monitor such levels. Care managers were not always aware of the presence or level of NHS resources which their users received and appeared to underestimate the frequency of resource inputs unless they were social workers, who in most respects had a more accurate picture of the care package. Nevertheless, social workers were liable to underrecord the presence or level of home care, possibly because it was arranged previously by another worker such as a home care manager, although they were less likely than other workers to overlook community nursing or the frequent deployment of delivered meals. Social workers appeared much more aware than home care managers of NHS resource inputs such as GP visits and chiropody, implying that their liaison with key NHS personnel was more effective.

Carer tasks

The agreement between user and carer over the full range of tasks performed by the carer, examined in this section, has the results presented in some detail. Both users and carers were asked what tasks the carer did for the user over the course of a week. This definition may have appeared ambiguous when, for example, a task was performed on some but not all weeks. It is presumably in such situations that the reports of users and carers are more likely to differ and when other factors, such as attitude to help of the user or carer, are likely to play a part in whether the task is included.

The comparison is shown in Table 6.6 and again excludes users who were severely cognitively impaired. Only twenty out of the thirty-two types of task monitored are shown, to facilitate clarity of presentation. Examining the overall totals, carers recorded most tasks somewhat more frequently than users. Nevertheless, in over half the tasks, the proportion for which both user and carer reported the task was greater than the proportion with disagreement. Agreement was generally better for clear-cut practical tasks directly affecting the user. In all but three tasks, the agreement as measured by kappa was significant at the 0.1 per cent level. Of these three tasks, changing

Table 6.6
Consistency between user and carer in identifying tasks performed by carer

Type of task	Overall total		Both interviews[a]	User interview only[1][b]	Carer interview only[2][c]	Neither interview[d]	Kappa		
	User %	Carer %	N %	N %	N %	N %	Coeff	S.E.[3]	Sig. t
Medical and toileting									
Injections/checks/treatment	7.3	5.5	2.6	4.5	2.6	90.4	0.385	.15	<.001
Changing continence pads	5.6	5.0	5.1	0.6	0.0	94.3	0.938	.06	<.001
Helping while on toilet	12.4	9.9	7.0	5.7	3.2	84.2	0.562	.10	<.001
Washing/lifting after soiling/wetting	9.9	9.6	5.1	5.1	4.5	85.4	0.463	.12	<.001
Personal care									
Washing/lifting generally	24.1	25.1	19.1	5.1	6.4	69.4	0.693	.07	<.001
Dressing/undressing	28.7	27.5	24.2	4.5	3.2	68.2	0.811	.05	<.001
Helping to toilet including lifting	13.9	14.9	10.2	3.8	5.1	80.9	0.644	.09	<.001
In/out of bed including lifting	16.8	20.8	13.4	3.2	7.0	76.4	0.622	.08	<.001
Housework									
Light housework	50.4	52.4	39.1	11.5	13.5	35.9	0.500	.07	<.001
Heavy housework	41.1	46.5	33.1	7.6	13.4	45.9	0.574	.07	<.001
Laundry of soiled bedding/clothes	36.5	36.9	24.8	11.5	12.1	51.6	0.492	.07	<.001

							S.E.	
Meals								
Preparing meals	55.0	57.5	48.4	6.4	8.9	36.3	0.690	.06	<.001
Shopping								
Taking out for shopping errands	45.5	34.7	29.5	16.0	5.1	49.4	0.565	.07	<.001
Shopping, prescriptions, errands	74.3	77.5	66.5	7.6	10.8	15.2	0.503	.08	<.001
Company and leisure								
Chatting/watching TV	79.0	97.5	78.3	0.6	19.1	1.9	0.122	.07	<.01
Taking out for pleasure trips	27.2	43.4	24.8	2.5	18.5	54.1	0.553	.07	<.001
Helping with administration								
Sorting/helping with bills/finance	54.9	65.1	49.0	5.7	15.9	29.3	0.554	.07	<.001
Other								
Providing medication reminders & review	21.7	31.6	17.2	4.5	14.0	64.3	0.531	.08	<.001
Keeping eye on them/check they are OK	45.3	57.4	36.1	9.5	21.5	32.9	0.388	.07	<.001
Helping talk about problems/make decisions	41.6	49.2	29.9	12.1	19.1	38.9	0.374	.07	<.001

Valid cases: 157. Missing cases: 10. Sample excludes users who were severely cognitively impaired.
For clarity of presentation, twelve out of the 32 tasks investigated were omitted from this table: changing bandages, changing catheters, etc., incontinence laundry, cutting toenails, helping with welfare benefits, arranging other services, reassessing user needs, reviewing help user needs, helping with home repairs, taking to appointments, helping learn social skills, helping learn practical skills.
1 User interview but not carer interview.
2 Carer interview but not user interview.
3 S.E. = standard error.

catheters and helping learn social skills only involved a few cases, while chatting and watching television appeared to be overlooked by the user for about one case in five although agreement was still significant at the 1 per cent level.

Kasten and Tennstedt (1997) have drawn attention to the disagreements which may arise between older people in the USA and their informal carers regarding the number of areas of informal care provided. It is, therefore, interesting to compare the levels of agreement found by these authors with those shown in Table 6.6. Overall, the concordance between the elderly and their carers over the types of task the carers performed was rather lower in Kasten and Tennstedt's study than in ECCEP. For example, their agreement for personal care of 0.46 is somewhat below our values for individual items which were typically 0.69 for washing or bathing and 0.66 for helping in and out of bed, while that for providing meals of only 0.31 compares with our much higher value of 0.69. Since the characteristics of the older people and their carers in the two studies are fairly comparable, the different levels of agreement may reflect differences in the style of data collection. While the present study collected data by face-to-face interview, Kasten and Tennstedt used telephone interviews.

Because of the relatively good agreement between user and carer, the numbers of cases in the two columns marked a/N and b/N showing disagreement were frequently insufficient for a logistic regression to be usefully carried out. These were restricted to instances where the number of cases was at least about 10 per cent of the total, amounting to a minimum of some sixteen cases showing disagreement.

Users but not carers specifying that carers performed tasks

When users but not carers indicated that the carer helped with two unrelated tasks — laundry of soiled bedding and clothes and supervision/check ups — the user was more likely to be male. This suggests either that male users tended to exaggerate the carer's help with these two activities or that female users withheld this information. A similar effect was found in the case of formal resources and the explanation may be once again that traditionally males are more aware of resource deployment than females. When users but not carers reported that carers help with taking the user for shopping or did shopping or small errands for the user, the user was much less likely to be cognitively impaired. Probably users who were cognitively impaired and some carers were failing to identify this help if it was not being offered every week. Kasten and Tennstedt (1997) also identified cognitive impairment as a cause of disagreement between users and carers, although only in connection with the performance of personal care tasks. These authors also found that tasks involving housekeeping, errands and transport all showed less disagreement between user and carer when they were co-residing. The reverse was found in the present study as regards taking out for shopping errands, with users reporting the task more frequently than their co-residing carers. When users but not carers reported that carers helped with the laundry of soiled bedding and clothes or with taking the user to appointments/helping them outside the home, the user was much less likely to have an independent attitude to help. Probably users with an independent attitude and carers were again failing to identify this help if it was not being offered every week.

Regarding carer characteristics, when users but not carers reported that carers assisted with light housework or helping user talk about problems or make decisions, the carer was more likely to be female. It is, therefore, likely that female carers tended to understate these activities. Thus, just as male users overstated certain tasks, perhaps because their traditional role made them more aware of them, so male carers also overstated some tasks, perhaps for a similar reason, while female carers more readily took these tasks for granted.

The heavier the commitments of carers, the less likely they were to understate their activities. Thus, when users but not carers specified that carers assisted with the laundry of soiled bedding and clothes, the carer was far less likely to have children under eighteen at home. Also, when users but not carers reported that carers helped with certain tasks, the carer was less likely to be in paid employment. The greater the stress experienced by carers, the more likely they were to overstate certain needs. This finding is similar to that of Long et al. (1998) for carer burden, which is closely related to stress. However, depression in carers led to their *understating* the role they played regarding certain tasks. This finding is the reverse of that found by Long and colleagues. When users but not carers specified that carers assisted with heavy housework, the carer was more likely to have an independent attitude to help. Also, carers with an independent attitude were more likely to understate their involvement with heavy housework.

Carers but not users specifying that carers performed task

Once again, female users were more likely to understate information on certain tasks such as offering pleasure trips. However, this appears to be at variance with that for Kasten and Tennstedt (1997), who found that male users were more likely to disagree with carers over running errands and the provision of transport, which would include pleasure trips.

When carers but not users reported that carers helped with a range of tasks, the user was much more likely to be married. This suggests that married users were much more likely to overlook certain types of help. The spouse of the user would have frequently been the carer, and married users were probably more likely to take some of their spouse's activities for granted, as being part of the couple's traditional division of labour. In the case of six varied types of task, users on a low income were more likely to overlook the help they receive from carers. These users would have faced only minimal charges for extra formal services, so might have underestimated their informal help in order to appear eligible for formal provision.

When carers but not users reported that the carer had assisted with chatting or watching television or in supervision and checking up, the user was more likely to have a lower geriatric depression score, suggesting that depressed users were less likely to overlook these two types of help. Similarly, it was found earlier that depressed users also overstated the need for help with ADL or IADL tasks and health problems. Interestingly, this is the opposite effect to that found for depressed carers, who appeared more likely to understate certain carer activities. Again, users with an independent attitude to help tended to understate activity, this time regarding the laundry of soiled bedding and clothes. This may have been out of embarrassment, which would be consistent with another finding from this study, that users with an independent attitude to help are more likely to understate the presence or frequency of faecal incontinence.

Turning now to carer characteristics, male carers once again appeared more likely to overstate their help, relative to females. When carers but not users identified help with laundry of soiled bedding and clothes, heavy housework or meal preparation, the carer was less likely to be married. Perhaps unmarried carers were more likely to overstate the help they provided with these tasks. Also, married carers would sometimes have the user as spouse, and so be more likely to regard what they did as part of the normal routine and hence be liable to understate their involvement. When carers but not users reported helping with the continent laundry, reassessing their needs or helping the user discuss problems or make decisions, the carer was less likely to be a non-relative, suggesting that these carers are less likely to overstate their activity. When carers but not users identified tasks performed by the carer, the carer was again much more likely to have more commitments, such as having children under eighteen at home or spending longer in paid employment. Again, stressed carers appeared to be more likely to overstate their activity. The findings that depressed carers and those with an independent attitude to help are less likely to overstate their activity were also confirmed.

Many of these results concurred with those found for when users but not carers specified the task, so the overall General Linear Model discussed next is based upon sound premises.

User and carer characteristics influencing carer task bias indicators

Results for carer tasks are shown in Table 6.7. With such a large number of tasks, it was especially valuable to study the results of an overall model in order to identify which predictors were common to the group. Individual items of carer task bias have been omitted from the table. Of the seven predictors which entered significantly, only one, ADL score, referred to the user. This variable might be expected to enter, since the greater the score, the more likelihood there is that carers would perform a greater range of tasks, and hence the greater the likelihood of any bias. Users were found to overstate tasks more the greater the ADL score. Kasten and Tennstedt (1997) found that while disability was a highly significant predictor of disagreement as regards personal care tasks, it predicted greater agreement for housekeeping tasks, so their results only partly confirm those of the present study.

As in the case of the need for help with ADL and IADL tasks, paid employment often appeared to lead carers to exaggerate the number of tasks they performed. However, the longer the hours per week spent in caring, the greater the tendency of carers to understate the number of tasks they performed overall, although for individual tasks the picture was a mixed one. Thus, helping user in and out of bed or to toilet, including lifting, or the laundry of soiled bedding or clothes were tasks which carers appeared to overstate, possibly due to the heavy nature of the activities which could include lifting, while the changing of catheters or continence pads were activities apparently understated. The majority of these tasks, whether over- or understated by the carer, in comparison to the user's account, have a common element of being demanding and possibly causing embarrassment to user or carer. Kasten and Tennstedt (1997) presented a more clear-cut result that the greater the number of hours of informal care per week, the greater the disagreement between user and carer over the number of areas of informal assistance. Moreover, while Kasten and Tennstedt found that users who did not co-reside with their carers were more likely to disagree with them, this predictor did not enter the model in Table 6.7.

The effect of carer stress apparently led carers to overstate the number of tasks they performed, particularly in regard to their Kosberg score, which reflects largely the carer's lifestyle problems. This was significant for a range of demanding tasks. Surprisingly, when the carer's health was affecting the tasks they performed, this generally had the effect of their understating tasks relative to the user, although the overall effect was significant only at the 10 per cent level. Since most of the carers with poor health and doing personal care were spouses, they were perhaps more likely to be stoical about all aspects of caring. Finally, when carers had an independent attitude to help they appeared more likely to understate the tasks they performed.

Some tentative conclusions regarding consistency between users and carers over reporting which tasks the carer carried out are now summarised. The

Table 6.7
Multivariate model of user and carer characteristics influencing bias in identifying carer tasks

| | User | Characteristics | | | | | |
| | Covariates | Factors | | Carer | | Covariates | |
	ADL score	Whether carer's health affects tasks done	Independent attitude to help	Hours per week in paid employment	Hours per week caring for user	Malaise score of carer stress	Kosberg score of carer stress
Overall F	1.53	1.41	1.34	2.45	2.63	0.30	0.30
F-test p	*	0.10	0.06	***	***	*	*

Valid cases: 157, Missing cases: 10.   Sample: Those carers with users who were not severely cognitively impaired.
This General Linear Model used the individual items of carer task bias as dependent variables, based on the 32 types of carer task listed in Table 6.6. The user and carer characteristics listed along the top of the table were those drawn from the predictor pools in Appendix Tables 6.1 and 6.2 which entered significantly.
Significance levels: *** p<0.001, ** p<0.01, * p<0.05, NS not significant.

overall model suggested that carers with more commitments apart from caring for user — more time spent in paid employment or in having children under eighteen at home — were more likely to report assistance they provide to user, and may possibly have been exaggerating this involvement. Moreover, stressed carers more frequently overstated their help, while carers with an independent attitude to help were likely to understate their activity.

There were further effects which, although not part of the overall model, appeared from the logistic regressions to affect subgroups of tasks. Thus, while male users were more likely than female users to report carer activity, married users were more likely to overlook certain types of help from the carer. Users who were cognitively impaired or depressed identified the carers' involvement less frequently with certain types of help. Users on a low income or with an independent attitude to help were more likely to overlook the help they received from carers. Female carers tended to understate their activities compared to males. Finally, carers who felt miserable or depressed or whose poor health affected the tasks they could perform, were more likely to understate the help they provided the user.

Problems caused by caring

The tasks carried out by the carer sometimes led to problems, either to the user or the carer. Both were asked whether the overall help provided by the carer caused problems to either of them, allowing the consistency between user and carer to be measured.

When problems were indicated, their nature was clarified from the point of view of both user and carer, and the consistency between these two views also determined. Uncertainties could sometimes arise if the user was unaware of some of the problems caused to carers by the tasks they performed, such as a carer forgoing promotion prospects at work in order to continue caring at the present level. Also, some demanding users may be unaware of the stress they cause their carers. Equally, carers may sometimes underestimate the extent to which their involvement can undermine the feelings of independence of users and add to their sense of being a burden.

The comparison excludes users who were severely cognitively impaired. Problems to the carer were reported about twice as frequently as those to the user. Individual problems caused to the user were overall more frequently reported by the carer than the user. This suggests that either users were sometimes reluctant to express problems they experienced such as loss of independence or their awareness of being a burden on others, or that carers were imagining the users as experiencing these problems when they were not present. Individual problems caused to the carer were much more frequently reported by the carer than the user. Presumably then users tend to be unaware of many of the problems caused by caring, although carers may be

Table 6.8
Multivariate model of user and carer characteristics influencing bias in identifying problems carer's help causes carer

| | Model | | Characteristics | Covariates | | | Carer |
| | Factors | | User Factors | | | | |
	Lives with principal informal carer	Children under 18 living at home	Often feels miserable or depressed	Age	Hours per week in paid employment	Hours per week caring for user	Kosberg score of carer stress
Overall F-test F	1.92 *	3.09 ***	2.06 *	1.92 *	1.84 *	2.72 **	2.40 **
Significance level, p, of F-tests on bias with individual problems							
Unable to give time to family	***	***	NS	NS	*	NS	***
Reduced leisure time	*	NS	NS	NS	NS	0.12	*
Do not see enough of friends	NS	0.08	NS	NS	NS	NS	NS
Lost earnings from work	0.15	NS	0.14	NS	***	NS	NS
Loss of job/limitations on future work	**	**	*	NS	0.13	*	*
Physical effort of caring (e.g. lifting)	***	0.11	***	*	NS	*	NS
Strain on relationship with user	0.07	NS	NS	NS	NS	0.11	0.17
Stress	**	NS	NS	NS	NS	NS	***

Loses sleep through attending to user	NS	NS	NS	NS	NS	NS	*
Loss of sleep through worry	***	NS	0.14	NS	NS	*	0.13
Financial cost	**	0.06	*	*	*	*	0.13
Cannot help other dependent person	***	NS	0.07	NS	*	0.12	0.17

Valid cases: 157. Missing: 10. Sample: Those carers with users who were not severely cognitively impaired.

This General Linear Model used the bias in identifying problems carer's help causes carer as dependent variables. The user and carer characteristics listed along the top of the table were those drawn from the predictor pool in Appendix Tables 6.1 and 6.2 which entered significantly.

Significance levels: *** $p<0.001$, ** $p<0.01$, * $p<0.05$, NS not significant

There is substantial inhomogeneity of variance. Also only three dependent variables have distributions close to normal and only three moderately close, out of twelve dependent variables. Nevertheless, the model appears reasonably robust.

exaggerating some of them. Overall agreement between users and carers on all these data was only fair, and for each item the proportion showing disagreement was always greater than that for which both parties identified the problem. Nevertheless, with the exception of four items, the remainder showed Kappa coefficients which were significant at the 0.1 per cent level.

Characteristics influencing bias indicators of the effects of carer activity on users

Differences in the pattern of predictors entering the logistic regressions to explain bias for individual effects of carers' activity on the user and the carer suggested that effects on the user and carer should be considered separately.

Only three predictors significantly affected the three types of problem carers' help can cause users. When user and carer lived together, carers understated these problems compared to users. This was particularly significant for awareness of being a burden on others, which is likely to be particularly acute hen user lives with carer. When the carer had children under eighteen living at home, carers also understated these problems compared to users, this being significant for loss of independence and awareness of being a burden on others. Perhaps parental responsibilities deflected their attention from some of the user's psychological needs, causing the carer to understate problems, while the user might feel a burden particularly in view of the carer having children at home to support. In contrast, when carers experienced stress through lifestyle problems, as measured by their Kosberg score, they tended to *overstate* the problems to the user, just as in the previous section they were found to overstate the tasks they performed.

As well as these three main predictors, other variables were found to enter the individual logistic regressions. Thus, female carers were more likely than males to overstate the loss of privacy their help caused the user. Also, carers whose health limited the tasks they could perform tended to overstate the problems which their help caused the user. Finally, carers with an independent attitude to help were less likely to report that their help had caused users problems, in particular with users feeling that they were a burden upon others.

Characteristics influencing bias indicators of the effects of carer activity on carers

Table 6.8 shows results for the effects of carer activity on carers, with the predictors relating almost entirely to the carers. These seven predictors include the three for the effects on users, although when carers had children under eighteen living at home, this had the opposite effect on bias to that for users. When users and carers lived together, carers tended overall to overstate their problems compared to users, also the opposite to the effect on users. Perhaps users who live with carers are more likely to take the carers' help for granted. However, the most significant item, the physical effort of caring (including lifting), proved to be an exception, with carers understating this compared to users.

In regard to carer characteristics, users appeared to be less aware of problems experienced by older carers, who would probably include spouses of users, even though these older carers would be more prone to physical frailty leading to greater physical demands of caring and probably to loss of sleep through worry too. Spending time in paid employment caused carers to overstate problems they experienced arising from their caring activities compared to users, particularly in regard to being unable to give sufficient time to their family and through lost earnings from work. Also, users may frequently be unaware of how caring activities cause the carer to cut back on some opportunities to earn more at work. Moreover, the longer a carer provided help to a user each week, the more likely carers were to overstate problems relative to users. This effect was significant in regard to loss of job or limitations on future work, the physical effort of caring, including lifting, and the financial cost of caring. The most significant predictor was the carer having children under eighteen living at home, which caused carers to overstate need relative to users, although this might be as a result of users being unaware of their carers' problems. The most significant effect of having children under eighteen living at home was in carers but not users reporting carers being unable to give time to their family.

The experience of stress through lifestyle problems, as measured by their Kosberg score, was apparently another reason for carers to overstate problems relative to users. This had a significant effect on six out of the twelve bias indicators. Carers who frequently felt miserable or depressed also overstated problems relative to users, this effect being significant with regard to loss of job or limitations on future work or especially the physical effort of caring, such as lifting.

Thus carers' commitments, such as hours per week in paid employment and hours per week caring for users and children under eighteen living at home, appeared to cause carers to overstate caring difficulties compared to users. Also, when carers felt stress through lifestyle problems, as indicated by their Kosberg score, they again appeared to overstate caring difficulties compared to users. Both these results confirm those found in the previous section for carer tasks. However, carers who felt miserable or depressed or found their care limited by poor health appeared to overstate caring difficulties compared to users, despite having been found in the previous section to understate the tasks they performed. These results may be compared with those of Long et al. (1998) in which increased carer hours were associated with carers overstating ADL needs compared to users, and increased carer burden meant carers overstating ADL and IADL needs compared to users. In both studies, depression in carers did not influence their judgement or bias in assessing the user's ADL and IADL needs, although in the present study it apparently led to their overstating the problems they experienced as a result of their caring activity, in comparison with the user's view.

As well as the predictors entering this equation, additional carer variables were found to enter the individual logistic regressions. Thus, female carers were more likely than males to overstate having suffered from the physical effects of caring, reflecting their weaker physique. Also, for spouse carers, wives may experience more physical problems in caring for their husbands than vice versa, not least because of the heavier build of the male.

These findings concerning the agreement between user and carer over the problems help provided by the carer affects both carer and user suggest the following conclusions. Regarding effects on the user, carers living with users or having children under eighteen living at home tended to overlook some problems caused to the user. If some carers were exaggerating the problems their help caused the user then these carers were much less likely to have an independent attitude to help. When carers but not users reported that users feel themselves to be a burden on the carer, the carer was likely to spend more time in caring for the user.

With respect to the effects on the carer, cognitively impaired users may be less aware of any strain in their relationship with the carer. Users may be less aware of carers suffering from the physical effects of caring or losing sleep through worry, when that carer is older. Female carers may tend to overstate the problems experienced by carers as well as users regarding the carer's help. Carers with additional commitments, whether these be children under eighteen at home or additional hours spent in paid employment or in caring for the user, are more likely to overstate the problems they experienced from caring. Carers under stress, suffering from frequent depression or whose help was affected by their health also have a strong tendency to overstate problems they experience through caring, in comparison with their perception by the user.

Carer stress

Care managers were asked whether they judged the principal informal carer to be under stress. Carers were asked about a range of different aspects of stress through the Malaise and Kosberg scales, for which scores were obtained. In order to compare results for carers and care managers, it was necessary to apply a suitable cut-off level to these two scales, in order that they each indicate whether the carer was significantly stressed. The consistency between the care manager level and each carer measure could then be tested in turn.

In the case of Malaise, the carer was taken as being stressed when the score was at least seven, the level termed 'critical stress' (Rutter et al., 1970). Regarding the Kosberg scale, the cut-off was taken as being at least six in order that the proportion in the 'stressed' category was approximately the same as for Malaise. Clearly the levels of the overall totals for the carer are arbitrary, depending upon the cut-off level selected. It would, therefore, be a mistake to draw any conclusions from the relative levels of the totals for the carer and care manager. Nevertheless, the subgroups identified showing inconsistency are likely to reflect particular characteristics of the user, carer and care manager which may be of interest. The cut-off levels actually selected make the care managers appear to have categorised almost twice as many carers as being stressed as the carers themselves. The overall agreement as measured by Cohen's kappa was insignificant using the Malaise cut-off, but was significant at the 0.1 per cent level when applying the Kosberg cut-off.

Because the Malaise and Kosberg scores are based on rating scales which are defined fairly objectively, they are less likely to provide values which can be distorted according to the characteristics of the carer, although some carer bias may still occur. However, the care manager's definition of the presence of stress in the carer is arbitrary and the response will depend to some extent on the ability of the care manager to detect lower levels of stress. Characteristics influencing bias introduced by carers and care managers may also include aspects of the user, which were therefore included in the predictor pool.

Examination of the logistic regressions predicting membership of either of the two groups of inconsistent cases suggested the following conclusions. Care managers may be more prone to overlook carer stress when the carer was not living with the user. Care managers may underestimate carer stress when the user has a demanding attitude to help, perhaps because they do not take fully into account the demands the user had placed on the carer. Carers who spent longer in paid employment were more likely to overstate their level of stress, while care managers may assume longer hours spent in caring indicate stress, even when the carer can cope without experiencing it. Female or spouse carers appeared less likely to report their stress symptoms, perhaps as a result of their more stoical attitude. Care managers may be failing to identify the presence of depression or physical health problems in carers or the part these play in increasing stress. Home care managers appeared to be less adept at recognising lower levels of stress in carers. Finally, some of the discrepancies between carers and care managers over the presence of carer stress may result from the time lapse between carer and care manager interviews, during which stress levels may have changed.

Discussion

This discussion of consistency has examined the concordance between older service users, their informal carers and their care managers over a range of functional and health needs of both user and carer, together with formal and informal resource inputs. This range is probably rather broader than in previous studies of consistency. These have been based primarily on more localised populations of older people in the USA (Long et al., 1998). In contrast, ECCEP is based on a stratified sample of 325 community-based elderly in care-managed schemes drawn from ten local authorities in England and Wales, and may be regarded as fairly representative of England and Wales generally.

The first stage in ECCEP analysis of consistency was to measure the extent of agreement between two respondents over the need or resource level being measured. Opportunities were sometimes available for such comparisons to be contrasted with similar ones made in other studies. Regarding ADL and IADL needs, comparisons between the reports of ECCEP users and carers were also made by Long and collegues in their American research. Both studies found agreement for ADL tasks to be better to that for IADL items. Moreover, the agreement in ECCEP was in general at least as good if not better than that found by Long and colleagues.

ECCEP analysis of consistency also examined agreement between users and care managers regarding mental health, for which users were interviewed using standard scales, while care managers gave an overall judgement of the presence of the disorders: cognitive impairment, depression or low morale. Levels of agreement were moderate for cognitive impairment but less good for depression and low morale. The agreement in ECCEP between the user's and care manager's reports of levels of cognitive impairment and depression was compared with that between self-report and interview evaluations found by Segal et al. (1998). Agreement for cognitive impairment in ECCEP was comparable to that found by these authors for their memory dimension, although other aspects of cognitive ability which were tested by them gave poor agreement. The agreement found in ECCEP for depression was much less than for cognitive impairment though overall probably still comparable with that found by Segal and colleagues which varied considerably depending on the scale used.

The agreement found in ECCEP between users and carers over the tasks which carers performed could be compared with that found by Kasten and Tennstedt (1997). Despite the fact that the tasks defined in ECCEP were much narrower, the agreement found was rather better than that found by Kasten and Tennstedt, perhaps reflecting our use of home interviews in preference to telephone interviews.

In the second stage of the analysis, ECCEP work followed Long and colleagues in adopting a multivariate approach to investigating the causes of bias between respondents. Long et al.'s community-based study also drew on a fairly general population of 340 frail elderly users and their carers in North Carolina, so provides a means of comparing results for England and Wales with this particular state. Long et al. restricted their study to comparisons between users and carers over functional capacity and health problems and the only causes of bias which they considered were a range of carer characteristics. ECCEP analysis has both extended this range and also included characteristics of the user and care manager when these were the respondents.

The simplest way of finding possible causes of bias was, for a particular need or resource, to use logistic regression to predict which characteristics might lead to a particular respondent and not the other from identifying the item. This was then repeated for those cases where the respondents who identified and failed to report the item were reversed. From these two dependent variables for each item a bias variable could be computed which took on the value −1 if the first but not the second respondent identified it, 0 if both respondents agreed and 1 if the second but not first respondent identified it. Similar bias variables were computed for IADL items and for physical health items by Long et al. The technique of General Linear Model was then adopted in identifying the characteristics which predicted overall bias for a group of indicators, such as bias in identifying the need for help with the group of four IADL needs. By this means, predictors which had a similar effect on a group of bias indicators could be identified.

ECCEP results of user-carer agreement over IADL needs share some common features with those of Long et al. While we identified a high Kosberg score of carer stress to be associated with these carers overstating need in relation to users, Long et al. found carer burden to have a similar association. Also, while our study showed carers spending more hours per week caring tend to overstate IADL need, Long et al. found a similar effect for ADL tasks though not IADL tasks. Neither study identified depression in the carer as being a significant cause of bias. While Long et al. found hours per week spent in informal caring to increase the tendency of carers to overstate certain problems, ECCEP, as well as replicating this result under certain circumstances, also found that other commitments of the carer, such as time spent in paid employment and having children under eighteen at home were also likely to cause carers to exaggerate need. One carer predictor not considered by Long et al. (the carer's demanding attitude to help) was also found to cause the carer to overstate two individual ADL needs.

Kasten and Tennstedt (1997) used logistic regression analysis to predict inconsistency between user and carer regarding which tasks were performed by the carer. In regard to the circumstances which appeared to cause bias, Kasten and Tennstedt found that carers putting in longer hours of informal care disagreed more with users over the number of areas of informal assistance, which is consistent with findings from ECCEP. Just as cognitive impairment caused users to understate need, it was found both by Kasten and Tennstedt and the present authors to lead to their underestimating carer involvement with certain tasks, although the types of task involved were found to be different in the two studies. However, while the American study found that carers co-residing with users were more likely to agree with them, this was not a significant effect in ECCEP. While Kasten and Tennstedt found that male users were more likely to overlook some of the tasks carried out by their carers, ECCEP results suggest the opposite effect: that female users were more likely to overlook tasks.

In regard to the influence of user characteristics, a study by Kiyak et al. (1994) found that over a period of months, users did not take account of the full extent of their deterioration as specified by their carers in reporting their ADL and IADL performance. This was particularly noticeable for those users suffering from cognitive impairment. The understating of needs by the cognitively impaired was also widespread in our study, though was not apparent for ADL and IADL needs. One explanation is that the strongest bias would be expected for the severely cognitively impaired, and these users were not interviewed about their functional capacity.

Conclusion

This study of consistency has implications for care management practice and community care policy more broadly. It has highlighted the fact that all participants in assessment — the care manager, the user and the carer — can introduce bias into the process depending on their individual characteristics and circumstances. Overall, it was found that certain sources of bias recur across several of the areas of need and resource deployment. While users with a demanding attitude to help are more likely to overstate problems, those with an independent attitude to help are more likely to withhold information. Similarly, while depressed users are more likely to overstate needs or carer tasks performed, cognitively impaired users are less likely to identify problems or resources received. Female users appeared less aware than males of the levels of formal and informal resources which they received. Extra commitments for carers such as having paid employment, spending longer hours in caring, or having children under eighteen at home may lead to their overstating problems and the tasks they perform. Carers who are stressed may tend to exaggerate problems and the tasks they perform. Social workers are more likely than home care managers to identify needs overall.

In the assessment of users and their carers it was found that the care manager is particularly liable to make errors in relation to key areas of need. In these areas the care manager should take particular care to ensure accuracy by building up a relationship of trust with the user, observing the user perform certain tasks, consulting informal carers, liaising with other professionals and agencies, and arranging extra specialised assessments where appropriate. The areas in which errors were most likely to take place — such as in relation to incontinence, depression and cognitive impairment — illustrate the need for multidisciplinary assessment or regular input from health professionals in the assessment and care planning process. This has implications for joint working, a theme we address in greater detail in Chapter 11.

This analysis of consistency also found that care managers may not always have an accurate picture of the levels of resource inputs to their clients, particularly when the worker was not involved in their mobilisation or in the provision of non-SSD inputs. When care managers do not have an accurate knowledge of resource inputs, they appear to overestimate their levels. In order to deploy resources effectively, care managers should be aware of not only resource levels but also the costs of all inputs to the care package, including those from outside the social services department.

The accurate assessment of the needs of the frail elderly in the community is clearly crucial in order to ensure that appropriate packages of care are offered. Evidence relating to differences in view between different respondents in this chapter further supports the need for full involvement of both users and carers in the assessment and care planning process. Because disagreements arise between users and carers in the assessment of need, it is worthwhile for both users and carers to be included in a care manager's assessment, so that any discrepancies immediately become apparent and can be investigated further. In instances where only the carer's judgement can be relied on, it would be helpful for assessors to take into account the circumstances of the carer, such as heavy commitments or undue stress, which might lead to bias.

In an ideal world, the care manager's report could have been regarded as an objective standard against which the responses of user and carer could be compared. However, findings from ECCEP suggest that care managers themselves can introduce bias, and that care managers' judgements can be influenced by their own characteristics. In particular, this analysis of consistency has found that care managers who were social workers were much more effective than home care managers in identifying need. This suggests that social workers should continue to be allocated to cases involving older people with complex needs, while the skills of home care managers are better suited to managing more straightforward cases. Although care managers appeared to make fewer errors in assessing need when they were social workers, some errors still remained. This suggests a need for more appropriate in-service training, particularly in assessment skills with the frail elderly. It is also important that workers have sufficiently low caseloads to allow them to carry out effectively the full range of care management tasks.

Appendix 6.1
Characteristics of Users, Carers and Care Managers, and Consistency

Appendix Table 6.1
The pool of characteristics of elderly person used to test for association with inconsistency

Type of comparison	Users who were not severely cognitively impaired User/ care manager	Users with a principal informal carer who were not severely cognitively impaired User/ carer
Age, mean in years ± SD	80.5 ± 7.3 (Range 65-98)	81.1 ± 7.0 (Range 65-98)
Sex, % female	74.0	69.2
Marital status, % married	22.2	34.5
Living alone, %	66.9	48.3
Has a principal informal carer, %	78.3	100.0
Living with principal informal carer, %	33.5	45.0
Living in sheltered accommodation, %	25.4	21.0
User's income, %		
Up to £60 per week	10.2	12.6
£61 to £100 per week	45.9	42.9
£101 to £175 per week	36.0	38.3
£176 to £275 per week	6.2	5.5
£276 to £325 per week	0.4	0.0
£326 to £450 per week	1.4	0.7
Received income support/housing benefit, %	37.7	36.1
Activities of daily living score, %		
0	48.4	37.6
1	22.9	24.2
2	15.6	18.5
3	5.8	8.9
4	5.3	7.9
5	2.1	3.0
Katzman score at least 11 (moderately cognitively impaired),[1] %	22.4	28.5
Geriatric depression score,[1] mean ± SD	5.73 ± 5.24 (Range 0-15)	6.09 ± 5.35 (Range 0-15)
Elderly person's perception of degree of ill health, %		
Better than other people my age	25.0	25.0
About right for my age	43.0	44.1
Worse than other people of my age	32.0	30.9
Independent attitude to help,[2] %	65.0	69.7
Demanding attitude to help,[2] %	9.1	6.1
Sample size	325	167

1 See Appendix 3.1 for user definition. Cognitive impairment could lead to users providing incorrect information on other matters. For example, the user may report his performance as it was years earlier.
2 An independent attitude may cause users to underestimate difficulties, while a demanding attitude may lead to users exaggerating problems.

Appendix Table 6.2

The pool of characteristics of the principal informal carer used to test for association with inconsistency

Age, mean in years ± SD	60.83 ± 13.94 (Range 19-89)
Sex, % female	73.5
Marital status, % married	80.8
Whether children under 18 living at home, %	12.2
In paid employment, %	37.6
Hours per week worked in paid employment, mean ± SD	13.42 ± 22.29 (Range 0-168)
Hours per week caring for user, mean ± SD	27.24 ± 37.28 (Range 1-168)
Relationship to user	
Spouse, %	29.3
Offspring, %	40.1
Other relative, %	18.3
Non-relative, %	12.3
Whether carer's health affects tasks done, %	27.6
Malaise score of carer stress,[1] mean ± SD	5.47 ± 4.22 (Range 0-19)
Kosberg score of carer stress,[2] mean ± SD	4.32 ± 4.00 (Range 0-15)
Whether carer often feels miserable or depressed,[3] %	23.7
Independent attitude to help,[4] %	56.7
Demanding attitude to help,[4] %	12.4
Sample size	167

Sample: Users with a principal informal carer who were not severely cognitively impaired.

Because the time lag between interviews of users and carers was on average three days, with a standard deviation of only one week, it was assumed that circumstances had not changed between the two interviews.

1 This aspect of stress was based more heavily on psychosomatic symptoms.

2 This aspect of stress was based more heavily on lifestyle problems.

3 This was one item of the Kosberg score which reflected depression.

4 An independent attitude may cause carers to underestimate difficulties, while a demanding attitude could lead to carers exaggerating problems.

Appendix Table 6.3
The pool of characteristics of the care manager used to test for association with inconsistency

Worker is a social worker or equivalent, %	46.4
Worker is a home care manager, %	30.8
Time lag between user and care manager interviews,[1] mean in weeks ± SD	11.12 ± 9.80 (Range -41 to 63)
Sample size	325

Sample: Care managers of users who were not severely cognitively impaired.
1 Because a substantial time interval frequently elapsed between user and care manager interviews, it cannot be assumed that circumstances had not changed. Therefore, when investigating reasons for inconsistency, time lag was included as a predictor, it being assumed that change is more likely the longer the time interval.

Notes

1 The odds ratio for a particular variable entering a logistic regression equation is the factor by which the probability of subgroup membership is increased when the value of that variable is increased by one unit.

2 One issue with the General Linear Model, however, was that it is designed to cope with dependent variables which are continuous, while our dependent bias variables have only three categories. Further requirements of GLM are that the distribution of each dependent bias variable is normal, and that the variance (or spread) of each dependent variable is homogeneous with respect to different combinations of values of the factors which enter each model as predictors. The approach adopted was to test for normality and homogeneity. If these conditions were met, then it was assumed that the dependent variables behaved as though they were continuous. If the conditions were not met, then it was necessary to demonstrate that by removing the dependent variables that violated these assumptions, the model was sufficiently universal for the coefficients and significance levels of predictors to remain substantially unchanged. It would appear that Long et al. (1998) also assumed that three category bias variables approximated to continuous variables in their use of Multivariate Analysis of Variance (MANOVA) to predict the causes of carer bias in detecting problems associated with the groups of IADL and physical health indicators.

3 These independent variables are either factors, which can take on two (or occasionally three) different values, or covariates — variables which can take on a continuous set of values or approximate to this.

4 One type of factor influencing responses of users and carers is their attitudes to help. Information on these attitudes was obtained from the interview of the care manager. In this particular study it was decided to focus on whether users or carers had an independent or demanding attitude to help. This was deduced from the response to the following question:

'Compared with other elderly people in similar circumstances does user tend to ask for more help or less help?'

If the answer was 'more', the user was classed as having a demanding attitude to help, and if 'less' an independent attitude. A similar question was used to judge whether the informal carer had a demanding or independent attitude to help.

5   In this particular model, an increase in any of the four predictors increased the overall probability of positive bias among the set of ADL indicators: that is, the probability that users and not care managers would have identified the need for help. However, in some of the models discussed later, increasing the value of some predictors would decrease this probability. Unfortunately, the results from these models do not indicate in which direction an increase in a particular predictor would affect bias. This direction was determined by separate analysis and mentioned in the text where appropriate.

6   Nevertheless, users who are depressed or ill at ease may underperform on the Katzman scale of cognitive impairment, while users who are cognitively impaired may deny some of the problems included in the measurement of depression or morale. Care managers may not have sufficient training to consistently detect these mental health problems, particularly when they are not substantial. In addition, the level of severity at which a mental health problem is deemed by the care manager to be present was left vague in the interview.

7   The resources considered and threshold levels used were local authority home help (two hours per week), domiciliary nursing visits (one per week), delivered meals (three per week), day care (one day per week), regular GP visits (one per fortnight) and regular chiropody (one appointment per quarter).

Introduction

The contribution of informal carers to the care of older people is widely acknowledged, and has been emphasised in the practice and policy guidance following the passage of the 1995 Carers (Recognition and Services) Act. The Act reinforces the provisions of the 1989 White Paper, which stipulated that service providers should make support for carers a priority, and that the assessment of needs should always take into account those of family, friends and neighbours. As the guidance states, knowledge regarding who provides informal care, what type of tasks are engaged in, and how much time the carer spends assisting the user is an important part of a comprehensive assessment. Chapter 4 outlined the need-related circumstances of principal informal carers. This brief chapter details the type and amount of support these carers provide, outlines assistance offered by other family members and friends, and describes some of the consequences of informal care, from the carer's perspective.

The nature of caring tasks varies according to the functional limitations or cognitive impairment of the user. A significant body of research has illustrated that informal support is also moderated by factors such as place of residence, gender and the relationship between user and carer. These studies have made consistent distinctions between sources of support for domestic and personal care tasks, with help for household activities coming from a wider network of family and friends, while assistance with personal care is in most cases provided by spouses or close female relatives (Wenger, 1992; Parker, 1993; Fisher, 1994; Twigg and Atkin, 1994).

Caring activities

In the ECCEP interviews with principal informal carers, these individuals were asked to indicate what they did to assist the user during the course of a week. Responses were for individual tasks, which were then grouped into eight categories of activity, ranging from medical and toileting assistance to help with administration.

Table 7.1 illustrates the activities that carers were engaged in, by interval need and cognitive impairment/behavioural disorder of the user. The general pattern of assistance is, not surprisingly, related to the needs of the user. Results show that more dependent users are receiving assistance from their carer with a wider range of tasks than more independent older people. It is worth detailing results for each activity in turn, as interesting differences do emerge.

Medical and toileting

Medical and toileting tasks include assisting the user in the bathroom, changing continence pads, catheters and bandages, and giving injections and other treatments. This type of care is required by only a minority of users, and thus only a small group of informal carers (28 per cent overall) perform these tasks. The health, functional ability and mental state of the user all influence which carers help with medical and toileting activities. The proportion of carers performing these tasks rises significantly among those caring for more dependent older people. The majority — 60 per cent — of carers looking after someone with critical interval needs and a cognitive impairment provide this type of assistance, as do just over one-third of those caring for someone with critical interval needs but without a cognitive impairment. Proportions are much lower — fewer than one in five — among all other groups of carers. Not surprisingly, it is those carers who live with the user who are more likely to be providing this help. When co-resident and non-co-resident carers were compared, 46 per cent of those living with the user were assisting with some form of medical or toileting task, while just 15 per cent of carers living separately engage in these activities.

Personal care

Personal care assistance is defined as help with washing or bathing, transferring to the toilet, help with dressing and undressing, assistance in and out of bed, cutting toenails and the laundry of soiled bedding or clothes. Most users requiring assistance with personal care activities are those in the short and critical interval need categories, and those with a cognitive impairment.

Table 7.1
Activities carer does for user, by interval need and cognitive impairment or behavioural disorder of user

Tasks done by carer for user	Critical		Short		Long		Total		Total
	CI/BD %	No CI/BD %	CI/BD %	No CI/BD %	CI/BD %	No CI/BD %	CI/BD %	No CI/BD %	n =
Medical & toileting	59.9	34.8	16.8	15.8	13.5	7.4	41.9	19.5	67
Personal care	85.4	74.6	67.1	36.9	46.0	32.4	74.7	55.1	149
Housework	80.1	82.8	86.3	58.0	46.0	51.1	68.9	64.0	156
Meals	75.9	78.7	52.1	56.2	39.3	38.9	64.2	58.2	144
Shopping	77.3	79.5	73.1	80.5	83.7	79.5	77.3	79.9	187
Company & leisure	97.5	100.0	89.9	98.1	100.0	95.6	96.0	98.0	230
Help with administration	76.6	75.4	73.1	73.0	56.7	53.3	72.6	67.7	165
Other	80.9	69.3	91.6	78.6	63.5	73.8	80.8	74.1	182
Total n =	55	48	23	52	14	45	93	144	237

Missing cases: 1. Sample: All carer interviews.

The carers of these users are thus most likely to be providing this type of help. Indeed, as Table 7.1 illustrates, there is a clear gradient across interval need categories, with the carers of critical interval need users with a cognitive impairment most likely to be providing this assistance (85 per cent).

When the carer's relationship to the user and their place of residence is considered, it is co-resident carers who are more likely to be helping with personal care. Just over 83 per cent of co-resident carers help with these tasks, compared with 48 per cent of carers living separately. Spouse carers are the largest group of carers providing this type of assistance: 85 per cent of spouse carers help with at least one personal care task, compared with 54 per cent of other female and 45 per cent of other male carers. While this is partially explained by the fact that spouse carers are looking after the most dependent users, there are other factors that must be considered. Considerable research in recent years has illustrated that intimate personal assistance, such as help with bathing, is assistance which many older people are reluctant to accept from family members other than their partner or close relative of the same sex (Fisher, 1994; Twigg and Atkin, 1994; Twigg, 1997). If the specific task of helping the user wash or have a bath is extracted from the personal care category, findings illustrate that 42 per cent of spouses provide this assistance, compared with 24 per cent of other female and 16 per cent of other male relatives. When co-residency is also considered, the role of female carers in general increases in importance. While 42 per cent of co-resident spouse carers helped with bathing, 45 per cent of other co-resident female and 26 per cent of other co-resident male carers were providing this assistance. Thus, ECCEP findings support those of other studies, suggesting that both gender, relationship and place of residence are important predictors of which informal carers provide help with personal care.

Housework

Domestic care assistance such as light and heavy housework and laundry is provided by a wider range of informal helpers than those involved in assisting with personal care. This type of help is also required by a higher proportion of users, including those who are otherwise fairly independent. Table 7.1 illustrates that just under two-thirds of carers are helping with housework. While those caring for more dependent users are still more likely to be providing this support, almost half of those looking after long interval need users are also helping with some form of housework. When the relationship between the user and the carer is considered, some gender differences are apparent, as other studies have suggested. Female carers (61 per cent) are more likely than male carers (51 per cent) to help with housework, although co-residency is a more important predictor: 81 per cent of carers living with the user help around the house, compared with 55 per cent of those that live separately.

Meals

Preparing meals for the user is, as Table 7.1 illustrates, a task which is similar to housework in the distribution of carer responses. While the carers of more dependent users were most likely to be preparing meals for the user, this was also a form of assistance provided by a significant proportion — over one-third — of carers of long interval need users. Again, meal preparation was a task engaged in by a higher proportion of co-resident (84 per cent) than non-co-resident carers (43 per cent). Among non-spouse carers, the gender differences found for assistance with housework were not as prevalent with meal preparation: 48 per cent of other male carers said they assisted with meals compared with 51 per cent of other female carers.

Shopping

Like housework and meals, shopping is a task with which most older service users require some assistance, whether merely in the form of transport, or whether the carer does the shopping for the user. However, there are some differences between shopping and domestic task assistance, particularly regarding which carers perform these tasks. As Table 7.1 illustrates, it is the carers of less dependent, long interval need users who are most likely to assist with shopping, rather than those looking after users with more complex needs, although the differences are small. One possible explanation for this pattern of informal support is that formal services received by more dependent users may include home help assistance with shopping as well as personal care tasks, while long interval need users who require assistance with shopping may be ineligible for formal support. An alternative explanation is that, as the majority of principal carers of critical interval need users are spouses who may themselves have mobility or transport problems, other informal supporters could be involved in shopping for these users. Another factor which may contribute to the high proportion of principal carers of long interval need users reporting that they shop for the user is place of residence. Less dependent users have a higher proportion of carers who do not live with them. While it is difficult for carers who live separately to provide the same level of personal and domestic assistance as those living with the user, shopping is a form of assistance which can be provided in the carer's own time and on a more predictable basis. Thus, it is not surprising that a higher proportion of carers who live separately from the user provide assistance with shopping (83 per cent) than those who live with the user (73 per cent).

Company and leisure

This category of activity differs slightly from the other activities engaged in by carers as it is less a form of assistance than a consequence of the relationship between user and carer. Company was defined as 'chatting or watching TV' and leisure as 'taking the user out for pleasure trips'. As Table 7.1 illustrates, carers of cognitively impaired users were slightly less likely than other carers to engage in these activities with the user, which is indicative of the change in relationship between user and carer that may occur as the user's mental state deteriorates. The fact that company and leisure activities primarily reflect the user/carer relationship rather than the functional abilities of the older person is clear, as there are few differences across interval need categories for company and leisure. The vast majority of carers — 97 per cent overall — engage in these activities with the user.

Help with administration and other tasks

As Litwak (1985) has suggested, the management of personal affairs is perhaps the only area of informal support which can be provided by individuals who do not have a close relationship with the user. Despite this, Table 7.1 illustrates that a high proportion (70 per cent overall) of principal informal carers take on this task. There is a relationship between the needs of the user and the carer's involvement in help with finances and benefits, carers of critical and short interval need users, and those with a cognitive impairment, are more likely than the carers of long interval need users to be providing this type of help.

Carers were also asked to list other types of tasks they did for the user. Not surprisingly, this list of other tasks was substantial, including liaising with formal services, keeping an eye on the user, talking through problems and taking the user to appointments. One particularly important task included in this list of 'other' activities was monitoring the medication of the user. Other recent studies have emphasised the crucial role of informal carers in supervising medication, as formal services may find it difficult to provide adequate support on a daily basis. An American study estimated that up to 53 per cent of informal carers of older people may be involved in medication monitoring (Stone et al., 1987) while a recent British study has detailed the implications of medication monitoring on carer strain, and emphasised the need for adequate support and guidance for carers from professionals (Goldstein and Rivers, 1996). Among ECCEP carers, one in three principal carers reported that they help the user with medication, with this proportion rising slightly to 38 per cent among the carers of users with a cognitive impairment. Medication monitoring was much more prevalent among co-resident carers (42 per cent) than carers who live separately (26 per cent).

Hours of assistance

Some types of informal care inputs require a significant time commitment from principal carers, while other types of support can be provided on an infrequent basis. ECCEP carers were asked to detail how many hours per week they spent providing support to the user.

Table 7.2 details the amount of time spent by different carers on tasks for the user. Carers were asked to estimate the number of hours they spent each week on each of the activities listed in the table. Hours for each activity were then combined to arrive at a total number of hours spent each week assisting the user. Some carers found it difficult to estimate the number of hours involved, but 70 per cent of the sample were able to do so, as Table 7.2 illustrates.

The majority of principal carers (56 per cent) are providing six hours or more of direct support to the user each week. Just 14 per cent assist the user for less than an hour per week. It is clear from Table 7.2, however, that the amount of care provided is heavily moderated by place of residence of the carer, and the relationship between the carer and the user. The difference in input between carers who live with the user and those who live separately is striking. Among those who are co-resident, 40 per cent are providing twenty hours or more assistance per week, while just 13 per cent of carers who live separately are providing this amount of help. Among co-resident carers, those reporting the highest number of hours of assistance are female carers other than the spouse of the user, the majority being daughters of the user who are living in the same household. Among these co-resident female carers, 77 per cent provide ten or more hours of help per week, while 57 per cent of spouse carers overall provide a similar level of assistance.

Naturally the hours of informal care provided are also closely associated with the needs of the user. Carers of critical interval need users report the highest number of hours or care per week (an average of 15 hours per week), followed by the carers of short and long interval need users. Carers of older people with a cognitive impairment or behavioural disorder also provide more hours of care per week than the carers of users without these mental health problems.

Carers were also asked how long they had been providing this level of assistance to the user. Responses are illustrated in Table 7.3. Over two-thirds of carers (70 per cent) reported that they had been providing this level of input for over a year. Interestingly, the relationship between duration of caring and the needs of the user was not clear, with the highest proportion of carers of less dependent, long interval need users indicating that they had been caring for a year or more. Carers of users with a cognitive impairment were, however, slightly more likely to indicate a long-standing commitment, suggesting the more gradual onset of the need for assistance as a result of mental health problems.

Table 7.2
Hours per week PIC helps user, by relationship to user and whether lives with user among community-based sample

Hours per week PIC helps, excluding leisure	Spouse/partner		Relationship to user Other female		Other male		Total
	With user %	Not with user %	With user %	Not with user %	With user %	Not with user %	n
Up to 15 mins	4.5	0.0	0.0	4.6	10.6	14.9	9
15 - 59 mins	18.4	29.3	7.5	5.0	10.6	0.0	15
1 hr - 2 hrs 29 mins	9.3	0.0	0.0	14.2	21.2	22.4	20
2 hrs 30 mins - 5 hrs 59 mins	4.7	0.0	14.9	23.2	0.0	40.4	29
6 hrs - 9 hrs 59 mins	7.0	0.0	0.0	26.0	10.6	7.5	27
10 hrs - 19 hrs 59 mins	23.0	0.0	18.0	15.9	10.6	7.5	28
20 hrs and over	32.8	70.7	59.6	11.2	46.9	7.5	39
Total n =	42	3	13	86	9	13	166

Missing cases: 72. Sample: All carer interviews.
Hours per week were obtained by summing up the times spent on seven types of activity: medical and toileting; personal care; housework; meals; shopping; help with administration; other. If one or more of the seven items was missing, then the sum was taken as missing.

Table 7.3
How long PIC has been providing the current level of help, by interval need and cognitive impairment or behavioural disorder of user among community-based sample

	Critical		Short		Long		Total
Length of time PIC has been helping	CI/BD %	No CI/BD %	CI/BD %	No CI/BD %	CI/BD %	No CI/BD %	n
Less than 4 weeks	0.0	0.0	4.0	0.0	0.0.	0.0	1
4 - 12 weeks	3.5	10.2	8.1	13.1	0.0	8.7	19
12 - 52 weeks	21.6	18.4	36.3	16.8	6.7	19.6	48
More than a year	74.8	69.3	51.7	70.0	93.3	69.5	168
Don't know	0.0	2.0	0.0	0.0	0.0	2.2	2
Total n =	55	48	24	52	14	45	238

Interval need

Missing cases: 0. Sample: All carer interviews.

Visits

As the evidence presented has illustrated, carers who live with the user are often those who provide the most intensive informal care inputs, and assist with the widest range of activities. However, carers who live separately from the user also have a significant contribution to make. One method of measuring this contribution is to examine the frequency and nature of visits between the user and the carer.

Carers who live separately were asked how many times per week they saw the user. Responses are illustrated in Table 7.4. Four out of ten carers reported seeing the user every day. The number of visits was, not surprisingly, closely linked to the needs of the user. Thus, 60 per cent of non-co-resident carers of critical interval need users reported seeing the user every day, compared with 37 per cent of those caring for a short interval and 23 per cent of those caring for a long interval need user. Visits were also more frequent overall if the user was cognitively impaired. Just one in ten carers reported that they saw the user once a week or less. This suggests that carers living separately were also providing an important and consistent level of support, one which is responsive to the specific needs of the user.

Carers living separately from the user were also asked if there had been any overnight visits between the user and the carer in the past week. Although the reasons for an overnight visit will vary, the incidence of this type of carer/user contact suggests that the user may have less predictable needs (for toileting or assistance with personal care) which the carer finds difficult to meet in short daytime visits. Not surprisingly, therefore, it was the carers of critical interval need users who reported the highest incidence of overnight visits. One in three carers of critical interval need users reported at least one overnight visit, compared with 15 per cent of non-co-resident carers overall. No carers of long interval need users reported an overnight visit in the week preceding the Time I interview.

Input from other informal carers

Many older people have more than one family member or friend who offers them support. Contributions from other informal carers can benefit not just the older person but often the principal carer as well, alleviating responsibility and providing the carer with a break. Help received from the user's wider support network is, however, moderated not just by the availability of other helpers, but also by factors such as the nature of the user's needs, the relationship between the carer, user and other helpers, and the health and circumstances of these helpers.

ECCEP principal informal carers were asked whether any other relatives or friends provided the user with assistance. Overall, 60 per cent of carers stated

Table 7.4
Number of times carer sees user, by interval need and cognitive impairment or behavioural disorder of user among community-based sample

Number of times carer sees user	Critical		Short		Long		Total
	CI/BD %	No CI/BD %	CI/BD %	No CI/BD %	CI/BD %	No CI/BD %	n
Every day	59.5	59.8	31.6	39.0	37.5	19.2	56
5 - 6 times a week	3.8	8.6	21.6	20.3	0.0	3.0	14
2 - 4 times a week	27.5	21.3	27.8	31.9	50.0	62.8	51
Once a week or less	9.2	4.3	12.6	8.7	12.5	15.0	15
Total n =	26	23	15	34	8	33	137

(Interval need)

Missing cases: 1. Sample: Carers who do not live with the user.

that there were other informal carers. This suggests that 40 per cent of carers are supporting the user on their own, without help from family or friends. Although interval need and cognitive ability were not strong predictors of the presence of other informal supporters, the relationship between the user and the principal carer did seem to affect which users had other carers. While spouse carers and other female carers were equally likely to report that the user received help from others (58 per cent), the proportion was much higher among other male carers (74 per cent). This suggests that male carers who are not the spouse of the user have more support from other sources in carrying out their caring tasks. This finding is similar to that found by Green (1988) in the analysis of the 1985 GHS, which indicated that male carers were more likely to receive support from other friends and family members than female carers (50 per cent compared with 35 per cent).When these carers are the sons of the user, other support is most likely to come from wives, sisters or other female relatives.

Table 7.5 illustrates the sources of additional informal support to users, by their relationship to the user. Like principal carers themselves, the vast majority of other helpers are female relatives. Daughters and sons each make up one-third of these other carers. Daughters-in-law make up 14 per cent of other supporters, many of whom will help their husband, who is the principal carer, provide assistance. Indeed, when the principal carer is a male relative of the user (other than a spouse), the proportion of daughters-in-law providing help rises to just under one-third.

Support does extend beyond the family network, with just under one in four other carers being a friend of the user (24 per cent). Friends are a more common source of support to users whose principal carer does not live with them, although the differences are small.

Principal informal carers were also asked to estimate the amount of time other carers helped the user each week. The amount of help provided is clearly related to the needs of the user, as Table 7.6 shows. Overall, carers other than the principal informal carer are providing a modest level of help, with just under half providing less than three hours assistance per week. One in three of these carers provides between one and two and a half hours of help each week. Just 17 per cent provide more than ten hours assistance.

However, the distributions do change according to the needs of the user. Users who are physically frail or have functional limitations are receiving a higher level of input from other informal carers. One in three of these carers providing assistance to someone with critical interval needs is helping for more than six hours per week, compared with just 15 per cent of those caring for long interval need users. The hours of assistance offered are particularly high if the user is cognitively impaired and has critical interval needs, in which case 50 per cent of other carers are helping for more than six hours per week. Thus, when help is available from a wider circle of family and friends, it

Table 7.5

Other family member and friends caring for the user as well as PIC, by relationship and whether living with user among community-based sample

Who else cares for the user other than PIC	Spouse/partner		Relationship to user Other female		Other male		Total
	With user	Not with user	With user	Not with user	With user	Not with user	n =
	%	%	%	%	%	%	
Spouse/partner	0.0	0.0	9.1	7.5	14.3	24.4	15
Daughter	55.2	63.1	36.4	25.2	14.3	12.2	47
Son	38.6	55.4	0.0	35.4	28.6	26.9	47
Daughter-in-law	10.3	0.0	9.1	13.2	28.6	33.0	21
Son-in-law	5.2	0.0	9.1	20.7	0.0	0.0	16
Brother/brother-in-law	5.2	0.0	0.0	0.0	14.3	6.1	4
Sister/sister-in-law	2.6	0.0	18.2	9.6	14.3	18.3	13
Grandchildren	12.9	0.0	9.1	17.9	28.6	20.8	23
Other relations	5.2	18.5	27.3	10.5	14.3	18.3	17
Friend	24.2	36.9	18.2	20.9	28.6	30.5	34
Total n =	38	5	11	65	7	16	142

Missing cases: 0. Sample: Carers whose user is helped by other family members and friends.

Table 7.6

How many hours do other helpers work per week, by interval need and cognitive impairment or behavioural disorder of user among community-based sample

| How many hours a week do other people help? | Interval need | | | | | | Total |
| | Critical | | Short | | Long | | |
	CI/BD %	No CI/BD %	CI/BD %	No CI/BD %	CI/BD %	No CI/BD %	n
Up to 1 hour	10.8	19.2	0.0	16.3	12.5	3.9	16
1 hr - 2 hrs 29 mins	18.7	35.0	46.6	27.7	50.0	36.0	46
2 hrs 30 mins - 5 hrs 59 mins	10.5	11.4	25.3	16.0	25.0	19.7	23
6 hrs - 9 hrs 59 mins	12.3	7.6	6.3	10.7	0.0	11.8	14
10 hrs - 19 hrs 59 mins	17.9	3.8	0.0	10.7	0.0	7.9	12
20 hrs and over	19.7	3.8	6.3	8.0	0.0	0.0	11
Total n =	32	26	15	36	8	25	122

Missing cases: 20. Sample: Carers whose user is helped by other family members and friends.

follows a similar pattern to help from the principal carer: the more complex the needs of the user, the more hours of informal care are provided.

Assistance provided by a wider network of family and friends is not always intended to benefit the user. In many cases, it is the carer who is being supported. In some instances other helpers will replace inputs from a principal carer, in order to provide him or her with a break. In other instances, other helpers will assist with a task that the principal carer finds difficult to do, either due to health problems or problems of access (such as lack of transport). In some cases, however, it is the carer him or herself who requires help with specific tasks due to functional limitations.

Principal carers were also asked whether they viewed other help as being intended for them, or for the user. Only a minority of carers — 14 per cent of those who reported that other helpers were involved — said that any of the help was provided specifically for them. Among those who acknowledged that they were receiving assistance, the majority indicated that it was shared equally with the user: 50/50. Almost all (90 per cent) of the principal carers who reported that they shared the help given to the user by other carers were spouses of the user. These principal carers are older people themselves, and thus more likely to have health problems or difficulties with some tasks, and require assistance.[1]

Other research has indicated that principal carers can be reluctant to let friends and family members provide assistance. In some cases, particularly when the carer is a spouse, this intention may be to protect the dignity of the user, by hiding the degree of his or her impairment from others (Tennstedt et al., 1989; Parker, 1993). In other cases, conflict between the principal carers and other family members may result in a reluctance to accept assistance. Alternatively, the principal informal carer may find over time that his or her social networks have been reduced by years of caring, resulting in an erosion of relationships with those who may have been able to provide assistance (Twigg and Atkin, 1994).

ECCEP carers who reported that other helpers were involved were asked if they thought the assistance provided by these individuals was adequate. In their opinion, should these friends or family members be providing more help? The vast majority of principal carers (84 per cent) reported that the other carers should not be doing any more to help the user, that their contribution was sufficient. Just 5 per cent of principal carers thought that other carers could be doing considerably more, while one in ten felt they could be doing some more. This proportion of carers who thought others could be doing some more to help rose slightly among cases with a cognitively impaired user, particularly if they had long interval needs. Although the differences are small, this may reflect the difficulties experienced by principal carers in looking after a user with mental health problems, particularly when that user is mobile, in which case aggressive behaviour or wandering could make it difficult for the principal carer to cope alone.

Caregiving and financial contributions

Caregiving can include an element of financial support. Many of the tasks which carers do for their older relative or friend involve some expense, such as providing transport, doing the shopping, helping with repairs or even just taking the user out for pleasure trips. Particularly in cases where the user is becoming cognitively impaired, the carer may find themselves paying bills or covering other expenses if the user is unable to manage his/her own finances.

Carers who do not live with the user were asked if they personally paid for any of the user's expenses. Findings are illustrated in Table 7.7. Non-co-resident carers were asked this question as the household expenses of carers who live with the user are difficult to separate, particularly when such a high proportion of co-resident carers are spouses. Among non-co-resident carers, one in four (24 per cent) reported that they paid some of the user's expenses. The most common contributions were towards household and personal goods such as groceries and toiletries. This suggests that some carers who are assisting the user with shopping may also be paying for the goods purchased. Paying bills on behalf of the user, such as for heating and lighting, was something that 13 per cent of non-co-resident carers reported that they did, while contributions towards other expenses were reported by 6 per cent of these carers overall. Across all three categories of living expenses, it is primarily the carers of more dependent users who are making a financial contribution. This is particularly the case for the carers of short and critical interval need users with a cognitive impairment.

Very few of these carers who live separately and contribute to the user's living expenses were able to specify how much they paid per month. Among those who were able to estimate a figure, the level of contribution was fairly low, with the majority indicating that they contributed between £8 and £16 per month (1995 prices).

Reciprocity is an important component of many caregiving relationships. Interaction between the carer and the older person can involve an exchange — either in the form of the carer providing help to a parent who once cared for them, or in the form of more immediate reciprocity. Some older people give their carer gifts or money in order to thank them for the support provided. ECCEP principal carers were asked if this type of exchange took place. Table 7.8 illustrates responses.

The vast majority of principal carers — 80 per cent — indicated that they receive neither money nor gifts from the user. Among the one in five users who did report receiving these presents, a slightly higher proportion received money (11 per cent) rather than gifts (9 per cent). Which carers receive these items is affected by the relationship between the user and the carer, rather than the needs of the user (although, not surprisingly, the carers of cognitively impaired users were slightly less likely than other carers to receive money or gifts). As Table 7.8 shows, very few spouse carers receive these presents from the user. Other female and other male carers are more likely to be given money or gifts by the user. Interestingly, almost all other male carers are receiving money in return for the help they provide, rather than gifts. The opposite is true for other female carers, a slightly higher proportion of whom are receiving gifts, rather than money.

Carers receiving money from the user were asked how often this occurred and what amount was involved. Responses were varied, but the most common response was payment on weekly basis, usually amounting to less than £20. Carers receiving gifts reported that these were given less frequently, on a monthly basis or less, with a similar value of £20 or below.

Consequences of informal inputs

The emotional, physical and financial costs of caring have been well documented (Qureshi and Walker, 1989; Twigg and Atkin, 1994; Healy and Yarrow, 1997). The act of caring can affect health, restrict opportunities and have adverse effects on family relationships. While specific outcomes for carers over time will be discussed in Chapter 10, it is worth mentioning here some of the problems which carers reported that they were experiencing at the time of the first ECCEP interview.

Some carers experience difficulty in helping the user with specific activities. Helping with personal care, for instance, can be difficult. If the carer is a spouse, assisting with personal care may interfere with normal marital roles. Alternatively, tasks which require a role reversal — such as cooking and housework for some male carers — may prove challenging. ECCEP carers were asked which tasks, if any, they found difficult to perform. Table 7.9 illustrates responses.

The majority of carers — two-thirds — reported that they had no difficulty with the tasks they performed for the user. The remaining one-third of carers did, however, report a problem. Not surprisingly, the tasks which the largest proportion of carers found difficult were personal care (15 per cent) and medical or toileting assistance (13 per cent). It was the carers of frailer users who reported a difficulty with these tasks in greater numbers than other carers. This is not surprising, as this type of assistance is required primarily by users in the short and critical interval need category, particularly when the user is both frail and has a cognitive impairment. Other tasks which carers said they disliked or had difficulty doing were activities in the 'other' category such as monitoring medication or taking the user to appointments (5 per cent of carers) and housework, which 4 per cent of carers described as difficult.

Overall, however, carers were comfortable with the various activities they did for the user. Only those tasks related to health — personal care, help with toileting, and medical assistance such as changing catheters and bandages — were described as difficult by a significant number of carers. This may relate to

Table 7.7

Which if any of the following items does carer personally pay for, by interval need and cognitive impairment or behavioural disorder of user among community-based sample

Living expenses carer pays for	Critical CI/BD %	Critical No CI/BD %	Interval need Short CI/BD %	Interval need Short No CI/BD %	Long CI/BD %	Long No CI/BD %	Total n =
Household and personal goods	82.1	50.0	100.0	75.0	0.0	16.7	26
Heating and lighting	53.7	50.0	45.3	50.0	0.0	16.7	18
Other	17.9	37.5	0.0	0.0	0.0	16.7	6
Total n =	13	8	4	8	2	6	41

Sample: Carers who do not live with the user (n=134) and who incur extra expenditure on user (n=41).

the fact that these activities not only get in the way of normal relationships between relatives and friends, but also involve a certain level of skill and knowledge. When carers were asked if they had received training of any kind from health or social care staff, just 7 per cent overall reported that they had been instructed in how to help the user. It may be that training (particularly relating to tasks such as lifting, and administering treatments) would alleviate the difficulty experienced by some carers, particularly those caring for more dependent users.

ECCEP carers were also asked if caring had created any problems in their lives, or in the lives of users. As Table 7.11 shows, the single largest group of carers — 52 per cent — said that caring had not caused any problems, just under half reported that there had been difficulties. For one in five carers — 18 per cent — it was the user who had been affected. These users may have been reluctant to accept assistance, or found it difficult to be assisted by the individual who had taken on the role of carer. For a larger proportion of respondents (38 per cent), however, assuming the role of carer had caused problems for the carer him or herself, rather than the user. Problems for the carer were particularly prevalent among those caring for more dependent users. Indeed, almost two-thirds (65 per cent) of those caring for someone with critical interval needs and a cognitive impairment reported that they had experienced problems as carers.

The carers who indicated that their role had caused them problems (38 per cent overall) were asked to state what they perceived as the consequences of caring. This was a multiple response question; the breakdown of responses is shown in Table 7.11. The most common response, mentioned by more than half of these carers (52 per cent) was that one of the consequences of caring was stress. Chapter 4 described the results from two standardised measures of carer stress, the Kosberg and Rutter scales. As scores from these scales illustrated, carers of more dependent users, particularly those with a cognitive impairment, are experiencing higher levels of strain. This is also reflected here in self-perceptions of stress. As Table 7.11 shows, carers of cognitively impaired users across all three interval need categories were more likely to report that stress was a consequence of caring. Indeed, 81 per cent of these carers looking after a user with short interval needs and a cognitive impairment stated that stress was a problem for them.

Among carers for whom caring had negative consequences, a similar proportion (51 per cent) reported that they had reduced leisure time as a result of looking after the user. On a related point, almost one in three of these carers (27 per cent) said that not having enough time for family and/or friends was also a problem. The physical effort of caring was identified as a problem by 42 per cent of respondents. This was particularly problematic for the carers of short and critical interval need users, many of whom may be providing assistance with basic activities of daily living. Other physical consequences for the carer were a lack of sleep due to worry (29 per cent) or due to having to

Table 7.8

Does carer frequently receive anything (money or gifts) from user for the help carer gives, by relationship to user and whether lives with user among community-based sample

Items received	Relationship to user						Total
	Spouse/partner		Other female		Other male		
	With user	Not with user	With user	Not with user	With user	Not with user	
	%	%	%	%	%	%	n
Money	1.5	0.0	11.8	13.3	21.1	30.9	26
Gifts	6.1	0.0	19.7	12.2	8.8	0.0	22
Nothing	92.4	100.0	72.5	76.4	70.1	69.1	184
Total n =	64	8	25	103	11	19	229

Missing cases: 9. Sample: All carers.

Table 7.9

What things does carer not like doing or has difficulty doing, by interval need and cognitive impairment or behavioural disorder of user among community-based sample

Things carer does not like doing or has difficulty doing	Critical		Interval need Short		Long		Total
	CI/BD %	No CI/BD %	CI/BD %	No CI/BD %	CI/BD %	No CI/BD %	n =
Medical/toileting	24.5	6.1	20.1	11.2	9.5	7.4	32
Personal care	27.3	11.1	16.1	18.7	9.5	4.4	37
Housework	7.1	2.0	4.0	3.7	0.0	4.4	10
Meals	4.3	0.0	0.0	5.6	0.0	0.0	5
Shopping	3.5	2.0	0.0	0.0	6.7	2.2	5
Company and leisure	1.8	2.0	4.0	1.9	0.0	0.0	4
Administration	1.8	0.0	0.0	0.0	0.0	2.2	2
Other	12.1	0.0	4.0	5.6	0.0	6.5	13
Don't know	0.0	0.0	5.7	1.9	0.0	0.0	2
No difficulty/dislike	46.1	78.7	58.1	66.3	83.7	79.5	159
Total n =	55	48	24	52	14	45	238

Missing cases: 0. Sample: All carers.

attend to the user (24 per cent). Again, the carers of more dependent users were more likely to report that lack of sleep was one of the consequences of caring.

Financial consequences were mentioned by only a small proportion of carers overall. Just 11 per cent of carers who reported problems with caring said that the financial cost was one of the consequences, although this proportion rose to 29 per cent among the carers of short interval need users with a cognitive impairment. In addition, just 9 per cent of these carers said that lost earnings from work were a problem, while 7 per cent reported that the loss of a job or limitations on future work were a concern. These proportions must be interpreted with caution, however, due to the prevalence of carers over retirement age in the sample. For older carers, lost earnings or job opportunities may not be as important as other problems caused by caring.

A more detailed analysis of some of the other consequences of caring will be offered in Chapter 10. We now turn our attention to the formal services which combine with informal inputs to form the overall level of support available to the older people taking part in ECCEP. These formal services are obtained from both the statutory and independent sectors, and are in many instances deployed to support or maintain the carer was well as the user. These services, and their associated costs, are described in the next chapter.

Note

1   Carers were also asked if they regularly received any *formal* services in their own right. Just sixteen carers (7 per cent of the community-based sample) reported that they did. Twelve received home helps, four received nursing visits in their own right and an additional three were visited by a voluntary worker. Half of these carers were the spouse of a user, four were other female carers and just two were other male carers.

Table 7.10
Whether the help user receives from carer causes problems, by interval need and cognitive impairment or behavioural disorder of user among community-based sample

Whether problems caused by caring	Critical		Short		Long		Total
	CI/BD %	No CI/BD %	CI/BD %	No CI/BD %	CI/BD %	No CI/BD %	n =
Yes, causes user problems	22.7	17.2	16.1	24.3	23.0	6.5	44
Yes, causes carer problems	64.9	35.7	41.9	22.5	29.8	24.9	90
No problems caused	22.0	55.3	46.0	62.6	70.2	70.7	124
Don't know	1.8	0.0	0.0	0.0	0.0	0.0	1
Total n =	55	48	24	52	14	45	238

(The "Critical", "Short", "Long" headers fall under the span *Interval need*.)

Missing cases: 0. Sample: All carers.

Table 7.11

In what way the help PIC gives causes problems to PIC, by interval need and cognitive impairment or behavioural disorder of user among community-based sample

	Critical		Short		Long		Total
Types of problems	CI/BD %	No CI/BD %	CI/BD %	No CI/BD %	CI/BD %	No CI/BD %	n =
Not enough time for family	31.7	11.5	42.4	41.7	0.0	17.5	24
Reduced leisure time	50.3	34.5	80.8	66.7	45.3	38.7	46
Not enough time for friends	31.7	25.3	28.8	25.0	32.0	8.8	24
Lost earnings from work	6.6	11.5	9.6	8.3	22.7	8.8	8
Loss of job/limitations on future work	14.3	5.7	0.0	0.0	0.0	0.0	6
Physical effort of caring	46.9	51.7	19.2	58.3	22.7	26.3	38
Strain on relationship with user	35.6	17.2	38.4	16.7	32.0	29.9	26
Embarrassment	13.1	0.0	9.6	0.0	0.0	0.0	6
Stress	55.8	28.7	80.8	66.7	54.7	29.9	47
Loss of sleep due to attending user	30.6	34.5	28.8	0.0	32.0	8.8	22
Loss of sleep due to worry	34.5	11.5	28.8	41.7	32.0	17.5	25
Financial cost	9.3	11.5	28.8	16.7	0.0	0.0	10
Carer unable to help other dependent	6.6	5.7	9.6	16.7	0.0	0.0	6
Other	0.0	23.0	0.0	0.0	22.7	8.8	6
Total n =	36	17	10	12	4	11	90

Missing cases: 0. Sample: All carers whose help causes them problems.

8   Formal and Independent Sector Inputs

Introduction

In addition to any support provided by informal sources, the older people who took part in ECCEP were also receiving formal services. One of the central aims of the study was to determine which users were receiving which services, in what amounts and in what combinations. Services came from three main types of provider: the social services department (SSD), the health service (NHS) and the independent sector, which included both private and voluntary organisations. This chapter describes in detail which services ECCEP users were receiving in 1995 and examines the relationship between need-related circumstances and service receipt. The mixed economy of care and the role of different providers are then discussed, followed by a description of the average weekly cost of individual services and care packages. Finally, evidence relating to service charges across ECCEP authorities is presented.

Use of resources

Despite the growth of the mixed economy, local authority social services departments remain the principal provider of social care services. ECCEP users receive a wide variety of SSD services. Table 8.1 illustrates the proportion of users receiving each type of service provided and financed by the SSD, and describes the average level of consumption.

As many other studies have shown, the home help service is the foundation upon which most care packages are built (Dexter and Harbert, 1983; Davies et al., 1990; Challis et al., 1995). It is the most widely received service, with 70 per cent of ECCEP users having a SSD home help in 1995. The average amount of service per week was just over six hours.

Evidence presented in Chapter 1 illustrated that the average number of home help hours per client has increased in recent years, while the number of clients (in relation to the proportion of people aged 65 and over) has decreased across England and Wales. In other words, the service has become more intensive, providing a higher level of help to fewer users. This change in service intensity is evident when we compare ECCEP findings with those of the Domiciliary Care Project (DCP). In DCP, the mean number of hours of home help for the *most* dependent users — those in the critical interval need category, with no principal informal carer — was just five hours per week. The fact that the mean level for ECCEP users *overall* is now higher — at over six hours per week — indicates just how the allocation of home help hours has changed in the past decade.[1]

As Table 8.1 shows, meals on wheels was received by 28 per cent of ECCEP users, with an average consumption of four meals per week. One in four ECCEP users were attending a day centre, on average just under twice a week. Occupational therapy services were received by one in five users, on average once every two months. ECCEP findings relating to day care and meals on

Table 8.1
Usage of SSD resources[1] around time of first care manager interview

Type of resource	Whether received		Mean consumption for those receiving			
	%	Missing cases	Units per week		Valid cases	Missing cases
Home care	70.3	3	6.20	hours	281	15
Sitting services	5.2	7	14.18	hours	21	1
Laundry services	3.0[2]	16	1.00	times	9	3
Delivered meals	28.1	9	4.38	meals	111	6
Occupational therapy[3]	20.2	31	0.14	visits	55	25
Technical input for sensory impairment	3.3	31	0.11	visits	7	6
Day care	24.4	10	1.76	days	101	0
Respite care[4]	17.8	5	0.80	days	72	3

Number of cases: 425. Source: Care manager interview.
1 Only resources provided and financed by the SSD are included.
2 Of twelve cases receiving an SSD laundry service, five services would launder articles soiled by urine or faeces, three would not, and it was not known whether the other four would or not.
3 Occupational therapy includes related technical input.
4 For respite care, units per week was calculated by dividing the total number of days of respite care by the number of weeks between referral and the care manager interview.

wheels are compared with findings from DCP in the next section of this chapter, relating to resources and needs.

Respite care was received by 18 per cent of users, with an average consumption of 0.8 days per week. This would be the equivalent of a one week stay in respite every nine weeks. The proportion of users receiving respite services is much higher than the proportion receiving respite in DCP. Just 5 per cent of users had short stays in residential care in the mid-1980s so the proportion has more than tripled in the ten intervening years. Other SSD resources received by ECCEP users were social work visits by someone other than the care manager (7 per cent of users), sitting services (5 per cent of users), technical input for sensory impairment (3 per cent) and laundry services (also 3 per cent of users). Although sitting services were received by a small group of users, the importance of overnight stays is evident, as the mean consumption per week totals fourteen hours.

Table 8.2 describes the usage of NHS services by ECCEP users. While the list is representative of the main health services used by older people, it is important to note the number of missing cases in the table before drawing any conclusions about generalisability. Care managers were unable to provide comprehensive information regarding health service usage in some cases, and there were also gaps in the accounts provided by users and carers, particularly in cases where the user was cognitively impaired. The limitations of ECCEP health data, and the retrospective Health Research Module undertaken to obtain more detailed information, have been described in Chapter 2. It is also important to note that the data relating to health service usage in this chapter refer to ongoing and regular contacts only, which may underestimate the actual usage of some services, particularly general practitioners, physiotherapy, speech therapy and chiropody. These services are used by many older people in the community from time to time, when required, rather than regularly. This type of usage is not captured in the ECCEP data presented here, something which should be considered when interpreting findings.

As Table 8.2 illustrates, nursing visits were the most commonly received NHS service among ECCEP users, with over a third visited by a nurse on average once a week. Other primary care services received included regular visits by or to a GP (15 per cent), regular chiropody appointments (14 per cent) and community physiotherapy (7 per cent).

The most commonly used hospital-based service was short-stay care, received by 17 per cent of ECCEP users. The average service receipt was similar to that of local authority respite care: a one-week stay every nine weeks. This type of care is often provided to more dependent service users with ongoing health needs who cannot be adequately treated as outpatients. Only 5 per cent of users had occupied designated NHS respite care beds.

As a proportion of the ECCEP sample were referred to a care manager prior to discharge from hospital, it is not surprising that some users were attending ongoing outpatient clinic (13 per cent) and day hospital (5 per cent)

Table 8.2

Usage of NHS resources around the time of first care manager interview

Type of resource	Whether received		Mean consumption for those receiving			
	%	Missing cases	Units per week		Valid cases	Missing cases
Nursing visits	38.5	22	1.06	visits	119	44
GP visits, regular and ongoing contacts	14.9	24	0.77	visits	38	25
Physiotherapy, regular and ongoing contacts	6.6	35	1.26	visits	18	10
Speech therapy, regular and ongoing	0.5	23	0.25	visits	1	1
Chiropody, regular and ongoing contacts	14.2	97	0.21	visits	37	23
Day hospital	5.3	13	1.50	attendances	20	3
Outpatient clinic	13.4	49	0.43	visits	38	18
Short stays in hospital	17.4	14	0.88	days	53	21
Hospice	1.1	31	0.23	days	2	3
NHS day care	2.4	287	2.30	attendances	10	0
NHS OT	7.9	31	0.22	contacts	24	9
NHS technical staff for sensory impairment	0.7	31	0.65	contacts	3	0
NHS respite care	4.6	19	0.97	days	16	3
NHS laundry	0.5	16	1.00	times	1	1

Total cases: 425. Source: Care manager interview. Service usage here refers to regular and ongoing contacts only.

appointments. When averaging over all users, outpatient visits took place once every four months. For those attending day hospital, mean attendance was one and a half days per week. Other services, such as speech therapy, NHS laundry services and NHS day care, were received by fewer than 5 per cent of users overall.

Independent sector services account for an increasing proportion of social care provision. While most of the expansion to date has been in the residential and nursing home sector, a more diverse range of community-based services are also becoming available. Despite these changes, however, independent sector services made up only a small proportion of care packages in 1995. Table 8.3 shows the services most commonly received from private and voluntary providers.

Table 8.3
Usage of independent sector resources around time of first care manager interview

Type of resource	Whether received		Mean consumption for those receiving			
	%	Missing cases	Units per week		Valid cases	Missing cases
Home care[1]	19.2	26	4.80	hours	55	0
Voluntary organisations[2]	7.4	14	0.94	visits	25	5
Volunteer[3]	9.1	37	1.40	visits	28	0
Warden of sheltered housing/ neighbourhood scheme[4]	12.0	11	-		-	-

Total cases: 425. Source: Care manager interview. Resources were included in this table only if received by at least 7 per cent of users.
1 Independent sector home care was provided by voluntary organisations, private organisations and private individuals formally arranged and paid for.
2 The main voluntary organisations involved were Age Concern (2.4 per cent of users) and the Crossroads Care Attendant Scheme (2.1 per cent of users).
3 Volunteers were from places of worship and community groups. The main source of volunteers was from places of worship. These visited 8.6 per cent of all users.
4 With regard to independent sector wardens, 9.5 per cent of all users had a housing association warden; the remaining 2.5 per cent had a warden from a private organisation.

Private home care was received by just under one in five users (19.2 per cent), with users receiving an average level of service of almost five hours per week. Support from wardens for those living in sheltered housing was received by 12 per cent of users overall. For 9.5 per cent of these users, the warden was an employee of a housing association, while in 2.5 per cent of cases, he or she was the employee of a private provider of sheltered housing. The only other independent sector services received by a significant number of users were visits from voluntary organisations or from other volunteers. In 9 per cent of cases, users were receiving visits from church or community group volunteers. In 7 per cent of cases, the visitors were from two main voluntary organisations: Age Concern and Crossroads.

Resources and needs

The proportion of users receiving specific services from the SSD, NHS and the independent sector varies. For most services, there are clear relationships between the level or frequency of service provided and the needs of the user.

Table 8.4

Usage of social care resources[1] around time of first care manager interview, by interval need and social support

	Critical		Short		Long		Total		Missing
	No PIC	PIC	No PIC	PIC	No PIC	PIC	No PIC	PIC	n =
Home care hours/week	9.24	7.80	6.65	4.79	3.75	4.09	5.82	5.72	20
Sitting service hours/week	3.02	2.68	0.00	0.30	0.03	2.99	0.80	2.12	11
Laundry service times/week	0.05	0.03	0.00	0.06	0.02	0.05	0.03	0.47	25
Delivered meals per week	2.16	1.22	2.84	1.28	1.12	1.25	1.78	1.24	18
Occupational therapy[2] visits/week	0.05	0.03	0.02	0.03	0.00	0.04	0.02	0.03	58
Technical input for sensory impairment visits/year	0.55	0.06	0.00	1.20	0.03	0.17	0.15	0.42	33
Day care days/week	0.34	0.96	0.32	0.69	0.12	0.47	0.22	0.72	5
Respite care[3] days/week	0.25	0.44	0.15	0.29	0.09	0.24	0.15	0.33	19

Number of cases: 425. Source: Care manager interview.

1 Although the SSD is one of the important providers of these resources, all other sources of these services are also included in the data presented in this table. By this means, the way in which the total quantity of each resource is distributed between different need groups is demonstrated.

2 Occupational therapy includes related technical input.

3 For respite care, units per week was calculated by dividing the total number of days of respite care by the number of weeks between referral and the care manager interview.

Social care

Table 8.4 illustrates the average level of social care service received by users, by interval need and social support.

What is immediately apparent in Table 8.4 is the intensity of service received by critical interval need users when compared with those in other need categories. With the exception of meals on wheels, all services are received more frequently by those with critical interval needs. Differences are most striking for home care, with 9.25 hours per week of service being received on average by critical interval need users without a carer, compared with 3.75 hours per week for those with long interval needs and no carer.

The level of service also differs slightly when the user is cognitively impaired or has a behavioural disorder. Although not shown here, these users are also receiving a more frequent service in relation to home care (7.42 hours per week compared with 5), day care, respite care and other social work visits.

When the presence or absence of a principal informal carer is considered, the picture is more mixed. As Table 8.4 shows, users who do *not* have a carer are receiving home care and meals on wheels slightly more frequently than those with a carer. This suggests a service response to need, as cooking and other domestic tasks are forms of help which carers often provide. Other service levels are also clearly responding to the needs of the carer as well as the user. Sitting services is the most obvious. While the average level of service receipt is less than one hour a week for users without a carer, this rises to just over two hours a week for users with a carer. Other services which may be providing a break for carers are day care (0.2 days per week for those without a carer, 0.7 days for those with a carer) and respite care, for which the level of service receipt doubles for users with a carer, compared to those without this informal support.

The distribution of social care resources is also related to the frequency and predictability of user needs. Older people with more complex needs may require services frequently, and at times which are not always easy for statutory services to accommodate. While this point will be dealt with specifically in relation to private home care providers later in this chapter, it is worth demonstrating the breakdown in home help provision across all sectors by the timing of provision. Table 8.5 illustrates mean hours of home care at different times of the week.

The relationship of user needs to provision out of normal office hours is clearly illustrated in Table 8.5. Users in the critical interval need category are not only receiving more home help hours on average: they are also more likely to be receiving these hours of help in the evening or at weekends. Whereas just over one quarter (29 per cent) of the home help hours received by long interval need users fall in the evening or at weekends, this proportion rises to 43 per cent among critical interval need users. Meeting the needs of these users

Table 8.5
Mean hours per week home care[1] received during office hours, evenings and weekends, by interval need

Period	Critical	Short	Long	Total
	%	%	%	n =
Weekdays before 5 p.m.	4.5	3.5	2.8	3.6
Weekdays after 5 p.m.	1.4	0.6	0.5	0.8
Weekends	2.0	1.1	0.7	1.3
Whole week	7.9	5.1	4.1	5.7
Valid n =	146	105	147	398

Missing cases: 27. Source: Time I care manager interview.
1 All sources of home care included: (a) social services department; (b) voluntary organisation; (c) private organisation; (d) private individual formally arranged and paid for but excluding informal carers.

clearly requires a level of service flexibility which providers are attempting to attain.

In relation to overall receipt of social care services, comparisons with the Domiciliary Care Project demonstrate some clear changes between the mid-1980s and mid-1990s. Service levels which can be easily compared relate to home help, meals on wheels and day care. It is important to point out that ECCEP users are, as a group, more dependent than those involved in DCP (Davies et al., 1997b). With that in mind, one assumption would be that the level of service received by users would thus be more intensive. This is the case for only one of the services: home help. The striking increase in home help hours per client, particularly for the most dependent users, has already been mentioned. To provide another example: whereas in DCP the mean number of home help hours provided to a user with no principal informal carer and short interval needs was four per week, the service level for a user with equivalent needs in ECCEP was almost seven hours per week.

In relation to day care and meals on wheels, however, the picture is one of reduction in service levels between DCP and ECCEP. In relation to meals, DCP found that long interval need users without a carer were receiving three meals per week on average. In ECCEP, these long interval need users were receiving just over one meal per week. Among users in the critical interval need category without a carer, the DCP mean was just under four meals per week, whereas the ECCEP mean was just over two meals per week. The receipt of meals on wheels appears to have declined across all interval need categories. A similar pattern is evident for day care. One additional difference in relation to this service, however, is that the ECCEP distribution appears more closely related to the user's circumstances than the DCP distribution. In DCP the mean attendance of approximately one visit per week did not vary significantly across interval need categories, and the relationship to presence/absence of a carer was not clear. In ECCEP, however, users with a carer are receiving a higher level of day care than users without carers across all interval need categories, suggesting that supporting the carer may be a clearer aim of care packages in the 1990s than in the pre-reform period.

Health care

Table 8.6 illustrates the distribution of NHS resources received regularly by ECCEP users. As would be expected with social care services, there is a relationship between interval need and the receipt of most health care resources.

As Table 8.6 shows, nursing visits, physiotherapy and day hospital services are all received more frequently by critical interval need users. In relation to nursing visits, for example, the average level of service across all critical interval need users with a carer was 0.86 visits per week (the equivalent of one visit every eight or nine days) compared with 0.27 visits per week (the equivalent of just over one visit per month) for long interval need users with a carer.

The services which do not demonstrate a close relationship with interval need are chiropody, outpatient visits, GP visits and short stays in hospital. Chiropody is a service which many older people use, usually on an infrequent basis. The need for chiropody among those already using the service would not be expected to change significantly with a decline in health or functional ability. Outpatient clinics are an important service for older people with health problems, as they can provide access to geriatricians and other specialist services.

One factor which does relate to the usage of outpatient clinics and indeed to short stays in hospital is the presence or absence of a principal carer. Attendance at outpatient clinics averages 0.03 visits per week for those with a carer, compared to 0.12 visits for those without a carer. It may be that without the supervision of a carer (who may provide assistance with tasks such as medication monitoring and following dietary or exercise regimes) the need for a follow-up outpatient visit is greater. When short stays in hospital are considered, the pattern is reversed. Those with a carer are receiving this service on a more frequent basis overall (0.13 days per week) than those without a carer (0.08 days). Short hospital stays may be providing carers with a break from looking after someone with difficult-to-manage health needs. Short stays were also more frequently received by users with a cognitive impairment (0.16 days per week on average) compared with other users (0.07 days per week). Nursing visits are the only other health resource for which a

Table 8.6
Usage of health care resources around the time of first care manager interview, by interval need and social support

	Critical		Short		Long		Total		Missing
	No PIC	PIC	No PIC	PIC	No PIC	PIC	No PIC	PIC	n =
Nursing visits/week[1]	0.86	0.84	0.41	0.77	0.27	0.32	0.53	0.54	64
GP visits/week	0.06	0.06	0.05	0.05	0.11	0.05	0.08	0.05	50
Physiotherapy visits/week	0.11	0.00	0.07	0.06	0.03	0.01	0.07	0.02	45
Chiropody visits/week	0.03	0.03	0.01	0.06	0.02	0.03	0.02	0.04	120
Day hospital attendances/week	0.12	0.15	0.06	0.11	0.03	0.05	0.07	0.09	15
Outpatients clinics visits/week	0.02	0.00	0.03	0.19	0.05	0.14	0.03	0.12	67
Short stays in hospital days/week	0.13	0.11	0.18	0.15	0.09	0.03	0.13	0.08	35

Number of cases: 425. Source: Care manager interview.

1 Includes only NHS nurses. One user was visited by a hospice nurse but no information was available on the frequency of visits; and one user had both NHS district nurse and private nurse visits, but the frequency of visits could not be separated for the two types of service providers. All other services refer to those provided by the NHS only.

relationship between service receipt and cognitive impairment is apparent: users with a cognitive impairment receive an average of 0.73 visits per week, compared with 0.45 visits for those without this impairment.

Voluntary sector

Table 8.7 illustrates the distribution of service receipt from voluntary organisations and sheltered housing wardens across the ECCEP user sample.

As Table 8.3 showed, 7.4 per cent of users receive support from Age Concern or the Crossroads Care Attendant Scheme. Table 8.7 shows these visits distributed across all users, including those not receiving the service. Critical interval need users were most likely to receive these services, particularly if there was no principal informal carer involved. Age Concern visits in particular were more likely to be received by users without a carer, as their visiting service is designed to offer companionship and support, particularly to older people who may be isolated or housebound. Crossroads services in contrast are often aimed at providing carer relief, by staying with the user while the carer takes a break. Thus, it is not surprising that their service is received only by users with a carer.

Other volunteers, from churches and community groups, were seen by 9 per cent of users overall. When these visits are distributed across all users, as Table 8.7 shows, it is evident that this form of support is also primarily provided to more dependent older people, particularly critical interval need users without a carer. There is also a relationship between warden services in sheltered housing and user's need-related circumstances. The users most likely to be living in sheltered housing where a warden is present were critical and short interval need users without a principal carer (32 per cent and 47 per cent respectively). In these cases, the warden may be fulfilling some of the functions of a carer, at least in the sense of being there to monitor and assist the user when necessary.

Table 8.7 also shows the breakdown of warden services by the two largest providers: local authority housing departments and independent sector housing associations. While the relationship between interval need, presence of a carer and the receipt of warden services in local authority sheltered housing is not clear, more distinct patterns emerge when the provider of housing is an independent association. Among the small group of users living in housing association properties, the largest proportion are short interval need users without a carer (26 per cent) followed by critical interval need users without a carer (14 per cent). Thus, users who are more physically frail and lack informal support are more likely to be living in independent sector sheltered housing with a warden. Interestingly, however, the vast majority of these users are not cognitively impaired. Only 4 per cent of users living in independent sector sheltered housing with warden services were cognitively

Table 8.7
Usage of voluntary organisations, volunteers and housing wardens, by interval need and social support

	Interval need								
	Critical		Short		Long		Total		Missing
	No PIC	PIC	No PIC	PIC	No PIC	PIC	No PIC	PIC	n =
Voluntary organisations visits/week	0.096	0.103	0.059	0.046	0.019	0.021	0.048	0.060	23
Crossroads[1] visits/week	0.000	0.088	0.000	0.000	0.000	0.000	0.000	0.034	18
Age Concern[1] visits/wk	0.096	0.000	0.059	0.011	0.016	0.005	0.047	0.004	21
Volunteers' visits/week	0.258	0.025	0.000	0.162	0.118	0.133	0.130	0.100	51
	%	%	%	%	%	%	%	%	
Warden of sheltered housing/neighbourhood scheme – proportion receiving	32.0	17.0	47.0	24.0	21.0	25.0	30.0	22.0	8
Housing department[2] – % receiving	9.2	6.4	10.5	10.3	6.9	10.7	8.3	9.0	8
Housing association[2] – % receiving	13.7	6.4	26.3	10.3	2.3	10.4	10.7	8.8	8

Number of cases: 425. Source: Care manager interviews.
1 Crossroads and Age Concern were the most frequently used voluntary organisations.
2 Housing departments and housing associations were the most frequent sources of sheltered housing wardens.

impaired. In contrast, a slightly higher proportion of those living in local authority sheltered housing with a warden were cognitively impaired (10 per cent) than not (8 per cent). These findings may suggest that independent sector sheltered housing is less able or willing to accommodate older people with mental health problems, even when warden supervision is available.

So far, Tables 8.5, 8.6 and 8.7 have shown how social care, health care and voluntary resources have been distributed according to interval need and social support. Each of these tables include independent sector resources. Since an expanding range of providers has had a substantial impact on the nature of services for the elderly, it is worth pausing at this point to consider further how independent sector resources were being deployed in 1995 in relation to users with different levels of need.

The mixed economy

ECCEP data were collected at a time when the mixed economy of care was becoming well established, with independent sector involvement expanding rapidly. Independent sector resources can account for a significant proportion of services in some care plans. These types of services do however appear to be used to support some groups of users more than others, particularly in instances when there are gaps in existing statutory services. An analysis which compares how independent sector and statutory resources have been deployed in response to need illustrates these patterns of utilisation.

Independent sector usage by interval need

The proportion of a selection of social care resources provided by the independent sector is shown in Table 8.8 with a breakdown by interval need. This table illustrates that the proportion of resources provided by the independent sector is considerable, ranging from 13 per cent for delivered meals to 74 per cent for sitting services, with 25 per cent of home care from this sector. Two extreme examples not included in the table are occupational therapy, which was not provided by the independent sector in any ECCEP cases, and luncheon clubs, which were always provided by this sector and were almost all voluntary.

When the breakdown by interval need is considered, resources showed differing trends. A greater proportion of independent sector home care was provided for short and critical interval need users (around 27 per cent) than for long interval need cases (only 19 per cent), with day care behaving in a similar fashion. In contrast, a greater proportion of respite care, laundry service and delivered meals were provided by the independent sector for long interval need users.

Table 8.8

Proportion of some key social care resources provided by the independent sector, by interval need

Type of resource	Critical %[1]	Short %	Long %	Total %	Missing n
Home care	27.7	26.6	18.8	25.1	27
Sitting services	61.7	17.2	95.5	74.4	1
Delivered meals	10.3	13.4	16.5	13.4	5
Day care	19.8	19.9	10.0	17.6	8
Respite care	23.0	26.2	35.6	27.0	14
Laundry service	18.5	28.6	71.4	41.2	6

Number of cases: 425. Source: Care manager interview.
1 Percentage due to independent sector calculated for each cell in table by dividing the amount of resource provided by the independent sector by the amount of resource from all providers for that particular cell.

Also, while the proportion of independent sector respite care was much greater for users with a principal informal carer (30 per cent) than for others (5 per cent), the reverse effect was found for meals on wheels, with 20 per cent of those without a carer receiving independent sector provision, compared to only 11 per cent of those with a carer. These two results suggest that the independent sector tends to be used more in cases where there is a particular need for the resource. Thus, the presence of a carer is more likely to indicate a need for respite care to provide some relief from caring while users without a carer are less likely to receive informal help with meals. Moreover, the proportion of respite care (77 per cent) and home care (40 per cent) provided to long interval need users with a cognitive impairment was particularly great. These are the users who are more likely to be mobile and hence at risk of wandering or endangering themselves or others: another high need group. A notable exception to this trend was found for sitting services, for which the proportion provided by the independent sector was much smaller for users who were cognitively impaired or behaviourally disturbed (17 per cent) than for others (91 per cent).

The community-based independent sector service which has seen the most rapid expansion in the past two decades has been home care. The growth in this sector is largely due to social services departments using their budgets to buy in private care. Initially this was often seen as a means of off-loading responsibility for lower need elderly users in order that social services departments could target their resources on those in greatest need. However, as the independent sector has grown, its home care resources have been used more comprehensively.

Table 8.9 illustrates how the proportion of home care hours provided by the independent sector varies with interval need and social support at different times of the week. The total columns show that independent sector involvement was smallest during office hours, was greater at weekends and greatest during the evening. This suggests that independent sector home care was seen as more flexible than inhouse provision, and more able to provide services outside of office hours.

Overall, users with a principal informal carer received a slightly higher proportion of independent sector home care (26 per cent) than those without (22 per cent), although the difference is very small. During office hours, cases without a principal informal carer receive a smaller proportion of independent sector home care, suggesting that statutory home care resources may be focusing on these users. When interval need is considered, it is evident that more dependent users, particularly those without a carer, are receiving a high proportion of independent sector home care during the evenings, again suggesting that statutory services may less able to respond to the needs of more vulnerable users out of office hours.

Although not shown here, findings also suggest that a greater proportion of independent sector home care was deployed on cognitively impaired or behaviourally disturbed users. For the week as a whole, 32 per cent of the home care received by these users was provided by the independent sector, compared to only 22 per cent for other users, and at evenings and weekends the difference was still greater. This result suggests again that the independent sector has greater flexibility, this time in being willing to care for a demanding group of users, particularly at inconvenient times.

The evidence, therefore, points to several conclusions regarding social service department use of independent sector home care. SSDs are using independent sector home care to fill the gaps in statutory provision. A greater proportion of users receive independent sector home care at times when statutory services have traditionally found it difficult to provide a comprehensive service: namely at weekends and particularly during the evening. Given the need among more dependent users for support at unpredictable and frequent intervals, it is thus not surprising that a greater proportion of independent sector home care is deployed to assist cognitively impaired users, and those with higher interval needs.

Average weekly costs

In addition to analysing the usage and distribution of resources, it is also important to consider the costs of services. While a more in-depth analysis of care package costs and related issues of equity and efficiency can be found in the ECCEP productivities work (Davies et al., 1999), descriptive findings are offered here. Weekly costs to the social services department are examined first,

Table 8.9

Proportion of home care hours provided by the independent sector[1] during office hours, evenings and weekends, by interval need and social support

Proportion of home care hours provided by independent sector	Interval need							
	Critical		Short		Long		Total	
	No PIC %	PIC %	No PIC %	PIC %	No PIC %	PIC %	No PIC %	PIC %
Office hours	18.2	24.8	22.2	24.5	13.2	17.8	17.3	22.8
Evenings	48.8	38.2	54.5	34.9	16.8	36.0	40.6	37.3
Weekends	29.3	29.1	36.3	26.3	2.1	26.7	24.3	28.1
Whole week	25.2	28.4	29.2	26.0	11.9	21.6	21.7	26.2
Total n =	20	123	17	89	40	106	77	318

Valid cases: 395. Missing: 30. Source: Time I care manager interview.

1 Independent sector includes voluntary organisations, private organisations and private individuals, formally arranged.

in relation to individual services and total weekly social care costs for different groups of users.[2] Costs to the NHS are then examined in the same manner. Finally, costs to different providers are combined in a discussion of total weekly package costs. Examples of care packages, and the relationship between costs and needs, are illustrated using a series of case studies which describe the circumstances of five ECCEP users and the amount and frequency of services they were receiving.

Average weekly SSD cost and its components

In calculating the cost of social care, it is important to consider that an increasing proportion of services are no longer provided directly by the social services department. Box 8.1 describes how costs to the SSD were determined, and explains how they are presented in the tables that follow.

Just as the needs of users vary considerably, so can overall social care costs. The distribution of total weekly SSD costs across the ECCEP sample is shown in Table 8.10, which illustrates that twenty[3] cases (5 per cent of the total) had zero SSD cost at the time of the first care manager interview, when costs of aids and adaptations were excluded. The median cost of £62.91 marks the point in the distribution at which there are equal numbers of cases with costs above and below this value. The lower quartile indicates the cost for which one quarter of the cases are cheaper than this value, and the upper quartile the cost for which one quarter of cases are more expensive than this value. The wide range in weekly cost between lower and upper quartiles of £25.26 to £124.19 is clear. Ten per cent of cases have costs above the upper decile of £189.03.

Table 8.10
Distribution of average gross[1] weekly cost to the social services department[2]

	£
Minimum	0.00 (20 cases)
Lower decile	8.42
Lower quartile	25.26
Median	62.91
Mean	91.56
Upper quartile	124.19
Upper decile	189.03
Maximum	849.90

Valid cases: 387. Missing cases: 38. Source: Care manager interview.
1 Costs are expressed gross (that is, before deducting user contributions).
2 All private sector resources received were assumed to have been purchased by the social services department.

Box 8.1
Calculating total SSD cost

Although the provider of a social care resource is not always the purchaser, information was not normally available to indicate when they were different. Thus, in calculating total SSD cost, it was not known whether any private sector resources used were purchased by the social services department or by the user. When users purchased private sector resources themselves, they would need the financial means to do so. The financial circumstances of users receiving private sector resources were, therefore, examined to test whether they were sufficiently poor to be unlikely to pay for these resources themselves. One convenient measure of poverty is whether the user receives income support or housing benefit. Out of the full sample of 300 cases for which both SSD costs and financial information were available, 38 per cent received this benefit. In comparison, for the subsample of these cases (61) receiving private sector resources, 32 per cent received benefit. Since this percentage is not much less than that for the full sample, this evidence does not suggest that private sector resources were confined to those who could afford to pay for them. Moreover, even when users did not receive this benefit, a high proportion were on relatively low incomes and with little or no savings. It was, therefore, felt that by assuming all private sector resources were paid for by the SSD, the total SSD cost was unlikely to have substantially overestimated. In the absence of more precise information on unit costs, it was assumed that those due to the private sector were the same as those for the social services department. By including private sector resources, gross weekly SSD cost (excluding the care manager's own time) was increased from £67.69 to £91.56.

The quantity of individual SSD resources consumed was occasionally missing. Because the costs of up to ten resources were summed to obtain the total, exclusion of a case whenever a component was missing would have resulted in a large number of missing values. It was, therefore, decided to exclude only those cases for which at least one of the four most costly resources provided by the SSD was missing, these being home care, delivered meals, day care and respite care. Other missing values were assumed to be zero. This resulted in 38 missing values for total SSD cost. Costs have been expressed gross (that is, without deducting client charges).

Despite the low overall mean of £91.56 per week, there were nine users (2.3 per cent of the total sample) with weekly costs above the equivalent cost of a week in a residential care home.

The average gross weekly cost to the social services department (including all private sector costs) of care packages is illustrated in Table 8.11. The total weekly SSD cost was somewhat greater for users with a principal informal carer (£95.78) than for those without (£74.43), reflecting the greater combined need of users and carers. It is worth emphasising that both these costs are much smaller than the average cost of a week in a residential care home, which was £382 in 1995 (Netten and Dennett, 1995).

The largest component of cost to the social services department was home care. The only other substantial cost contributions were from day care, respite care and sitting services. While respite care for users with a principal informal carer cost double that of those without, day care and the sitting service cost three times as much for users with a carer. These results suggest that respite care and particularly day care are in many cases used to provide the carer with a break, as well as provide activity for the user.

The combined weekly cost of day care, respite care and sitting for users with a principal informal carer amounted to £43, approaching that for home care (£48). The cost of meals (whether hot or frozen) to the social services department was slightly greater for cases without a principal informal carer (£4.51) than for those with one (£3.14). This may reflect the fact that informal carers are sometimes willing to provide meals themselves. Table 8.11 also shows that the cost of sheltered accommodation provided by the SSD when averaged over all cases was greater for users without a principal informal carer, totalling £3 per week. Remaining cost components were all low.

When interval need is considered, Table 8.11 shows that costs rose with the level of dependency. Among users without a carer, weekly social care costs amounted to £45 for users with long interval needs, and rose to £129 among those with critical interval needs. For users with a carer, cost between long and short interval need remained unchanged, but again increased sharply between short and critical interval need from £78 to £121. The relatively high cost of critical interval need cases for users with no carer arose mainly from the much greater quantity of home care consumed by these cases (£83 per week), reflecting their lack of informal help with personal care tasks as well as household tasks.

Other costs which varied with interval need were those for day care, which increased steadily from £13 per week for long interval need users with a carer to £22 among critical interval need users with a carer. It is at short and critical interval need that users tend to be less mobile and more confined to home, often resulting in higher levels of carer stress, so that the benefits of day care to both user and carer become greater. It is thus not surprising that the cost of both respite care and sitting services also increased steadily through the interval need categories, and were again considerably higher for users with a carer. It is thus evident that day care, sitting services and respite resources were being targeted towards more dependent users, as well as aiming to relieve their carers.

Table 8.11

Average gross[1] weekly cost of services provided by the social services department, by interval need and social support

	Critical		Short		Long		Total	
	No PIC[2] £	PIC £	No PIC £	PIC £	No PIC £	PIC £	No PIC £	PIC £
Weekly cost								
Total SSD cost[3]	128.68	120.82	81.17	78.00	45.37	80.57	74.43	95.78
SSD cost components[3]								
Home care	82.89	63.69	56.06	40.80	30.59	34.66	49.54	47.78
Delivered meals - hot	5.38	2.76	5.67	2.92	2.34	2.53	3.98	2.73
- frozen	0.19	0.39	1.55	0.34	0.23	0.49	0.53	0.41
Day care	7.35	22.16	8.68	18.40	4.18	13.19	6.03	18.14
Respite care	10.30	17.70	8.30	12.64	5.15	10.75	7.17	14.01
Sitting service[4]	15.89	13.45	0.00	1.71	0.00	15.96	3.93	11.13
Laundry service	0.17	0.09	0.17	0.21	0.08	0.16	0.12	0.15
Occupational therapy	0.69	0.33	0.47	0.29	0.05	0.43	0.31	0.35
Tech. input for sensory impairment	0.23	0.03	0.00	0.54	0.01	0.07	0.06	0.18
Sheltered accommodation[5]	5.60	0.00	0.00	0.00	2.68	2.10	2.77	0.71
Other social work[6]	0.00	0.23	0.26	0.14	0.06	0.22	0.09	0.20

Valid cases: 385. Missing: 40.

1 Costs are expressed gross (that is, before deducting user contributions). 2 PIC stands for principal informal carer.

3 Includes private sector resources which are assumed to be purchased by the social services department.

4 The large contribution of sitting service to the total cost was brought about by relatively few high consumers of this service, including one requiring it day and night all week and another for nearly this amount.

5 Sheltered accommodation has been included in the total cost only when provided by the SSD.

6 Other social work excludes care managers' visits. Each social work visit is assumed to be associated with one hour client-related activity.

Costs to the SSD also vary when the user is cognitively impaired. Table 8.12 illustrates the breakdown of average weekly cost to the social services department by interval need and cognitive impairment or behavioural disorder.

As the total columns in Table 8.12 illustrate, the cost of social care services for users with cognitive impairment or behavioural disorder is considerably higher (£115 per week) than for users without these conditions (£82 per week). Most of the increased expenditure is due to greater spending on home care, day care and respite care for these users. The extra use of day care and respite care is evidence of a response by the SSD to the particular need to provide relief to the carers of this very demanding user group.

It is worth noting that costs were not uniformly higher for cognitively impaired cases. Occupational therapy cost rather less per week for these users (£0.27) than for the others (£0.37), suggesting that this service was aimed mainly at coping with physical rather than mental incapacity. Similarly, technical input for sensory impairment was focused primarily on users without cognitive impairment or behavioural disorder (£0.20 per week) than those with these problems (£0.06 per week). Sheltered accommodation provided by the SSD was used entirely for users who were not cognitively impaired or behaviourally disturbed, reflecting the difficulty experienced by sheltered housing wardens in providing adequate supervision and preventing disturbance to other residents in cases of cognitive impairment.

When a user is both physically more frail and has a cognitive impairment, it is evident from Table 8.12 that overall social care costs are higher. The total weekly cost to the SSD for users with both critical interval needs and a cognitive impairment was £136, in contrast to a weekly cost of £67 for non-impaired users with long interval needs. Greater use of home care, sitting service and day care resources account for most of the increase in weekly cost. A service received by very few users — social work input other than that provided by the care manager — was also concentrated on cognitively impaired users with critical interval needs, suggesting a greater need for counselling or other types of direct intervention in these cases involving users with complex needs.

Average weekly costs to the NHS

Based on information regarding receipt of NHS services at Time I, it is possible to estimate weekly package costs for health as well as social services. For those cases for whom adequate information regarding receipt of health services exists, the average cost of the NHS component of a care package was just over £36 per week. As with social care costs, however, health service costs vary according to the needs of the user.

Table 8.12

Average gross[1] weekly cost (£) of services provided by the social services department, by interval need and presence of cognitive impairment or behavioural disorder

Weekly cost	Critical		Interval need Short		Long		Total	
	CI/BD[2]	No CI/BD	CI/BD	No CI/BD	CI/BD	No CI/BD	CI/BD	No CI/BD
Total SSD cost[3]	135.98	108.41	79.88	78.30	88.05	67.11	115.48	81.65
SSD cost components[3]								
Home care	76.91	55.67	38.51	44.69	50.25	30.27	64.37	41.50
Delivered meals - hot	3.37	2.82	1.22	3.90	4.13	2.23	3.22	2.90
- frozen	0.18	0.59	0.10	0.66	0.54	0.39	0.25	0.53
Day care	25.50	15.41	19.71	15.96	17.81	8.88	22.72	12.79
Respite care	18.31	15.60	18.75	10.36	13.69	8.04	17.26	10.78
Sitting service[4]	10.89	16.19	0.81	1.52	1.28	13.77	6.97	10.70
Laundry service	0.07	0.13	0.36	0.17	0.00	0.17	0.10	0.16
Occupational therapy	0.31	0.43	0.25	0.34	0.17	0.35	0.27	0.37
Tech. input for sensory impairment	0.07	0.05	0.11	0.52	0.02	0.06	0.06	0.20
Sheltered accommodation[5]	0.00	1.46	0.00	0.00	0.00	2.78	0.00	1.58
Other social work[6]	0.36	0.05	0.07	0.17	0.16	0.18	0.26	0.14

Valid cases: 387. Missing: 38.
1 Costs are expressed gross (that is, before deducting user contributions).
2 CI/BD stands for cognitively impaired or behaviourally disturbed.
3 Includes only resources provided and paid for by the SSD. Independent sector resources purchased by the SSD are excluded.
4 The large contribution of sitting service to the total cost was brought about by relatively few high consumers of this service.
5 Sheltered accommodation has been included in the total cost only when provided by the SSD.
6 Other social work excludes care manager's visits. Each social work visit is assumed to be associated with one hour client-related activity.

The first portion of Table 8.13 illustrates overall NHS package costs by interval need and social support. There is a clear gradient across interval need categories in relation to mean package cost. While critical interval need users without a carer received on average almost £45 per week of services, this fell to just under £28 for long interval need users with a carer. Thus, it is evident that frailer users are more likely to be receiving a more costly health service package, both due to the frequency and type of service provided.

The relationship between NHS package costs and the presence of an informal carer is, however, not as clear as between package costs and interval need. There was a small difference in weekly mean cost: the health care package of users with a carer totals on average £35 per week, compared with almost £40 for users without a carer.

Table 8.13 also illustrates the average weekly cost of health service packages broken down by individual service. Nursing visits make up the single most significant component of health package costs, averaging just under £13 per week. This is followed by day hospital and then outpatient costs. Although these two hospital-based services are used by a relatively small proportion of users, their unit cost is high, which accounts for their price in relation to other services.

When interval need is considered, service costs for critical interval users are higher for most services, reflecting more frequent use. Nursing visits, for instance, demonstrate a clear relationship with the interval need, with the average weekly cost of nursing visits for critical interval need users without a carer at £21 per week, compared with £9 per week for similar users with long interval needs. Services which show little or no increase in cost with interval need are GP visits and chiropody.

Whether the user has a principal informal carer or not does affect the distribution of specific services, which in turn has an impact on service cost. For instance, day hospital and outpatient services account for a larger proportion of package costs among users without a carer. Conversely, as with SSD respite services, NHS respite care is more likely to be received by users with a carer, and thus account for a higher service cost. One interesting finding is that average physiotherapy costs per week were just over £5 per week for users with a carer, compared to less than £1 for those without. Community physiotherapy services are often only provided on a short term basis, and in some cases are withdrawn before the user has received the full benefit of treatment. It is possible that carers were acting as advocates for the user in obtaining a continuation of physiotherapy, or were responsible for seeking the service in the first place.

Table 8.14 illustrates the same breakdown of NHS weekly cost and its components, by interval need and cognitive impairment/behavioural disorder, rather than social support. The contrast between the cost of care packages for users with a cognitive impairment and those without is small: users with these mental health problems were receiving an average weekly

Table 8.13
Average gross weekly cost to the NHS and its components, by interval need and social support

Weekly cost	Critical		Short		Long		Total	
	No PIC[1] £	PIC £	No PIC £	PIC £	No PIC £	PIC £	No PIC £	PIC £
Total NHS cost	44.80	43.35	42.65	31.24	35.55	27.57	39.89	35.39
Nurse visits	21.26	17.97	11.55	10.38	8.92	7.82	12.57	12.90
GP visits	2.82	2.55	1.71	2.58	2.47	5.70	2.31	3.50
Day hospitals	15.55	8.87	7.60	6.11	5.18	2.76	8.31	6.30
Chiropody	0.59	0.58	0.78	0.23	0.66	0.49	0.68	0.46
Physiotherapy	0.00	3.19	1.53	2.46	0.26	1.11	0.60	5.38
Outpatients clinics	0.63	2.19	19.48	3.71	18.00	6.67	14.48	3.93
NHS day care	0.00	2.20	0.00	0.59	0.00	1.60	0.00	1.59
NHS respite care	3.59	5.36	0.00	4.96	0.00	0.46	0.82	3.79
NHS occupational therapist	0.38	0.44	0.00	0.21	0.07	0.97	0.12	0.54
n =	11	90	15	56	22	62	48	208

Number of cases 256. Missing cases: 169. The sample includes cases with at least one health care input. When all health service inputs are missing, the total cost is set to missing. When some health service inputs are missing, these are reset to zero. Source: Care manager interview.

1 PIC stands for principal informal carer.

Table 8.14

Average gross weekly cost to the NHS and its components, by interval need and whether cognitively impaired or behaviourally disturbed

Weekly cost	Critical		Short		Long		Total	
	CI/BD[1] £	No CI/BD £	CI/BD £	No CI/BD £	CI/BD £	No CI/BD £	CI/BD £	No CI/BD £
Total NHS cost	42.89	43.56	37.85	32.61	20.48	31.95	37.02	35.62
Nurse visits	18.67	17.67	12.99	10.05	12.03	7.09	16.21	11.19
GP visits	3.58	1.90	7.20	1.21	0.43	6.00	3.50	3.25
Day hospital	6.98	11.83	12.21	5.00	0.00	4.19	6.33	6.12
Chiropody	0.77	0.39	0.46	0.32	0.21	0.61	0.59	0.45
Physiotherapy	1.41	4.12	1.64	2.42	1.28	0.76	1.42	2.29
Outpatients clinics	2.72	1.34	0.99	8.52	1.15	11.93	2.07	7.68
NHS day care	3.37	0.62	2.36	0.00	3.67	0.49	3.26	0.37
NHS respite care	5.10	5.14	0.00	4.88	1.57	0.00	3.43	3.09
NHS occupational therapist	0.31	0.55	0.00	0.21	0.05	0.89	0.20	0.57
n =	90	11	56	15	62	22	208	48

Valid cases: 256. Missing: 169. Source: Care manager interview.
1 CI/BD stands for cognitively impaired or behaviourally disturbed.

health care package costing £37 per week, compared with just under £36 per week for users without a cognitive impairment or behavioural disorder.

For users with a cognitive impairment, nursing is one of the few services which does demonstrate a clear difference in frequency of visits, and thus weekly cost. Whereas users with a cognitive impairment were receiving nursing visits averaging £16 per week, users without these mental health problems received services costing £11 per week.

Physiotherapy, outpatient clinics, and occupational therapy make up a relatively small proportion of weekly health costs, but it is interesting to note that these services were received more frequently (thus costing more overall) by users who were *not* cognitively impaired. As rehabilitation is a component of all these services, it may be that users who are severely cognitively impaired or have a behavioural disorder are less likely be able to retain and thus benefit from the new treatments or regimes which these services can provide. Conversely, the weekly costs of NHS day care, respite care and day hospital services were slightly higher for users with a cognitive impairment than those without. These services fulfil a monitoring function, relieving carers while providing treatment: factors which make these health services particularly valuable for older people with a cognitive impairment. Day hospital accounts for a higher proportion of package costs than the other two services, averaging just over £6 per week across all groups of users.

Total weekly package costs

Health and social care costs combine to make up the total weekly cost of each care package. The distribution of care package costs among ECCEP cases was broad, with an average total weekly cost of £138 per user.[4] In order to illustrate how care package costs were distributed across ECCEP users, five case studies have been selected. These case studies describe the individual circumstances of users, the services they were receiving, and the associated costs. The five case studies reflect the approximate distribution of cases. These cases have not been chosen as 'typical' or representative of other packages with similar costs, but rather provide some examples of how resources are combined to support individual users. The cases were extracted from a total of 243 for whom there was adequate information regarding the receipt of both health and social care services. The packages described were those being received by each user at Time I. Thus, 1995 prices have been used to calculate gross weekly package costs. The distribution of package costs is shown in Figure 8.1.

The distribution of total weekly costs varies, again depending on the needs of the user. Although not shown here, package costs rise with interval need, and are higher for users with a cognitive impairment. Each case is represented in Figure 8.1 by a bar. The higher the bar, the more costly the total weekly cost of services, reflecting the complexity of needs. The percentage distribution of

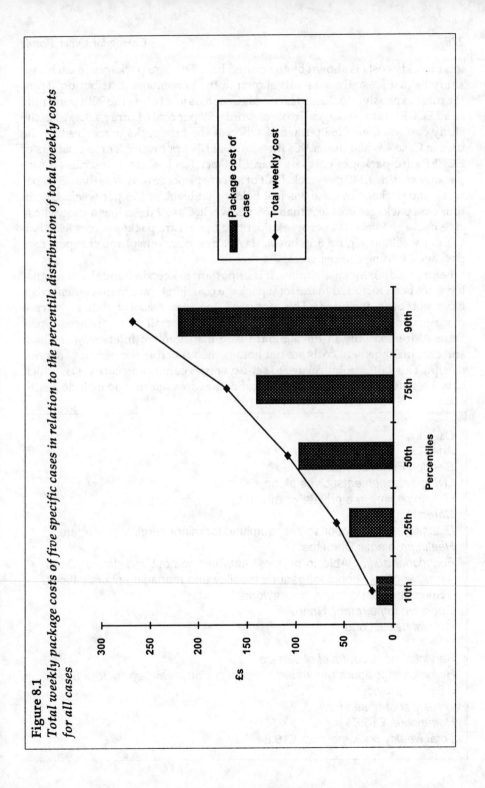

Figure 8.1
Total weekly package costs of five specific cases in relation to the percentile distribution of total weekly costs for all cases

total weekly costs is shown by the dotted line. The care packages in each case study lie just *below* the intervals shown in the percentage distribution. Thus, the most expensive package described (Case 5) is just below the 90th percentile of all ECCEP care packages. In other words, 90 per cent of care packages in the study cost *less* than £268 per week, whereas the care package received by the user in Case 4 is just under this threshold, at £221 per week. Three-quarters of ECCEP care packages cost less than £171 per week. Case 4 describes a care package costing £140 per week. Half of all care packages cost less than £108 per week: the package in Case 3 is just below that level, at £96 per week. One in four care packages cost less than £58 per week. Case 2 describes a user whose care package totals £44 per week. Just one in ten care packages cost less than £21 per week, as Figure 8.1 shows. Case 1 describes one of the cheapest care packages, costing £16 per week.

Before reading the case studies, it is important to keep in mind the items that have not been included in the total package cost. First, care management costs have not been included. This occurred for two reasons: details of care management tasks and time were not available for all cases as these topics were addressed only in the standard care management interviews (n=200); and care management costs are not homogeneous across the period of service receipt. This latter point relates to set-up versus continuing care costs, which have been described in Chapter 5. Second, the cases selected do include health

---

Case 1
Age: 75
Gender: Female
Living arrangements: Lives alone
Housing: Lives in a privately rented flat
Carer: None
Discharged from hospital: Yes, admitted for minor surgical procedure
Health problems: Diabetes
Functional ability: Able to do most activities without assistance. Does however find shopping, general mobility and managing stairs difficult. She does not do heavy housework.
Cognitive impairment: None.
Interval need: Long

Services received, level of service
Home care: 2 hours per week. Visits occur on weekdays before 5 p.m. SSD is provider.
Weekly cost of services
Home care: £16.84
Total weekly package cost: **£16.84**

Case 2
Age: 88
Gender: Female
Living arrangements: Lives alone
Housing: Lives in house which she owns
Carer: Close friend
Extent of carer input: Carer lives nearby and visits twice a week on average. As well as providing companionship, the carer does some shopping and errands for the user, helps with repairs in the home, monitors the user's situation and provides transport to take the user out and to appointments.
Discharged from hospital: No, community referral
Health problems: Depression, cognitive impairment
Functional ability: Able to do most activities unaided. Is able to manage general mobility, stairs and money matters with difficulty. Needs help with transport, shopping, errands and heavy housework.
Cognitive impairment: Moderate to severe.
Interval need: Long

Services received, level of service
Home care: 4.5 hours per week. Visits occur Monday to Friday before 5 p.m. (3.5 hours per week) and on weekends (one hour per week). SSD is the provider.
Meals: Frozen, two provided each week by SSD.
Weekly cost of services
Home care: £40.41
Frozen meals: £3.80
Total weekly package cost: **£44.21**

care costs. It is possible, however, that some services have been excluded, particularly relating to GP visits. Issues concerning ECCEP health data were addressed in Chapter 2. Finally, as other PSSRU costing exercises have emphasised, it is important that any comparisons of cost information should be comprehensive, meaning like should be compared with like (Netten et al., 1997; Knapp, 1993). The package costs presented here cannot be accurately compared with residential or nursing home costs as housing, food and heating costs have not been included. Comparing community care costs with those of institutional care also involves estimating the monetary value of informal care inputs, which has not been attempted here.

Case 3
Age: 79
Gender: Male
Living arrangements: Lives with wife
Housing: Owner-occupied bungalow
Carer: Spouse
Extent of carer input: Intensive. Changes continence pads, helps with toileting and transfers, washes soiled linen as well as household washing, prepares meals, shops, collects pension and other errands, liaises with services, helps with medication and offers companionship.
Discharged from hospital: Yes. General medical problems following a stroke.
Health problems: Stroke, urinary incontinence.
Functional ability: User has difficulty bathing, dressing, transferring, negotiating stairs, toileting and general mobility. Needs help with meals, transport, managing medication and money. Does no shopping, errands, or heavy housework.
Cognitive impairment: None.
Interval need: Critical

Services received, level of service
Home care: 7.25 hours per week. Visits occur Monday to Friday before 5 p.m. (5.75 hours per week) and on weekends (1.50 hours per week). SSD is the provider.
Nursing visits: 2 visits per week (each 45 minutes) by a district nurse.

Weekly cost of services
Home care: £48.41
Nursing visits: £48.00
Total weekly package cost: **£96.41**

Case 4
Age: 85
Gender: Female
Living arrangements: Lives alone
Housing: Lives in sheltered housing owned by the local authority
Carer: Daughter
Extent of carer input: Moderate level of support. Carer assists with housework, shopping, errands, transport and provides companionship.
Discharged from hospital: No, community referral.
Health problems: Senile dementia.
Functional ability: Can do most activities unaided. Does not however do any shopping, errands, heavy housework, managing money or managing medication, and relies on others for transport.
Cognitive impairment: Moderate
Interval need: Short

Services received, level of service
Home care: 2.50 hours per week. Visits occur Monday to Friday before 5 p.m. SSD is the provider.
Nursing visits: One visit per quarter from a district nurse.
Day care: Two visits per week to an SSD day centre.
Chiropodist: One visit per quarter.
Respite: Two visits since referral (one 7 days, one 14 days) to an SSD residential care home.
Voluntary services: Attends a church lunch club twice a week.

Weekly service costs
Home care: £21.05
Nursing visits: £2.66
Day care: £66.00
Chiropodist: £1.33
Respite: £49.30
Total weekly package cost: **£140.34**

Case 5
Age: 81
Gender: Female
Living arrangements: Lives alone.
Housing: Lives in a house which she owns
Carer: No carer
Discharged from hospital: No, community referral
Health problems: Arthritis and urinary incontinence
Functional ability: Is able with difficulty to wash, transfer, go to the toilet
and move around the house. Requires assistance with bathing,
dressing, errands, meals and drinks. Does not do any housework or
attempt to go down stairs.
Cognitive impairment: None
Interval need: Short

Services received and level of service
Home care: 17.75 hours per week. Visits take place Monday to Friday
before 5 p.m.: (9.5 hours per week), weekday evenings (3.75 hours)
and weekends (4.50 hours per week). SSD is the provider.
Nursing visits: One visit per week (30 minutes) from a district nurse.
Day care: One day per week (mid week) at an Age Concern day centre.
Chiropody: One visit per quarter.

Weekly cost of services
Home care: £170.24
Nursing: £16.00
Day care: £33.00
Chiropody: £1.35
Total weekly package cost: **£220.57**

Charging

Charging users for domiciliary services is not a new development, yet it has become a particularly contentious issue during the 1990s. While government proposals introduced in 1998 are now attempting to rectify some of the problems by forming a national framework for charging and introducing new inspection arrangements, at the time of the first ECCEP interviews in 1995 charges for social care services remained a thorny issue. Estimates at that time suggested that charges accounted for 14 per cent of local authority income, and that local authorities were recovering approximately 9 per cent of the gross costs of domiciliary services for the elderly from charges (Baldwin and Lunt, 1996). Research during the 1990s highlighted the complex range of issues which charging evokes: from questions about the relationship between central and local government, to issues of entitlement, the divisions between health and social care, and fears of reduced take-up as a consequence of charging (Baldwin and Lunt, 1996; Bennett, 1996; Chetwynd et al., 1996).

ECCEP users, carers and care managers were asked about service charges, their amount and the structure of payments. Table 8.15 illustrates the overall proportion of users, across all study sites, who were reported by care managers to be paying charges for the social care service received. What is evident from the table is that most users were paying a charge: approximately two-thirds of users for most services. Meals on wheels was the service for which the highest proportion of users (79 per cent) were charged. This was followed by SSD home care (69 per cent) and day care (68 per cent). Respite care was paid for by just over half of the users receiving it, perhaps because eligibility for respite care charges may be means-tested in the same manner as

Table 8.15
The proportion of users receiving particular resources[1] who are charged for those resources

Service	Provider	Proportion of users receiving resource who pay charges	
		Number receiving	% charged
Home care	SSD	289	69.2
Home care	Private organisation	66	62.6
Delivered meals	SSD	116	78.8
Day care	SSD/Voluntary org.	140	67.6
Respite care	SSD	109	53.5

Valid cases: 410. Missing: 15.
1 Resources were included only if received by at least 10 per cent of users. NHS resources were excluded since these generally incur no charges.

residential care, excluding a higher proportion of users than other services (such as meals) which may be charged at a flat rate.

What these overall figures mask is the varied experience users had of charging. Variation was not based on needs-related circumstances: no clear patterns were found between interval need, social support, cognitive impairment and whether or not the user was charged. Instead, the variation was caused by differences between local authorities.

As other recent research has shown, charging policy varies enormously across local authorities. This is evident from the findings shown in Table 8.16, which illustrate the proportion of users charged for particular services they were receiving, in each of the ECCEP study areas. While the majority of users are charged for services in some authorities, users living elsewhere may be paying no charges at all.

The proportion of users charged for SSD home care ranges from all users in some authorities (Authorities A, C, H and I) to less than one in ten in other authorities (Authorities F and G). Other areas may apply a means-test to home care charges and thus most but not all users are liable. For instance, 83 per cent of users were charged in Authority J, while 67 per cent were charged in Authority D and E.

For delivered meals, all authorities were charging the majority of users with the exception of Authority I, where just 42 per cent of users were paying directly for this service. Day care and respite care, however, provide the clearest examples of extreme variation between all authorities. For day care, one authority (I) charged all users, while three others (B, J and D) charged more than two-thirds of users. An additional four authorities charged fewer than half their users for day care, while one (F) did not charge anyone for day care, although the sample size here was very small. For respite care, the patterns were similar. Although all authorities were charging some users for the service, the range was again very wide: from 17 to 83 per cent of users.

Another way of looking at non- is to examine which authorities were charging a high proportion of users for all services, compared with those who charged very few users overall. Authorities B, D and J charged more than half their users for all services, with H and A also levying charges on a substantial proportion of users. Authorities I, C, and E were more variable, but F and G were exceptional in the *low* proportions of users charged, across all services except meals on wheels.[5] Baldwin and Lunt (1996), in their study of five English authorities, identified features which influenced charging policy. These ranged from the political composition and control of the authority, to the level of opposition from local user groups. One conclusion they did reach, however, was that authorities which had made a commitment to the concept of a mixed economy of care were more likely than other authorities to be 'moving towards the market rate for services' (Baldwin and Lunt, 1996, p.32). It may be that one or more of these factors would help illuminate the origins of contrasting charging policies across the ECCEP authorities. The study has

Table 8.16
The proportion of users receiving particular resources[1] who are charged for those resources, by local authority

	Home care		Delivered meals	Day care	Respite care	Missing cases
	SSD	Private org.	SSD		SSD	n
Authority A						
n =	29	1	12	7	4	0
% charged	100.0	0.0	83.3	42.9	50.0	
Authority B						
n =	69	4	28	50	42	2
% charged	97.2	25.0	74.3	90.2	67.6	
Authority C						
n =	9	15	1	7	7	2
% charged	100.0	100.0	100.0	40.5	28.6	
Authority D						
n =	7	22	3	13	11	2
% charged	67.4	44.5	66.7	73.9	52.6	
Authority E						
n =	18	1	3	3	0	0
% charged	67.4	0.0	66.7	41.4	-	
Authority F						
n =	49	1	19	9	7	6
% charged	4.0	0.0	90.0	0.0	28.6	
Authority G						
n =	30	0	15	10	11	1
% charged	6.5	-	93.5	9.6	17.5	
Authority H						
n =	26	1	7	11	6	1
% charged	100.0	100.0	85.7	43.8	83.3	
Authority I						
n =	29	4	12	11	9	1
% charged	100.0	25.0	42.3	100.0	55.6	
Authority J						
n =	22	18	11	19	13	0
% charged	82.6	78.3	73.7	84.5	52.2	

Number of cases: 425.
1 Resources were included only if they were received by at least 10 per cent of users overall. NHS resources were excluded since these have no charges.

collected detailed information on these factors which will the subject of future analysis. What is clear from Table 8.16, however, is that ECCEP users living in different parts of the country in 1995 were subject to very varied charging policies, both between authorities and also between individual services.

Care managers were asked what the response of users and carers had been towards charging. Two-thirds of care managers reported that clients had not raised any objections to charges, while an additional 19 per cent pointed out that the user was not liable. Just 1 per cent of care managers reported that the user had been liable but refused to pay. Some users and carers did, however, express particular worries regarding charges, with 7 per cent of care managers reporting that clients were resentful, and 5 per cent reporting that clients were anxious about their ability to pay. Users without a carer were particularly anxious about charges, with 12 per cent of the case managers of these clients reporting that the user was anxious, and an additional 9 per cent stating that the user was resentful. Anxiety may be higher among users without carers because the lack of informal support means these users have no one to depend upon if they decide not to pay for formal services. Lack of informal support may contribute to a feeling among these users that they have no choice but to pay for care, even if they disagree with the principle of charges or have difficulty meeting the cost.

User and carer views regarding service charges provide one important indicator of how differences in the nature of community care provision can affect the manner in which services are perceived, and accepted. The next chapter explores in more detail the views of users concerning the services they received from a range of providers. These views were obtained during Time II interviews, after services had been in place for more than six months. Users were able at that point to provide an assessment of the impact of the care package on both their ability to cope at home and a variety of other issues relating to quality of life. Other key outcomes for users, such as survival in the community and improvements in health and functional ability, are also discussed in the next chapter.

Appendix 8.1. Unit Costs, 1994-1995 Prices

All unit costs are taken from Netten and Dennett (1995), unless otherwise stated.

Appendix Table 8.1
Social care services[1]

Service	Cost	Notes
Home care[2]	£8.42 per hour	Monday to Friday before 5 p.m. (SSD)
	£10.94 per hour	Evenings and weekends (SSD)
Day care	£33.00 per day	Based on SSD unit price
Hot meals	£2.80 per meal	
Frozen meals	£1.90 per meal	
Laundry service	£3.30 per visit	
Sitting services	£5.00 per hour	Same SSD unit price used for daytime and evening
SSD occupational therapy	£22.00 per visit	Same unit price used for technical input for sensory impairment
Other social work	£27.00 per hour	
Sheltered accom.	£110.00 per week	
Respite care	£378 per week in a residential care home (£54 per day)	Unit cost includes cost of care, building and oncosts, and addition of 5% to account for overhead cost of other services provided by the facility.

1 All costs take account of time spent in activities associated with each unit of resource, such as travelling, administration, telephone calls and meetings, unless stated below.
2 Home care daytime unit cost based on Netten and Dennett (1995) price for SSD home care. Evening and weekend costs are estimated as 30 per cent above daytime costs, based on other costing exercises in three local authorities in England (Hallam and Netten, 1996). Standard hourly cost was used for SSD total weekly cost tables, while standard and out-of-hours rate was used in case studies, to obtain as precise individual costings as possible.

Appendix Table 8.2
Health care services

Service	Cost	Notes
Nursing visits[1]	£17.32 per visit	Half hour domiciliary visit
Day hospital[2]	£57 per attendance	Transport costs not included
Outpatient clinic	£89.91 per attend.	Transport costs not included
General practitioner[3]	£31 per contact	Applies to routine visits
Chiropodist	£16 per visit	Routine domiciliary visit
NHS physio-therapist	£23.00 per contact	Routine domiciliary visit
NHS OT	£23.00 per visit	Domiciliary visit
NHS day care	£33.00 per attend.	Transport costs not included
NHS respite care	£54 per day	

1 The cost of nursing visits was obtained by averaging unit costs for different grades of nurses, as information regarding the type of nursing service received was not available for all users. See unit cost details below. Information was available for the type of nurse received by users profiled in the individual case studies (district nurses), in which case Netten and Dennett's district nurse rate of £16 per half hour visit was applied.

2 Transport costs to day hospital, outpatient clinics and day care were not included in the unit cost. Some users will access these services by bus, by taxi or by car. However, ambulances may have been used in a minority of cases. Netten and Dennett (1997) provide an average cost per patient journey, by ambulance (patient transport service) of £33.59.

3 Routine contacts with the GP were assumed to be equally divided between surgery and domiciliary visits, giving a unit cost as the average of £16 and £46.

Unit cost details

When unit costs were not available in Netten and Dennett (1995), they were derived as follows.

1. *Costing care manager time.* This was based on the cost per hour of client-related activities corresponding to the job status of the care manager. Job status was classed into many categories, and for simplicity these were divided into (a) social worker or equivalent; and (b) non-social worker (with less responsibility). Netten and Dennett (1995) cost a social worker as £20 per hour of client-related activity. Because some of the job descriptions in category (a) would suggest rates of pay somewhat more than for a social worker, the unit cost was raised by one-third to £27. Netten and Dennett (1997) cost a social work assistant as £14 per hour of client-related activity, which, after deflating by their PSS inflation index, works out at £13 per hour in 1995. Because some of

the job descriptions in category (b) would suggest rates of pay slightly more than for a social work assistant, the unit cost was raised by one quarter to £16.

2. *Time spent by social work staff excluding the care manager.* It was assumed that these should be costed at the same rate as category (a) care managers: namely £27 per hour.

3. *Laundry services.* The unit cost for the Lewisham Care Management Scheme for an incontinent laundry service of £13.22 was used (Challis et al., 1997). Because most ECCEP users in receipt of the laundry service received one visit per week, this unit cost translated into £3.30 per week.

4. *Technical input for sensory impairment.* This referred to input from mobility officers and technical officers specialising in sensory impairment or communication problems. This level of expertise was felt to be equivalent to that for occupational therapy and related technical input, for which Netten and Dennett (1995) present a unit cost of £22 per visit (local authority based).

5. *Sitting service.* The unit cost for the Lewisham Care Management Scheme (Challis et al., 1997) for a night sitter of £6.90 per hour was reduced slightly to include less expensive day sitting and exclude London weighting effects to give £5 per hour.

6. *Sheltered accommodation.* Netten and Dennett (1995) quote unit costs for local authority sheltered housing and very sheltered housing. It was assumed that the former unit cost of £111 per week was more representative.

7. *Delivered meals.* Hot meals and frozen meals were costed separately. Netten and Dennett (1995) only present a unit cost for hot meals of £2.80 per meal. It was assumed that frozen meals would amount to two-thirds of this: namely £1.90 per meal.

8. *SSD respite care.* It was assumed that this had the same unit cost as for long-term residential care in a local authority care home of £54 per day (Netten and Dennett, 1995).

9. *Nursing visits at home.* Nurses were of four types: district nurses, nursing auxiliaries, community psychiatric nurses and health visitors (all NHS). Most visits were by district nurses. Netten and Dennett (1995) present unit costs for each of these types. Assuming each visit lasts for half an hour, these unit costs were as follows: district nurse £17 per visit; nursing auxiliary £7 per visit; community psychiatric nurse £23.50 per visit; health visitor £24 per visit. An overall unit cost was obtained as a mean of the unit cost for each of these four categories, weighted according to the number of users visited by each type of nurse. It amounted to £17.32 per visit.

10. *GP appointments.* When care managers were interviewed, it was not specified whether these appointments were at the surgery or home visits.

Results from the General Household Survey for higher need elderly suggest that GP appointments for ECCEP users would have been split roughly equally between the surgery and the home. Netten and Dennett (1995) provide unit costs of £16 for a surgery visit and £46 for a domiciliary visit, so the mean of £31 was used for ECCEP cases.

Notes

1   There are several explanations for this growth in the number of hours of home help provided per user since the mid-1980s. One important source has been the changing role of the home help service — from one which provided assistance with domestic tasks such as cleaning and shopping, to one which has begun to cross the boundaries between health and social care — with home helps now increasingly providing assistance with personal care and medical and toileting actitivies. These tasks are by their nature more intensive and require longer visits — for some users, at the expense of assistance with household tasks. This change was being experienced by local authorities both before and during the reforms. See in particular the 1987 Social Services Inspectorate Report *From Home Help to Home Care*, which was informed by the interim report of the Domicliary Care Project.

2   In presenting costs to the social services department, care management costs have been considered separately in Chapter 5, as their level, unlike individual service costs, depends strongly on whether a care package is still being set up or whether a continuing care period has been reached when all services were in place.

3   Out of these twenty cases with zero SSD cost, seven did not have all services in place, three had been admitted to hospital and three to a care home. A further four cases received voluntary sector provision: three voluntary day care and one voluntary lunch club. One user had received an SSD aid, while another attended NHS day care and NHS respite care which may have been arranged following negotiations between the care manager and health service professionals. One zero SSD cost case remained, and since the information on a substantial proportion of resources was missing for this case, the true cost may have been non-zero.

4   While the average package for ECCEP users cost £138 per week, the range of costs was from just over £1 per week (a user who had received one occupational therapy assessment and two pieces of equipment since referral, but no other services) to £683 per week (in the case of a critical interval need user with complex needs receiving multiple services). It should be noted that the most expensive SSD cases are excluded from this analysis because health care utilisation data were not available.

5   Although variation in charging policy is always based on a complex set of circumstances, political commitment is one causal factor which is relevant in the case of Authority G. This authority made an early pledge (from 1948) to free home help for the elderly: a commitment that still applies to the majority of users today, despite long periods of consultation for change. This example highlights the importance of historical as well as political factors in shaping local charging policy.

Introduction

There is now an increasing emphasis in social care research upon outcome measurement. This is partially in response to criticisms that, in the past, the field has been dominated by studies which focused on service delivery and decision-making processes rather than the efficiency or effectiveness of services or the extent to which they improved the lives of users and carers. In part the traditional process focus in social care research has been due to the fact that defining social care outcomes is problematic, as improvements in welfare are not easy to measure and are often dependent upon subjective assessments. Evaluating outcomes is, however, an area which the PSSRU has maintained as a priority (particularly through the production of welfare approach) and has consistently pursued in studies from the mid-1970s onwards. This chapter focuses on findings relating to a range of outcomes for ECCEP users, while the subsequent chapter addresses outcomes specifically related to carers.

This chapter and the next should be placed in the context of ECCEP as a study with several branches of work. The aim of this monograph is to present a wide range of findings by means of straightforward statistical analysis, accompanied by clear text which places the findings in context. In contrast, ECCEP also contains a complementary body of work which explores the effectiveness and efficiency of community care for older people through more complex statistical modelling. Findings from this work can be found in Davies and Fernández (1999). The productivities work has outcomes as its focus. It provides specific information regarding which services, in which combinations, produce what types of outcomes for which users and carers. ECCEP descriptive work does not attempt to replicate or repeat findings from the productivities research. Instead, it describes a wider range of outcomes which require a broader interpretation.

This chapter describes outcomes for users which are of significance in the policy and practice context. It is important to note that some of the domains relate to *states*, while others are *change* outcomes. State outcomes are those which captured the respondent's perceptions at one interview, while change outcomes relate to a comparison of responses between the two interviews. In computing means of change, analysis has been restricted to respondents for whom data were available at both Time I and Time II interviews. This allows us to draw conclusions about how things have changed for users since services were put in place.

The distinction between state and change outcomes has resulted in this chapter being divided into four main sections: destinational outcomes, quality of life at Time I, changes in health status, and quality of life at Time II. *Destinational outcomes* describe which users died, entered institutional care or remained in the community at two points in time: twelve months post-referral, and at Time II. *Quality of life at Time I* explores a range of state outcomes relating to the user's perception of control, relationships and satisfaction with services at the time of the first interview. The next section focuses on a range of change outcomes under the heading *changes in health status*. Finally, *quality of life at Time II* explores other change outcomes which detail differences in users' perceptions of control, relationships and satisfaction between the two interviews, as well as describing findings from questions relating to quality of life which were raised only during the Time II interview.

Destinational outcomes

The length of time which older users remain in the community before death or transition to institutional care is an important outcome indicator of service effectiveness. Given that the aim of community care policy is to maintain older people in their own homes, any estimation of the extent to which this has been achieved must include information about the length of time in which the user was able to remain at home. Thus, destinational outcome measures have been consistently employed in the evaluation research literature, including a series of PSSRU studies (Davies and Knapp, 1981; Davies and Challis, 1986; Davies et al., 1990).

Whether the user remains at home, enters a care home or dies is naturally determined by a wide range of factors, of which service effectiveness is just one. Identifying the impact of services on how long the user remains at home, and indeed the role of specific inputs in facilitating this, is not something dealt with here. Statistical analysis of this type has been undertaken and findings presented in the ECCEP productivities work (Davies and Fernández, 1999). The data presented here, in contrast, detail which users were remaining in the community and receiving services at two specific points in time. First, destinational outcomes for users one year after the initial referral date to social services are presented. Second, findings relating to the location of users at the second stage of data collection — approximately six months after the initial ECCEP interview — are described.

Location twelve months post-referral

Evaluating outcomes involves the measurement of change in specific directions, based upon clearly identifiable criteria (Jones and Borgatta, 1972). In ECCEP, the measurement of change is based around data collected at regular intervals within the longitudinal design of the study. Time I and Time II represent the intervals in ECCEP, plus subsequent tracking data collected at four-monthly stages. These intervals correspond with the set up and continuing care periods of the care management process, but do not by their nature correspond with significant changes in the experience of the users and carers being interviewed. This point is particularly salient in relation to destinational outcomes. Users were referred and assessed at different times, began receiving services at different times, and in some cases, ceased receiving services at different times. In order to capture these changes and compare destinational outcomes it is necessary to identify a common starting point from which progress can be accurately measured. In ECCEP, this point is the referral date: the date at which users were referred to social services and the care management process began. Thus, mapping the location of users one year after their initial referral captures their individual progress at comparative intervals.

Table 9.1 illustrates the location of users one year after their initial referral date to social services. Among the original community-based sample of older people, 13 per cent died during the year following referral. Among users who died, the majority (62 per cent) passed away between 20 and 52 weeks after referral, with just 6 per cent dying within ten weeks of the referral date. In addition to the users who did not survive, Table 9.1 shows that 10 per cent of

Table 9.1
Location of user twelve months post-referral

Location of user	%	n =
Dead	12.6	53
In care home	9.8	41
Living in the community	56.6	237
Other	20.8	87
Total	100.0	418

Missing cases: 1.

users moved from their own homes into a care home during the first year. This is a small proportion of the overall sample and suggests that the vast majority of users avoided institutionalisation and remained in the community, with temporary or long-term support from formal services. Indeed, 57 per cent of users were still living at home and still receiving social care services one year post-referral. The remaining 21 per cent of users were no longer receiving services from the same SSD one year later for a variety of reasons. The most common reasons were either because they had regained independence and no longer required help (an example would be users who had recovered following discharge from hospital), the user or carer had refused services, or because the case was closed to care management but the user was still receiving services from other sources.

Destinational outcomes twelve months post-referral do reveal a relationship between interval need and the location of the user. This is not surprising as the link between functional disability and mortality or institutionalisation is well established (Carriere and Pelletier, 1995; Davies et al., 1990; Wachtel et al., 1987). Among users who had either died or moved to a care home within the first year following referral, the largest proportion had critical interval needs (38 per cent) followed by those with short (21 per cent) and long interval needs (13 per cent). Among users still receiving services and living in the community, long (59 per cent) and short (60 per cent) interval need users were present in higher proportions than critical interval need users (51 per cent).

Neither cognitive impairment/behavioural disorder nor the presence of a principal carer was found to be associated with the destinational outcomes of death or institutionalisation. Indeed, a higher proportion of those without a cognitive impairment died or entered an institution (56 per cent) than those with a cognitive impairment (44 per cent). There is, however, an interaction effect between cognitive impairment and interval need, in that users with both critical interval needs and a cognitive impairment were far more likely to have died or entered an institution (43 per cent) than users with a cognitive impairment but fewer functional limitations (29 per cent among short interval need users with a cognitive impairment, and 21 per cent among long interval need users with a cognitive impairment). The lower proportions of these last two groups of users leaving the scheme may partly reflect their relative physical fitness, with the need for help in performing tasks being due to their cognitive impairment rather than physical disability.

When the presence or absence of a principal carer is considered, higher proportions of death or institutionalisation were found among users with a carer than those without a carer. The one exception to this was among short interval need users, where 26 per cent of users without a carer died or entered a care home, compared with 21 per cent of those with a carer, but the numbers are too small to be significant. While at first glance the fact that the presence of a carer has not resulted in higher rates of survival in the community may seem surprising — given the body of research establishing the role of social support in preventing institutionalisation — it is important to consider that ECCEP users with a carer are overall more dependent than those without a carer, as detailed in Chapter 3. Indeed, users with carers were found to be more dependent (even controlling for interval need) in several other PSSRU studies preceding ECCEP, including the Kent Community Care projects and DCP. Thus, while informal support is undoubtedly assisting users in maintaining independence, it may not be able to compensate entirely for the impact of poor health and functional limitations on destinational outcomes.

Location at Time II

Findings relating to the user's location at Time II differ somewhat from destinational outcomes at twelve months post-referral. Time II interviews took place six or more months following the original Time I interviews, which themselves took place on average three months after the original referral date (for user and carers) and six months post-referral (for workers). Thus, while Time II information regarding the user's location is valuable (detailed information exists from user, worker and care manager interviews at this juncture), it is important to keep in mind that users had been receiving services for varied lengths of time when the interviews took place.

Table 9.2 illustrates the location of users at the time of the second worker interview. Based on their knowledge of the case, care managers were able to identify any changes in the user's place of residence since the Time I interview. It is evident from the table that over two-thirds of users (70 per cent) were still living in the community, at the same address as at Time I. While the majority of these users were still receiving services at that address, it is important to note that the 70 per cent also includes those who had remained in the community but no longer required services arranged by the SSD. A very small group of users — less than 3 per cent — also remained in the community but had either moved house, moved in with others or changed their accommodation to sheltered housing.

Another group of users — 13 per cent — had died between the first and second worker interview. This is the same proportion as identified in the destinational outcomes twelve months post-referral. As with twelve-month outcomes, the proportion of users identified by care managers to have died varied with interval need: 18 per cent of users with critical interval needs had died, compared with 11 per cent of short and long interval need users respectively. Moves to institutional care were reported for 13 per cent of users overall, with a slightly higher proportion moving to residential than nursing home care, and three individuals moving to long-stay NHS care. Given that the majority of worker Time II interviews took place more than one year after the user had been referred to social services, it is perhaps not surprising that a slightly higher proportion of users had moved to institutional care by Time II

Table 9.2
Location at Time II, by interval need and social support among community-based sample

Location at Time II	Critical		Short		Long		Total
	No PIC %	PIC %	No PIC %	PIC %	No PIC %	PIC %	n =
User at Time I address	48.3	62.3	66.7	72.8	78.2	77.6	231
User died at Time I address	28.7	16.0	20.0	9.4	10.2	11.5	44
Moved to own home	0.0	2.4	0.0	1.3	0.0	0.0	3
Moved to another's home	0.0	0.0	0.0	1.3	0.0	0.0	1
Moved to sheltered accommodation	0.0	0.0	0.0	1.3	0.0	2.1	3
Moved to long-term residential care	5.7	10.1	13.3	5.1	3.4	5.7	23
Moved to nursing home	0.0	8.1	0.0	7.6	3.4	3.1	19
Moved to NHS facility	5.7	0.0	0.0	1.3	4.8	0.0	3
Moved elsewhere	11.5	1.0	0.0	0.0	0.0	0.0	3
Total n =	17	96	15	77	29	93	330

Missing cases: 9.

than at twelve months post-referral. The proportion of users moving to institutional care shows a clear gradient by interval need: from 10 per cent of long interval need users moving to a care home, to 17 per cent of critical interval need users. Again, a slightly higher proportion of users with a carer (14 per cent) than without a carer (12 per cent) were in institutional care by Time II, although the differences are small.

Institutionalisation rarely occurs as a result of one causal factor but rather as a response to gradual decline combined with significant events, such as hospitalisation, an accident or the loss of a carer. Care managers whose client had moved to a care home were asked in a multiple response question to identify the causes of the move. Changes in health status were the most frequently mentioned reason, with 72 per cent indicating the user's failing health as a cause, while 65 per cent mentioned increasing dependence. An additional 16 per cent of care managers mentioned an injury to the user, which had contributed to the decision.

Changes in informal support were mentioned as a cause of admission by a significant proportion of care managers: 37 per cent stated that the carer had reduced their input, while 5 per cent reported that the carer had died. Loneliness or grief on the part of the user — possibly resulting from bereavement — was mentioned by 16 per cent of care managers. Environmental factors also contributed to the move for some users, with 21 per cent of care managers reporting that the user felt unsafe at home,[1] while damage to the user's place of residence had prompted a move in 5 per cent of cases.

Quality of life at Time I

Quality of life and its determinants are often poorly defined, relating to a range of factors which are notoriously difficult to measure but which are central to human existence. Studies of older people living in the community have most commonly employed the term quality of life to describe social and environmental factors which influence physical and psychological well-being (Hughes, 1990). These factors relate to both human and material resources which are available to the older person, as well as their personal resources in terms of physical and mental health. Thus, psychological concepts such as locus of control and self-efficacy have been linked in some studies to quality of life, as have measures of self-perceived health, and the extent of social support and networks.

In ECCEP, three main areas relating to quality of life at Time I (and, as a later section will describe, Time II) are discussed here. They include: choice and control, social inclusion and relationships, and satisfaction. Choice and control relate to users' evaluations of the degree of influence they have over their own lives and aspects of the care management process. Care managers' perceptions of the attitudes of users and carers are also relevant to this theme. Social inclusion and relationships are important components of quality of life; the findings presented here relate to the user's own evaluation of his/her opportunities to meet people and maintain existing relationships. Finally, satisfaction is an important component of quality of life, both general satisfaction relating to living independently in the community, and satisfaction with care management arrangements and services received.

Choice and control

The extent to which individuals feel that they have control over their own lives and actions, rather than those actions being monitored or sanctioned by others, can have a significant impact on quality of life. Several recent studies have highlighted the fact that feelings of choice and control are central to older people's own definitions of independence and thus their determination to remain living in the community (Langan et al., 1996; Clark et al., 1998). Yet even among older people who are cognitively intact, it is acknowledged that the freedom to make choices can diminish in later life, as health and functional ability deteriorate and the need for assistance arises. ECCEP users were asked to what extent they felt they had control over their own lives. Findings by interval need and social support are illustrated in Table 9.3.

Almost two-thirds of users (64 per cent) reported that they did feel free to run their life the way they wished. A clear gradient across interval need categories is evident. While 75 per cent of long interval need users felt in control, this proportion dropped to 65 per cent among those with short interval needs and to just half (50 per cent) of critical interval need users. This suggests that feelings of control are closely related to disability. Loss of function and the dependence on others that is associated with this involves a relinquishing of control over some aspects of life, particularly when the loss of function results in a need for assistance with personal care.

Another interesting finding shown in Table 9.3 relates to the role of informal support and feelings of control. Across interval need categories, users with a carer were less likely than those without a carer to state that they felt free to run their own lives. In fact, a minority (48 per cent) of critical interval need users with a carer stated that they felt in control. This suggests that the presence of a principal carer may remove some sense of self-sufficiency or independence from older people who have this type of available support. In contrast, users without a main carer may find that accepting formal services does not require the same loss of feelings of control. This may be particularly the case if the user is paying for services, or feels that he/she has some influence in determining the type or timing of assistance received.

Table 9.3
Percentage of users who feel free to run their lives the way they want, by interval need and social support among community-based sample

| | Interval need | | | | |
Presence of carer (PIC)	Critical %	Short %	Long %	Total %	Total n =
No PIC	67	72	81	76	72
PIC	48	64	72	61	277
Total	50	65	75	64	
Total n =	111	99	140		350

Missing cases: 67.

Choice and care management

Users were, in general, more positive in their responses regarding control or influence during the care management process than when faced with the more general question regarding their assessment of control in daily life presented in Table 9.3. As stated in Chapter 5, the vast majority of users (88 per cent) felt that they had a say in the plans being made during the assessment process, and two-thirds (68 per cent) felt that they were offered some degree of choice in the services offered by the care manager following assessment.

Chapter 5 (Table 5.31) also detailed users' responses when asked how they perceived their role in decision-making with the care manager. Was the care manager someone in charge, who told them what to do, or did the user feel that the exchange was one between equals, or did the user view the care manager as someone whose job it was to get the services the user wanted? Findings indicated that most users — over two-thirds — felt that they were treated as an equal in decision-making with the care manager. In addition, a higher proportion of users (16 per cent) viewed their own position as one of control (asking for services which the care manager should then obtain) rather than passivity (just 9 per cent indicated that the care manager was someone in charge, making the decisions). It is interesting that more dependent users were slightly more confident of their role as decision-makers in the care management process, particularly those with a principal carer. Although the differences are small, this pattern may reflect more extensive contact between care managers, users and carers when needs are complex. Users with carers may also feel more confident during the decision-making process, due to the availability of alternative support.

Worker perceptions of choice and control

Care managers who received a standard interview (n=200) were also asked a series of questions about the role of users and carers in decision-making, and to compare the particular case in question with other, similar cases. Questions related to how demanding clients were and how knowledgeable they were about existing services.

Table 9.4 illustrates whether care managers thought that, compared with other elderly people in similar circumstances, the user tended to ask for more or less help. This question was designed to illicit from care managers their opinion regarding whether the user was more anxious to get attention and services than other similar users. Interestingly, the majority of care managers (65 per cent) reported that the user was *less* demanding than others. Just over one in four (28 per cent) stated that the user asked for a similar amount of help, and 6 per cent reported that the user in question was more demanding than others. Table 9.4 also shows an interesting relationship with both interval need and social support. There is a clear gradient across interval need categories, with more dependent users being less demanding: 75 per cent of critical interval need users were described by care managers as asking for less help than similar users, compared with just over half (57 per cent) of long interval need users. In addition, users without a carer were overall slightly less demanding than those with a carer. No critical or short interval need users without a carer were described as asking for more help than users in similar circumstances. Reasons for these responses can only be hypothesised with this type of analysis, but it is possible that more dependent older people without regular informal support are reluctant to ask for substantial input from social services, either in an effort to retain their independence, or due to the belief that they will not be able to afford the corresponding charges.

Care managers were also asked if users and carers had been either ignorant or knowledgeable about available services *prior* to receiving information during assessment. The importance of available information about services has been emphasised by the Social Services Inspectorate, who have set and applied information standards in their inspections (SSI, 1993, 1998). Adequate information is required if individuals are to exercise choice and become involved in the care planning process. ECCEP care managers described just over a third of users (38 per cent) and carers (37 per cent) as knowledgeable about available services, with the largest proportion of users (41 per cent) and carers (42 per cent) described as ignorant. Interestingly, users with a carer were more frequently described as ignorant (46 per cent) than those without a carer (24 per cent). It may be that older people living alone or managing without regular informal support are by necessity more aware of formal services even before they are assessed, whereas those with carers do not acquire this knowledge until their needs have changed to the extent that informal support is no longer sufficient.

Table 9.4
Whether user asks for more or less help than other similar users, by interval need and social support among community-based sample

| Whether user asks for more or less help than similar users | Interval need | | | | | | Total |
| | Critical | | Short | | Long | | |
	No PIC %	PIC %	No PIC %	PIC %	No PIC %	PIC %	n =
More	0.0	11.5	0.0	5.5	5.4	3.9	12
Same	0.0	15.1	17.2	32.9	36.6	40.9	53
Less	100.0	73.4	82.8	61.6	58.1	55.2	123
Total n =	4	55	9	43	24	50	188

Missing cases: 12. Sample: Standard care manager interviews (n=200)

Relationships and social inclusion

An important indicator of quality of life is the extent and nature of relationships which older persons have with those around them. Social contact may become increasingly important as needs change and the ability to engage in activities previously enjoyed diminishes. As other research has shown, requiring assistance can have a detrimental effect on relationships between older people and informal carers, as well as restricting available social networks as visits and activities become more difficult to engage in (Lawton et al., 1989; Wenger, 1990; Twigg and Atkin, 1994). Two significant bodies of gerontological theory — disengagement theory (Cumming and Henry, 1961) and activity theory (Havighurst, 1963) — debate the importance of maintaining these social contacts and engaging in social activities during the ageing process. While disengagement theory postulates that 'withdrawing' from some aspects of social life is a natural part of ageing, activity theorists reject this and instead suggest that maintaining networks and engaging in activities is vital to healthy ageing and the maintenance of life satisfaction. Applying these theories raises questions about which aspects of life are seen as 'natural' areas for withdrawal from social activity, and which areas are affected by intervening factors such as poverty and disability. Thus, it is interesting to observe users' views concerning their relationships with those around them, both at Time I when service intervention was just beginning, and, as we shall discuss later in this chapter, to observe changes in these relationships over time.

First, users were asked at Time I whether they had people around them to whom they could turn in times of real need, such as during an emergency. Over two-thirds of users reported that they did have such a person. The difference between users with a carer (69 per cent) and those without a carer (67 per cent) was very small. This suggests that the availability of emergency help is not dependent upon having one principal source of informal support, but rather is a type of assistance which can be obtained from a wider network of individuals. Clearer differences were, however, apparent when the availability of informal support was combined with interval need categories. While 82 per cent of long interval need users with a carer stated that they knew people who could help them, this proportion fell to 59 per cent among critical interval need users without a carer. Frailer users, particularly those without a carer, are less able to get out of the home and maintain contacts with others in the community, which may contribute to their doubts about whether support would be available in a time of real need.

Table 9.5 illustrates responses from users regarding whether they had people around them of whom they could easily ask small favours. Again, the differences between users with a carer and without are very small. There is, however, an interval need effect, with a greater proportion of more independent users reporting that this type of help was available to them.

Table 9.5
Percentage of users who have people around of whom they can easily ask small favours, by interval need and social support among community-based sample

| | Interval need | | | | | | Total | |
| | Critical | | Short | | Long | | | |
	No PIC %	PIC %	No PIC %	PIC %	No PIC %	PIC %	No PIC %	PIC %
Percentage of users	58.8	66.4	57.9	66.0	75.7	76.2	67.1	69.4
Total n =	17	122	19	97	37	101	73	320

Missing cases: 7. Sample: Cases with a user or proxy interview.

While 76 per cent of long interval need users without a carer said they had people around them they could ask for small favours, this proportion fell to 59 per cent among critical interval need users without a carer.

While social support, in general, is important for older people living in the community, the availability of a confidante contributes significantly to the maintenance of a good quality of life. The loss of this type of support through widowhood or other events can have significant psychological implications, particularly relating to morale and depression. Table 9.6 illustrates the proportion of users who reported that they had a confidante at Time I. The importance of principal carers in fulfilling this role is evident from the table. While a high proportion of users without a carer (64 per cent) said they did have a confidante, this grew to 85 per cent among users with a carer, with the pattern being consistent across interval need categories. Critical interval need users without a carer were the group least likely to report that they had someone around in whom they could confide, with just 53 per cent of these users stating that they had a confidante. The absence of this support among the frailest users underlines the important contribution formal services can make — particularly through regular contact with the same social worker or home help — in assisting this group of users.

Broader social contacts are also important in maintaining quality of life. Users were asked how satisfied they were with the available opportunities to meet people and socialise on a regular basis. Table 9.7 illustrates the responses, which demonstrate a clear relationship with interval need. It is the more independent, long interval need users who report the highest levels of satisfaction with their chances to meet people. While three out of four long interval need users described themselves as satisfied or very satisfied with their chances to socialise, this proportion fell to under two-thirds among critical interval need users, a finding which emphasises the link between functional independence and the ability to maintain social contacts.

Satisfaction and unmet need

The extent to which health and social services provide the type of support that older people want and require has an impact on quality of life. Satisfaction with the help received can both contribute to an acceptance of that assistance and the maintenance of morale. A significant body of research has found, however, that determining real levels of satisfaction among older people can be difficult. This is related to both low expectations of services and to the fear that dissatisfaction expressed will lead to a withdrawal of support (Abramson, 1988; Allen et al., 1992; Cox, 1996). The experience of chronic illness or disability can also lower expectations and demands, similar to the causal process described by Rodman (1963) as 'value stretch'. In order to address some of these issues, both ECCEP users and carers were asked a series of

Table 9.6

Percentage of users who have people around in whom they can confide, by interval need and social support among community-based sample

| | Interval need | | | | | | | | | | |
| | Critical | | Short | | Long | | Total | | | | |
	No PIC %	PIC %	No PIC %	PIC %	No PIC %	PIC %	No PIC %	PIC %			
Percentage of users	52.9	80.5	72.2	87.2	64.9	87.0	63.9	84.6			
Total n =	9	118	18	94	37	100	72	312			

Missing cases: 16. Sample: Cases with a user or proxy interview.

Table 9.7

How satisfied are users with the available opportunities to meet people and socialise, by interval need and social support among community-based sample

	Interval need							
	Critical		Short		Long		Total	
	No PIC	PIC	No PIC	PIC	No PIC	PIC	No PIC	PIC
	%	%	%	%	%	%	%	%
Very satisfied	33.3	16.8	11.1	14.4	34.2	28.7	28.2	20.2
Satisfied	33.3	42.5	49.9	59.4	39.5	42.5	40.8	47.8
Neither satisfied or dissatisfied	13.3	17.3	22.2	5.2	10.5	11.5	14.1	11.5
Dissatisfied	20.0	15.0	5.5	14.4	13.2	12.6	12.7	14.0
Very dissatisfied	0.0	8.4	11.2	6.5	2.6	4.6	4.3	6.5
Total n =	15	81	18	74	37	7	69	240

Missing cases: 15. Sample: Users who were not severely cognitively impaired.

questions relating to both satisfaction with the care management process (detailed in Chapter 5), with services and with their ability to remain living independently in the community. Questions relating to the need for support which was not met by existing services at Time I were also asked, in order to identify any unmet need following the initial assessment process.

First, users were asked about their overall satisfaction with the way in which social services had *assessed their needs and tried to help*. Satisfaction levels were high, with 80 per cent of users reporting that they were either satisfied or very satisfied. There were no significant differences relating to interval need, although users with a carer were slightly more likely to report that they were satisfied or very satisfied with the assessment and help (80 per cent) than users without a carer (72 per cent).

Users were also asked to assess their satisfaction at Time I with their own ability to remain living independently in the community. Table 9.8 illustrates that the vast majority of users were either very satisfied or satisfied with their ability to remain at home. It is interesting that the difference between the responses of users with a carer and those without are not significant. Other recent research found that older people living in the community described the availability of informal support as one of the most important factors permitting them to remain at home (Mack et al., 1997). Our results suggest that users may not view the presence or absence of a principal informal carer as a crucial determining factor in their own ability to continue living in the way they wish.

Table 9.8 does, however, show a relationship by interval need. Long interval need users were most satisfied with their ability to remain living at home, with 59 per cent of those with a carer and 43 per cent of those without a carer stating that they were very satisfied with their ability. Short interval need users without a carer were the least confident: 17 per cent of these users reported that they were dissatisfied with their ability to remain at home. This underlines the relationship between confidence in the future and the need for assistance. Those users who require regular help at home have lost some of the optimism evident among those whose needs are still infrequent.[2]

Services were, however, viewed by users as playing a key role in their ability to remain living independently in the community. Over half of users overall, excluding those with a severe cognitive impairment, reported that services helped them to remain at home 'to a great extent', while an additional 37 per cent reported that they assisted 'to a degree'. Just 7 per cent of users stated that services made no difference to their ability to continue living at home.

While user satisfaction both with services and the ability to remain at home was high overall, some respondents did identify needs which remained unmet at the time of the first interview. Table 9.9 illustrates the services which users felt they still required. Just over one in three users identified a need for more services. The most common unmet need was for aids and adaptations, which 15 per cent of users said they had expected but not received. As there can be a

Table 9.8

User satisfaction with their ability to live at home in the way that they want, by interval need and social support among community-based sample

Satisfaction of user with own ability to live at home	Interval need							
	Critical		Short		Long		Total	
	No PIC %	PIC %	No PIC %	PIC %	No PIC %	PIC %	No PIC %	PIC %
Very satisfied	38.5	37.8	16.6	36.9	59.0	42.7	44.3	39.3
Satisfied	53.8	45.5	55.5	47.0	33.3	46.1	42.8	46.2
Neither satisfied or dissatisfied	0.0	11.6	11.1	6.7	5.1	5.6	5.7	7.9
Dissatisfied	7.7	5.1	16.8	8.1	2.6	4.5	7.2	5.8
Very dissatisfied	0.0	0.0	0.0	1.3	0.0	1.1	0.0	0.8
Total n =	13	76	18	72	38	5	68	235

Missing cases: 21. Sample: Users who were not severely cognitively impaired.

Table 9.9
Services expected by user from social services but not provided sufficiently or at all, by social support among community-based sample

Services expected but not provided	No PIC %	PIC %	Total n =
Home support	15.9	10.2	11
Day care	5.4	0.0	1
Monitoring and sitting	5.4	5.1	5
Alarms, aids and adaptations	5.4	17.8	15
Help with garden and outside of house	5.3	4.4	4
Advice	5.3	0.0	1
Rehousing	5.3	2.5	3
Residential accommodation	5.4	0.0	1
Other	15.8	5.7	7
Total n =	9	27	36

Missing cases: 5. Source: Version 2 of the user questionnaire only for users who were not severely cognitively impaired.

long delay in obtaining some aids, particularly community alarms, it is likely that a proportion of these users had been assessed as requiring an aid or adaptation, but had not as yet received one by the time of the first interview. A need for home support was mentioned by 11 per cent of users overall, rising to 16 per cent among users without a principal carer who would be less likely to have an alternative source of assistance with domestic help of the kind home helps provide. Other services were each requested by fewer than 10 per cent of users, such as sitting services (5 per cent of users) and help with the garden or the outside of the home (also identified as an unmet need by 5 per cent of users).

Changes Time I to Time II

Health status

In the period between the first and second interview, many users experienced changes in their need-related circumstances. In order to capture these changes and consider the contribution of services to the observed change, interview responses to questions posed at both Time I and Time II were compared. The first group of these change outcomes to be examined relates to the health status of the user. Health outcomes have been divided into three categories: changes in functional ability, physical health, and mental health.

In the absence of intervention, the average performance of a group of elderly people would be expected to deteriorate over time in each of these three categories of need. However, the deployment of resources may have the effect of slowing this rate of deterioration or even of reversing the trend to give some improvement. The measurement of outcomes allows these rates to be compared for users with differing levels of interval need and social support.

Changes in functional ability

The probability of reporting problems with activities of daily living[3] increases with age (Peek et al., 1997). However, in a general population, increases in both ADLs and instrumental activities of daily living[4] are very gradual (Anderson et al., 1998). By being offered suitable types of help, this trend in the frail elderly can be slowed or reversed in the short-term, affecting general mobility and ability to perform ADLs and IADLs.

An ADL score was calculated by counting how many of the following five activities the user could not manage unaided: bathing/all over wash, dressing/undressing, transfer, toileting, and feeding.[5] This yielded a score which ranged between 0 and 5. The increase in ADL score, therefore, had a maximum range of between -5 and 5. This increase has been broken down by interval need and social support in Table 9.10.

Table 9.10 illustrates overall ADL score increased very slightly (0.06) from its mean value of 1.28 at Time I. The overall variation with interval need indicates that while short and long interval need users showed an increase in ADL score of around 0.12, critical interval need users showed a decrease of 0.13, indicating an improvement. One possible explanation might be that a greater proportion of critical interval need users were recovering from an acute illness, and thus an improvement in ADLs over time would be expected. The improvements may also be due to targeting more resources on this group of older people with complex needs. Improvements among users also varied with social support. As Table 9.10 shows, while users with a principal carer showed a mean *increase* in ADL score of 0.09, those without a carer demonstrated a mean *decrease* of 0.05. This suggests that in instances where users were not already receiving substantial informal support, there was greater scope for achieving an improvement in ADL performance through care management intervention or, again, that care managers target more resources on this subgroup. These two effects combine to yield the greatest improvement (-0.33) for critical interval need users with no carer. However, in view of the relatively high standard errors, these inferences must remain tentative.

Table 9.10
Increase in ADL score between Time I and Time II, by interval need and social support among community-based sample

| | Interval need | | | | | | | | |
| | Critical | | Short | | Long | | Total | | |
	No PIC	PIC	No PIC	PIC	No PIC	PIC	No PIC	PIC	Total
Mean	-0.33	-0.10	0.13	0.13	-0.03	0.19	-0.05	0.09	0.06
Standard error of mean	0.62	0.22	0.59	0.19	0.03	0.07	0.13	0.09	0.08
Total n =	6	37	8	38	28	54	42	130	172

Missing cases: 39. Sample: 211 users at home at Time I and Time II excluding those with no user or proxy interview.

The changes in ADL score are of course brought about by changes in the individual activities of daily living, and some of these are now considered. While a slightly higher proportion of dependent users became independent than vice versa with regard to bathing and transfer, there was a small overall deterioration for dressing, toileting and feeding. In relation to dressing and toileting, this net deterioration only occurred at short and long interval need. Moreover, it was those without a carer who were more likely to become independent with dressing (14 per cent). In contrast, those with a carer became more dependent (15 per cent) than independent (5 per cent). These results again suggest that more resources were being targeted on those in greatest need, particularly if they lacked informal help.

An IADL score was calculated by counting how many of the following seven activities the user reported they could not manage unaided: shopping, meal preparation, making a hot drink, preparing a snack, heavy housework, light housework and handling own money. This yielded a score which ranged between 0 and 7. The increase in IADL score, therefore, had a maximum range of between -7 and 7. This increase has been broken down by interval need and social support in Table 9.11.

Table 9.11 illustrates that there was an overall improvement in IADL functioning of 0.28 from the Time I score of 1.21. The much smaller standard error of only 0.10 suggests that this improvement is statistically significant. Once again, the improvement increased with interval need, being only 0.10 for long interval need but around 0.46 at short and critical interval need, although this difference was of only marginal statistical significance in relation to the standard errors. In contrast to ADL change, overall improvement in IADL performance was slightly greater for users with a principal carer (0.31) than for those without one (0.17). This suggests the possibility that users may have lost the ability to perform certain IADL tasks because the carer had previously completely taken them over; care managers may then have advised these carers to assist the user in relearning these tasks. An alternative explanation for these improvements in IADL score is that when users were asked about their need for help with IADLs, some had interpreted this as their overall need shortfall, so ignored the needs which were already being met.

In relation to changes in individual instrumental activities of daily living, the proportion of users who became more independent was either equal to that becoming dependent (preparing snack and managing finances) or exceeded it for remaining items (shopping, meal preparation, preparing hot drink, and heavy and light housework), leading to a net improvement. With regard to meal preparation, making a hot drink and light housework, this improvement was only found at short and critical interval need, again suggesting that more resources were targeted at the higher need users. The one exception was the need for help in managing finances, for which short and critical interval need users showed a net deterioration while a majority of long interval need users improved.

Table 9.11

Increase in IADL score between Time I and Time II, by interval need and social support among community-based sample

	Interval need									
	Critical		Short		Long		Total		
	No PIC	PIC	No PIC	PIC	No PIC	PIC	No PIC	PIC	Total
Mean	-0.17	-0.47	-0.50	-0.47	-0.11	-0.09	-0.17	-0.31	-0.28
Standard error of mean	0.31	0.31	0.57	0.24	0.19	0.13	0.16	0.13	0.10
Total n =	6	36	6	37	27	53	39	127	166

Missing cases: 45. Sample: 211 users at home at Time I and Time II excluding those with no user or proxy interview.

Changes in physical health

Physical health has an important influence on both functioning and mental health. As Anderson and colleagues (1998) remind us: 'Morbidity holds a primary position in the disablement process and has a complex association with disability'. Table 9.12 shows which health problem the user reported that they had suffered from in the six months leading up to the Time II user interview.

Table 9.12 illustrates the prevalence of health problems among users in the six months preceding the Time II interview. The most common category, musculo-skeletal problems, consisted mainly of arthritis, and occurred for over one-third of cases. Circulatory problems, affecting 23 per cent of users, included heart problems and hypertension. While other skeletal problems are correlated with a slow decline in functional ability, circulatory problems are associated with a more rapid decline (Anderson et al., 1998). Respiratory problems, which occurred in 17 per cent of users, covered bronchitis, emphysema and asthma. Eyesight and hearing problems were other significant items.

In view of the expected strong association between physical health and physical functioning, it is perhaps surprising that many of these health items

Table 9.12
Health problems in the previous six months reported by user at Time II among community-based sample

Health problem	%
Any nervous system problem	8.9
Cataracts/glaucoma/other eyesight problem	15.6
Deafness/tinnitus/other hearing problem	10.2
Any circulatory problem	22.8
Any respiratory problem	17.3
Any digestive problem	12.2
Genito-urinary/excretory	12.0
Musculo-skeletal problems	36.6
Cancer/other internal growth/tumour	2.2
Diabetes	2.8
Flu/cold/chest infection/pneumonia	7.3
Other health problems	19.2
No health problems	34.0
Total n =	175

Sample: 175 users interviewed at Time II and not severely cognitively impaired.

did not show a clear relationship with interval need. One reason was the relatively low proportions reporting each condition, requiring rather bigger sample sizes for a positive association between ill health and disability to emerge. Nevertheless, nervous system disorders, which include severe conditions such as stroke and Parkinson's disease, were more frequent at critical interval need (13 per cent) than at short and long interval need (7 per cent). Also, the presence of genito-urinary problems (including incontinence) was more frequent at critical and short interval need (16 per cent) than at long interval need (8 per cent). Seventeen per cent of all users had sustained an accident or injury, such as a fall or road accident, in the last six months. Fourteen per cent of users had been a hospital inpatient between the two user interviews.

The increase in the number of health problems reported by the care manager between Time I and Time II, a period which averaged 46 weeks, is given in Table 9.13. Overall, users were perceived to have an increase of 1.22 in the number of health problems at Time II compared to 2.59 problems present at Time I. As Anderson et al. (1998) point out, the number of chronic diseases and illnesses increases with prevalent and incident disability. It is, therefore, likely that a growth in this number over time would also increase with disability and hence with interval need. Although not all the health problems reported by the care manager are necessarily chronic, it can be seen from Table 9.13 that this change in the number of health problems increased from 1.01 at long interval need to 1.44 at critical interval need, although the relatively large confidence intervals made this difference not quite statistically significant. This increase was greater for users with a principal carer, although the difference was again not statistically significant. None of the six groups in the table showed a decrease in number of health problems. One possible explanation for this is that because care managers are not trained to identify the full range of medical problems, they take longer to become aware of all the health problems suffered by the users they supervise, and thus may have underestimated the number of health problems affecting the user at Time I.

Because many aspects of risk in frail elderly people are related to health, risk has been addressed in this section. According to a Canadian study of frail elderly people in the community (Mack et al., 1997), the most important factors affecting the ability of these older people to remain at home were health, adequate finances and a social network to provide companionship and help. Moreover, Williams and colleagues (1991) comment that it is not possible to assess the risks to independent living among older people without first knowing which resources they have available. For example, loss of capacity to cook may not be a problem if meals on wheels is readily available. Thus, care management intervention can minimise the risk to the elderly person by offering suitable resources to combat problems.

Table 9.14 shows the increase in the number of risk items identified by the care manager between Time I and Time II. The number was obtained by

Table 9.13

Increase in number of user's health problems reported by care manager at Time I and Time II, by interval need and social support among community-based sample

Increase in health problems	Interval need								Total
	Critical		Short		Long		Total		
	No PIC	PIC	No PIC	PIC	No PIC	PIC	No PIC	PIC	
Mean	0.88	1.54	0.69	1.31	1.23	0.95	0.99	1.27	1.22
Standard error of mean	0.64	0.30	0.44	0.25	0.39	0.22	0.28	0.15	0.13
Total n =	15	82	13	70	23	80	51	231	281

Missing cases: 56. Sample: Cases with a care manager interview at Time I and Time II.
More precisely, this increase is obtained by subtracting the number of health problems during the past twelve months reported by the user at Time I from the number of those problems during the past six months reported by the user at Time II. The overall mean number of health problems was 2.59 at Time I and 3.80 at Time II. The number of health problems was obtained using a checklist of 35 items together with an 'other' category. These include four items of mental disorder: senile dementia, other cognitive impairment, depression and other mental ill health. Examining the distribution of the increase in number of health problems, 18 per cent of cases showed a decrease in the number of problems, 24 per cent showed no change, and 58 per cent showed an increase.

counting how many of fifteen items of risk were present at each interview. Overall, there was a decrease in the number of risk items of 0.98 (almost 1) from the mean value at referral/review of 3.31. Critical interval need cases showed the greatest reduction in risk items (-1.89), this result being statistically significant. Although there was no overall dependence on the presence of a principal carer, critical interval need cases without a carer showed a significantly greater reduction in number of risk items than those with one, this amounting to almost 4. It is reassuring that this most vulnerable of the six groups has responded so effectively to care management intervention. The result suggests that these users at greatest risk are being effectively targeted in this respect, probably as a result of the type of eligibility criteria used (Blackman and Atkinson, 1997; Clark et al., 1998).

Changes in mental health

Three aspects of mental health have been considered in this section: cognitive impairment, depression and morale. Cognitive impairment was measured using the Katzman scale. This produced a score of between 0 and 28 in response to six questions relating to the user's orientation in time, short-term memory and other cognitive skills. Scores of 11 and over were taken to indicate moderate cognitive impairment, and 22 and over severe cognitive impairment. The various medical conditions leading to cognitive impairment are usually progressive and untreatable (with the important exception of acute confusional state). Nevertheless, certain circumstances can exacerbate these conditions, so that the removal of these circumstances could lead to an improvement. Thus, while moving house could exacerbate disorientation, the maintenance of an unchanging environment could minimise such disturbance. Moreover, reminding the user about such things as the time of day and other aspects of orientation are can lead to certain short-term improvements. Other evidence suggests that depression can contribute to a poor score on the Katzman scale. Conversely, if care management intervention is able to reduce depression effectively, cognitive performance on the Katzman scale is likely to improve.

Table 9.15 shows the mean increase in the user's Katzman score between the Time I and Time II user interviews, a period averaging 34 weeks. The whole group showed a mean decrease of 2.35 from the Time I value of 10.12. This decrease was statistically significant in relation to the standard error of 0.68. This decrease was significantly greater for critical interval need cases (5.07) than for short or long interval need cases (around 1.0). The presence of a principal carer led to differences which were just statistically significant. While users with a carer showed a decrease in Katzman score of 3.06, those without showed an increase of 0.38. If it is assumed that the reduction in Katzman score between Time I and Time II is largely the effect of recovery of

Table 9.14

Increase in number of risk items reported by care manager between referral/review and Time II, by interval need and social support among community-based sample

Increase in number of risk items	Critical		Short		Long		Total		Total
	No PIC	PIC	No PIC	PIC	No PIC	PIC	No PIC	PIC	
Mean	-3.83	-1.55	0.49	-0.27	-0.64	-1.00	-0.99	-0.97	-0.98
Standard error of mean	1.38	0.38	1.00	0.36	0.44	0.40	0.56	0.23	0.21
Total n =	9	52	14	45	17	55	40	153	193

Missing cases: 57. Sample: Cases with a standard or brief care manager interview at Time I and Time II (n=250).

Table 9.15

Mean increase in user's Katzman score between Time I and Time II, by interval need and social support among community-based sample

Increase in Katzman	Interval need						Total		
	Critical		Short		Long				
score	No PIC	PIC	No PIC	PIC	No PIC	PIC	No PIC	PIC	Total
Mean	-0.30	-5.81	0.88	-0.95	0.47	-2.17	0.38	-3.06	-2.35
Standard error of mean	3.42	1.79	1.14	1.12	1.28	1.05	1.05	0.80	0.68
Total n =	9	59	8	47	29	71	46	178	224

Missing cases: 0. Sample: Users with Time I and Time II interview (n=224).

some users from a crisis period at Time I, then one possible inference is that users having the support of a carer are more likely to improve following the crisis than those with no such support. The combination of these two effects led to the greatest decrease in Katzman score for critical interval need cases with a carer (5.8). Katzman scores only increased — by a small amount — for long and short interval need cases without a carer.

Table 9.16 examines the proportions of users whose Katzman score decreased by more than 5, when broken down by interval need and social support. Overall some two-thirds of cases had scores which changed by less than this amount, with a greater proportion of the remainder showing decreases (22 per cent) than increases (14 per cent). A likely explanation for this high proportion of cases showing a substantial decrease in Katzman score is that users were initially being tested during or soon after a crisis period when they were likely to be at their most confused and disorientated. Any recovery since then is likely to be largely spontaneous, though in some measure a result of the stable environment and stimulation offered by care management intervention.

Although not shown here, the proportion of cases showing a decrease in cognitive impairment was much greater for critical interval need cases (34 per cent) than for short or long interval need (16 per cent), which may result from the greater severity of problems experienced by critical interval need cases at the time of the first interview. Decreases were also much more frequent for users with a principal carer (26 per cent) than for those without one (5 per cent). This difference was maintained at all levels of interval need.

Depression is one of the most common mental health problems for those aged 60 and older (Blazer et al., 1987). In comparison to early onset cases, depression in later life is less influenced by genetics and more by environmental factors such as loss of self-esteem, meaningful roles, or significant others, as well as declining social role contacts due to functional and financial limitations. By ameliorating some of these environmental causes, effective care management intervention can reduce or reverse the increase in depression with age. As well as this care management effect there may also be, as with cognitive impairment, a spontaneous recovery in some users from a crisis at Time I. Depression was measured by means of the shortened fifteen item version of the geriatric depression scale (GDS) (Yesavage, 1988), though was only asked of a small subset of 35 users at both Time I and Time II. However, five of these fifteen questions were asked of 177 users at both these times. The Pearson correlation coefficient between the five and fifteen question scales was very high, being 0.90 at Time I and 0.88 at Time II. It was, therefore, decided to use the five question scale as a proxy for the fifteen question scale, scaling it up by the appropriate factor, 2.94. This scaled-up proxy version of GDS is shown in Table 9.17 broken down by social support.

Table 9.16

Proportion of users with a decrease in Katzman score of greater than 5 from Time I to Time II, by interval need and social support among community-based sample

| Decrease in Katzman score greater than 5 | Interval need | | | | | | | | Total | |
| | Critical | | Short | | Long | | | | | |
	No PIC	PIC	No PIC	PIC	No PIC	PIC			No PIC	PIC	Total
Percentage	15.0	36.7	0.0	18.6	3.3	21.6			5.1	25.8	21.5
Total n =	9	59	8	47	29	71			46	178	224

Missing cases: 0. Sample: Users with Time I and Time II interview.

Table 9.17

Mean increase in short geriatric depression score, by social support among community-based sample

Increase in short geriatric depression score	No PIC	PIC	Total
Mean	-0.21	0.50	0.35
Standard error of mean	0.56	0.38	0.32
Total n =	41	136	177

Missing cases: 47. Sample: 224 users at home at Time I and Time II.
A proxy score was obtained using the five items drawn from the shortened fifteen point GDS. The score obtained was then scaled up by a factor of 2.94. If one item is entered as 'don't know' or 'no response', that item is given the value 0.5. If more than one item is entered as 'don't know' or 'no response', the GDS is set to missing.

Table 9.17 illustrates that there has been an overall mean increase in depression score of 0.35 at Time II from the Time I value of 6.05. This increase is very small and comparable with the standard error of 0.32. The increase was greater for users with a carer, with a *decrease* of -0.21 for users without a carer contrasting with an *increase* of 0.50 for those with a carer. However, this contrast was not quite sufficient to be significant in relation to the standard errors. Thus, there may be greater scope for a reduction in depression for cases without a carer, perhaps because more resources are targeted on these users.

Finally, improvements in morale were measured using the PGC morale scale (Lawton, 1975). This version produced a scale with a range of 0-17 with high scores indicating high morale, so improvement in morale could vary between -17 and 17. Table 9.18 shows the mean improvement broken down by interval need and social support. Overall, there was a small improvement in morale of 0.60 from its Time I value of 8.68. This improvement was significant when the standard error of only 0.25 was taking into account, and increased with interval need from 0.44 at long interval need to 0.99 at critical interval need, although the increase was not sufficient to be statistically significant. Overall, the increase in morale was very slightly greater for users with a carer, although the difference became much greater for critical interval need users. Thus, care management intervention may be most successful in improving morale in cases of critical interval need with a carer, although the effects from this type of simple analysis were too small to be statistically significant. Statistical modelling on the other hand has clearly found (Davies and Fernández, 1999) that the effect specifically from services on morale was greatest for users with a cognitive impairment, again most marked when the user also had critical interval needs and a carer.

Table 9.18

Improvement in PGC morale score from Time I to Time II, by interval need and social support among community-based sample

Improvement in PGC morale score	*Interval need*						Total		
	Critical		Short		Long				
	No PIC	PIC	No PIC	PIC	No PIC	PIC	No PIC	PIC	Total
Mean	0.43	1.11	-0.25	0.69	0.62	0.36	0.43	0.66	0.60
Standard error of mean	0.63	0.67	1.93	0.60	0.60	0.32	0.50	0.29	0.25
Total n =	9	39	8	43	28	65	45	148	193

Missing cases: 31. Sample: Users at home at Time I and Time II (n=224).

Quality of life at Time II

Service receipt over time can have a marked impact on the quality of life of older people. Effective care management interventions can assist the user in maintaining independence within his/her own home, sustaining existing or new relationships, and retaining satisfaction with life and the support offered. Changes in quality of life over time are by their nature difficult to measure, as is the role of services in bringing about these changes. It is possible, however, to describe findings related to changes in the three indicators of quality of life introduced earlier in this chapter: choice and control; relationships and social inclusion; and satisfaction and unmet need. Like health outcomes and outcomes for carers, these change measures relate to differences in the responses of users and carers between Time I and Time II interviews, reflecting an average period of service receipt of just under nine months between interviews.

Changes in choice and control

Receiving formal services for the first time can affect older people's feelings of autonomy. Accepting assistance implies some measure of dependence, which involves a loss of control (Challis, 1981). Particularly if services are means-tested or subsidised, older people can be made to feel that they are relying on welfare, which can undermine their sense of self-sufficiency (Langan et al., 1996). Exchange or power theory has been applied as a framework in other PSSRU studies (Davies and Knapp, 1981; Qureshi et al., 1989) for understanding changes in control experienced by older people receiving services. These theories, particularly work by Dowd (1975, based on Blau, 1964) postulate that the power of the older person in relation to his/her social environment can diminish when this environment involves structured assistance (such as in a care home or receiving regular home care), reducing the influence of the older person and placing him/her in a position of compliance. The nature of services themselves can also affect feelings of choice and control: for instance, the timing of some services can impose restrictions, by forcing some older people to adapt their own routines to fit those of the service provider.

Not all the evidence relating to the receipt of formal services and feelings of control over time is, however, negative. Other research has indicated that effective care management can empower older people to make their own choices about any help required. The provision of some forms of assistance (particularly aids and adaptations, or assistance with instrumental activities) can actually improve feelings of independence by allowing people to 'help themselves' (Clark et al., 1998). Accepting formal services can also liberate some older people from reliance on their families for support.

ECCEP users were asked at both Time I and Time II whether they felt they were free to run their own life in the way they wished. Changes in the responses are illustrated in Table 9.19.

Table 9.19 illustrates changes in users' feelings of control over their own lives. There was a slight reduction in the confidence of users since the first interview, an average decrease of 3 per cent overall from 64 per cent at Time I. Interestingly, it was users without a carer who reported the more significant reduction in their feelings of control, particularly short interval need users without a carer (31 per cent). These older people may have been unused to receiving support prior to their referral and were more likely to be living alone than users with carers. The acceptance of care-managed interventions may have involved a significant change in the lives of these older people who had previously valued their ability to cope alone. Thus, formal service intervention resulted in a loss of some of their feelings of independence.

The only group of users who reported an improvement in their feelings of being free to run their own lives at Time II were critical interval need users with a carer: the relatively small standard error indicating that this result was significant. These are users who have functional limitations and may have complex needs. Users at this level of need, even with the regular support of a carer, may be aware of the role formal services are playing in allowing them to remain living in the community. Although some improvement must be attributed to diminished health problems or the recovery of function over time (particularly for those users discharged from hospital) a new or augmented package of services for these users may be adding to their feelings of control in the home, assisting them with tasks they could not otherwise perform. Particularly as other evidence suggests that a larger proportion of resources are being concentrated on users with complex needs, the finding of greater feelings of control at Time II may indicate that services are a central factor in permitting these older people to run their lives as they wish.

Changes in relationships and social inclusion

Service intervention can in some cases significantly change the social circumstances of older people. Numerous studies have described the important role that home helps and other workers play in providing users with companionship and monitoring, as well as assistance with tasks (Dexter and Harbert, 1983; Davies and Challis, 1986; SWSI, 1996). Attendance at day centres, respite facilities and day hospital can give isolated users new opportunities to socialise. It has also been argued that service intervention can strengthen existing social networks over time, by supporting carers, accessing transport and improving user morale (Twigg and Atkin, 1994; Healy and Yarrow, 1997).

Table 9.19

Increase in percentage feeling free to run life from Time I to Time II, by interval need and social support among community-based sample

	Critical		Short		Long		Total
	No PIC %	PIC %	No PIC %	PIC %	No PIC %	PIC %	n =
Mean	- 8	20	- 31	- 12	- 3	- 6	- 3
Standard error of mean	18	9	25	8	7	6	4
Total n =	9	39	8	43	28	65	193

Missing cases: 31. Sample: Users at home at Time I and Time II (n=224).

This question — 'Do you feel free to run your life the way you want?' — forms part of the PGC morale scale.

Table 9.20

Change in availability of people from whom users can ask small favours between Time I and Time II, by social support among community-based sample

	No PIC %	PIC %	Total n =
Always had someone	51.2	60.5	98
Not now, before yes	20.9	7.7	19
Not before, now yes	16.3	24.9	38
Never had anybody	9.3	6.9	13
Don't know	2.3	0.0	1
Total n =	42	127	169

Missing cases: 0. Sample: Users at home at Time I and Time II and not severely cognitively impaired at both these times.

At Time I, users were asked a series of questions relating to access to wider social support networks and opportunities to socialise. These responses can be compared with those at Time II, in order to assess the degree of change some months after the new care package was put in place.

A small proportion of users reported a change by Time II in the availability of people they could turn to in an emergency or time of real difficulty. While 8 per cent of users indicated that the people available for emergency assistance at Time I were no longer available at Time II, a much larger proportion — 16 per cent — indicated that they now felt there were people they could turn to in a time of real difficulty, whereas at Time I they had been unable to identify such sources of support. Thus, while the proportion of users reporting a change is small, there has been an overall improvement.

Change is also apparent in the proportion of users identifying people they can easily ask for small favours. Table 9.20 illustrates changes between Time I and Time II. While the overall picture is one of stability — 58 per cent of users stating that they still have this form of support and 7 per cent indicating that it was not available at either Time I or Time II — over a third of users reported a change. The proportion of users reporting that they now have people they can ask for small favours (23 per cent) is more than double that indicating that they had lost this form of support since services were put in place (11 per cent). Improvements were more prevalent among users with a carer (25 per cent) than those without a carer (16 per cent). This may be due to service intervention aimed at relieving the carer which has put the user in contact with a wider range of people, through day care, respite or lunch club attendance.

The proportion of users indicating that they have a confidante also improved since Time I, as Table 9.21 illustrates. While 71 per cent of users indicated at both Time I and Time II that they had someone in whom they

Table 9.21

Change in the availability of people in whom user can confide from Time I to Time II, by social support among community-based sample

| | No PIC | PIC | Total |
	%	%	n =
Always had someone	53.5	76.2	119
Not now, before yes	11.6	6.9	14
Not before, now yes	16.3	10.7	20
Never had anybody	16.3	4.6	13
Don't know	2.3	1.5	3
Total n =	42	127	169

Missing cases: 0. Sample: Users at home at Time I and Time II and not severely cognitively impaired at both these times.

could confide, an additional 12 per cent gained a confidante between the two interviews, while the smaller proportion of 8 per cent indicated a loss. It was users without a carer who were much more likely to report that they have gained a confidante: 16 per cent of users without a carer said they now had someone in whom they could confide, compared with 11 per cent of users with a carer. Although the numbers are small, these users may be identifying a home help or other contact established through care management intervention as a confidante, particularly if they live alone.

Table 9.22 illustrates changes in users' opportunities to meet people and socialise between Time I and Time II. While 41 per cent of users indicated that their opportunities remained the same, the majority of users did report a change. The proportion of users reporting an increase (31 per cent) and those reporting a decrease (27 per cent) in their chances to meet people were similar, with the overall picture being one of slight improvement. While the presence or absence of a carer was not found to be a significant factor, it is clear from Table 9.22 that there is an interaction effect between interval need and the presence of a carer for some groups of users. More dependent (short and critical interval) users without a carer were overall much more positive about their new opportunities to socialise and meet people than other users. Although the actual numbers are small, the marked improvement suggests that services were helping to compensate for any functional limitations that previously prevented these users from getting out and meeting people. Without the availability of a principal carer, these opportunities may have been limited in the past, due to problems of transport, access and confidence. Aspects of the care package fully implemented by Time II may have improved this important aspect of quality of life for a particularly vulnerable group of older people.

Table 9.22

Change in the opportunities to meet people and socialise from Time I to Time II, by interval need and social support among community-based sample

	Interval need						Total
	Critical		Short		Long		
	No PIC	PIC	No PIC	PIC	No PIC	PIC	n =
	%	%	%	%	%	%	
Got worse	0.0	22.0	25.0	29.4	32.1	29.2	44
No change	60.0	46.7	37.5	38.2	42.9	38.0	67
Improved	40.0	31.3	37.5	32.4	25.0	32.8	51
Total n =	5	35	8	33	27	53	162

Missing cases: 7. Sample: Cases with user interviewed in community at Time I and Time II, and not severely cognitively impaired at both these times.

Changes in satisfaction and unmet need

Findings relating to user satisfaction at Time I reflected opinions about services and their effects shortly after (re-)referral. These initial impressions can alter over time, as users become more aware of longer-term changes due to care management intervention. Thus, satisfaction with services and the ability to live independently was assessed at Time II, and responses to some of these questions were compared with Time I answers.

Table 9.23 illustrates user assessments of their contact with social services during the six months preceding the Time II interview. The table shows responses for users with a carer, and those without a carer. For the group overall a significant proportion of users — 61 per cent — described their experience with social services as favourable. While only 10 per cent indicated that their experience had been negative in the past six months, an additional 29 per cent did describe their experience as mixed. Thus, for four out of ten users, some aspects of their contact with social services were not entirely positive.

Users without a carer were slightly more critical of their experience than those with a carer: 14 per cent of users without a carer described the contact they had with services as unfavourable, compared with 9 per cent of those with a carer. This pattern is similar to that at Time I, when users were asked a slightly different question relating specifically to satisfaction with the way in which their needs had been assessed and met. It may be that users with a carer are aware that services are addressing the carer's needs as well as their own. As other research has suggested, older people requiring assistance are often concerned about any strain or burden meeting their needs has placed on their relatives and friends. Interventions from formal services that are perceived as

Table 9.23

Experience of social services over last six months at Time II, by social support among community-based sample

Experience of social services over last six months	No PIC %	PIC %	Total n =
Favourable	55.6	62.6	98
Mixed	30.6	28.0	46
Unfavourable	13.9	9.3	17
Total n =	35	125	160

Missing cases: 64. Sample: Cases with user interviewed in community at Time I and Time II (n=224).

alleviating the carer's responsibilities can be highly valued by some older service users (Brody, 1981).

Users and carers were asked at both Time I and Time II whether the services received helped the user to remain living at home. At Time I, just over half of users agreed that services helped them 'to a great extent' to remain at home, while an additional 37 per cent said that services were helping 'to a degree'. Just 7 per cent of users indicated that services were making no difference or not helping at all. Table 9.24 illustrates changes in user responses between the two interviews. The single largest group of users gave the same response at both Time I and Time II (54 per cent). Among those users who indicated a change, however, the proportion reporting an improvement in the extent to which they felt that services helped them remain at home was greater (29 per cent) than those reporting a deterioration (17 per cent). Thus, by the time the care package had been in place for several months, users were overall more confident that services were making a significant contribution to the maintenance of their independence.

Table 9.24 also illustrates a clear pattern by interval need, with more dependent users indicating greater confidence in the role of social services than less dependent users. When combined with the presence or absence of a carer, it is evident that critical and short interval need users without a carer were particularly pleased with input from social services over time. Indeed, 57 per cent of critical interval need users without a carer and 37 per cent of short interval need users without a carer reported that they were more confident at Time II that services were instrumental in allowing them to live as they wished. It is interesting to reflect on findings relating to this indication of user satisfaction in conjunction with the overall improvements in functional and mental status among more dependent users (discussed in the health status section of this chapter). The targeting of more intensive resources on these users is thus having not only a rehabilitative effect, but is also making an impact on some aspects of quality of life.

Unmet need

A final indicator of changes in quality of life over time is the extent to which users report unmet needs for assistance. Some interventions — particularly aids and adaptations and other services with a waiting list — are not always immediately available. This can result in a continued need for additional assistance, even after the initial care package has been in place for several months.

Users were asked which, if any, services they needed but had not received by Time II, or needed more of. Users selected their responses from a list of 27 possible services, choosing any that applied. Just over half — 51 per cent — of users interviewed at Time II answered this question and were able to identify

Table 9.24
Change in extent that help allows users to live as they would like from Time I to Time II, by interval need and social support among community-based sample

| Did ability of help to improve user's life increase | Interval need | | | | | | Total |
| | Critical | | Short | | Long | | |
	No PIC %	PIC %	No PIC %	PIC %	No PIC %	PIC %	n =
Got worse	14.3	16.0	25.0	11.4	24.0	16.4	27
No change	28.6	53.5	37.5	60.0	56.0	54.4	88
Improved	57.1	30.5	37.5	28.6	20.0	29.2	48
Total n =	7	36	8	34	24	53	163

Missing cases: 6. Sample: Cases with user interviewed in community at Time I and Time II, and not severely cognitively impaired at both these times.

services which they still required.[6] A resulting count of service shortfall among these users found that the average number of services still needed per user was 2.48.[7] There was no clear interval need effect, but users with a carer reported unmet need for a slightly higher number of services (2.53) than did users without a carer (2.33), although the differences are small. What is perhaps more significant is the type of services which respondents indicated they still needed.

Table 9.25 illustrates the services which users reported they still needed but which had not been provided by Time II. As this was a multiple response question, totals exceed 100 per cent. The table lists only those services which a significant number of users indicated were still required, with the 'other' category accounting for a variety of services which only a small number of respondents said were still needed.

The most common unmet need at Time II was for cleaning services. This need was particularly prevalent among less dependent, long interval need users, 44 per cent of whom said they needed some or more of this service. These less dependent users may not qualify for cleaning as a result of tightened eligibility criteria. However, as another recent study has described (Clark et al., 1998), help with housework remains a priority for most older

Table 9.25
Services which users still require at Time II

Service required but not provided	%	Total n =
Help with cleaning	36.3	32
Safety/alarm system	20.9	19
Companionship	18.7	17
Help with shopping	16.5	15
General support at home	16.5	15
Disability equipment	14.3	13
Transport	14.3	13
Help with personal care	13.2	12
Someone to check that I am OK	13.2	12
Help with garden and outside of house	9.9	9
Other	50.5	45
None	2.2	2
Total n =		89

Missing cases: 86. Sample: 175 users interviewed in community at Time I and Time II, and not severely cognitively impaired at Time II.

people using services, even though this assistance is becoming less readily available.

Another type of assistance which was traditionally provided by home helps but is now less widespread is assistance with shopping, which 16 per cent of users selected as an unmet need. Again, this service was requested by a higher proportion of long interval need users (26 per cent) and also those without a carer, who may require assistance with this task but have fewer available informal sources of help. Aids and adaptations were mentioned by a significant proportion of users as an unmet need: first, for safety alarms, which may have a waiting list of some months; and second, for disability equipment, which was mentioned as an unmet need by slightly more users without a carer (19 per cent) than with a carer (13 per cent). A relatively small proportion of users mentioned assistance with personal care or other intimate tasks as an unmet need (13 per cent), suggesting either that they were unwilling to identify these tasks as something they could not do for themselves, or that services were meeting these needs.

Conclusion

ECCEP illustrates that the first few weeks and months following the implementation of a care package can be a period of significant change for older service users. For some users — just under one in four — initial service intervention is insufficient or unable to prevent the outcome of death or institutionalisation within a year of referral. For the majority of older people in the study, however, the implementation of services signals the beginning of a period in which positive changes in functional ability, mental and physical health and social circumstances can be observed. This chapter has described some of these changes, and highlighted their implications. It is useful to summarise some of these findings and to illustrate how a pattern emerges across user groups in relation to the impact of services. When these findings are considered in conjunction with the ECCEP productivities results (Davies and Fernández, 1999), conclusions can be drawn about the efficiency and effectiveness of services in the post-reform period.

Outcomes for users show clearly that the impact of services is more marked among those with complex needs, particularly users at the critical and short interval level, and those without a carer. This is particularly the case in relation to improvements in health status, and in relation to social inclusion and relationships. These improvements suggest both that resources are indeed being targeted on the most vulnerable older people, and that they are having a positive effect over time.

While functional ability, physical health and mental health would be expected to gradually decline over time without intervention, ECCEP evidence demonstrates small but important improvements in several key indicators in the months between Time I and Time II. In regard to functional capacity, the ability to perform ADLs declined slightly for the sample as a whole but improved among critical interval need users and those without a carer. IADL score improved slightly for all groups, particularly short and critical interval need users. While some of this improvement can be attributed to recovery following a crisis or discharge from hospital, more dependent users have also clearly benefited from care management interventions designed to maximise their capacity for independent living. This is perhaps most evident in the reductions care managers reported in relation to risk items. Critical interval need users again recorded the most significant decrease, particularly those without a carer. Risk items included falling, not eating well, wandering, loneliness and other factors, all of which can be addressed by a carefully constructed care plan.

Improvements in mental health are also evident among more dependent users, although the relationship with the presence or absence of a principal carer is not as clear. While evidence to date does not suggest that social care services can reverse decline relating to cognitive impairment, it is known that the maintenance of a stable environment and regular assistance with daily tasks can improve orientation and alleviate related conditions, such as depression. Thus, we see a slight improvement in cognitive ability — measured by the Katzman scale — for users overall between Time I and Time II, with the improvement again most marked among critical interval need users. Morale also improved for the sample overall, the improvement increasing with interval need.

Clear benefits from care management intervention are also evident in relation to the social circumstances of users. For each indicator of social inclusion — the availability of people to turn to in an emergency, people to ask for small favours, the availability of a confidante and the opportunity to meet people and socialise — improvements were evident between Time I and Time II for the user sample as a whole. Improvements were most marked for a variety of user groups, with more dependent users benefiting to a greater extent in most instances. Those without a carer also showed the most marked improvement regarding the availability of a confidante and the opportunity to meet people and socialise, suggesting that services are performing a social support function and providing users with the means to broaden their available networks. These benefits for users were reflected in satisfaction levels. Although a significant minority of users described their experience of social services at Time II as mixed, they were more willing at the second interview to recognise the impact that services were having on the maintenance of their independence. A higher proportion of users at Time II than at Time I reported that services were allowing them to live as they wished, with critical and short interval need users without a carer reporting the most significant improvement in satisfaction levels.

Thus even at the descriptive level, there is compelling evidence to suggest that services are having an impact on users' lives, and that this is recognised by users themselves. It is important to note, however, that not all indicators evidenced an improvement between Time I and Time II (an example is that a smaller proportion of users felt in control of their lives at the second interview than they had when services were first introduced) and that some older people clearly experienced fewer benefits than others. In particular, the emphasis the system is currently placing on more dependent users may to some extent be at the expense of those with fewer limitations. This is particularly evident in indicators such as unmet need, in which a high proportion of long interval users reported that the level of basic services — such as cleaning and shopping — they were receiving at Time II was inadequate. This complex relationship between the need-related circumstances of the user and the impact of services is further developed in the ECCEP productivities work, which supports this finding that outcomes are improving, but that not all users are benefiting in equal measure.

Evidence from ECCEP also demonstrates benefits for carers, although findings are more mixed. Outcomes for carers are dealt with in the next chapter.

Notes

1   Feeling unsafe at home can be related to more than the physical environment for some users. While factors associated with the home or neighbourhood do contribute to feeling unsafe (such as steep stairs or a high crime rate), personal factors also affect perceptions of safety. Examples would be living alone, or lacking available informal support.

2   Although, as we shall describe later in this chapter with reference to Time I/Time II comparisons, the provision of regular help over time can improve confidence levels for some users.

3   Activities of daily living are those relating directly to personal care.

4   Instrumental activities are those which do not relate directly to personal care but form an important part of daily living such as housework, laundry, shopping and meal preparation.

5   In selecting those cases which needed help with individual ADLs or IADLs, ambiguity arose when the activity was classed as 'not done', since this did not clarify whether the user could perform the task without help if they had to. In what follows, 'not done' has been treated as not needing help. This assumption was justified since tasks whose performance was highly correlated with the task in question were normally rated as able without help when the original task was classed as 'not done'.

6   While 51 per cent of the user sample responded to the question relating to unmet need for specific services, two of the users who responded chose the response 'none' when asked to identify which services they still required. These two cases have been included in Table 9.25.

7 Unfortunately, it is not possible to compare the service shortfall count between Time I and Time II as only a subsample of users (n=36) were asked about the specific services they felt they still required at Time I. In contrast, all users without significant cognitive impairment were asked about service shortfall at Time II.

10 Outcomes for Carers

Introduction

Input from formal services can make a significant difference in the lives of informal carers. Regular assistance for the user can alleviate strain, particularly if this involves help with tasks which the carer previously performed but found difficult or time-consuming. Formal service intervention can allow the carer more time for friends and family, or for employment. Other research has suggested that the breaks from caring which services provide can also improve the carer's own physical and mental health (Wenger, 1990; Twigg and Atkin, 1994; Ashworth et al., 1996). However, service intervention does not always yield positive outcomes for carers. Inflexible or inappropriate services can increase stress, particularly if the carer continues to balance work and caregiving responsibilities (Neal et al., 1997). Service intervention can also aggravate conflict between the user and carer, particularly if the user has been reluctant to accept services and feels assistance should be provided by family members (Noelker et al., 1998). Thus, the measurement of outcomes for carers involves an assessment of both the positive and negative impact of services on a variety of relevant indicators.

The previous chapter, Outcomes for Users, outlined the difference between state and change outcomes in ECCEP. State outcomes are derived from information gathered from the respondents during one interview, while change outcomes compare responses between Time I and Time II interviews. This chapter presents findings relating primarily to change outcomes for carers, the one exception being the section relating to carer satisfaction, which contains both state and change outcomes. As with findings relating to outcomes for users, it is important to remember that the descriptive statistics used here do not attempt to determine whether services themselves are responsible for the changes observed, or to what extent. This has been undertaken for a similar set of key carer indicators in the ECCEP productivities work (Davies and Fernández, 1999) which examines the complex relationship between needs, resources and outcomes. Instead, the descriptive findings detailed here describe a wider range of outcomes which require a broader interpretation. This descriptive work should be considered in conjunction with the productivities findings, in order to gather a more comprehensive picture of outcomes for carers.

This chapter illustrates some of the changes in carer circumstances between the user's referral to social services and the continuing care period, when services had been in place for six months or more. First, changes in principal carer inputs are described, as well as differences in the amount and frequency of support provided by secondary carers. Second, changes in carer stress — both self-perceived stress and stress scores — are discussed. Third, the issue of carer employment is raised, and any reductions in hours or the incidence of employment are detailed. Changes in breaks from caring are described next, followed by changes in the user/carer relationship over time. Finally, carer satisfaction with services both at Time I and between Time I and Time II is discussed, and the issue of whether services are meeting the needs of carers as well as users is examined.

Changes in informal inputs

Carer input changes over time as a result of altered circumstances, user needs and the availability of other sources of support. At Time I, carers were involved in supporting a user who had just begun to receive a package of formal services, either as a new referral, or as a continuing case with significant changes to the service package. By Time II, the new service package was fully in place and any benefits for the user and/or carer as a result of these services were becoming apparent.

Carers who live separately from the user were asked if they saw their older relative/friend more or less frequently at Time II. Only those carers who were interviewed at both Time I and Time II were asked this question. As at Time I, not all carers who live separately were able to estimate the frequency of contact, which accounts for the smaller sample size in Table 10.1. Among the carers who did respond, however, half reported that the frequency of visits had remained the same. For one in five carers, the number of visits had *decreased*. A reduction in support was particularly prevalent among the carers of users who were less dependent: those without a cognitive impairment, and those who with short and long interval needs. Just under one in three carers did, however, report an *increase* in the number of times they saw the user per week. Increases were more apparent among the carers of more dependent older people. Indeed, 43 per cent of carers of critical interval need users with a cognitive impairment described an increase in their visits between Time I and

Table 10.1

Whether carer sees user more often at Time II than Time I given that carer and user do not live together, by interval need and cognitive impairment or behavioural disorder of user among community-based sample

Does the carer see the user more often at Time II than Time I?	Interval need						Total	
	Critical		Short		Long			
	CI/BD	No CI/BD	CI/BD	No CI/BD	CI/BD	No CI/BD		
	%	%	%	%	%	%		n =
More	42.9	22.2	38.9	23.5	33.3	24.5		19
The same	42.9	66.7	40.7	47.1	50.0	51.0		34
Less	14.3	11.1	20.4	29.4	16.7	24.5		15
Total n =	7	9	10	17	6	20		67

Missing cases: 0. Sample: Carers interviewed at Time I and Time II and not living with user.

Time II. This increased support may have been necessary to adapt to a deterioration in the user's condition, or to meet needs not addressed by formal services.

As at Time I, all carers were asked at Time II which tasks they performed for the user. Differences were found between the activities of some carers. An interesting pattern emerged of a general reduction in the amount of medical, toileting and personal care tasks which carers were performing for users, while the number of carers providing help with domestic tasks, particularly housework, actually grew over the same period.

Table 10.2 illustrates changes in the number of carers providing personal care assistance to users between Time I and Time II. The dominant pattern is one of stability. For just under one-third of carers, however, there was some change. Fewer carers were providing personal care assistance at Time II than at Time I, with just over one in four reporting that they had stopped providing this type of support to the user. Just 6 per cent of carers who previously had not been providing this type of assistance had started helping with personal care between Time I and Time II.

This overall reduction in the number of carers helping with personal care is most marked among those who were caring for users with a cognitive impairment, over one-third of whom were no longer providing this type of help. When interval need is considered, it was the carers of users in the short interval need category who were most likely to report a reduction in their involvement. Interestingly, a similar pattern emerged for medical and toileting assistance. A slightly larger group of carers (13 per cent) stated that they had ceased providing this type of help between Time I and Time II than reported they had begun providing it between the two interviews (9 per cent). The reduction was particularly apparent among the carers of users with a cognitive impairment, 20 per cent of whom reported that they were helping with medical and toileting activities at Time I, but had ceased to do so by Time II. Again, reductions were more common among the carers of short interval need users, and also critical interval need users, rather than among the carers of more independent, long interval need users.

Table 10.3 illustrates changes in the number of carers providing assistance with housework between Time I and Time II. The pattern is significantly different from that found for personal care and medical/toileting activities. Again, most carers gave the same response at Time I and Time II, but instead of there being an overall reduction in the number of carers providing this assistance, there has been a slight increase. Overall, 15 per cent of carers who were not doing housework for the user at Time I had started to do so by Time II. The increase was particularly prevalent among the carers of less dependent users: those without a cognitive impairment or behavioural disorder, and those caring for short and long interval need users.

When changes in other forms of domestic assistance are considered — such as meals and shopping — there is an even clearer pattern of growth in the

Table 10.2

Change in the personal care services the carer provides from Time I to Time II, by interval need and cognitive impairment or behavioural disorder of user

Changes in help with personal care	Critical CI/BD %	No CI/BD %	Short CI/BD %	No CI/BD %	Long CI/BD %	No CI/BD %	Total n =
Still providing help	56.5	70.4	40.3	30.8	17.5	15.3	55
Providing help at Time II but not at Time I	3.8	3.3	8.1	7.7	7.2	10.4	9
Providing help at Time I but not at Time II	35.9	13.2	32.2	26.9	31.9	22.2	34
No help at Time I or Time II	3.8	13.2	19.4	34.6	43.4	52.0	36
Total n =	26	30	12	25	13	28	134

Missing cases: 2. Sample: Carers for whom there were both Time I and Time II interviews.

Table 10.3

Change in the help with housework the carer provides from Time I to Time II, by interval need and cognitive impairment or behavioural disorder of user

Changes in help with housework	Critical CI/BD %	Critical No CI/BD %	Short CI/BD %	Short No CI/BD %	Long CI/BD %	Long No CI/BD %	Total n =
Still providing help	66.4	86.8	86.4	57.7	24.7	46.5	81
Providing help at Time II but not at Time I	11.4	6.6	16.1	26.9	14.5	18.8	21
Providing help at Time I but not at Time II	9.2	3.3	19.4	0.0	24.7	0.0	9
No help at Time I or Time II	13.0	3.3	8.1	15.4	36.2	34.7	24
Total n =	26	30	12	25	13	28	135

Missing cases: 1. Sample: Carers for whom there were both Time I and Time II interviews (78 per cent of the Time I sample were also interviewed at Time II).

number of carers engaged in these tasks between Time I and Time II. Indeed, no carers reported that they had stopped helping with either meals or shopping between the two interviews. Instead, one in ten carers who had not been shopping for the user at Time I had begun doing so by Time II, while the same proportion who had not been providing the user with meals at Time I began doing so by Time II. Increases were particularly apparent among the carers of less dependent users.

Thus an interesting picture of change in informal inputs emerges between when formal services were being put in place at Time I, and in the continuing care phase at Time II. Overall visits from carers who live separately increased in frequency. More specifically, there were changes in the number of carers doing specific tasks for their older relative or friend. There was a clear reduction in the number of carers providing help with health-related tasks (medical and toileting, and personal care) while the number of carers providing help with domestic, or instrumental, tasks increased overall. Changes in informal health-related inputs were most marked among the carers of more dependent users, particularly those with a cognitive impairment. In contrast, carers of less dependent users began to assist with domestic tasks in greater numbers. These descriptive results present only one aspect of change in informal care over time, and there are many other factors which must be considered before drawing conclusions. Despite this, these results do raise questions about the relationship between formal service receipt and informal care inputs, which suggest several possible explanations.

An important explanation for changing informal care inputs is that users' needs alter over time, prompting adjustment in the type and frequency of support offered by carers. Older service users may find their functional and cognitive abilities lessening, which can result in the need for greater assistance with all tasks. Thus, allowing for changes in carers' circumstances, we would expect to see an increase in informal care inputs over time. However, the fact that *fewer* carers of the more dependent users are providing assistance with health-related tasks at Time II could be attributed to recovery of function for some users, or to formal services affecting informal inputs. If formal services are the cause, the changes seen in the number of carers helping with medical and toileting assistance, as well as personal care, suggest that services have stepped in to meet the health and personal care needs of more dependent older people at home, relieving their carers. These findings support evidence that services, particularly intensive services, are now being targeted at older users with complex needs (Bauld et al., 1998c; Davies et al., 1997a).

In contrast, the increase in the number of carers assisting with domestic tasks suggests that formal services may not be assisting all users with these activities. Findings indicate that it is the carers of less dependent users who are helping with domestic tasks in increasing numbers. These less dependent users, particularly those who are not cognitively impaired, may not be eligible for a level of home care which would provide shopping and cleaning services.

Instead, some informal carers are stepping in to provide this help as users' functional abilities change over time.

Changes in other informal inputs

In addition to the nature of support offered by principal carers, the amount and type of help provided by a wider network of family and friends can also vary over time. Principal carers were asked about these secondary inputs at Time I, and findings were described in Chapter 7. Carers were asked the same questions at Time II, and a comparison of their responses thus reveals any change in inputs from the wider informal network. Results are shown in Table 10.4 .

Overall, the picture is one of stability in receipt of help from other informal carers over time. In just over half of cases, the assistance provided by other helpers at Time I continued to be provided at Time II. In an additional 29 per cent of cases, the principal carer was coping alone without other informal carers at both Time I and II. Thus, in 80 per cent of cases, there was no change between the two carer interviews.

Among those cases in which there was a change in the support provided, there was, however, a relationship between the needs of the user involved and whether more or less support was available. Carers of more dependent users reported that less support was available over time, whereas those caring for long interval need users recorded an increase in help. Thus, among carers of critical interval need users with a cognitive impairment, 21 per cent reported that help from other informal supporters was no longer available, while just 7 per cent of these carers reported an increase in the availability of help. In contrast, 17 per cent of carers of long interval need users without a cognitive impairment reported that help from other informal supporters had increased by Time II, whereas just 5 per cent of these carers reported that this help was no longer available.

Other British studies, particularly the work of Wenger (1989, 1994) and Finch and Mason (1993), have argued that secondary carers — friends/neighbours and more distant relatives in particular — may reduce their involvement as users' needs become more complex, particularly when help with personal care is required, or behavioural difficulties develop. The reduction in availability of other informal support reported by the principal carers of more dependent users at Time II may in part be a reflection of this phenomenon. Although the numbers are small, the fact that the loss of support is most evident among critical interval and cognitively impaired users suggests that, as users' needs increase, the availability of support from a wider social network may diminish.

An alternative explanation concerns service receipt. By Time II, the care package for all users was in place. Reductions mentioned above in the number

Table 10.4
Change in the help user gets from other family members and friends from Time I to Time II, by interval need and cognitive impairment or behavioural disorder of user among community-based sample

Changes in help family gives	Critical		Interval need Short		Long		Total
	CI/BD	No CI/BD	CI/BD	No CI/BD	CI/BD	No CI/BD	
	%	%	%	%	%	%	n =
Help before and now	30.5	47.4	63.8	65.4	57.9	50.3	69
Help now	7.6	3.3	7.2	15.4	0.0	16.8	13
Helped before	20.6	13.2	7.2	3.8	0.0	4.7	12
Never helped	41.3	36.2	21.7	11.5	34.9	28.2	40
Don't know	0.0	0.0	0.0	3.8	7.2	0.0	2
Total n =	26	30	13	25	13	29	136

Missing cases: 0. Sample: Principal informal carers who were interviewed at both Time I and Time II and who reported that other informal helpers were involved at one or both interviews.

of principal carers providing personal care and medical and toileting support suggests that some user needs are being met by targeted formal services. The reduction in help from other informal carers could thus be as a result of increased service receipt. If formal services are in place and appear to be meeting needs, secondary helpers may feel that their input is no longer as necessary, and may withdraw their assistance.

Changes in carer stress

Given the changes in the type and amount of support provided by principal and secondary carers between Time I and Time II, corresponding changes in related aspects of carer circumstances would be expected. Other studies have consistently shown carers to be more at risk of mental health problems, particularly stress and depression, than other adults of a similar age (Strawbridge et al., 1997; Hocker et al., 1998). Chapter 4 described the subjective and objective measures used to estimate the strain carers in the study were experiencing. At Time I, carers overall were found to be experiencing moderate to high levels of malaise and stress, with the carers of more dependent users — those with critical interval needs, and particularly those with a cognitive impairment or behavioural disorder — having significantly higher stress scores than other carers. It is possible to compare scores between Time I and Time II for the main indicator of stress used: the Kosberg Cost of Care Index (Kosberg and Cairl, 1986).

Table 10.5 illustrates the mean change in carer stress scores between the first and second interviews. At Time I, the mean stress score for all carers was 4.92. Since then, carers experienced a slight decrease in stress, -0.41 on average. Although the decrease was not substantial, it does suggest that, over time, services may alleviate some of the strain experienced by carers. The largest decrease in mean score was recorded among the carers of long interval need users without a cognitive impairment or behavioural disorder. At Time I, cares looking after users with these needs had a mean stress score of 3.28. The overall decrease of 1.73 is substantial, reducing their Kosberg score to 1.55, which represents a very low level of stress overall. This is perhaps not surprising as long interval need users without a cognitive impairment are the most independent among the ECCEP sample, and thus require a lower level of assistance. They may also be new referrals to social services. The implementation of services for these users may have meant relief for carers who were previously acting as the main or only source of assistance.

An improvement in stress score was not found for all carers. Among those looking after more dependent users, there has been an increase in the level of stress. For example, carers of users with a cognitive impairment, who had a high mean stress score at Time I (6.57 overall), reported a further increase between Time I and Time II, although this increase was small, averaging 0.12.

Table 10.5
Change in Kosberg carer stress score from Time I to Time II, by interval need and cognitive impairment or behavioural disorder of user

Change in Kosberg carer stress score from Time I to Time II	Critical		Interval need Short		Long		Total
	CI/BD	No CI/BD	CI/BD	No CI/BD	CI/BD	No CI/BD	n =
Mean	0.63	0.83	0.68	-1.22	-1.46	-1.73	-0.41
Standard error of mean	1.08	0.47	0.85	0.73	0.94	0.66	0.33
Total n =	20	23	10	22	10	24	111

Missing cases: 3. Sample: Carer interviews at Time I and Time II and user in community at Time I and Time II (n=114).

The largest single increase between Time I and Time II was recorded for the carers of critical interval need users without a cognitive impairment, averaging 0.83 overall. These critical interval need users require a high level of support, on an unpredictable basis. Their needs include assistance with personal care but also with a variety of other tasks. While social services were providing some types of assistance to these users, carer input was still significant (Time I interviews found that carers of critical interval need users were providing an average of fifteen hours assistance per week). This level of input, combined with other factors, results in higher levels of strain. Services and other sources of support were clearly insufficiently successful in alleviating carer stress for this particular group between Time I and Time II, although these results should be interpreted in conjunction with findings from the ECCEP productivities work, findings relating to the contributions of services and risk factors to levels of carer stress (Davies and Fernández, 1999).

Objective measures of stress are only one method of estimating the effect of caregiving over time. Subjective measures of burden are also important, particularly as the carer's own assessment of their situation has been found to have a significant effect on the actual impact of caregiving (Lawton et al., 1989; Wenger, 1990). In other words, the degree to which the carer views looking after the user as problematic can affect the degree of stress experienced and influence other factors, such as willingness to continue caring. Principal carers were asked a series of questions about their own perceptions of problems caused by caring at both Time I and Time II.

Table 10.6. illustrates changes in the proportion of carers who reported that caring caused problems for them. The single largest group of carers — 57 per cent — reported at both Time I and Time II that the help they provided to the user did not cause problems, represented by the 'never' category in Table 10.6. An additional 14 per cent of carers — the 'always' category — indicated at both Time I and Time II that caring was problematic. Thus, for over two-thirds of carers, there was no significant change in their perception of burden between the two interviews.

Just over one in four carers did, however, report a change in their perception of caregiving between interviews. For 13 per cent of the sample, caring had become a problem by Time II, whereas their previous assessment had been that it was not problematic. The carers reporting an increase in burden were most likely to be caring for someone with a cognitive impairment, particularly if the user had short interval needs. Just under one in five carers of short interval need users reported an increase in burden, compared with 11 per cent of critical and 10 per cent of long interval need carers.

The proportion of carers reporting a *reduction* in burden was slightly higher than those reporting an increase. Overall, 17 per cent of carers stated that caring had been problematic for them at Time I, but that things had improved since then. There was a clear gradient across interval need categories in relation to this reduction in burden, with 22 per cent of the carers of critical

Table 10.6

Whether providing help to the user caused the carer problems between Time I and Time II, by interval need and cognitive impairment or behavioural disorder of user

Whether help caused carer problems	Critical		Short		Long		Total
	CI/BD	No CI/BD	CI/BD	No CI/BD	CI/BD	No CI/BD	
	%	%	%	%	%	%	n =
Now	9.6	12.5	23.2	17.4	13.6	8.1	14
Never	42.4	62.5	38.4	43.5	76.8	74.2	63
Always	24.0	4.2	28.8	13.0	9.6	9.7	15
Then	24.0	20.8	9.6	26.1	0.0	8.1	19
Total n =	20	23	10	22	10	24	111

Missing cases: 3. Sample: Carer interviews at Time I and Time II and user in community at Time I and Time II (n=114).

interval need users reporting a reduction, compared with 21 per cent of the carers of short and 6 per cent of the carers of long interval need users. Thus, a significant proportion of those looking after physically dependent users had experienced a positive change in their perceptions of caring by Time II. However, this was not so clearly the case for those looking after someone with a cognitive impairment. Just 14 per cent of these carers reported an improvement, compared with 18 per cent of those caring for someone without this impairment, although the differences are small.

Carers were also asked to describe the aspects of their lives which they perceived to be affected by caregiving at both Time I and Time II. Reflecting the overall reduction in burden mentioned above, carers reported a net decrease in the number of problems caused by caring. Table 10.7 lists these problems and illustrates the proportion of carers who reported that their particular difficulties had been alleviated by Time II.

As Table 10.7 illustrates, just over one in four carers (28 per cent) were able to report a reduction of burden relating to at least one specific areas of their lives. The most common improvement was in self-perceived stress, with 11 per cent of carers reporting that they felt less stressed at Time II. A similar proportion of respondents — 10 per cent — stated that they had received relief from the

Table 10.7
Reduction in carer's problems caused by helping user from Time I to Time II

Problems which improved by Time II	%	n =
Insufficient time for family	6.9	8
Reduced leisure time	8.6	10
Don't see friends enough	1.7	2
Lost earnings from work	1.7	2
Loss of job (prospects)	0.9	1
Physical effort of caring	10.4	12
Strain on relationship with user	7.3	8
Embarrassing tasks	1.7	2
Stress	11.2	13
Sleep lost through tasks	6.9	8
Sleep lost through worry	6.9	8
Financial cost	3.5	4
Other needy family	2.6	3
Other	0.9	1
No reduction	72.0	81
Total n =	100.0	113

Missing cases: 1. Sample: Carer interview at Time I and Time II and user in community at Time I and Time II (n=114).

physical effort of caring since Time I. A break from lifting, bathing the user or otherwise physically caring may have been provided by home care or nursing services. Similarly, the 7 per cent of carers who reported that they were losing sleep less frequently by Time II may have been benefiting from respite, or other intervention such as continence services.

In the period between the two interviews, some carers also reported a reduction in problems relating to family and relationships which had previously been caused by caring responsibilities. For example, Table 10.7 shows that 9 per cent of carers reported having more leisure time by the second carer interview, and 7 per cent reported that they had more time for their family. Just over 7 per cent of carers also said that previous problems they had experienced in their relationship with the user had improved since Time I, although, as evidence later in this chapter will illustrate, this improvement was not apparent across the whole carer sample. Despite this, and although the actual numbers reporting a reduction in specific problems are small, the decrease in problems reported by carers overall (a mean decrease of 0.18 problems per carer) does suggest that there has been a general reduction in carers' own estimations of the problems caused by caring since users were referred to social services.

Among the minority of carers who reported an *increase* (23 per cent) in the number of problems they experienced as carers from Time I to Time II, the areas which more than 5 per cent of these carers reported had become more problematic were reduced leisure time (11 per cent) and sleep lost through worry (7 per cent). Carers of users with a cognitive impairment were more likely than other carers to report that these problems had become worse in the period between the two interviews.

Changes in carer employment

There is now a considerable literature which examines the effect of changes in carer employment upon caring activities and, to a lesser degree, one which evaluates the impact of caring responsibilities upon employment. The argument supporting the first type of analysis has been that employment limits the time which family members can devote to caring. This argument is related to fears about rising female participation in the labour market and the possibility of a resulting shortage of primary carers. Research evidence (much of it American) examining the effect of employment on caring is mixed: some studies have found that employment, particularly full-time employment, does limit the hours of caring provided and causes some carers to modify the type of support they offer (Brody and Schoonover, 1986), while other evidence suggests that the distinction between full and part-time work, and the availability of secondary caregivers, are key factors to consider before making the assumption that employment results in reduced informal care inputs

(Doty et al., 1998). Other research has found no evidence that employed women are less likely to become carers, and a recent study has even argued that employment can alleviate the stress of caregiving, enabling the carer to continue providing support (Martire et al., 1997).

Large-scale studies which have examined the effect of caring on employment have found little evidence that either women or men who become carers give up their jobs in large numbers. Instead, certain groups of carers have been found to reduce their working hours to accommodate caring responsibilities or have been found to be more likely to take time off to fit in caring tasks (Neal et al., 1997; Pavalko and Artis, 1997). Thus, it is interesting to map changes among employed ECCEP carers over time. Findings at Time I indicated that just over one-third of carers were in employment. At Time II, carers were again asked to report whether they were employed and to record any changes in their working patterns since the first interview.

Table 10.8 illustrates that 36 per cent of the carers who were interviewed at both Time I and Time II were employed, and that no change in their employment status had occurred since the first interview. As at Time I, carers of less dependent users were more likely to be employed. This was particularly the case among carers of users without a cognitive impairment, 41 per cent of whom were employed at both Time I and Time II, compared with 27 per cent of the carers of cognitively impaired users. While these differences in the proportion of carers in employment may be due to the demands of caring for someone with mental health problems, it is also important to keep in mind the large number of spouse carers in the ECCEP sample, the vast majority of whom were retired and were more likely to be caring for a user with a cognitive impairment and short or critical interval needs than other younger carers.

The number of carers whose employment status changed between Time I and Time II was very small. Three people, representing just 3 per cent of the sample, had stopped working between Time I and Time II, while two carers who were not previously working had started a new job by Time II. Thus, overall, there was little change in the employment status of carers during the months following the implementation of a new or revised package of services.

As the effect of changing user needs on carer employment can result in modified working hours rather than the cessation of employment, principal carers were also asked a series of questions about their hours of employment and time off from work. Among the carers working at both Time I and Time II, only one in four (ten people) provided reliable information about their working hours during both carer interviews. This small sample does not allow us to draw any significant conclusions about the impact of caring or formal service intervention on carers working hours over time. However, among those carers for whom information about working hours exists, the overall picture was of a reduction in hours since Time I, on average 1.15 hours fewer worked per week. Although this is a very slight change, it does suggest that

Table 10.8

Change in carer's employment status from Time I to Time II, by interval need and cognitive impairment or behavioural disorder of user among community-based sample

Carer's employment status	Critical CI/BD %	No CI/BD %	Short CI/BD %	No CI/BD %	Long CI/BD %	No CI/BD %	Total n =
			Interval need				
Still employed	28.8	16.7	52.0	47.8	0.0	60.5	40
Not employed anymore	0.0	8.3	9.6	0.0	0.0	0.0	3
Working now	9.6	0.0	0.0	0.0	0.0	0.0	2
Still not working	61.6	75.0	38.4	52.2	100.0	39.5	65
Total n =	20	23	10	22	10	23	110

Missing cases: 4. Sample: Carer interview at Time I and Time II and user in community at Time I and Time II (n=114).

some carers were still adapting their own routines to accommodate the changing needs of users over time, despite intervention from formal services.

Changes in breaks from caring

Regular breaks are important for all carers, but particularly those who live with the user. Co-resident carers are often unable to have adequate time for themselves, with the result that existing social networks can be eroded and the carer's mental and physical health affected (Tennstedt et al., 1989; Twigg and Atkin, 1994). Providing support to carers was one of the stated aims of the 1990 community care reforms, which became more explicit with the passage of the 1995 Carers Act. Formal services can provide support to carers in a variety of ways, but putting in place interventions which provide a break (such as respite care) is a particularly important function of social services.

At Time I, a significant proportion of ECCEP carers (18 per cent) reported that they had not had a break away from home in the past year, but wished they could take one. When asked if looking after the user had been the primary cause of not taking a break, over two-thirds of these carers agreed that this was the case. Carers were asked the same question at Time II, and responses are shown in Tables 10.9.

Table 10.9 illustrates the proportion of carers who reported at Time II that they had taken a break away from home in the previous six months. While just under half of the carers interviewed (48 per cent) had taken between one and three breaks away from home, the remaining 52 per cent had not been away at

Table 10.9
Frequency carer has had a break away from home in the last six months, by cognitive impairment or behavioural disorder of user among community-based sample

Frequency of breaks	CI/BD	Not CI/BD	Total
	%	%	n =
One	29.5	33.1	35
Two	4.9	7.1	7
Three or more	4.9	12.7	11
None — wish I could	43.9	26.0	35
None — don't want	16.8	21.2	21
Total n =	40	69	109

Missing cases: 5. Sample: Carer interviews at Time I and Time II and user in community at Time I and Time II (n=114).

all. Just under one in three carers overall reported that they had not been away, but wished they could. As Table 10.9 demonstrates, the proportion who had not been away but wished they could rose substantially when the user involved had a cognitive impairment or behavioural disorder. Indeed, 44 per cent of those caring for someone with a cognitive impairment had not had a break. This rose to 48 per cent among those caring for a user with cognitive problems and long interval needs. These users are physically more able than others, but their mental state may place them at risk of accidents and wandering, limiting the ability of the carer to leave them alone at any time.

When carers who had not taken a break (but indicated that they wished they could) were asked if looking after the user was the reason, just over half of interviewees indicated that caring was the cause. There was a clear gradient relating to interval need, with critical interval need users almost twice as likely as the carers of long interval need users to report that caring was the reason for not taking a break. Caring responsibilities were also more likely to restrict breaks among those looking after a cognitively impaired user. When the relationship between the user and carer and their place of residence was considered, it was found that those living with the user (66 per cent) were more likely to report that the reason they had not had a break was due to caring responsibilities than those living elsewhere (43 per cent), particularly co-resident female carers, all of whom stated that the reason they had not had a break was due to caring.

Thus those carers providing the greatest input and caring for more dependent users were most likely to report both that they had not taken a break in the past six months, and that the responsibility of caring for the user had been the reason. These results suggest that, six months or more post-referral, care-managed interventions were not managing to provide all carers with an adequate level of respite to allow them to get away from home, even for a few days. It is clearly those carers who are most in need of a break — those providing high levels of care to users with complex needs — who remain unable to get away, despite their wish to do so.

Changes in user/carer relationship

A positive relationship between user and carer can become more difficult to sustain as the user's needs change, particularly when cognitive impairment or a behavioural disorder is involved. As research has found that a good carer/user relationship is one of the best predictors of a sustained commitment to caring (Lechner, 1992), it is particularly important that care manager intervention involves the implementation of services which support rather than undermine this relationship.

Principal carers were asked to reflect on any changes in their relationship with the user since the recent package of services had been put in place.

Results are shown in Table 10.10. The overall picture was one of stability, with 79 per cent stating that the relationship had not changed since the implementation of a new or revised care package. Among those carers who did indicate a change, however, a slightly larger proportion stated that the relationship had deteriorated (12 per cent) rather than improved (9 per cent). The proportion indicating a deterioration was much larger among the carers of users with a cognitive impairment (18 per cent) than those without (9 per cent). This perhaps reflects the increasing burden experienced by those caring for someone with a mental impairment, particularly as the user becomes less aware of their condition over time, and traditional forms of interaction are no longer possible (Seltzer et al., 1997). While care management can address this deterioration by providing the carer with respite and other support, it may not be able to compensate for the loss of the relationship as it once was.

There is also a slight interval need effect evident in Table 10.10, with the carers of critical interval need users being more likely to report a deterioration than those caring for short or long interval need users. The combination of cognitive impairment and critical interval needs emerges as a predictor of deterioration in the user/carer relationship during the six months preceding the Time II interval for a significant proportion of carers: 26 per cent of carers looking after a user with these characteristics reported a deterioration in the relationship over time.

The carers most likely to report an improvement in their relationship with the user were those looking after less dependent older people. Among carers of users with short (13 per cent) and long (12 per cent) interval needs without a cognitive impairment, an improvement was recorded. Care management intervention may be realising gains for these users and their carers by providing basic services (such as home care and day care) which alleviate strain without damaging existing arrangements between the user and the carer.

Cessation of caregiving

Not all carers are able to continue providing support to the user indefinitely. In some cases, changes in circumstances or the needs of the user result in the principal carer giving up their role. By the second interview a small group of carers (10 per cent of the original carer sample) were no longer providing support to the user. Care managers were asked, in a multiple response question, to identify the reason for this withdrawal of informal support.

Table 10.11 illustrates the reasons why the 24 carers who had been providing regular assistance to the user at Time I were no longer doing so by Time II. The single most common reason for the loss of informal support was the death of a carer, which workers indicated had occurred in eight cases. The loss of a carer occurred in more cases where the user had critical interval needs (42 per cent)

Table 10.10

How has the relationship changed with user over the last six months, by interval need and cognitive impairment or behavioural disorder of user among community-based sample

Change in relationship with user over the last six months	Interval need						Total
	Critical		Short		Long		
	CI/BD	No CI/BD	CI/BD	No CI/BD	CI/BD	No CI/BD	
	%	%	%	%	%	%	n =
Improved	11.6	4.2	9.6	13.0	0.0	12.1	10
Not changed	62.4	83.3	80.8	82.6	90.4	78.2	87
Deteriorated	26.0	12.5	9.6	4.3	9.6	9.7	13
Total n =	20	23	10	22	10	24	111

Missing cases: 3. Sample: Carer interviews at Time I and Time II and user in community at Time I and Time II (n=114).

Table 10.11

Reason previous carer could no longer care for user, by interval need among community-based sample

Reason for cessation of caring	Critical %	Short %	Long %	Total n =
Previous carer died	41.7	25.6	29.3	8
User & carer further apart	0.0	10.6	0.0	1
Previous carer too ill	33.3	21.2	0.0	6
Caring tasks too hard	33.3	21.2	41.4	7
Carer got exhausted	25.0	10.6	0.0	4
Carer needed time with family	0.0	0.0	29.3	1
Carer needed temporary breaks	8.3	0.0	0.0	1
Other	8.3	31.9	0.0	4
Total n =	12	9	3	24

Missing cases: 3. Sample: Cases whose original carer withdrew between Time I and Time II.

than either short (26 per cent) or long (29 per cent) interval needs. A higher proportion of those caring for someone with critical interval needs are spouse carers, and thus older people themselves. Illness was also a common cause of the carer giving up: care managers indicated that illness had been a factor in 30 per cent of cases.

Just under half of care managers also indicated that exhaustion and inability to cope with caring had been a factor in the previous carer withdrawing his/her support by Time II. While 30 per cent of care managers said the carer had found caring tasks too difficult, an additional 16 per cent indicated that the carer had been just too exhausted to continue. In another two cases, the carer had given up because they needed more time with their family or more frequent breaks. Although these carers account for only 13 cases overall, the fact that inability to cope was the reason for withdrawing support does suggest that service intervention following the user's (re-)referral was not sufficient for this small number of cases. Help either came too late, or in a form unsuited to sustaining existing caring arrangements.

Carer satisfaction

Chapter 9 provided detailed information regarding user satisfaction with services over time. Carers were also asked a range of questions relating to satisfaction, both at Time I and Time II. Satisfaction levels at Time I would capture the carer's first impressions of the care management process and the initial impact of services, while Time I/Time II comparisons indicate any improvement or deterioration in satisfaction after the care package had been in place for six months or more.

Satisfaction at Time I

Principal carers were first asked about the manner in which social services had assessed their needs and tried to help. As with users, carer satisfaction levels were high, with 73 per cent of carers reporting that they were either satisfied or very satisfied. However, those looking after someone with a cognitive impairment were less satisfied across all three interval need levels (39 per cent stating they had mixed feelings or were dissatisfied) than were those caring for someone without a cognitive impairment (just 20 per cent of whom stated that they had mixed feelings or were dissatisfied).

Table 10.12 illustrates carer satisfaction levels with the help and support *provided* to the user by social services. At Time I, the vast majority of carers interviewed were looking after a user for whom all services were in place. Thus, this question attempts to capture the carer's perceptions of the adequacy of this initial package of services. As the table shows, the vast majority of carers again reported that they were satisfied or very satisfied (76 per cent), with satisfaction levels slightly higher among the carers of users without a cognitive impairment. The carers of the frailest users — those with critical interval needs and a cognitive impairment — reported the lowest levels of satisfaction overall, with just over one in four of these carers describing themselves as having mixed feelings, being dissatisfied or being very dissatisfied.

Carers who reported that they had health problems or required services in their own right were also asked how satisfied they were with the extent to which social services had addressed their needs, rather than the user's. Satisfaction with this aspect of the care management process was slightly more mixed, as Table 10.13 illustrates.

As Table 10.13 shows, 61 per cent of these carers described themselves as satisfied or very satisfied with the manner in which social services had taken account of their own needs as carers. Again, satisfaction levels were lower among the carers of users with a cognitive impairment, 17 per cent of whom were dissatisfied or very dissatisfied. Overall, the carers of more dependent users reported lower levels of satisfaction, particularly those caring for someone with a cognitive impairment and critical or short interval needs. Carers of long interval need users were happier with social services' treatment of their own needs: 71 per cent of these carers described themselves as satisfied or very satisfied.

Table 10.12

Carer satisfaction with help and support from social services, by interval need and cognitive impairment or behavioural disorder of user among community-based sample

Satisfaction of carer with help and support from social services	Interval need						Total
	Critical		Short		Long		
	CI/BD	No CI/BD	CI/BD	No CI/BD	CI/BD	No CI/BD	
	%	%	%	%	%	%	n =
Very satisfied	28.7	37.1	21.9	24.3	7.2	30.1	60
Satisfied	42.2	45.8	56.2	61.5	71.1	44.8	110
Mixed feelings	16.7	10.5	8.8	12.1	0.0	17.6	28
Dissatisfied	4.8	2.2	8.8	2.0	7.2	7.5	10
Very dissatisfied	5.6	2.2	4.4	0.0	14.5	0.0	7
Don't know	2.0	2.2	0.0	0.0	0.0	0.0	2
Total n =	49	45	22	48	13	39	216

Missing cases: 22. Sample: Carers interviewed at Time I (n=238).

Table 10.13

Carer satisfaction with how social services took account of their own needs, by interval need and cognitive impairment or behavioural disorder of user among community-based sample

Satisfaction of carer with SSD help to meet own needs	Interval need						Total
	Critical		Short		Long		
	CI/BD	No CI/BD	CI/BD	No CI/BD	CI/BD	No CI/BD	n =
	%	%	%	%	%	%	
Very satisfied	30.1	18.9	0.0	21.1	41.4	53.2	26
Satisfied	31.7	58.4	25.0	36.8	24.3	20.0	36
Mixed feelings	20.3	7.6	50.0	36.8	17.2	13.3	20
Dissatisfied	4.1	11.4	12.5	0.0	0.0	6.7	6
Very dissatisfied	9.8	3.8	12.5	5.3	17.2	0.0	6
Don't know	4.1	0.0	0.0	0.0	0.0	6.7	2
Total n =	24	26	8	19	6	15	96

Missing cases: 8. Sample: Carers who reported that they had health problems or needed assistance in their own right.

Table 10.14

Whether PIC needed help to enable him/her to look after user which has not been provided by interval need and cognitive impairment or behavioural disorder of user among community-based sample

Presence of CI/BD	Interval need			Total
	Critical %	Short %	Long %	n =
CI/BD	37	25	23	92
Not CI/BD	26	12	15	144
Total n =	101	76	59	236

Missing cases: 1. Sample: Carers interviewed at Time I (n=238).

Carers were also asked about unmet need for services (to help them look after the user) at Time I. A smaller proportion of carers than users indicated an unmet need for services: 23 per cent of carers, compared with just over a third of users. As Table 10.14 shows, however, there was a clear gradient across interval need categories, with just 17 per cent of the carers of long interval need users reporting unmet needs, rising to 32 per cent among the carers of critical interval need users. Carers of users with a cognitive impairment were also more likely to report unmet needs. The carers who most frequently identified a need for additional formal services to help them assist the user were the carers of critical interval need users with a cognitive impairment — more than one in three of these carers reporting that they required additional services. Because the carer's need for help increased with the functional and cognitive impairment of the user, the broadly similar trend reported for the carer's satisfaction with help (presented in Table 10.12) is to be expected.

Among the 23 per cent of carers who reported unmet needs, the specific service most frequently mentioned was respite care, mentioned by just over a third of these carers. Most (24 per cent) wanted respite services which would give them a break during the day, while others (11 per cent) required respite to give them an overnight break. The need for both day and night respite was more frequently mentioned by the carers of users with a cognitive impairment than other carers. Another service mentioned by a significant proportion of carers who indicated unmet needs was assistance with physically demanding tasks, such as lifting the user (27 per cent). This type of assistance could be provided by either a home care worker, nursing auxiliary or district nurse. The need for this service was particularly prevalent among the carers of users with critical interval needs (33 per cent), who are most likely to be caring for a user who needs help with personal care. Carers of critical interval need users are also more likely to be older people themselves, and thus may find help with lifting particularly valuable as a means of avoiding back strain or injury. Other forms of assistance — such as individual counselling (13 per cent), training with various tasks (6 per cent) and referral to a support group (4 per cent) — were mentioned as unmet needs by only a small proportion of carers.

Changes in carer satisfaction

As with users, some changes were noted in carer satisfaction levels in the six months or more between the two interviews. These changes related to satisfaction with services, and with any unmet need for additional support.

Table 10.15 illustrates changes in carer satisfaction with services between Time I and Time II. It is worth restating that, at Time I, 79 per cent of carers said that they were either satisfied or very satisfied with the help and support provided by social services. By Time II, just under half of carers (47 per cent) had retained the same opinion of services between the two interviews, with an additional 22 per cent saying that their level of satisfaction had improved. Among those carers whose views changed, however, a slightly higher proportion felt their satisfaction with services had deteriorated (32 per cent).

Interestingly, it was the carers of users without a cognitive impairment who were much more likely to report *lower* levels of satisfaction at Time II than at Time I. Among the carers of users without a cognitive impairment, 38 per cent said their opinion of services had deteriorated, compared with just 20 per cent of those looking after someone with a cognitive impairment or behavioural disorder. This may reflect a desire for more respite or other forms of intervention among the carers of users without mental health problems, who may feel that their needs have been neglected in the care management process.

Carers were also asked to identify any unmet need at Time II. Among carers, the question referred to any outstanding needs for assistance to help them look

Table 10.15
Whether carer more or less satisfied with the level of service the user receives at Time I and Time II, by cognitive impairment or behavioural disorder of user among community-based sample

Change in satisfaction	CI/BD %	Not CI/BD %	Total n =
Deteriorated	20.2	38.2	32
The same	43.5	49.2	47
Improved	36.3	12.5	22
Total n =	39	62	101

Missing cases: 13. Sample: Carer interview at Time I and Time II and user in community at Time I and Time II (n=114).

after the user. Overall, 16 per cent of carers reported that there were services which they still required at Time II. This represents a reduction in unmet need since the first interview, when 23 per cent of carers reported that more assistance was required to look after the user. Among the small group of carers who still reported unmet needs at Time II, there remained a relationship between the needs of the user and the extent to which carers still required support. As at Time I, carers of users with a cognitive impairment were more likely to have unmet needs. There was also a clear relationship with interval need, with service shortfall being most marked among the carers of the most dependent users: those with critical interval needs and a cognitive impairment.

The small group of carers who reported unmet needs at Time II was also asked which services were still required. As at Time I, the most frequently mentioned types of help mentioned were assistance with physically demanding tasks, such as lifting and bathing (required by 9 per cent of carers overall at Time II), and day or night respite, which was mentioned by 4 per cent of carers overall. What is encouraging, however, is the relatively small number of carers identifying any unmet needs for assistance at Time II. Although those caring for more dependent users required some changes to the care package, most other carers clearly felt that services were providing an adequate level of support.

Finally, carers were also asked at both interviews whether services were helping the user to live as he/she wanted. As Chapter 9 described, users (particularly more dependent users) responded very favourably to this question at both interviews, with an overall improvement reported by 26 per cent of users at Time II, rising to 57 per cent among critical interval need users without a carer. A comparison of carer responses between Time I and Time II demonstrates a less favourable pattern than was evident for users. While 26 per cent of carers said their view of the role of services in maintaining the user's independence had improved, a similar proportion (28 per cent) indicated that it had deteriorated. This deterioration was most prevalent among the carers of more dependent users, particularly those with critical interval needs, 32 per cent of whom reported a deterioration, compared with 23 per cent of those caring for long interval need users. A deterioration was also more likely to be reported by carers of someone with a cognitive impairment (34 per cent) than without (24 per cent).

Thus the greater confidence which more dependent users had at Time II regarding the role of services in keeping the user at home does not appear to be as prevalent among carers. When this finding is placed in context with the other outcomes for carers previously discussed in this chapter, a pattern does emerge. Carers of more dependent users — particularly those caring for someone with a cognitive impairment — demonstrate a rise in stress scores between Time I and Time II, a slight rise in self-perceived burden, a deterioration in their relationship with the user and a continued lack of breaks away from their caring responsibilities. Although the changes are relatively small and are measured over a short (on average, nine-month) period, immediate benefits of care management interventions overall are not apparent among the carers of more dependent users. This lack of immediate improvement has, not surprisingly, affected carers' perceptions of service effectiveness overall. It is important, however, that these findings be assessed in line with those from ECCEP productivities work, which do demonstrate clear benefits for some groups of carers, particularly when specific services are provided (Davies and Fernández, 1999).

Conclusion

The evidence presented here demonstrates positive outcomes for carers following the implementation of a care package, although the benefits are less clear for carers than they are for users. In relation to the key change indicators — carer stress, carer employment, breaks from caring, the user/carer relationship and carer satisfaction — improvements are not consistent across groups of carers, particularly in relation to those caring for more dependent users. Comparisons of carer stress scores between Time I and Time II illustrate a slight decrease in stress overall but an increase in stress among those caring for someone with a cognitive impairment, particularly someone with critical interval needs. Similarly, although subjective burden decreased among the carer sample as a whole, it increased among those looking after a user with a cognitive impairment, a higher proportion of whom identified caring as a problem at Time II than at Time I.

Other indicators support this pattern of reduced improvement among the carers of more dependent users. Carers of cognitively impaired users, critical interval need users and users who are co-resident were more likely than other carers to report that they had not had a break (due to caring responsibilities) in the six months preceding the second interview, despite their desire to take one. In addition, the proportion of carers reporting a deterioration in their relationship with the user since Time I was much larger among the carers of users with a cognitive impairment than other carers, again particularly if the user had critical interval needs and a cognitive impairment. One in three carers reported at Time II that their satisfaction with services had deteriorated, with dissatisfaction again more prevalent among the carers of cognitively impaired users.

Thus while the service system is clearly prioritising support to those users most in need of services, the benefits are not as immediately evident for their carers. The ECCEP productivities work does demonstrate that specific interventions, such as social work input, or respite care, have powerful effects on stress levels among certain groups of carers (Davies and Fernández, 1999). However, the descriptive evidence presented here illustrates that, across a wider range of variables, the outlook for carers is complex, varied and by no means uniformly positive. Findings suggest that the system is not entirely compensating for the difficulties of caring for an older person with complex needs. As those needs change over time, service interventions are not managing to alleviate the problems experienced by all carers who continue to provide a high level of input. Naturally, the world of post-reform community care is a changing one, as the final chapter in this volume will outline. The outlook for carers may continue to improve as the provisions of the 1995 Carers (Recognition and Services) Act are fully implemented and other policies designed to help carers are put in place. ECCEP evidence would suggest that there is indeed considerable scope for improvement.

11 Conclusion

Evaluating Community Care for Elderly People began just after the provisions of the 1990 NHS and Community Care Act were fully implemented in 1993. Thus, the study and its findings, both the descriptions in this volume and the results from statistical modelling (Davies and Fernández, 1999), represent an assessment of community care in the post-reform period. Since then, however, a new and potentially broad-reaching set of reforms has begun to be introduced following the election of a Labour government in May 1997. These reforms have been outlined in a series of consultation documents, White Papers and the report of the Royal Commission on Long Term Care. They propose changes in the organisation and delivery of social services, in the relationship between health and social care, and in the funding structure of the long-term care system. The reforms represent not only the desire of a new government to fulfil election pledges and to promote a new agenda but also an attempt to address the weaknesses which remain in the post-1990 community care system. ECCEP has a significant contribution to make in examining and revealing the weaknesses as well as the strengths of community care. An assessment of the experiences of users, carers and care managers in the post-1990 system has been undertaken in the preceding chapters. It is worth now summarising some of these findings in the context of the proposed new set of changes. Five themes in particular relate both to ECCEP and the current reforms. These are the effectiveness and quality of services, prevention and rehabilitation, care management, joint working, and addressing the needs of carers.

Effectiveness and quality of services

In November 1998, the White Paper *Modernising Social Services* was published. It set out a series of national objectives for social care into the next millennium, in relation to service provision, care management and coordination with other agencies, particularly the NHS. Two of the national objectives listed in the paper emphasise the continued importance of the principles of independence and choice as central to services offered to users and carers. In relation to independence, the White Paper specified a national objective as 'To enable adults assessed as needing social care support to live as safe, full and as normal a life as possible, in their own home whenever feasible' and in relation to choice, 'to allow for choice and different responses for different needs and objectives.' These two objectives echo those clearly expressed in the 1990 reforms and represent a continued emphasis both on the importance of domiciliary care provision and on matching services from a range of providers to the varied needs of older people. ECCEP evidence can significantly contribute to establishing a picture of how successful the post- 1990 system has been in both maintaining older people in their own homes, and in delivering services which effectively meet the needs of users.

In relation to maintaining older people at home, findings demonstrate that, one year after referral to social services for a new or revised care package, the vast majority of ECCEP users remained in the community, receiving services. Just 13 per cent of users had died, and only 10 per cent had entered a care home during that year. What is perhaps more significant, however, is the clear relationship which emerges throughout the study in relation to the effectiveness of the system in matching the needs of users with the services deployed to meet them. In contrast to the mid-1980s and findings from the Domiciliary Care Project, the post-1990 system placed considerable emphasis on matching resources to needs in four distinct ways: targeting, tasks, flexibility, and indicators of quality.

Targeting

Community care services are currently being targeted towards users with more complex needs, rather than providing a basic level of coverage to all older people in need of social care services. One of the most obvious pieces of evidence to support this is found in the distribution of resources between different user groups in ECCEP. Users who are physically more dependent — those with critical interval needs — were receiving all social care services more frequently than other users, with the sole exception of meals on wheels. Home care services in particular were targeted on these users, with a critical interval need user receiving on average 9.25 hours of home care, compared with 3.75 hours among users with long interval needs. Users with a cognitive impairment were also receiving a higher level of home care (7.42 hours per week on average, compared to five hours for users without a cognitive impairment) and also of day care, respite care and social work visits. A slightly higher proportion of social care resources were also directed towards users without a carer in the case of home care and meals on wheels, although other services which traditionally aim to relieve carers (such as respite and sitting services) were received in larger amounts by users with informal support.

Comparisons of service receipt with the Domiciliary Care Project more clearly demonstrate the shift in emphasis towards users with more complex needs and away from a uniform, basic level of provision. The distribution of home care resources in particular has shifted. Whereas short interval need users without a carer received an average four hours of home care in the mid-1980s, this had grown to an average of seven hours per week in the mid-1990s. Comparisons with DCP also illustrate a shift away from some services, particularly meals on wheels which is now received by fewer users overall than a decade ago, towards others, particularly day care and respite care. Just 5 per cent of DCP users had short stays in respite care during the 1980s, whereas by the mid-1990s this proportion had tripled. Day care attendance in DCP was found to differ very little between user groups, whereas in ECCEP it was clear that this service was at least some of the time aiming to relieve carers: users with a carer were receiving a higher level of day care across all interval need categories in ECCEP.

Tasks

In addition to a greater proportion of social care resources being targeted at more dependent users, it is also evident that the nature of the assistance given has changed in the period since the 1990 reforms. As other recent research has argued, the emphasis on maintaining more dependent users at home has resulted in a changing role for the home help service — away from household maintenance activities and shopping towards the provision of bathing and personal care assistance (Twigg, 1997; Clark et al., 1998). While it is clear that many ECCEP users requiring this type of assistance were receiving it from their carers (just under two-thirds of carers reported providing assistance with personal care, and one in four helped with medical and toileting activities at Time I), others became recipients of this type of help from formal services following the implementation of a care package. The evidence to demonstrate the effects of this type of help being directed particularly towards more dependent users can be found in the discussion relating to changes in informal care inputs over time. Carers interviewed at both Time I and Time II described a shift in the nature of activities they did for the user after the care package had been in place for several months. There was a general reduction in the amount of medical and toileting help and assistance with personal care that carers were providing by Time II, in contrast with an increase in the number of carers providing help with domestic tasks. In relation to personal care, one in four carers who had been providing this help had ceased to do so by Time II, with the changes most marked among the carers of more dependent users, particularly those with a cognitive impairment. Similar reductions were evident among the carers who had been providing medical and toileting help at Time I, with reductions again more common among the carers of more dependent users. While changes in informal care inputs are just one indicator of the pattern and effect of services, this evidence does suggest that some users with more complex needs were receiving assistance with a particularly challenging range of tasks which they had previously relied on informal carers to provide.

Flexibility

The 1989 White Paper Caring for People and the subsequent NHS and Community Care Act emphasised the need to develop a mixed economy of care in order to promote user and carer choice as well as stimulate improvements in services through competition. As numerous other studies have demonstrated, the range of social care providers has expanded, but the expansion has been primarily in relation to independent home care services, with regional variation in provision remaining marked. Evidence from ECCEP detailed in Chapter 8 does demonstrate that the SSD remained the provider of the vast majority of social care provision in 1995, but that developments in independent sector home care and voluntary and independent sectors day care, respite care and sheltered housing had taken place. What is perhaps most interesting in relation to both the quality and effectiveness of services, however, is the role which independent sector services were playing in relation to statutory provision, and which users they were assisting.

Analysis of independent sector home care usage in ECCEP reveals that these services were playing a significant role in assisting more dependent users to a greater extent than others. This is in contrast to the image of private sector home care in the 1980s, which was of a service as a cheap alternative to provide help with basic tasks. While just under one in five ECCEP users were receiving independent sector home care, these providers were responsible for 25 per cent of home help hours overall. This was due to the fact that more dependent users — those with critical and short interval needs — were receiving a higher proportion of home care from independent sector providers. These users have needs which necessitate service provision at more frequent and less predictable times, notably after hours and at weekends. These are the times at which SSDs may find it difficult to provide services, and thus may turn to the independent sector to fill gaps in existing statutory provision.

The flexibility of services available from different providers is something which the reform process begun in 1997 wishes to preserve. Both the social services White Paper and the subsequent report of the Royal Commission on Long Term Care emphasise the need to retain the benefits of a mixed economy of care. As the Royal Commission report describes: 'better value for money can be obtained within the existing system, but in recognising the different circumstances, needs and wishes of individuals we do not advocate a single model. There should be a tapestry of accessible provision from which, within limitations, people may choose, confident that their needs can be met' (Royal Commission on Long Term Care, 1999, 8.2). This 'tapestry of provision' is likely to include an increasing number of voluntary and private social care providers in the future. An important difference between the enthusiasm for the mixed economy expressed in the 1990 reforms and the changes proposed for the new millennium do, however, rest in the manner in which all provision — both statutory and independent — will be monitored and evaluated to assess the quality of care being provided. Along with the continued importance of the Social Services Inspectorate, Audit Commission and reviews commissioned by the Department of Health, a new performance management framework is proposed. Its emphasis will be on outcomes rather than on processes, with a particular emphasis on quality indicators, an area in which ECCEP findings also have a significant contribution to make.

Quality indicators

A consultation document on the new performance management framework for social services was published in February 1999. It stated that the framework would provide local authorities, central government and others with the means to assess performance across a range of indicators (Department of Health, 1999, 1.7). The framework was presented as a means of achieving 'best value'[1] across services by setting authority-wide objectives, conducting regular reviews and establishing a new statistical performance assessment framework which would allow authorities to be compared and monitored over time, and for interface issues with the NHS to be examined through the development of some common indicators. A set of indicators central to this proposed framework and relevant to community care for older people concerns the quality of services, including assessing user/carer perceptions and experiences of services by focusing on the extent of their involvement in assessment and review, and measuring levels of satisfaction.

User/carer involvement

The fact that the new performance management framework proposes to include indicators of user and carer involvement and empowerment highlights the growing recognition of the importance of this theme throughout the 1990s. While the principle of empowerment or involvement was included in the 1989 White Paper, there was no statutory obligation placed on authorities to include users and carers in decision-making or in any way attempt to monitor or measure their input. Despite the vague nature of the concept of empowerment, however, findings from ECCEP suggest both that the issue gradually grew in importance across authorities following the implementation of the reforms, and that users, and to a lesser extent carers, were included in the assessment and review process.

Chapter 5 on care management in this volume details findings of policy and practice discussions with managers and workers in each of the authorities in the study. These groups were asked to rank service outcomes in order of priority for two periods: 1992-1994, when the reforms were in the process of being implemented, and 1995-1997, when implementation should have taken place. For the earlier period, the outcome ranked across groups as the most important was 'a real chance for users to stay at home, rather than enter a care home'. For the period 1995-1997, this outcome was replaced in ranking with what had been the second choice for the earlier period 'empowerment, choice and control over their own lives for users'. The importance of empowering users was thus recognised by managers and workers across authorities, at least in principle.

Users, carers and care managers were asked about their experience of user and carer involvement in assessment during the first round of ECCEP interviews. Both care managers and users reported relatively high rates of involvement. Among care managers, 70 per cent reported that users had been involved to a considerable extent in assessment, with an additional 17 per cent reporting some involvement. A similar proportion (71 per cent) of users themselves reported that they had a say in assessment, although the proportions were slightly lower (60 per cent) among more dependent users: those with critical interval needs. Users were also asked about their perceptions of the role of the care manager in decision-making, with two-thirds reporting that they saw them as someone with whom to discuss choices, as an equal, and fewer than 9 per cent saying that the care manager was someone 'in charge', who made decisions on the user's behalf.

Carers were also positive about the role of the care manager in decision-making, with 71 per cent of them reporting that they saw the care manager as an equal in discussions, and again just 9 per cent perceiving the care manager as someone in charge. Carer involvement was also assessed by asking about the extent and nature of contact with the care manager, and the incidence of separate carer assessment. Findings relating to the level of contact were also generally positive, with 78 per cent reporting some contact either in person or by phone. Levels of contact were higher among carers who lived with the user, and those looking after more dependent users. Findings relating to the incidence of separate assessment for carers were, however, not as positive, a point to which we shall return later in relation to care management.

Satisfaction

In introducing the new performance management framework, the 1998 social services White Paper stated that local authorities would be expected to carry out satisfaction surveys of users and carers, as part of their assessment of the quality of services. The performance management consultation document further developed this idea by announcing the government's intention to develop a small set of national survey questions relating to satisfaction, which would be agreed by the Department of Health in collaboration with local government for inclusion in local authority surveys by April 2000. ECCEP assessed several aspects of both user and carer satisfaction which will be relevant to future satisfaction measures, both as one approach to selecting questions and as a reflection of users' and carers' perceptions of the quality of community care in the 1990s.

Three distinct aspects of user satisfaction were measured in ECCEP, both at Time I and at Time II, once the care package had been in place for several months. Users were asked about their satisfaction with the way care managers had assessed their needs and tried to help, with their own ability to remain living independently in the community, and with the specific role of services in helping them to remain at home. Not surprisingly, overall rates of satisfaction were high, with eight out of ten users describing themselves as very satisfied or satisfied with the assessment and help provided and their ability to live independently. In addition, less than one in ten users at Time I reported that services had made no difference in their ability to remain at home. These high levels of satisfaction only partially reflect the overall picture, however. This is due first to the fact that users with a cognitive impairment were excluded from this line of questioning; second because, as other research has repeatedly shown, older people are reluctant to criticise services and as a result dissatisfaction may be underreported; and finally because there were subtle but important differences between groups of users in satisfaction levels through time. By Time II, a significant proportion of users — one in four — reported that their experience of social services over the past six months had been mixed, unfavourable or very unfavourable, suggesting that there was some disappointment with services once the care package was in place, perhaps as a result of unmet need. This dissatisfaction by Time II was slightly more marked for users without a carer than others. When asked about the role of services in helping them remain living at home, more users reported an overall improvement in their opinion by Time II. Improvements were more marked among users with critical and short interval needs than long interval need users, however, possibly reflecting the effects of targeting resources towards more dependent users in order to help them remain at home.

Carer satisfaction was also measured through a series of questions relating to the assessment of the user's needs, assessment of the carer's own needs, satisfaction with the help provided by social services, and satisfaction with the role of services in helping the user live as he/she wanted. The majority of carers stated that they were satisfied in response to each question, but satisfaction levels were lower overall than those reported by users, particularly in relation to the assessment of the carer's own needs. In contrast to users, carers of users surviving in the community were overall slightly less satisfied with services at Time II than Time I. The most consistent pattern to emerge from the carer satisfaction questions, however, relates to the responses of the carers of more dependent users, particularly those with a cognitive impairment. These carers reported lower levels of satisfaction in relation to the services provided, the assessment of their own needs and the ability of services to help keep the user at home. For instance, when asked if they were satisfied with the help provided by social services for the user, just over one in four carers of someone with critical interval needs and a cognitive impairment reported that they either had mixed feelings, were dissatisfied or were very dissatisfied. Carers of more dependent users were also less confident in the ability of services to help the user remain at home by Time II than at Time I. These results suggest that, particularly for those looking after an older person with complex needs, the services offered were not always sufficient.

Prevention and rehabilitation

Despite progress made since the introduction of the 1990 community care reforms, evidence from other research suggests there are still a significant number of older people entering residential or nursing home care for whom admission could have been preventable, if the right services had been available and provided at the appropriate time (Audit Commission, 1997). In addition, the proportion of older people entering hospital as emergency admissions has risen throughout the 1990s. The rising number of older people in hospital has contributed towards the pressure for early discharge, often without adequate provision for rehabilitation. The outcome of many hospitalisations thus remains residential or nursing home admission. This cycle of seemingly preventable admissions and discharges was detailed in a 1997 Audit Commission *Coming of Age*, as 'the vicious circle' (Audit Commission, 1997). The report argued that the starting point for this pattern was the targeting of social care resources on older people with more complex needs, while the proportion of older people receiving lower level services had been reduced. The Audit Commission and more recently the Royal Commission on Long Term Care have argued that this focus away from prevention and low-level support has contributed to the problems in the current system, and similarly that rehabilitation opportunities are missed both in hospital and in the community which have further contributed to the pressure on hospital beds and continued admissions to institutional care.

In response to this assessment of weaknesses in social care and at the interface between health and social care, the 1998 social services White Paper identified 'better preventative services and a stronger focus on rehabilitation' as part of its overall programme of action for adult services. The intention to improve provision both at entry into the system and in follow-up is also reflected in the National Priorities Guidance issued for both health and social services for the period from 1991-2001. Of the eight main priorities, one relates to the development of preventative strategies, and another to the development of rehabilitation services. ECCEP has evidence to contribute in relation to both these themes. While readers should turn to the productivities work (Davies and Fernández, 1999) for a discussion of which services were benefiting which users in relation to both prevention and recovery over time, descriptive findings in this volume do highlight the shift away from low-level to more intensive and selective support — and which users benefited — as well as detailing some of the gaps which users, carers and care managers identified in relation to both preventative and rehabilitative services.

Prevention

Earlier PSSRU studies highlighted the role of low-level help — particularly relating to domestic tasks, monitoring and companionship — in maintaining older people in their own homes, particularly those with less complex needs, who could be supported with relatively few resources as long as these were provided on a consistent basis (Davies and Challis, 1986; Qureshi et al., 1989).[2] The emphasis that the post-1990 system has placed on supporting those with more complex needs has meant that the distribution of resources, particularly in relation to home care, has shifted away from providing a basic service to less dependent users to concentrating provision on those most in need. ECCEP evidence supports this argument in a variety of ways, some of which have already been touched upon in this chapter. In relation to the potentially preventative nature of low-level services, however, two important points should be noted. The first is that ECCEP clearly illustrates that less dependent users, namely those with long interval needs and in some instances those without a cognitive impairment, are not benefiting from current patterns of provision to the same extent as more dependent users. The second is that there are obvious gaps in the provision of basic services, gaps which users and carers identify and which in some cases result in informal carers giving help that formal services will no longer provide.

In relation to outcomes from services, evidence in Chapter 9 detailed changes in users' functional ability, health status and quality of life between Time I interviews when the care package was being implemented, and Time II when services had been in place for several months. In relation to the majority of these indicators, more dependent users, particularly those with critical interval needs, showed greater improvements than less dependent users. With reference to changes in functional ability over time, for instance, the only group of users to report an improvement in the performance of ADLs between Time I and Time II were those with critical interval needs. While users overall evidenced a slight improvement in IADL performance between the two interviews, long interval need users showed no improvement in relation to meal preparation, making a hot drink and housework, suggesting measures to improve a user's task performance were either not provided or were insufficient to result in the positive changes experienced by more dependent users with these tasks over time. In relation to mental health, users with long interval needs showed no significant improvement in either Katzman cognitive impairment score, depression, or morale, whereas some improvements were apparent among frailer users. Quality of life measures such as having someone in whom to confide, and the ability to meet people and socialise, were areas in which more dependent users reported some improvement overall between Time I and Time II, but again no significant change was apparent among long interval need users. While it is important to be cautious when interpreting these results, given the small sample sizes for some indicators and the descriptive nature of the analysis conducted, it is nevertheless evident that the level of help provided to less dependent users was insufficient to result in measurable improvements between Time I and Time II interviews.

ECCEP users were also asked to identify any unmet needs for services during both interviews. The gaps in provision most commonly identified were clearly related to low-level support, primarily with domestic tasks. At Time II, when the care package should have been fully implemented for all users, just over half (51 per cent) were able to identify at least one outstanding need for assistance. The most common type of help requested was assistance with cleaning (36 per cent). Shopping was also mentioned by a proportion of users (16 per cent). The need for help with both these tasks was most marked among less dependent, long interval need users, who as a result of changing eligibility criteria may not have been able to receive these services. Interestingly, changes in carer input over time support this pattern of gaps in provision. By Time II, a group of carers (15 per cent of the sample) had started doing housework for the users, whereas they had not been engaged in this task at Time I. The increase was most marked among the carers of less dependent (short and long interval) users without a cognitive impairment. A similar increase was also evident for meals and shopping. What this pattern suggests is that informal carers were providing a type of assistance which the implemented care package could not offer to a sufficient extent. The question which this evidence does not answer is to what extent lack of formal assistance with these basic tasks would contribute to future deterioration or problems among older service users. This is an issue which future research will need to address if the issue of prevention in social care provision is to be properly understood.

Rehabilitation

While the effects of targeting since the 1990 reforms may have reduced the potential benefit of services to less dependent older people, what ECCEP evidence does demonstrate is that improvements across a range of indicators were evident for users with more complex needs. In the period between setting up a new or revised care package and Time II interviews six or more months later, users with short and critical interval needs — and in some instances those with a cognitive impairment — reported small but important improvements in functional ability, mental health, a reduction in risk factors and improvements in several indicators relating to quality of life. These improvements are detailed in Chapter 9. They are rehabilitative effects — improvements which in most cases were due to a range of factors — but in which the provision of both social and health care resources played a part.

One area relating to rehabilitation in which ECCEP evidence suggests problems still exist, however, is in relation to the provision of aids and adaptations. Gaps in provision were raised during both user interviews. By Time II, when the care package should have been fully in place, a significant proportion of users who identified unmet needs reported that they still required aids or adaptations to assist them at home. Just under one in four users (21 per cent) who identified an unmet need was waiting for a safety or alarm system, and 14 per cent were waiting for some form of disability equipment. These types of aids can make a significant difference to the ability of older people to retain their independence within the home, and thus constitute an important aspect of the rehabilitative potential of social care services. The delay in providing these basic pieces of equipment has been highlighted by other recent research which informed the conclusions of the Royal Commission on Long Term Care, who state in their report: 'We have heard over and over again how a quick intervention with the appropriate aid or appliance could ensure independence and improve quality of life — small amounts of money preventing the later expenditure of larger sums' (Royal Commission on Long Term Care, 1999, 8.23). The Commission has recommended that budgets for equipment be available from a single pool for both health and social services, and that local authorities should be able to make loans for aids and adaptations to certain groups of older people. In conjunction with a health and social care partnership grant set out in the social services White Paper (which will aim to improve the planning and provision of rehabilitation services), these recommendations are consistent with a continued commitment to assist more older people to remain in their own homes, for as long as possible.

Care management

The system of care management put in place by the 1990 reforms has served as the mechanism for matching services from a range of providers with the needs of users and carers living in varied circumstances. While recent evidence from other PSSRU studies has found that the core tasks of care management have been interpreted and implemented in different ways in different parts of the country (Challis et al., 1998a), it is a concept which still represents a coordinated response to assessing needs and planning interventions to meet them. A continued commitment to care management is evident in the policy documents at the close of the decade, despite the recognition of important weaknesses in the current system. This commitment is emphasised in the 1998 social services White Paper which describes one of the national objectives for social services as 'to identify individuals with social care needs who are eligible for public support, to assess those needs accurately and consistently, and to review care packages as necessary to ensure that they continue to be appropriate and effective' (Department of Health, 1998c). The need to make the best use of care management by improving the consistency and reducing the variation in arrangement is a theme echoed in the report of the Royal Commission, as well as in the launching of the Department of Health's 'Fair Access to Care' initiative from April 2000, which will focus on improving the performance of the core tasks of care management in order to provide users and carers with a more accessible and reliable system.

Assessment

The variation in care management arrangements which the Royal Commission report in particular highlights as a problem for the development of a more efficient system of assessment, service delivery and review is evident from ECCEP findings. There was considerable variation in the type of worker who identified him/herself as a care manager, although social workers and home care managers/organisers did make up the majority of those carrying out care management tasks. Similarly, the type of assessment which ECCEP users were given differed considerably, from initial, simple or fast track to complex and full multidisciplinary assessments. Despite these differences in local practice arrangements, however, it is worth emphasising that a pattern of assessment is evident in the study which relates directly to needs and reflects the targeting of resources towards more dependent users. Thus, older people with more complex needs were more likely to have a qualified social worker as their care manager; cases involving these older people took longer to set up and accounted for a larger proportion of the worker's time, even in the continuing care phase; and more complex cases resulted in higher care management costs.

Evidence relating to the assessment of carers' needs in ECCEP was mixed. While care managers reported that a significant proportion of care packages (45 per cent) were aimed at supporting both the user and the carer with an additional 9 per cent designed to support primarily the carer, the separate assessment of carer needs was something which rarely took place. Just 16 per cent of carers felt they had a separate assessment, and there was inconsistency between carers and care managers in identifying which carers were more likely to have their needs assessed, with care managers reporting that those looking after more dependent users received special consideration, while carers of long interval need users were the group most likely to report that they had a separate assessment. Part of the explanation for these findings does lie in the fact that ECCEP fieldwork was conducted before the implementation of the 1995 Carers (Recognition and Services) Act was completed, which made the carer's right to ask for a separate assessment a statutory obligation of local authorities.

Review

Findings from the Domiciliary Care Project highlighted the fact that review was one part of the care management process which was consistently neglected across authorities, and often relegated to a task which home help managers/organisers were expected to perform. In contrast, ECCEP identified improvements in the incidence of review. By Time II, the majority of cases (60 per cent) had been reviewed, particularly in instances where the user had more complex needs and a carer involved. Care managers reported that user involvement in review was commonplace, with users involved in 80 per cent of cases, and carers or family/friends in 54 per cent of cases. Worker involvement was somewhat different: just two-thirds of care managers who had assessed the user said they had been involved in the review, which suggests some separation of care management tasks, with review officers becoming involved. Multidisciplinary review was also rare, with GPs involved in just 5 per cent of reviews, and a similar level of involvement reported for community nurses.

It is important to point out, however, that despite an improvement in the proportion of cases being reviewed between the mid-1980s and following the community care reforms of 1990, the fact that four out of ten ECCEP users had still not had their case reviewed six or more months following assessment still suggests room for improvement. The 1998 social services White Paper criticises current practice and argues: 'Once services are provided, they are often not reviewed. This again contributes to a culture of dependency rather than one of enablement. A great deal of effort is put into initial assessment of care needs, but after that there may be very little review of progress to see whether the user's needs have changed or whether the services are providing the best outcomes' (Department of Health, 1998c, 2.0). The White Paper has proposed that reviews following initial assessment should now be required to take place every three months, and the Royal Commission report has taken this one step further by incorporating the three month review into a new framework for means-testing for long-term care funding, which would see the value of the older person's home disregarded following admission to a residential or nursing home until the review had been conducted and opportunities for rehabilitation or redirection back to domiciliary care fully explored.

Consistency

The detailed analysis of consistency of views between care managers, users and carers described in Chapter 6 has highlighted some of the potential problems involved in relying on professional judgements to inform decisions regarding the care plan, or to assume that the view of either the carer or the user represents the whole picture. Findings revealed important areas of inconsistency between the views of care managers and users in particular, which emphasises the importance of including the user in decision-making around assessment and care planning. Factors relating to the needs and circumstances of users and carers were also found to affect their contributions to the assessment and care planning process. For instance, users had a tendency to understate their needs if they were cognitively impaired, while users with a demanding attitude to help were found to be more likely to exaggerate their problems. When the user was depressed, it was also found that they would overstate their needs, or exaggerate the nature and proportion of tasks performed by the carer. In cases where the carer was involved, his or her own circumstances were found to affect responses. Carer stress, hours per week spent caring, and other factors such as whether the carer was employed were found to influence responses.

It is interesting to note that the Royal Commission on Long Term Care directly addresses these issues of differing perceptions between users, carers and professionals. Their report states: 'Older people, like everyone in society, have rights to make their own choices of lifestyle. There can be no doubt that there will be times when people's choices will conflict with the views of their carer or the care manager. It will be essential for potential risks to be properly and sensitively managed within formal arrangements' (Royal Commission on Long Term Care, 1999, 8.31) The Commission report recommends that opportunities to develop advocacy arrangements at a local level be explored to assist older people and their carers during the assessment and care planning process. Another suggestion put forward by the Royal Commission and also mentioned in the social services White Paper is the importance of multidisciplinary involvement in order to address some of these issues of accuracy in assessment. There is considerable evidence in the ECCEP consistency analysis to suggest that care managers do indeed have problems identifying some areas of user need more than others, particularly in relation to health problems, depression, morale and cognitive impairment. Given the importance of accurate assessment of need for a well-planned care package, it is clear that the involvement of other agencies, particularly health professionals, in assessing the needs of some groups of users is important. This relates to the theme of joint working, to which we now turn.

Joint working

The Domiciliary Care Project outlined in some detail the problems of interface between health and social care in the mid-1980s (Davies et al., 1990). At the case level, problems centred around boundaries between tasks conducted by community nurses and home helps, particularly in relation to personal care. At the agency level, problems centred around a lack of joint planning, exacerbated by the absence of a lead agency for community care and limited use or availability of joint finance. The 1990 reforms attempted to address these interface issues by identifying local authorities as lead agencies in coordinating community care services, stipulating the need for joint community care plans, and arranging for some transfer of resources from the NHS to social services following the closure of long-stay beds. Despite these and other changes, however, the problematic relationship between health and social care remains the focus for reform at the close of the decade.

Joint working and ECCEP findings

Both the importance of partnership between health and social care and the limited evidence that it was occurring in relation to care management for older people is evident from ECCEP findings. Users in the study had a high incidence of health problems: care managers reported an average of 2.59 health problems per user, with the most prevalent being arthritis and rheumatism, heart disease and respiratory problems. By Time II, the number of health problems experienced by users had increased slightly rather than declined following the implementation of the care package. Not surprisingly, more dependent older people, particularly those with critical interval needs, were more likely to have health problems and thus required input from health services in order to remain living in the community. The role of health problems in leading to admission to residential or nursing home care was also evident from findings. Care managers of users who had moved to institutional care by Time II identified failing health as the most common cause (it was a factor in 72 per cent of cases), with increasing dependence and an injury to the user also mentioned by a significant proportion of workers.

Despite the high incidence of health problems in the ECCEP sample and the relationship between health and case complexity, health professionals were involved in assessment and review in only a small minority of cases. When care managers were asked who had been involved in the assessment process, just over half (58 per cent) indicated that other professionals had been included. In most cases, however, these professionals were other social care staff, including home care managers. Health professional involvement was limited to occupational therapy or rehabilitation staff in 17 per cent of cases, hospital nurses in 12 per cent of cases, and community nurses in 8 per cent of cases, despite the fact that four out of ten ECCEP users received community nursing services as part of their care packages. Other health professionals, including GPs, were involved in the assessment in less than one in ten cases. As we have already mentioned in this chapter, findings relating to health professional involvement in review were even less encouraging, with reported involvement limited to GPs and community nurses in 5 per cent of cases.

The relative absence of any input from health professionals in assessment and review suggests that, at the case level, the division between health and social care was still prevalent in the mid-1990s. Given the findings relating to consistency in Chapter 6, this lack of joint working is a cause for concern. The inability of a significant proportion of care managers, particularly those without a social work background, to identify both physical (particularly hearing impairment, speech impairment and blood pressure) problems and mental (particularly cognitive impairment and depression) health problems suggests that opportunities to provide users with services appropriate to their needs may have been lost. For example, care managers identified depression in just 13 per cent of the user sample, whereas the use of a standardised measure (the geriatric depression scale) indicated that severe depression was present in 21 per cent of cases overall. Given the considerable research evidence that the identification of depression is an important precondition for treatment and decisions relating to appropriate services, lack of recognition of this problem in care planning for older people could have serious consequences (Thompson, 1996).

New agenda for joint working

Research evidence at the case level from ECCEP is compatible with other recent studies which have identified persistent structural constraints to joint working between health and social care (and indeed with other agencies such as housing), despite the intention of the 1990 reforms to improve the situation (Audit Commission, 1997). At the close of the decade, the new series of reforms are trying to address this problem by creating opportunities for partnership working across a range of agencies, with a particular focus on better joint working between social services and the NHS. As the social services White Paper explains: 'The Government has made one of its top priorities since coming to office to bring down the "Berlin Wall" that can divide health and social services, and to create a system of integrated care that puts users at the centre of service provision' (Department of Health, 1998c, 6.5). This commitment to partnership has been included in a wide range of new policy documents. Within the National Priorities Guidance for both health and social services from 1999-2001, 'interagency working' is one of the key principles. Both the social services White Paper and the NHS White Paper published in December 1997 include the statutory duty of partnership as a central component of the proposed reforms. Other reform documents and initiatives, including Better Services for Vulnerable People, National Service Frameworks for different care groups, Health Action Zones, Health Improvement Programmes and the formation of Primary Care Groups are all based on a framework of joint planning and working.

Perhaps the most significant causal factor in the failure of the 1990 reforms to improve joint working was the lack of a firm financial framework for the development of shared means of assessment and service delivery. The key document relating to the new proposals for joint working published in September 1998 — *Partnerships in Action* — sets out the intention to establish pooled budgets between health and social care and to formalise this new arrangement in legislation. Pooled budgets would allow funds relating to areas currently on the periphery of community care — such as housing, and aids and adaptations — to be brought together in a single pot. Pooled budgeting is also presented as a mechanism for encouraging greater flexibility among health and social care staff involved in assessment and care planning, by facilitating access to a variety of services better able to meet the range of needs that older people may have. Thus, at the end of the decade, changes are proposed which may finally begin to address some of the restrictions placed on assessment and care planning for older people which both DCP and ECCEP have identified. It will be the task of future research to assess whether these reforms meet their objectives.

Addressing the needs of carers

Chapter 1 outlined how the position of carers in community care has shifted from one of relative anonymity in the policy documents of the 1970s and early 1980s to a position of greater prominence in the 1990s. The Griffiths report of 1988 recognised the contribution of carers to maintaining older people at home but made no real suggestions about how they should be supported. The 1989 White Paper and subsequent NHS and Community Care Act went one step further by recognising their need for support and their right to be involved in needs assessment and care planning. The position of carers was brought further towards the centre of community care policy in 1995 with the passage of the Carers (Recognition and Services) Act, which formalised their right to a separate assessment. Important investments in services and information for carers have since taken place in different parts of the country; national and local carers associations have grown in numbers and in prominence; and a significant body of research now exists relating to the needs, roles and expectations of the carers of older people. Despite this progress, however, there is now widespread recognition that the community care reforms failed to develop core services for carers sufficiently, made continued assumptions about their availability and roles, and failed to adequately respond to the varied needs of carers for support and respite (Twigg, 1998; Parker, 1999).

The reforms proposed for the new millennium attempt to respond to the criticisms of the treatment of carers in the post- 1990 system by stating an explicit commitment to invest in more support for carers. The social services White Paper states as one of its national objectives: 'To enable informal carers to care, or continue to care, for as long as they and the service user wish', and stipulates an overall programme of action designed to offer more support to carers. This action centres around a new system of support set out in the document *Caring About Carers: A National Strategy for Carers*, which the Department of Health published in early 1999. The Carers Strategy drew on research evidence and consultation with carers and community groups in proposing a new approach with three strategic elements: information, support, and care. The three elements represent a recognition of the need to provide carers with adequate and accessible information about services, benefits and standards; to ensure that they are involved in planning and providing services; and to set aside specific funds to develop services which give carers a break, and provide local authorities with new powers to provide additional services which carers may need. The strategy begins to address an ambitious agenda, but one which ECCEP evidence relating to the experience of carers in the mid-1990s suggests is indeed required if the informal sector is to continue to provide the bulk of care for older people. Two specific arguments from the study support this need for change. The first relates to the central importance of carers in supporting older people in the community, and the second asserts that the post-1990 system, while demonstrating clear benefits for some users, was not supporting their carers to the extent required.

The importance of informal care

The central importance of informal support in assisting older service users to remain in the community is demonstrated by a wide range of ECCEP findings. Evidence from Time I interviews, which took place during the implementation of the care package, reveal the extent of existing informal inputs. First, the relationship between the needs of users and the presence or absence of a principal carer is clear. The vast majority of users (81 per cent) were able to identify a principal carer: someone who provided them with regular assistance, on at least a weekly basis. However, the likelihood of both having a carer and living with others rose as the needs of the user became more complex. Thus, while three out of ten older people with long interval needs and no cognitive impairment lived alone without a principal carer, just one in ten users with critical interval needs and a cognitive impairment lived alone without a carer. These older users with complex needs require assistance frequently and often at unpredictable times, and thus need consistent and easily accessible support of the kind offered by a co-resident family member. Without this type of support, the possibility of remaining in the community is reduced, and admission to residential or nursing home care becomes much more likely.

Second, ECCEP evidence, like so many other studies, highlights the role of close relatives, particularly female relatives, in providing care. Women made up 72 per cent of the carer sample in the study, and the vast majority of carers were either the daughter or son (in-law) of the user (45 per cent) or a spouse (31 per cent). Friends and neighbours made up just 8 per cent of principal carers overall, although this proportion was further reduced in cases where the user was more dependent. Most ECCEP carers were older people themselves, with 52 per cent of the sample between the ages of 61 and 90. The age profile of carers has implications for the type and amount of support offered to both the carer and the user, a fact reflected in the high proportion of carers reporting health problems of their own as well as difficulty with particular tasks, such as lifting and bathing the user.

Third, the amount and type of support offered by carers was found to be closely related to the needs of users, and involved significant inputs over a long period of time. Time I interviews found that over 70 per cent of carers had been looking after the user for a year or more, and the majority (56 per cent) were providing six or more hours of assistance per week. Co-resident carers were providing more support, particularly co-resident female carers. Not surprisingly, the carers of more dependent users were more likely to be engaged in providing help with tasks such as personal care and assistance with medical and toileting activities, whereas those looking after less dependent users were assisting with instrumental tasks such as shopping and housework, although domestic assistance was something in which the vast majority of carers were engaged on a regular basis.

Thus the significant contribution of principal carers to supporting older service users in the community is clear from ECCEP findings at Time I. While none of this evidence is surprising, what is worth emphasising are the patterns which emerged in informal inputs and in the experiences of carers following the implementation of the care package, by the time of the second interview.

These patterns illustrate the extent to which some carers were supported by formal services, while others continued to experience problems despite the assistance provided.

Insufficient support for carers

Chapter 10 presented evidence relating to outcomes for carers following implementation of the care package. A consistent pattern emerged across a range of indicators relating to carer stress, carer employment, breaks from caring and the user/carer relationship which demonstrated that improvements were not consistent for all groups of carers. In particular, those looking after more dependent users, particularly users with a cognitive impairment, were experiencing more problems following care management intervention than they had before the new care package was in place, at Time I. By the second interview, the carers of more dependent users recorded higher stress scores overall, reported increased burden, were less likely to have taken a break in the past six months than other carers, and reported a deterioration in their relationship with the user. Combined with the lower rates of satisfaction with services reported by these carers and mentioned above, it is evident that the benefits which more dependent users demonstrated by Time II as a result of targeted service inputs were not shared by their carers.[3] In other words, although there is clear evidence from ECCEP that more dependent users were receiving higher levels of formal services and demonstrated some improvement in functional ability, mental health and quality of life indicators over time, the equivalent improvements were not as evident among their carers. This suggests that the community care service system put in place following the 1990 reforms has succeeded in maintaining more dependent older people in their own homes, but has failed to adequately support their carers.

Specific areas in which clear improvements are needed and which the Carers Strategy and other reforms are seeking to address are support with specific tasks which carers find difficult, the carer's right to have their own health needs met, and the chance for more carers to take a break from caring.

More support for carers

In relation to tasks which carers find difficult, it is evident from ECCEP findings that some activities are more problematic for carers that others. While one-third of carers in the study reported that they did find some tasks difficult, half of those carers said the difficulty lay in supporting the user with personal care tasks, while a slightly smaller but still significant proportion reported that the difficulty was with medical and toileting assistance. These types of activities often require knowledge and training which carers may not have; indeed, only a tiny proportion of ECCEP carers (7 per cent), reported that they had received training with any of the tasks they performed for the user. Some activities may also be physically demanding. Just under half of the ECCEP sample identified specific problems caused by caring, and while the most common problem listed was stress, a significant proportion of carers (42 per cent of those listing problems) also stated that the physical effort of caring was difficult to cope with.

Adequate services and appropriate training for carers are particularly important when the carer has health problems of his or her own. The majority of ECCEP carers (58 per cent) reported that they had experienced health problems in the year preceding the first interview, and just over half of these individuals reported that their health problems affected their ability to care. Those providing most support — carers of more dependent users, and co-resident carers — were most likely to have health problems of their own.

In order to provide adequate support to carers and to address their own needs, the Royal Commission on Long Term Care argued that 'on the grounds of equity and justice we believe carers need more support. They need to be actively engaged in the process of needs assessment, and where possible services to support them must be considered' (1999, 8.24). The Commission recommended that assessments become 'carer blind' — providing services based on the level of need of the user, rather than assumptions of what the carer was already providing or could provide — in order to ensure that the presence of informal support would not lead to a failure to offer adequate services. Although it is questionable to what extent this recommendation will be embraced in future policy decisions, it is also evident from the Carers Strategy that a commitment both to better assessment of carers' own needs and more comprehensive provision of services has been made, with the promise of future legislation which will provide local authorities with new powers to provide services to carers. One area in which specific proposals are already in place, backed up by ear-marked funding, is in relation to breaks for carers.

ECCEP evidence demonstrates that carers were often not able to take a break from their responsibilities, particularly if the older person they cared for had a cognitive impairment, and particularly if they were co-resident. Even when the care package had been put in place by Time II, one in three carers reported that they had not had a break away from home in the past six months, but wished they could take one. This proportion rose to four out of ten carers when the user had a cognitive impairment or behavioural disorder. The need to take a break also arose in relation to unmet need among ECCEP carers: at both interviews, respite care was the service most frequently mentioned as an unmet need, again particularly among the carers of more dependent users. This recognition that current levels of respite for carers may be patchy or inadequate is reflected in the reforms at the close of the decade. Announced in the social services White Paper and detailed in the Carers Strategy is a new programme to provide carers with a break. This will consist of a special grant totalling £120 million between 1999 and 2001, which will be directed towards the development of respite, sitting and other services which allow carers to have time for themselves away from caring responsibilities. This may constitute a tentative first step towards more adequately addressing carers' needs within the changing system of community care for older people.

Conclusion

It is clear that the system of community care for older people and their carers is poised for further transformation in the new millennium. In thinking about designing and implementing new policies and procedures to improve the equity, efficiency, quality and responsiveness of services for future generations of users and carers, a number of key findings highlighted in this volume are worth emphasising. First, the community care reforms introduced in the early 1990s have demonstrated the capacity of the system to achieve real change. The greater emphasis on care management and planning has resulted in scarce resources being targeted more effectively than hitherto towards those older people with the greatest needs, and there is clear evidence that this resulted in tangible benefits for users. Second, the findings in this book also make the point that in a system where resources in relation to needs have been tightly constrained for many years, any successes will have their associated costs. In so far as targeting has achieved many gains for particular groups of users, it may have been at the expense of appropriate investments in prevention and rehabilitation that have imposed costs on other parts of the health and social care system and added to the burdens placed on some carers. Finally, this book provides clear evidence of the enormous range and complexity of the needs of users and carers and the variation in the formal responses to them. Any serious commitment to developing new policies and procedures to make more effective use of resources, therefore, must continue to identify and evaluate this complexity. We believe that the singular strength of this volume lies in its attempt to give voice to the experiences of users, carers and care managers. The challenge for the future is to empower all of those most critically affected by policy changes so that they can articulate their needs, preferences and experiences in the more certain knowledge that the policy and practice community is willing and able to listen and learn and respond in entirely new ways.

Notes

1 'Best Value' is a principle spanning several policy areas whose central meaning is the duty to deliver services to clear standards, covering both quality and cost, by the most effective, economic and efficient means available (Department of Health, 1999, 7.14). The Best Value approach applies to all local government functions and is set out in the 1998 White Paper, *Modern Local Government: In Touch with the People.*

2 Findings from the Kent Community Care Project illustrate that low level support was particularly effective with certain characteristics of users, such as the clinically depressed.

3 As Chapter 10 argued, however, it is evident from the ECCEP productivities work (Davies and Fernández, 1999) that some services are being provided which have been successful in reducing levels of stress among certain groups of carers. These services include respite, day care and social work input. It is important that these effects in relation to the single outcome indicator of Kosberg carer stress be considered in conjunction with broader findings from the simple statistical analyses presented in this volume.

References

Abramson, J. (1988) Participation of elderly patients in discharge planning: is self-determination a reality?, *Social Work*, September-October, 443-8.

Adams, R. (1996) *The Personal Social Services: Clients, Consumers or Citizens?*, Longman, London.

Allen, I., Hogg, D. and Peace, S. (1992) *Elderly People: Choice, Participation and Satisfaction*, Policy Studies Institute, London.

Anderson, R., James, M., Miller, M., Worley, A. and Longino, C. (1998) The timing of change: patterns in transitions in functional status among elderly persons, *Journal of Gerontology*, 53B, 1, S17-S27.

Arber, S. and Ginn, J. (1990) The meaning of informal care: gender and the contribution of elderly people, *Ageing and Society*, 10, 429-54.

Arber, S. and Ginn, J. (1991) *Gender and Later Life: A Sociological Analysis of Resources and Constraints*, Sage, London.

Arber, S. and Ginn, J. (1995) Gender differences in informal caring, *Health and Social Care in the Community*, 3, 19-31.

Ashworth, M., Nafista, M. and Corkery, M. (1996) Respite care in an intermediate care centre: the views of patients and carers, *Health and Social Care in the Community*, 4, 4, 234-45.

Audit Commission (1986) *Making a Reality of Community Care*, Audit Commission, London.

Audit Commission (1992) *The Community Revolution: Personal Social Services and Community Care*, Audit Commission, London.

Audit Commission (1997) *The Coming of Age: Improving Care Services for Older People*, Audit Commission, London.

Baldwin, S. and Lunt, N. (1996) *Charging Ahead: The Development of Local Authority Charging Policies for Community Care*, Joseph Rowntree Foundation, York.

Bauld, L. (1997) Older patient participation in multi-disciplinary decision-making: discharge planning in Scotland and British Columbia, in

Healthy Aging: Challenges in Changing Times, Nova Scotia Centre on Aging, Halifax.

Bauld, L., Chesterman, J., Davies, B., Judge, K. and Mangalore, R. (1998a) Needs-related circumstances of users and carers, Discussion Paper 1410, Personal Social Services Research Unit, University of Kent at Canterbury.

Bauld, L., Chesterman, J., Davies, B., Judge, K. and Mangalore, R. (1998b) Care management at the case level, Discussion Paper 1430, Personal Social Services Research Unit, University of Kent at Canterbury.

Bauld, L., Chesterman, J., Davies, B., Judge, K. and Mangalore, R. (1998c) Outcomes for users and carers, Discussion Paper 1482, Personal Social Services Research Unit, University of Kent at Canterbury.

Bebbington, A. and Davies, B. (1983) Equity and efficiency in the allocation of personal social services, *Journal of Social Policy*, 12, 3, 309-30.

Bebbington, A., Charnley, H., Davies, B., Ferlie, E., Hughes, M. and Twigg, J. (1985) PSSRU Domiciliary Care Project: project summary, Discussion Paper 403, Personal Social Services Research Unit, University of Kent at Canterbury.

Bebbington, A., Charnley, H., Davies, B., Ferlie, E., Hughes, M. and Twigg, J. (1986) The Domiciliary Care Project: meeting the needs of the elderly, Discussion Paper 456, Personal Social Services Research Unit, University of Kent at Canterbury.

Bennett, F. (1996) *Highly Charged: Policy Issues Surrounding Charging for Non-Residential Care*, Joseph Rowntree Foundation, York.

Bernard, M. and Phillips, J. (1998) Social policy and the challenges of old age, *The Social Policy of Old Age: Moving into the Twentieth Century*, Centre for Policy on Ageing, London.

Blackman, T. and Atkinson, A. (1997) Needs targeting and resource allocation in community care, *Policy Studies*, 18, 2, 125-38.

Blalock, H., Jr (1960) *Social Statistics*, McGraw Hill, London.

Bland, R. (1994) EPIC – A Scottish case management experiment, in M. Titterton (ed.) *Caring for People in the Community: The New Welfare*, Jessica Kingsley, London.

Bland, R. and Hudson, H. (1994) *Providing Home Support to Frail Elderly People*, EPIC, Final report, University of Stirling.

Bland, R. (1997) Keyworkers re-examined: good practice, quality of care and empowerment in residential care of older people, *British Journal of Social Work*, 27, 585-603.

Blau, P. (1964) *Exchange and Power in Social Life*, Wiley, New York.

Blazer, D., Hughes, D. and George, L. (1987) The epidemiology of depression in an elderly community population, *The Gerontologist*, 27, 218-87.

Brink, T., Yesavage, J., Lum, O., Heersema, P., Adey, M. and Rose, T. (1982) Screening tests for geriatric depression, *Clinical Gerontologist*, 1, 37-44.

Brody, E. (1981) Women in the middle and family help to older people, *The Gerontologist*, 21, 471-9.

Brody, E. and Schoonover, C. (1986) Patterns of parent-care when adult daughters work and when they do not, *The Gerontologist*, 26, 372-81.

Burden, R. (1980) Measuring the effects of stress on mothers of handicapped infants, *Child Care, Health and Development*, 6, 111-23.

Carers National Association (1997) *Still Battling? The Carers Act One Year On*, Carers National Association, London.

Carriere, Y. and Pelletier, L. (1995) Factors underlying the institutionalisation of elderly persons in Canada, *Journal of Gerontology*, 50B, S164-S172.

Carver, V. and Edwards, J. (1972) *Social Workers and their Workload*, National Institute of Social Work, London.

Centre for Health and Social Research (1997) *The Carers (Recognition and Services) Act 1995 and Crossroads Care Attendance Schemes: A Baseline Survey*, CHSR, Glenrothes, Fife.

Challis, D. (1981) The measurement of outcome in social care of the elderly, *Journal of Social Policy*, 10, 179-208.

Challis, D. (1994a) Case management: a review of UK development and issues, in M.Titterton (ed.) *Caring for People in the Community: The New Welfare*, Jessica Kingsley, London.

Challis, D. (1994b) Care management: factors influencing its development in the implementation of community care, Discussion Paper 1027, Personal Social Services Research Unit, University of Kent at Canterbury.

Challis, D. (1999) Assessment and care management: development since the community care reforms in the UK, in G. Wistow and M. Henwood (eds) *Evaluating the Impact of Caring for People, With Respect to Old Age*, Research Volume Three, The Stationery Office, London.

Challis, D. and Davies, B. (1980) A new approach to community care for the elderly, *British Journal of Social Work*, 10, 1-18.

Challis, D. and Davies, B. (1986) *Case Management in Community Care*, Gower, Aldershot.

Challis, D., Chessum, R., Chesterman, J., Luckett, R. and Traske K. (1990) *Case Management in Social and Health Care: The Gateshead Community Care Scheme*, Personal Social Services Research Unit, University of Kent at Canterbury.

Challis, D., Chesterman, J., Darton, R. and Traske, K. (1993) Case management in the care of the aged: the provision of care in different settings, in J.Bornat et al. (eds) *Community Care: A Reader*, Open University Press, Buckingham.

Challis, D., Darton, R., Johnson, L., Stone, M. and Traske, K. (1995) *Care Management and Health Care of Older People: The Darlington Community Care Project*, Arena, Aldershot.

Challis, D., von Abendorff, R., Brown, P. and Chesterman, J. (1997) Care management and dementia: an evaluation of the Lewisham intensive case management scheme, in S. Hunter (ed.) *Dementia: Challenges and New Directions. Research Highlights in Social Work 31*, Jessica Kingsley, London.

Challis, D., Darton, R., Hughes, J., Huxley, P. and Stewart, K. (1998a) Emerging models of care management for older people and those with mental health problems in the UK, *Journal of Case Management*, 7, 4, 153-60.

Challis, D., Darton, R., Hughes, J., Stewart, K. and Weiner, K. (1998b) *Care Management Study: Report on National Data*, Social Services Inspectorate, Department of Health, London.

Chappell, N. (1990) Aging and social care, in R. Binstock and L. George (eds) *Aging and the Social Sciences*, third edition, Academic Press, New York.

Chesterman, J., Challis, D. and Davies, B. (1994) Budget-devolved care management in two routine programmes. Have they improved outcomes?, in D. Challis, B. Davies and K. Traske (eds) *Community Care in the UK and Overseas: New Agendas and Challenges*, Ashgate, Aldershot.

Chesterman, J., Bauld, L. and Judge, K. (1999) Consistency between frail elderly people, their informal carers and care managers in reporting levels of need and resource inputs, Discussion Paper 1518, Personal Social Services Research Unit, University of Kent at Canterbury.

Chetwynd, M., Ritchie, J., Reith, L. and Howard, M. (1996) *The Cost of Care: The Impact of Charging Policy on the Lives of Disabled People*, Joseph Rowntree Foundation, York.

City of Manchester (1981) *Hospital Social Workers: A Study of Patterns of Work and Use of Time*, City of Manchester Social Services Department.

Clark, H., Dyer, S. and Horwood, J. (1998) *That Bit of Help: The High Value of Low Preventative Services for Older People*, Policy Press, London.

Committee on the Management of Local Government (1967) *Reports of the Committees on the Management of Local Government*, Volumes 1-5, (The Maud Report), HMSO, London.

Cox, J. (1996) It's a lifeline, *Elderly Care*, 8, 1, 13-15.

Cumming, E. and Henry, W. (1961) *Growing Old: The Process of Disengagement*, Basic Books, New York.

Dalley, G. (1998) Health and social welfare policy, in M. Bernard and J. Phillips (eds) *The Social Policy of Old Age: Moving into the 21st Century*, Centre for Policy on Ageing, London.

Davies, B. (1968) *Social Needs and Resources in Local Services*, Michael Joseph, London.

Davies, B. (1974) Proposal for a Kent Community Care Project, KCCP Paper 1, Personal Social Services Research Unit, University of Kent at Canterbury.

Davies, B. (1990a) Community care in Australia and elsewhere: the future, in A. Howe, E. Ozanne and C. Selby-Smith (eds) *Community Care Policy and Practice: New Directions in Australia*, Monash University Press, Melbourne.

Davies, B. (1990b) New priorities in home care: principles from the PSSRU experiments, in A. Howe, E. Ozanne and C. Selby-Smith (eds) *Community Care Policy and Practice: New Directions in Australia*, Monash University, Melbourne.

Davies, B. (1992) *Care Management, Equity and Efficiency: The International Experience*, Personal Social Services Research Unit, University of Kent at Canterbury.

Davies, B. (1994a) The production of welfare approach: conceptual framework and methodology, Discussion Paper 1121, Personal Social Services Research Unit, University of Kent at Canterbury.

Davies, B. (1994b) On the targeting of care management: some implications of a PSSRU research synopsis of the task at the SSI workshop on Targeting Care Management, Discussion Paper 1176, Personal Social Services Research Unit, University of Kent at Canterbury.

Davies, B. (1995) Case management for elderly people: the Kent Community Care Project (KCCP) and its descendants in their international context, *Hong Kong Journal of Gerontology*, 9, 1.

Davies, B. and Baines, B. (1992a) Targeting and the silting-up of resources in the community-based social services: consequences of alternative policies, Discussion Paper 770, Personal Social Services Research Unit, University of Kent at Canterbury.

Davies, B. and Baines, B. (1992b) On the silting up of social services department resources and the stability of need states in a cohort of new recipients of community-based social services, Discussion Paper 815, Personal Social Services Research Unit, University of Kent at Canterbury.

Davies, B. and Challis, D. (1980) Experimenting with new roles in domiciliary service: the Kent Community Care Project, *The Gerontologist*, 20, 3, 288-99.

Davies, B. and Challis, D. (1981) Evaluating community care: a production of welfare approach, in E. Goldberg and N. Connolly (eds) *Evaluating Social Care*, Heinemann, London.

Davies, B. and Challis, D. (1986) *Matching Resources to Needs in Community Care*, Ashgate, Aldershot.

Davies, B. and Chesterman, J. (1995) How care management confers benefits: estimates of the direct and indirect effects from the channelling and PSSRU community care experiments, Discussion Paper 1161, Personal Social Services Research Unit, University of Kent at Canterbury.

Davies, B. and Chesterman, J. (1999) *Budget-devolved Care Management in Two Routine Programmes*, Ashgate, Aldershot, forthcoming.

Davies, B. and Fernández, J. with Nomer, B. (1999) *Equity and Efficiency Policy in Community Care: Needs, Service Productivities, Efficiencies and their Implications*, Ashgate, Aldershot.

Davies, B. and Knapp, M. (1981) *Old People's Homes and the Production of Welfare*, Routledge and Kegan Paul, London.

Davies, B. and Knapp, M. (1988) The Production of Welfare Approach: some new PSSRU arguments and results, *British Journal of Social Work*, 18.

Davies, B. and Reddin, M. (1978) *Universality, Selectivity and Effectiveness in Social Policy*, Heinemann, London.

Davies, B., Bebbington, A. and Charnley, H. (1990) *Resources, Needs and Outcomes in Community-Based Care*, Avebury, Aldershot.

Davies, B.,Warburton, R.W. and Fernández, J. (1995) Do different care management approaches affect who gets what?, Preliminary results from a comparative British Study, *Care Plan*, December.

Davies, B., Fernández, J. and Nomer, B. (1997a) Has increasing service inputs per client improved equity and efficiency in UK community care?, Paper presented at the 50th Annual Scientific Meeting of the Gerontological Society of America, Cincinnatti, Ohio, November.

Davies, B., Judge, K., Bauld, L., Chesterman, J., Fernández, J., Kesby, S., Mangalore, R., Nomer, B. and Saunders, R. (1997b) Evaluating community care for elderly people: a summary of baseline data, Discussion Paper 1372, Personal Social Services Research Unit, University of Kent at Canterbury.

Davies, B., Fernández, J. and Nomer, B. (1998) Needs and service productivities in post-reform community care, Discussion Paper 1429, Personal Social Services Research Unit, University of Kent at Canterbury.

Davis, A., Ellis, K. and Rummery, K. (1997) *Access to Assessment: Perspectives of Practitioners, Disabled People and Carers*, Joseph Rowntree Foundation and the Policy Press, Bristol.

Department of Health (1989) *Caring for People: Community Care in the Next Decade and Beyond*, HMSO, London.

Department of Health (1995) *Statistical Bulletin: Community Care Statistics 1995*, Statistical Bulletin 1994/95, Government Statistical Service, London.

Department of Health (1996a) *Health and Personal Social Services Statistics for England*, HMSO, London.

Department of Health (1996b) *Statistical Bulletin: Residential Accommodation Statistics 1996*, Government Statistical Service, London.

Department of Health (1997) *Community Care Statistics 1996*, Statistical Bulletin 1996/97, December 1997.

Department of Health (1998a) *Health and Social Services Statistics*, England 1998, Government Statistical Service.

Department of Health (1998b) *Community Care Statistics 1997*, Statistical Bulletin 1997/98, April 1998.

Department of Health (1998c) *Modernising Social Services*, The Stationery Office, London.

Department of Health (1999) *A New Approach to Social Services Performance: Consultation Document*, The Stationery Office, London.

Department of Health and Social Security (1963) *Health and Welfare: The Development of Community Care*, HMSO, London.

Department of Health and Social Security (1976) *Priorities for Health and Personal Social Services in England*, HMSO, London.

Department of Health and Social Security (1987) *Public Support for Residential Care: An Analysis of Policy, Resourcing and Service Management*, Social Services Inspectorate, DHSS, London.

Department of Health Social Services Inspectorate (1991) *Care Management and Assessment: Practitioner's Guide*, HMSO, London.

Department of Social Security (1997) Carers, *Family Resources Survey Great Britain 1995-96*, HMSO, London.

Dexter, R. and Harbert, A. (1983) *The Home Help Service*, Tavistock, London.

Doty, P., Jackson, M. and Crown, W. (1998) The impact of female caregivers' employment status on patterns of formal and informal eldercare, *The Gerontologist*, 38, 3, 331-41.

Dowd, J. (1975) Age as Exchange: A preface to theory, *Journal of Gerontology*, 30, 584-94.

Finch, J. and Groves, D. (1983) (eds) *A Labour of Love*, Routledge and Kegan Paul, London.

Finch, J. and Mason, J. (1990) Filial obligations and kin support for elderly people, *Ageing and Society*, 10, 2, 151-76.

Finch, J. and Mason, J. (1993) *Negotiating Family Responsibilities*, Routledge, London.

Fisher, M. (1994) Man made care: community care and older male carers, *British Journal of Social Work*, 24, 659-80.

Fitting, M., Rabins, P., Lucas, M. and Eastham, J. (1986) Caregivers of dementia patients: a comparison of husbands and wives, *The Gerontologist*, 26, 248-52.

Fraser, D. (1973) *Evolution of the British Welfare State*, Macmillan, London.

Ginn, J. and Arber, S. (1992) Elderly living at home: the relationship of social and material resources to service use, in F. Laczko and C. Victor (eds) *Social Policy and Elderly People*, Avebury, Aldershot.

Glaser, K., Murphy, M. and Grundy, E. (1997) Limiting long term illness and household structure amongst people aged 45 and over: Great Britain, 1991, *Ageing and Society*, 17, 3-19.

Goldberg, E.M., Mortimer, A. and Williams, B. (1970) *Helping the Aged: A Field Experiment in Social Work*, Allen and Unwin, London.

Goldberg, E.M. and Warburton, R.W. (1979) *Ends and Means in Social Work*, Allen and Unwin, London.

Goldstein, R. and Rivers, P. (1996) The medication role of informal carers, *Health and Social Care in the Community*, 4, 3, 150-58.

Gostick, C., Davies, B., Lawson, R. and Salter, C. (1997) *From Vision to Reality in Community Care: Changing Direction at the Local Level*, Arena, Aldershot.

Grant, G., Nolan, M. and Ellis, N. (1990) A reappraisal of the Malaise Inventory, *Social Psychiatry and Psychiatric Epidemiology*, 25, 170-78.

Green, H. (1988) *Informal Carers: General Household Survey 1985*, HMSO, London.

Griffiths, R. (1988) *Community Care: An Agenda for Action*, HMSO, London.

Hallam, A., and Netten, A. (1996) Costs methodology for an evaluation of community care arrangements for older people with dementia, Discussion Paper 1119, Personal Social Services Research Unit, University of Kent at Canterbury.

Harding, T. (1999) Caring for People five years on: what have we learned about the impact of the 1993 reforms on the care of frail elderly people?, in

G. Wistow and M. Henwood (eds) *Evaluating the Impact of Caring for People, With Respect to Old Age*, Research Volume Three, The Stationery Office, London.

Hardy, B., Leedham, I. and Wistow, G. (1996) Care manager co-location in GP practices: effects upon assessment and care management arrangements, in R. Bland (ed.) *Developing Services for Older People and their Families*, Jessica Kingsley, London.

Harris, A. (1968) *Social Welfare for the Elderly*, HMSO, London.

Havighurst, R. (1963) Successful aging, in R. Williams, C. Tibbits and W. Donahue (eds) *Processes of Aging*, Volume 1, Atherton, New York.

Healy, J. and Yarrow, S. (1997) *Family Matters: Parents Living with Children in Old Age*, Policy Press, London.

Henwood, M. and Wistow, G. (1999) Introduction and overview, in *Evaluating the Impact of Caring for People, With Respect to Old Age*, Research Volume Three, The Stationery Office, London.

Henwood, M., Wistow, G. and Robinson, J, (1996) Halfway there? Policy, politics and outcomes in community care, *Social Policy and Administration*, 30, 1, 39-53.

Herzog, A. and Wallace, R. (1997) Measures of cognitive functioning in the AHEAD study, *Journal of Gerontology*, 52B (Special Issue), 37-48.

Heyman, R. (ed.) (1995) *Researching User Perspectives on Community Health Care*, Chapman Hall, London.

Hoyes, L., Lart, R., Means, R. and Taylor, M. (1994) *Community Care in Transition*, Joseph Rowntree Foundation, York.

Hughes, B. (1990) Quality of life, in S. Peace (ed.) *Researching Social Gerontology*, Sage, London.

Hunt, A. (1970) *The Home Help Service in England and Wales*, Government Social Survey, HMSO, London.

Hunter, D. (1994) The impact of the NHS reforms on community care, in M. Titterton (ed.) *Caring for People in the Community: The New Welfare*, Jessica Kingsley, London.

Isaacs, B. and Neville, Y. (1976) The needs of old people: the 'interval' as a method of measurement, *British Journal of Preventative and Social Medicine*, 30, 79-85.

Isaacs, B. and Thompson, J. (1960) Holiday admissions to a geriatric unit, *The Lancet*, 30 April, 969-71.

Isaacs, B., Livingstone, M. and Neville, Y. (1972) *Survival of the Unfittest: A Study of Geriatric Patients in Glasgow*, Routledge and Kegan Paul, London.

Joint Initiative for Community Care (JICC) (1993) *Care Management: Identifying the Training Needs*, Joint Initiative for Community Care, Milton Keynes.

Jones, W. and Borgatta, E. (1972) Methodology of evaluation, in E. Mullen and J. Dumpson (eds) *Evaluation of Social Intervention*, Jossey-Bass, San Francisco, California.

Kanten, D., Mulrow, C., Gerety, M., Lichtenstein, M., Aguilar, C. and Cornell, J. (1993) Falls: an examination of three reporting methods in nursing homes, *Journal of the American Geriatrics Society*, 41, 662-6.

Kasten, L. and Tennstedt, S. (1997) *With whom do you talk? Differences between elder and caregiver report of long-term care*, Gerontological Society of America's 50th annual scientific meeting, Cincinnati, Ohio, November.

Kay, D., Beamish, P. and Roth, M. (1964) Old age mental disorders in Newcastle-upon-Tyne, Part I: a study of prevalence, *British Journal of Psychiatry*, 110, 146-58.

Kiyak, H., Teri, L. and Borson, S. (1994) Physical and functional health assessment in normal aging and in Alzheimer's Disease: self-reports vs family reports, *The Gerontologist*, 34, 324-30.

Knapp, M. (1993) Principles of applied costs research, in A. Netten and J. Beecham (eds) *Costing Community Care: Theory and Practice*, Ashgate, Aldershot.

Kosberg, J. and Cairl, R. (1986) The cost of care index: a case management tool for screening informal care providers, *The Gerontologist*, 26, 3, 273-8.

Laing, W. (1993) *Financing Long-Term Care: The Crucial Debate*, Age Concern, London.

Landis, J. and Koch, G. (1977) Agreement measures for categorical data, *Biometrics*, 12, 153-7.

Langan, J., Means, R. and Rolfe, S. (1996) *Maintaining Independence in Later Life: Older People Speaking*, Anchor Press, Oxford.

Lawton, M. (1975) The Philadelphia Geriatric Center Morale Scale: a revision, *Journal of Gerontology*, 30, 85-9.

Lawton, M., Morton, H., Moss, M., Rovine, M. and Glickman, A. (1989) Measuring caregiving appraisal, *Journal of Gerontology*, 44, 3, 61-71.

Lechner, V. (1992) Predicting future committment to care for frail parents amongst employed caregivers, *Journal of Gerontological Social Work*, 18, 69-84.

Lewis, J. and Glennerster, H. (1996) *Implementing the New Community Care*, Open University Press, Buckingham.

Lewis, J., Bernstock, P. and Bovell, V. (1995) The community care changes: unresolved tensions in policy and issues of implementation, *Journal of Social Policy*, 24, 1, 73-94.

Lewis, J. and Meredith, B. (1988) *Daughters Who Care: Daughters Caring for Mothers at Home*, Routledge and Kegan Paul, London.

Litwak, E. (1985) *Helping the Elderly. The Complementary Roles of Informal Networks and Formal Systems*, Guilford Press, New York.

Long, K., Sudha, S. and Mutran, E. (1998) Elder-proxy agreement concerning the functional status and medical history of the older person: the impact of caregiver burden and depressive symptomatology, *Journal of the American Geriatrics Society*, 46, 1103–1111.

Mack, R., Salmoni, A., Viverais-Dressler, G., Porter, E. and Garg, R. (1997) Perceived risks to independent living: the views of older, community-dwelling adults, *The Gerontologist*, 37, 6, 729-36.

Maclean, U. (1989) *Dependent Territories: The Frail Elderly and Community Care*, Nuffield Provincial Hospitals Trust, Leeds.

Magaziner, J., Simonsick, E., Kashner, T. and Hebel, J. (1988) Patient proxy response comparability on measures of patient health and functional status, *Journal of Clinical Epidemiology*, 41, 1065-74.

Martire, L., Stephens, M. and Atienza, A. (1997) The interplay of work and caregiving: relationships between role satisfaction, role involvement and caregiver's well-being, *Journal of Gerontology*, 52B, 5, S279-S289.

McNeil, B., Keeler, E. and Adelstein, S. (1975) Primer on certain elements of medical decision-making, *The New England Journal of Medicine*, 293, 211-15.

Means, R. (1997) Home, independence and community care: time for a wider vision?, *Policy and Politics*, 25, 4, 409-17.

Means, R. and Smith, R. (1998a) *Community Care: Policy and Practice*, second edition, Macmillan, London.

Means, R. and Smith, R. (1998b) *From Poor Law to Community Care: The Development of Welfare Services for Elderly People 1939-1971*, The Policy Press, London.

Meredith, B. (1993) *The Community Care Handbook: The New System Explained*, Age Concern, London.

Midwinter, E. (1994) *The Development of Social Welfare in Britain*, Open University Press, Buckingham.

Ministry of Health (1963) *Health and Welfare: The Development of Community Care. Plans for the Health and Welfare Services of the Local Authorities in England and Wales*, HMSO, London.

Moriarty, J. and Webb, S. (1997a) How do older people feel about assessment?, *Journal of Dementia Care*, Sept/Oct, 20-22.

Moriarty, J. and Webb, S. (1997b) *Part of their Lives: An Evaluation of Community Care Arrangements for People with Dementia*, National Institute of Social Work, London.

Neal, M., Ingersoll-Dayton, B. and Starrels, M. (1997) Gender and relationship differences in caregiving patterns and consequences amongst employed caregivers, *The Gerontologist*, 37, 6, 804-816.

Netten, A. and Dennett, J. (1995) *Unit Costs of Health and Social Care 1995*, Personal Social Services Research Unit, University of Kent at Canterbury.

Netten, A. and Dennett, J. (1997) *Unit Costs of Health and Social Care 1997*, Personal Social Services Research Unit, University of Kent at Canterbury.

Netten, A., Darton, R., Forder, J. and Baines, B. (1997a) Cross-sectional survey of residential and nursing homes for elderly people: interim report, Discussion Paper 1339/2, Personal Social Services Research Unit, University of Kent at Canterbury.

Netten, A., Hallam, A. and Knight, J. (1997b) Costings, in J. Moriarty and S. Webb (eds) *Part of their Lives: An Evaluation of Community Care Arrangements for People with Dementia*, National Institute of Social Work, London.

Noelker, L., Ford, A., Gaines, A., Haug, M., Jones, P., Stange, K. and Mefrouche, Z. (1998) Attitudinal influences on the elderly's use of assistance, *Research on Aging*, 20, 3, 317-38.

Office of Population Censuses and Surveys (OPCS) (1991) *Census*, HMSO, London.

Office of Population Censuses and Surveys (OPCS) (1992) *General Household Survey: Carers in 1990*, OPCS Monitor SS 92/2, HMSO, London.

Office of Population Censuses and Surveys (OPCS) (1994) *General Household Survey 1994*, HMSO, London.

Office of Population Censuses and Surveys (OPCS) (1997) *General Household Survey 1995*, HMSO, London.

Parker, C., Morgan, K., Dewey, M. and the Analysis Group of the MRC CFA study (1997) Physical illness and disability among elderly people in England and Wales: the Medical Research Council cognitive function and ageing study, *Journal of Epidemiology and Community Health*, 51, 494-501.

Parker, G. (1993) *With this Body: Caring and Disability in Marriage*, Open University Press, Buckingham.

Parker, G. (1999) Impact of the NHS and Community Care Act (1990) on informal carers: briefing paper for the Royal Commission on Long Term Care for the Elderly, in G. Wistow and M. Henwood (eds) *Evaluating the Impact of Caring for People, With Respect to Old Age*, Research Volume Three, The Stationery Office, London.

Pavalko, E. and Artis, J. (1997) Women's caregiving and paid work: causal relationships in late mid life, *Journal of Gerontology*, 52B, S170-S179.

Peek, C., Coward, R., Henretta, J., Duncan, R. and Dougherty, M. (1997) Differences by race in the decline of health over time, *Journal of Gerontology*, 52B, 6, S336-S344.

Petch, A. (1996) Developing skills in care management: a slow process, in R. Bland (ed.) *Developing Services for Older People and their Families*, Jessica Kingsley, London.

Pilgrim, D. (1993) Anthology: policy, in J. Bornat et al. (eds) *Community Care: A Reader*, Open University Press, Buckingham.

Quine, L. and Charnley, H. (1987) The malaise inventory as a measure of stress in carers, conference paper, Centre for Research in Health Behaviour, University of Kent, Canterbury.

Qureshi, H. and Walker, A. (1989) *The Caring Relationship: Elderly People and their Families*, Macmillan, Basingstoke.

Qureshi, H., Challis, D. and Davies, B. (1989) *Helpers in Case-managed Community Care*, Ashgate, Aldershot.

Redmond, E., Rudd, A. and Martin, F. (1996) Older people in receipt of home help: a group with high levels of unmet health needs, *Health and Social Care in the Community*, 4, 6, 347-52.

Reker, G.T (1997) Personal meaning, optimism and choice: existential predictors of depression in community and institutionalised elderly, *The Gerontologist*, 37, 6, 709-716.

Renshaw, J., Hampson, R., Thomason, C., Darton, R., Judge, K. and Knapp, M. (1988) *Care in the Community: The First Steps*, Gower, Aldershot.

Richardson, A. and Higgins, R. (1991) *Doing Case Management: Learning from the Wakefield Case Management Project*, Nuffield Institute of Health Services Studies, University of Leeds.

Robbins, D. (ed.) (1993) *Community Care: Findings from Department of Health Funded Research* 1988-1992, HMSO, London.

Rodman, H. (1963) The lower class value stretch, *Social Forces*, 43, December, 205-15.

Roth, M. and Kay, D. (1956) Affective disorders arising in the seniors. Part II: physical disability as an aetiological factor, *Journal of Mental Science*, 102, 141-50.

Rowntree, B. (1947) *Old People: Report of a Survey Committee on the Problems of Ageing and the Care of Old People*, The Nuffield Foundation, Oxford University Press.

Royal Commission on Long Term Care (1999) *With Respect to Old Age*, The Stationery Office, London.

Ruck, S. (1958) Unpublished accounts of visits to local authority welfare departments, given to Bleddyn Davies.

Rutter, M., Tizard, J. and Whitmore, I. (1970) *Education, Health and Behaviour*, Longman, London.

Scottish Office Social Work Services Inspectorate (SWSI) (1996) *A Service in Transition: The Report of an Inspection of Local Authority Home Help Services for Older People*, HMSO, Edinburgh.

Seebohm, F. (1968) *Report of the Committee on Local Authority and Allied Personal Services*, Cmnd 3703, HMSO, London.

Segal, D., Hook, J., Matsuoka, C., Dover, C. and Bogaards, J. (1998) *Comparison between self-report and interview assessments of anxiety, depression and cognitive impairment in older adults*, Gerontological Society of America's 51st annual scientific meeting, Philadelphia, PA, November.

Seltzer, B., Vasterling, J., Yoder, J. and Thompson, K. (1997) Awareness of deficit in Alzheimer's disease: relation to caregiver burden, *The Gerontologist*, 37, 14, 20-24.

Sheldon, J. (1948) *The Social Medicine of Old Age*, Oxford University Press, London.

Social Services Inspectorate (SSI) (1987) *From Home Help to Home Care: An Analysis of Policy, Resourcing and Service Management*, HMSO, London.

Social Services Inspectorate (SSI) (1993) *Social Services for Hospital Patients III: Users and Carers Perspective*, SSI, Department of Health, London.

Social Services Inspectorate (SSI) (1998) *Getting Better? Inspection of Hospital Discharge (Care Management) Arrangements for Older People*, SSI, Department of Health,, London.

Social Services Inspectorate/Social Work Services Group (SSI/SWSG) (1991) *Care Management and Assessment: Practitioner's Guide*, HMSO, London.

SPSS (1997) *SPSS Advanced Statistics 7.5*, SPSS Inc.

Stone, R., Cafferata, G. and Sangl, J. (1987) Caregiver of frail elderly: a national profile, *The Gerontologist*, 27, 5, 616-26.

Strawbridge, W., Wallhagen, M., Shema, S. and Kaplan, G. (1997) New burdens or more of the same? Comparing grandparent, spouse and adult-child caregivers, *The Gerontologist*, 37, 4, 505-10.

Tennstedt, S., McKinlay, J. and Sullivan, L. (1989) Informal care for frail elderly: the role of secondary caregivers, *The Gerontologist*, 29, 5, 677-83.

Tester, S. (1996) *Community Care for Older People: A Comparative Perspective*, Macmillan, London.

Thompson, L.W. (1996) Cognitive-behaviour therapy and treatment for late-life depression, *Journal of Clinical Psychiatry*, 57 (Supplement 5), 29-37.

Tierney, A., Closs, J., Hunter, M. and Macmillan, H. (1993) Experiences of elderly people concerning discharge from hospital, *Journal of Clinical Nursing*, 2, 179-85.

Titmuss, R. (1968) *Commitment to Welfare*, Allen and Unwin, London.

Townsend, P. (1957) *The Family Life of Old People*, Pelican, Harmondsworth.

Townsend, P. (1962) *The Last Refuge: A Survey of Residential Institutions and Homes for the Aged in England and Wales*, Routledge and Kegan Paul, London.

Twigg, J. (1985) Domiciliary Care Project, PSSRU Newsletter, Spring 1985, Personal Social Services Research Unit, University of Kent at Canterbury.

Twigg, J. (1989) Models of carers: how do social care agencies conceptualise their relationship with informal carers, *Journal of Social Policy*, 18, 1.

Twigg, J. (1997) Deconstructing the 'social bath': help with bathing at home for older and disabled people, *Journal of Social Policy*, 26, 2, 211-32.

Twigg, J. (1998) Informal care of older people, in M. Bernard and J. Phillips (eds) *The Social Policy of Old Age*, Centre for Policy on Ageing, London.

Twigg, J. and Atkin, K. (1994) *Carers Perceived: Policy and Practice in Informal Care*, Open University Press, Buckingham.

Wachtel, T., Fulton, J. and Goldfarb, J. (1987) Early prediction of discharge disposition after hospitalisation, *The Gerontologist*, 27, 1, 98-103.

Wagner, G. (1988) *Residential Care: A Positive Choice, Report of the Independent Review of Residential Care*, HMSO, London.

Walker, A. (ed.) (1982) *Community Care: The Family, the State and Social Policy*, Blackwell and Robertson, Oxford.

Walker, A. (1993) Community care policy: from consensus to conflict, in J. Bornat et al. (eds) *Community Care: A Reader*, Open University Press, Buckingham.

Walker, A. and Maltby, T. (1996) *Ageing Europe*, Open University Press, Buckingham.

Webb, A. and Wistow, G. (1987) *Social Work, Social Care and Social Planning: The Personal Social Services Since Seebohm*, Longman, London.

Wenger, G.C. (1989) Support Networks in Old Age: Constructing a Typology, in M.Jefferys (ed) *Growing Old in the Twentieth Century*, Routledge, London.

Wenger, G.C. (1990) Elderly carers: the need for appropriate intervention, *Ageing and Society*, 10, 197-219.

Wenger, G.C. (1992) *Help in Old Age. Facing Up to Change. A Longitudinal Network Study*, Liverpool University Press, Liverpool.

Wenger, G.C. (1994) *Support Networks of Older People: A Guide for Practitioners*. Centre for Social Policy Research and Development, University of Wales, Bangor.

Wenger, G.C. (1995) A comparison of urban and rural support networks: Liverpool and North Wales, *Ageing and Society*, 15, 59-81.

Williams, J., Drinka, T., Greenberg, J., Farrell-Holtan, J., Euhardy, R. and Schram, M. (1991) Development and testing of the assessment of living skills and resources in elderly community-dwelling veterans, *The Gerontologist*, 31, 84-91.

Woods, R. and Macmillan, M. (1994) Home at last? Impact of a local 'homely' unit for dementia sufferers on their relatives, in D. Challis, B. Davies and K. Traske (eds) *Community Care: New Agendas and Challenges from the UK and Overseas*, Arena, Aldershot.

Wright, F. (1986) *Left to Care Alone*, Gower, Aldershot.

Yesavage, J. (1988) Geriatric Depression Scale, *Psychopharmacological Bulletin*, 24, 4, 709-711.

Younghusband, E. (1959) *Report of the Working Party on Social Workers in the Local Authority Health and Welfare Services*, HMSO, London.

Index